THE DIAMOND APPRAISED

CRAIG R. WRIGHT
& TOM HOUSE

SIMON AND SCHUSTER
NEW YORK   LONDON   TORONTO
SYDNEY   TOKYO

SIMON AND SCHUSTER

SIMON & SCHUSTER BUILDING
ROCKEFELLER CENTER
1230 AVENUE OF THE AMERICAS
NEW YORK, NEW YORK 10020

DESIGNED BY KATHY KIKKERT
MANUFACTURED IN THE UNITED STATES OF AMERICA

1 3 5 7 9 10 8 6 4 2

LIBRARY OF CONGRESS CATALOGING IN PUBLICATION DATA
WRIGHT, CRAIG R.
THE DIAMOND APPRAISED / CRAIG R. WRIGHT & TOM HOUSE.
P. CM.
1. BASEBALL—UNITED STATES—HISTORY. I. HOUSE, TOM. II. TITLE.
GV863.A1W75 1989
796.357'0973—dc19   88-34898
ISBN 0-671-67769-1   CIP

TO THE MEMORY OF MY GRANDFATHER,
LEROY "GRAMPS" HILER.

—C.R.W.

TO ALL THE BASEBALL JOCKS AND EX-JOCKS
WHO FEEL FOR THE GAME LIKE I DO.

—T.H.

CONTENTS

ACKNOWLEDGMENTS

The sharing of our interest, joy, and knowledge of baseball is a natural as a team sport. That's a pleasant thought to remember as I gratefully acknowledge all those who assisted in preparation of this book. Bill James has been more than just a sabermetric colleague; he's always been an encouraging friend, and it is largely from his repeated urgings that I found the confidence to write this book. At times there were very trying circumstances surrounding the creation of this book; editor Jeff Neuman dropped a couple of balls in the early innings, but I never lost confidence in him, and as far as I'm concerned, he ended up the hero of the game. The Texas Rangers were exceedingly gracious in helping in any way possible, including almost limitless access to their library and records. STATS Inc. was just as free in its cooperation.

In looking through my various files behind this book, I recognize things which I identify directly with the assistance of the following people: Pete Palmer, John and Sue Dewan, Dick Cramer, Lloyd Johnson, John Blake, Eddie Robinson, John McMichael, Bobby Bragan, Davis Jackson, Dave Driscoll, Bob Garvey, Tom Grieve, Sandy Johnson, Bobby Valentine, Mike Stone, Gary Gillette, Wayne Krivsky, Bill Zeigler, Stan Reynolds, Judy Johns, John Leonard, Charlene Homuth, Gene Sunnen, Eric Nadel, Taunee Paur, Mark Holtz, Don Zminda, John Welaj, Wayne Stivers, Burt Hawkins, the late Bill

Veeck, Jr., and Paul Richards. Most of those folks also deserve kudos for their friendship and moral support, and in that vein let me also thank Sean and Cindy, Steve and Catherine, Susie, Andrea, the Robinson family, the ever supportive Wright clan (who could fill a page of their own), Shadow the Wonder Cat, all the guys on the V-Ball team, the Big Brothers of Arlington Softball team, and Jeff Ridlen, the best LB a guy could have.

—Craig Wright

I'd like to thank Tom Grieve, Mike Stone, and Bobby Valentine for allowing me to try new ideas in a sports environment that's too often bound (and gagged) by tradition; my wife, Karren, my daughters, Brittany and Brooke, and my son, Bryan, who understood even when this project took more of my time away from them; the athletes who listened and tried to follow what we've been up to; and Jeff Neuman, my editor and friend, who kept the book alive through two publishers and more than a few storms along the way.

—Tom House

FOREWORD

In the last few years I have reached the age at which they have begun to overturn laws that were passed within my memory. In my memory the speed limit has headed upward (I assumed it would always head upward) and downward and now upward again. The death penalty has been abolished (such a FINAL word, abolished) and now has come back to life. The draft was abolished and now it is struggling back. The drinking age has gone from twenty-one to eighteen and back to twenty-one. Schools that in my memory were forced into unhappy collectives called unified school districts are being splintered into smaller schools. Educational theory has spun like a top. New math has come and gone and earned a spot in pedagogical infamy. Required classes have given way to optional curricula, and options have given way to requirements.

In my childhood—I am less than forty, but not much less—we were taught to believe in the march of progress, a progress that proceeded in an orderly fashion like a man climbing a staircase. It is the shock of adulthood to discover instead that we are witnessing not progress but merely shifts in the balance of credibility between competing world views. We live in a society in which 52% is a mandate and 54% a landslide. I talked to my uncle about it; he is in his late eighties, and he can remember some laws that were repealed and re-instituted five or six times in his lifespan. Thomas Jefferson wrote that the history of mankind is like that of "the horse in his mill, (going) round and round the same beaten circle . . . I heard once a very old friend, who had troubled himself with neither poets nor philosophers, say the same thing in plain prose, that he was tired of pulling off his shoes and stockings at night, and putting them on again in the morning." It is not that we do not progress, perhaps, but that we progress like a catamaran heading into the wind, sailing at 45 degree angles to the headwind—and 90 degree angles to the course we charted just moments ago.

This book is about the tension between two views of the world of baseball, one looking northeast and one looking northwest, yet both fighting a strong north wind. Craig Wright and Tom House both believe that baseball could benefit from paying more attention to the facts and less to received wisdom, but they differ on which facts should be noted most carefully. Tom and Craig both believe that baseball needs to be more open in weighing its options, but they have rather different ideas about what options baseball should be open *to*. Both men believe that baseball should make room among the old ways to try out the new, but they disagree a little on the draft list.

This book is baked Alaska—cold and delicious inside, hot and delicious outside, but what really makes it work is the contrast. There will be times in this book when you will disagree with each man. There will be times when you think both of them have missed the boat. But you have to enjoy the process of seeing the baseball world drawn into sharp focus from such different perspectives, from the inside and the outside, from the distance of history and from the pressure of the moment's needs. Sometimes you will think that there should be more give and take between the two of them, and then you realize that there can't be, that they are proceeding from such different views of the baseball world that the reconciliation of minor points is impossible, like trying to find the same building in Los Angeles and New York, like trying to turn a sailboat every few inches so that it sails almost directly into the wind. It doesn't work that way, but it works.

Bill James
Winchester, Kansas
November, 1988

INTRODUCTION

In 1981, I made a critical career decision that I regret from time to time, although for the most part it has served me well. That's the year I endorsed the word "sabermetrics," and "sabermetrician" became my working title in professional baseball.

When I first began working in baseball, I wasn't doing anything different from what I am right now—though I hope I am doing it a bit better. I approached baseball questions through a concentrated study of available evidence, and Eddie Robinson, an old-school baseball executive, had an interest in adding that perspective to the more traditional approaches. I was hired by the Texas Rangers on a trial basis and successfully proved the value of my method.

At the time I had no title and would sign in simply as "baseball consultant." If I was uncertain about what I was, I was very clear about what I was not. I never aspired to be a statistician; I chose not to be educated as a statistician—outside the normal scientific training—and I firmly refused such a title or any derivative such as "statistical analyst." I was involved in the study of baseball by dealing with ideas and evidence; numbers were just a minor tool to be called on when needed, much like a screwdriver or a monkey wrench.

In *The 1980 Baseball Abstract,* Bill James was feeling the same need for a distinct title for his work and christened it "sabermetrics"—sound the trumpets, release the pigeons. I cannot say the term hit me as a revelation. I had that *Abstract* for nearly a year before I considered endorsing the term. But the more I thought about it, the better it sounded. I had always felt a great affinity for Bill's work and felt it was by far the closest image of my own. In fact, one friend who had read one of Bill's early books had asked whether I was using "Bill James" as a pen name.

Sabermetrics: The first part is the pronunciation of the acronym for SABR (the Society for American Baseball Research), while the second part signifies measurement. It's an unusual etymology for a word to be based on an acronym, but it is not unheard of; "scuba" comes from "self-contained underwater breathing apparatus." My final acceptance came when I realized that the study of baseball would literally translate to baseballology, and no one was going to take seriously a business card that read "Baseballologist."

It also turned out that people were going to have a hard time accepting the term "sabermetrician." The three major newspapers in Dallas and Fort Worth refused to use either "sabermetrics" or "sabermetrician" until the summer of 1984. Within the Ranger organization itself, some people balked at using the term. The general manager had to step in and overrule one employee who was refusing to allow my business cards to be printed with that title. The editor of the Ranger media guide insisted on using "statistician" in place of "sabermetrician" for several years. He stopped only when I pointed out that every job description I had with the Rangers was titled "sabermetrician" and every organizational chart, except his, listed me by that same title. *The Sporting News Baseball Guide* began using the title in 1983, though they misspelled it as "sabremetrician" for a couple of years despite my attempts at correction.

Here in the late 1980s the term is beginning to settle in as a word with a specific meaning in a limited field. Certainly it is recognized by the seven thousand or so members of SABR. Both "sabermetrics" and "sabermetrician" have been used in hundreds of newspapers and magazines including *Time* and nearly every general sports periodical.

My one regret is the way the meaning of "sabermetrics" is evolving. Because of the popularity of James's books, folks began imitating what they saw as the key to his success. Rather than looking at what made his work different from, say, that of the Elias Sports Bureau, they noticed there were an awful lot of numbers in his books. This seems to have led to an explosion of baseball statistics that, frankly, I find rather offensive.

I'm not so bothered by all the people writing books with a lot of baseball statistics in them—some of which are quite good. My biggest complaint is with the folks in the daily media. They wad up numbers and throw them back and forth without any real sense of perspective. They raise the statistical noise level to new heights with a bunch of irrelevant numbers, and then with pompous certainty they use them to make connections that don't exist. And, heaven help us, a lot of the fans are imitating such drivel, writing it to *The Sporting News* and talking it at the ballpark. Yeah, it's ugly, it's out of hand, it does take some of the fun out of the game, and I cringe to see it associated in any way with sabermetrics.

We've come a long way since the day when baseball statistics were just the fascinating creatures that made the phenomenon of baseball cards work, when "a chart of numbers that would put an actuary to sleep can be made to dance if you put it on one side of a card and Bombo Rivera's picture on the other." Ironically, the man who wrote that was Bill James.

I have a certain amount of hope that this book might restore some sanity to the wild use of baseball statistics—get away from numbers for numbers' sake and bring the focus back to the thoughtful process of understanding the evidence surrounding our questions. At worst, I expect to make the distinction between what sabermetrics is meant to be and how it is generally perceived. James once wrote, "Sabermetrics is the field of knowledge which is drawn from attempts to figure out whether or not those things people say [about baseball] are true." Bill has written a number of fine essays trying to capture the essence of sabermetrics, yet in that simple sentence he captures best the spirit of the work as well as the central platform of every other field of scientific inquiry. And yes, having said that, I must confess that I view sabermetrics as a science—not a rock-hard science of solid laws and principles that can be measured out to the tenth decimal point as in physics and chemistry, but rather a soft science in the nature of sociology or psychology.

My foreword for *The 1985 Baseball Abstract* was my attempt to define sabermetrics and James's virtues as a sabermetrician from my stance of sabermetrics as a gentle science.

> Sabermetrics is the scientific research of the available evidence to identify, study and measure forces in professional baseball. . . . The real tools of the trade fall under scientific methodology. Besides statistical techniques and applications, that includes things like rules of evidence, rules of logic, testing theories and measures by internal consistency, relation to known quantities and qualities, and common sense. It also includes creeds like, "Objectivity when possible but do the best you can before you do nothing," "The obvious is usually wrong" (this is a slight exaggeration of the reality that the obvious is wrong often enough to check it out), "Science is synthesis before analysis," and "Always remember to have fun" (Einstein's rule for having a good time).
>
> . . . Bill has the sharp, open, independent mind necessary to pursue truth rather than a consistency of belief. Yet he is able to temper what could be a ruthless, egotistical and joyless pursuit with the attitude that separates true scientists from technicians. With an almost Zen-like simplicity he loves his subject enough to synthesize while analyzing, to know that nothing stands alone. Everything has two frames of reference: what it seems to be as a single entity, and what it is in the reality that knows no such separations. In the back of every true scientific mind is a circus juggler seeking the whole. It is in these spaces that we touch the mystery, that we are taught humility and a respect for our own ignorance.

That is the nature of scientific inquiry, and, at its best, it is the nature of sabermetrics. Sabermetrics has been a part of the game for a long time in various guises. In his own way John McGraw was a sabermetrician; certainly Branch Rickey was. It exists not just to help the performance of the professionals, but also to enhance our understanding and enjoyment of the game. The extent to which this happens is up to the individual. To the president of the Jose Cruz Fan Club, all he may care about is knowing that in the context of his home park, Cruz was one of the best offensive players of his generation. For the frequent critic of the local front office, he may want to sink his teeth into learning about the value of players in their career context, or how offensive performance varies by defensive position. Others will be interested in the information underlying an unusual managerial move. There is no ceiling to the rewards other than the ambition of the seeker. Rather than being stripped of her mystery and mystique, baseball becomes the girl we met at the dance years ago. Getting to know her, building our intimacy, only heightens our pleasure and appreciation.

The work itself I consider a cross between detective work and archeology. Although folks like to hear about specific players and the best estimate of their futures—which is a lot like handicapping horses—the most important sabermetrics work involves the more basic issues, where we can learn something that can be used over and over and enrich our whole feel for the game.

Those are often the questions that bring out the detective in me. We generally don't have the answers because they are hard to get to; it's like a tough murder case without witnesses, the one in which the district attorney doubts the case can be solved. I like the challenge of building a case from circumstantial evidence. You can't start out worrying about making an airtight case; you can't afford to think that way. If you do, you'll generally end up learning nothing. Instead, start with the stance that you don't know anything, and any bit of knowledge you can come up with, no matter how small, is better than what you have. Acknowledging your ignorance frees your mind and gives you the will to deal with hair samples, blood types, and other seemingly trivial pieces of information. The investigation rolls along, and, more often than not, you find yourself finally getting a handle on the case. Those are the sweetest moments of all: the sense of wonder that "something" has come out of what appeared to be nothing.

You may not be able to prosecute the case—yet—but you learn enough that you can begin to focus and spend less time running down dead-end alleys. Finally there may come a day when you can show the D.A. a web of evidence that answers the question beyond a reasonable doubt. This is the same D.A. who started off saying, "What is this hair sample crap? I can't make a case on hair samples." Very satisfying.

In this book you will see a number of topics touched on in which the consensus has been that we are incapable of learning anything from the available evidence. By the time you finish this book, I hope you will not only know and enjoy more about baseball, but that you will be less likely to ever again accept a question as unanswerable.

The archeologist comes out with the realization that baseball is more than just the game played yesterday, today, and tomorrow. The roots of baseball go back well over a hundred years, and the man who would understand baseball must know that evolution just as the student of modern culture and civilization studies history. But this is more than just studying history; in a sense, archeologists create history by bringing the past to life with an understanding not realized before. I can't begin to count the number of times I've successfully turned to the past for a better understanding of the present.

In this book you will see both styles of inquiry in action. I hope we can also demonstrate how sabermetrics and professional baseball have begun to work together. Sabermetrics is slowly but steadily gaining ground in the decision-making process of more and more baseball organizations. Where the real change is taking place is not in hiring sabermetricians, but in the attitudes of those in the decision-making roles. It reminds me of the days when baseball was first faced with negotiating with agents rather than directly with the players. The deals were more complicated, more money was at stake, and the negotiations were much harder. In some cases, teams tried hiring special negotiators, but the real trend was to train the GM or some other member in baseball operations to handle such high-powered negotiations. I can see the same thing happening with sabermetrics. I see some interesting books popping up on the desks of front-office personnel and even in the offices of the field managers. If you listen closely, you can even hear in the way they talk that there is a greater awareness of the sabermetric approach and the field of established knowledge that is part of sabermetrics.

This book is another piece of evidence that this blend of sabermetrics and professional baseball is not only appropriate but actually happening. With an eye toward the enjoyment of the reader, both the serious and casual fan, we have selected a variety of topics to be viewed from both the sabermetric perspective and from the dugout. It is through this process that we may quickly realize that our similarities are greater than our differences, and possibly we may catch a glimpse of the future of baseball as it lightly learns more about itself.

HOUSE:
BASEBALL'S WAY

"It's not my way, his way, or your way, it's baseball's way, Tommy, baseball's way!" and he'd poke my chest with his gnarled ex-catcher's finger for emphasis. That was Clyde McCullough's response whenever I would ask, "Why?" and he didn't have a ready answer. Please note I said a *ready* answer, because eventually he would always come up with one. Fifty years in the game from his "dirt dog" perspective put some awesome information in his memory bank, and I would try to tap the resource whenever I could. Our paths crossed many times. Clyde loved baseball, loved to talk, and I'd give odds right now that he's in heaven convincing Saint Peter that baseball is bigger than the sum of its parts. "A flow, Pete, a *feeling* just waiting to be expressed on the diamond of life. Why do you think it's called a baseball diamond, Pete? Because it's precious, a jewel for the fans, and the players provide the sparkle. Fans buy the sparkle, Pete, and it's up to the game to make it shine. . . ." Et cetera, et cetera, and ad infinitum. I hope Saint Peter has a durable chest.

Clyde's right; baseball *is* bigger than the sum of its parts. *Synergy* is the word. As an athlete, my purpose was to learn, experience, and perform. As a coach now, my purpose is to identify, comprehend, and teach as many of the critical parts of the game as possible—to work with, not against, the synergy of the game. And it's the fans' role to watch, to appreciate, to enjoy.

In this book, I've tried to respond to some of the observations and studies that Craig has made so diligently. We've made an agreement to disagree, in book form. Craig can look deeply at the facts and figures of the game, and some of his conclusions are fascinating. But he's never played the game on the big-league level; I can provide a practical response to his theoretical observations. Of course, I'm not Clyde McCullough. I know that baseball has its way, but I also know that baseball perpetuates its own internal inconsistencies. Tradition in baseball is an excuse for tunnel vision. There are absolutes in baseball, but a lot fewer than most baseball people think. I always keep in mind Clarke's Laws, which demonstrated that the flow of revolutionary ideas in any field follows three steps:

First exposure: "It's impossible—don't waste my time."
Second exposure: "It's possible but not worth doing."
Third exposure: "I said it was a good idea all along."

I truly believe that the only way to discover the limits of the possible in baseball is to go beyond them into the impossible. I know Cy Young probably rolls over in his grave whenever one of my pitchers throws a pigskin in horsehide territory, but tradition doesn't invalidate the principle that you can't make a football spiral without proper mechanics.

I've always been a pitcher or involved with pitchers, for thirty years now at all levels, from Little League to the major leagues, both as a player and an instructor. As an amateur, I played in high school, in college, and in various summer leagues. As a professional, I played for the Braves, Red Sox, and Mariners. As an instructor, I've taught pitching for fifteen years to kids of all ages and abilities at the San Diego School of Baseball. I spent a year as a high school coach, five years teaching in the minor leagues for the Astros and Padres, and I'm now the major-league pitching coach for the Texas Rangers. I've had five knee surgeries, in addition to the usual day-to-day injuries that affect any athlete.

If I have a fetish, it's physical conditioning. I've used my body as an experimental laboratory for the last twenty years, trying many things, keeping the best. At five feet, nine inches I've weighed as much as 205 and as little as 160. I've documented the effects of not lifting weights as opposed to year-round lifting programs on Nautilus, Universal, and dead weights.

My formal educational background has nothing to do with baseball.

I have a B.S. in management (primarily focusing on behavioral sciences), an M.B.A. in marketing, and a Ph.D. in psychology. I've found surprising parallels between business and baseball in the psychology of stress and performance.

So if I say that performance comes when preparation meets opportunity, I'm not just parroting back something I've read on a clubhouse wall. I am *for* the game, but not so much *of* it that I lose the forest for the trees. I believe in the absolutes and the integrity of baseball, but I'm not afraid to question them and look for new ones.

And, of course, I'm the answer to a trivia question. For a while, I had to get used to not being just Tom House, but Tom House, the-guy-who-caught-Aaron's-715th-home-run. Kind of like my old friend Clyde McCullough, the-only-man-to-play-in-the-World-Series-but-not-the-regular-season-in-a-year.

With all this in mind, you can see I'm not like every other baseball guy. And you can imagine how refreshing it was for me to run into Craig Wright and his sabermetrics. Here was a "partner in crime," some company in my commitment to a different look at baseball. We do not, as you will see, agree on everything. In fact, part of the strength of our relationship is being able to take different routes in our efforts to interpret baseball's traditions. I am a field man; he's a researcher. We're both trying to find contemporary truths; he quantifies, I quibble. But like Clyde, we both love the game and enjoy the sparkle of the diamond.

We're neither of us looking to rebuild the wheel. We just want to grease the hub so that "baseball's way" will turn a little more efficiently than it would if we hadn't come along.

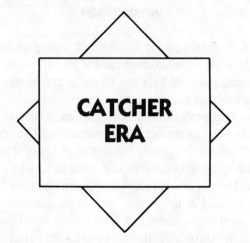

CATCHER ERA

In 1982 I read a very interesting article contrasting the attitudes found in Japanese baseball and in American baseball. The central point was that in Japan they emphasize the idea that a team is more than the sum of its parts. Players are evaluated not just on their individual accomplishments, but also by their impact on their teammates and, ultimately, the team itself. The strongest example of this principle is their attitude toward catchers. When a pitcher is struggling in a game, the Japanese manager will sometimes change the whole battery, or perhaps leave the pitcher in and just change catchers. And in their statistical records, many teams keep track of the number of runs allowed per nine innings caught for each of their catchers—a catcher ERA, or CERA.

I fell in love with the idea the minute I read it. I had always felt that an infielder's ability on the double play could not be evaluated without taking into account the other infielders who are part of the play, and this pales next to the importance of the symbiotic relationship between the catcher and the pitcher. The Japanese concept of CERA speaks to something I think we all understand on an almost instinctual level: that the real value of a catcher is not so much in throwing out base runners, fielding bunts, or preventing passed balls, but in his working relationship with the pitcher and defense.

Granted, a catcher must have some minimum level of arm strength and agility, but beyond those bare necessities, the lion's share of his value isn't in his obvious physical skills. Nor is it just a case of how the catcher calls the game. The catcher leads the pitchers, and by the nature of that relationship he exerts a certain control over the pitcher's psyche—and don't think the catchers don't know it. Does this quote sound familiar? "Some you have to challenge, some you pat on the back, and others you kick in the butt. Most need all three from time to time." That could be Roger Bresnahan talking about pitchers the day he invented shin guards, or the voice of Tony Pena, Jr., in the year 2001.

But it isn't just the pitcher that the catcher is trying to manipulate, even though you'll never hear a good catcher discuss his other main target. Catchers quickly go dumb when it comes to their attempts to influence the umpires. They are not eager to advertise what sells best when noticed least. While some umpires learn to ignore the supposedly innocent ramblings of a catcher's chatter, few escape being hypnotized by the glove of a good catcher. The mark of the master is the illusion whereby balls become called strikes. Learning to catch the ball so it looks like a strike may do more toward preventing runs than throwing out the extra base runner once a week that is the difference between the best- and worst-throwing catchers.

The best catchers learn to heighten the illusion of strikes by "framing" the close pitches within the strike zone by where and how they catch the ball. They know that the less they move the more it looks as though the pitch went where it should, and thus should be a strike. They diligently practice catching the low pitches without turning the glove down to catch a ball just below the strike zone. They know if they have to drop the glove down, the umpire will automatically call it a ball, low. Some catchers believe they get more calls if they help the umpire anticipate where the pitch is supposed to go, and they set an obvious target at the risk of tipping off the batter as well. That's why a catcher doesn't mind the umpire putting his hand lightly on his upper back. This lets the umpire feel the catcher's movement and direction, which not only keeps him out of the catcher's way when blocking or chasing tough pitches, but lets the catcher relay the location of his pitch call with just a subtle shift of his frame.

Still, this is all speculation and theories in the dark. Can these things be measured? Does CERA expose meaningful, consistent differences? Does it add to our understanding of the game? You don't have to work with the measure very long to realize that a responsible study of CERAs can help us, but it isn't an easy battle to win respect for the concept. Whenever a form of measurement is first introduced into a gray area, it often embarrasses the very experts that it must count on to be accepted as legitimate.

The simple truth is that most baseball experts don't even try to weigh this aspect of a catcher's defense; instead, they focus solely on the things that they can see: agility behind the plate, the number of passed balls, and, above all else, the catcher's throwing ability. When it comes to actual evidence, all they want to hear is how many runners he threw out. They automatically assume that the catcher who excels in that department is also outstanding in his overall defensive contribution. That's a lot like evaluating hitters by how fast they run; there's a correlation, but you wouldn't want to live by it. A lot of teams have great hitters who don't run well, and about 40% to 45% of them have their best CERA with the catcher who is *not* their best at stopping the running game. That's a stunning fact for folks who routinely give Gold Glove votes according to the percentage of runners thrown out.

One of the largest public controversies I got caught up in revolved around a catcher with awesome tools who came out on the wrong side of the CERA ledger. In 1984 *Sport* asked me to cast a Gold Glove ballot based on my defensive evaluation of the 1983 performances. My selections differed in some cases from the actual awards, but it was my selection of Rick Dempsey over Lance Parrish that set off fireworks.

In and of itself, a vote for Dempsey was hardly earthshaking. Seventeen of the actual voters selected Dempsey, thirteen took Bob Boone, and twenty-five voted for Parrish. In May, I was interviewed by a Dallas reporter, and we talked about the reasoning behind my ballot, particularly the point that I hadn't given Parrish much consideration because the Tigers' won-lost record and ERA were much poorer when Parrish was behind the plate in 1983 then when the reserves were catching. Rather than being a new trend, this was also true in 1981–82.

Well, that was absolute heresy at the time. Nineteen eighty-four was the Year of the Tiger, and Detroit was having one of the best first halves in the history of baseball. The reporter's paper sat on the story for roughly six weeks so it could be run when the Tigers came into town. The story was naturally edited to create the greatest interest. Comments on my part like, "Lance was, without a doubt, number one in shutting down the running game," never made it to print. They went and got smirking comments from Sparky Anderson and even sought out Tony Kubek, who gave a rather scathing reaction: "It's the old things with numbers. Figures don't lie, but liars figure. Lance Parrish throws with anybody in the league. He has learned to call a good game. He is a big guy, so he has trouble with low balls. But even Rick Dempsey, who is so cocky, conceded to me two weeks ago that Parrish is now the best."

I'm sorry, but that didn't help the discussion. As far as helping to understand the evidence and its significance, it's just a bunch of noise—a little slander, a little opinion, and no response to the evidence. It wasn't as if I had invited an attack by making an emotional sweeping point in a disrespectful manner; I bent over backward to present it in a way that would invite the skeptical into the discussion. I did not say Parrish was a bad defensive catcher. I did not say he called a bad game. I did not even say he didn't deserve the Gold Glove award. What I said, and I quote from the article, is, "I would not vote for Lance Parrish. I can't be too hard on the man because I don't know who's to blame for this: [for 1981–83] the Tigers are 63–29, a winning percentage of .685, with the reserve catchers starting. With Parrish catching, they were 172–169, barely .500. I know that Parrish is the DH when he's not catching, and, yeah, that helps the lineup, but it shouldn't make that kind of difference over three years. And, interestingly, the staff's ERA has been higher each of the last three years when Parrish catches. I've got to have some questions about his defensive ability [being Gold Glove caliber]."

Yet no one—not Parrish, not Anderson, not Kubek, not the reporter—ever made even the slightest attempt to try to explain why

Parrish's performance was so poor in 1981–83 relative to the Tigers' reserve catchers. They simply buried their heads in the sand and said, "It can't be." Ironically, I was the only one willing to ask and investigate the questions that might disarm the evidence.

Was it chance? Always a possibility, but not likely in a sample of this size and with such internal consistency. Did he catch a poorer set of Tigers pitchers? No, in fact when I set out to balance that factor I discovered that Anderson had a habit in all three years of matching Parrish with better pitchers than those assigned to the reserves. Did he catch more against the stronger teams? Yes, Anderson did have a slight trend of resting Parrish against the weaker teams, but in weighing the impact it was a much smaller effect than the edge drawn from working with the better pitchers. Were the Tigers' reserve catchers exceptionally good defensively, which made Parrish look less impressive by comparison? Yes, my research indicated that Bill Fahey in particular was one of the best defensive reserves in the league—despite a below-average throwing arm. But obviously a Gold Glover should be able to stand up better than that even to a group of talented reserves.

Why was there a drop in the pitchers' effectiveness with Parrish behind the plate? I didn't feel I was in a position to pinpoint the specific cause, but I did know this: I was not casting my Gold Glove ballot for a catcher who had such an unanswered question hanging over his head when the next-best catcher did not. In 1983 Dempsey had been the primary catcher on a World Championship club; the Orioles were 68–41 (.624) with a 3.52 ERA in games he started at catcher, and 30–23 (.566) and a 3.85 ERA when he did not. There were mitigating circumstances to account for part of that difference, but a good chunk of it appeared simply to be the presence of Dempsey behind the plate. That earned him my Gold Glove vote.

That evidence wasn't going to change anything either. I'm sure the reaction of Anderson and Kubek would be essentially the same as with the numbers on Parrish: They're meaningless. Shortly after that article appeared, I wrote a letter to Sparky Anderson that included this paragraph: "On a positive note, *if* the evidence is indicative of Parrish's effect on the pitchers, it also seems to indicate improvement over the last three seasons [each year the gap in comparative ERA was smaller]. *If* the evidence is meaningful, Parrish's comparative record should also improve with the absence of Bill Fahey [who was released and retired during the 1983 season]. He's the rascal who seemed to be in there for all the good games."

And that's exactly what happened. In each of his seasons with Detroit (1981–83), Bill Fahey's CERA was never over 3.00, and overall was a full run less than Parrish's for that period. In 1984, Marty Castillo became the Tigers' number two catcher. Castillo was a converted catcher, a former third baseman with very little experience behind the plate; in 1983, three-fourths of his defensive appearances were at third base and shortstop.

Castillo turned out to be a disaster behind home plate. The Tigers were a .681 club in 1984 with Parrish and Dwight Lowry catching, 12–15 (.444) when Castillo started there. On a team that led the league with a 3.49 ERA, Castillo's CERA was well over 4.00. It wasn't a fluke. In 1985, the Tigers were 7–12 (.368) in games Castillo started at catcher, and again his CERA was comfortably over 4.00.

Naturally, and as predicted, Parrish's comparative CERA was vastly improved in 1984. In 1985, an adjustment for the quality of the pitchers caught helped him come out about even in CERA. But much of this improvement came from the change in reserve catchers—particularly Castillo in place of Fahey. Dwight Lowry and Doug Melvin were the other reserves during those two years, and both had better CERAs than Parrish.

Parrish missed nearly half of 1986 with a back injury but had what I consider his best season in CERA. In 1987, his first year in the National League, reserve catcher Darren Daulton was more successful working with the Phillies' pitchers, but Parrish has had the edge in 1988 through the end of July. From 1987 to July '88, a careful control of the pitchers worked with shows that Parrish has had a 4.12 ERA compared with 4.07 for the Phillies' reserve catchers.

That covers a lot of ground, a lot of seasons, different catching corps, different pitchers, and even different leagues. Did the measure of CERA respond in an unreasonable manner that would suggest it's meaningless? No, when accepted for its strengths and weaknesses, it made sense, had a predictive note, and left us knowing something that we didn't know before. Despite Parrish's impressive control of the running game, there is no evidence to suggest that his overall defensive impact is exceptional, and over the span of 1981–88 it balances out as being pretty much average at best.

This case study does bring out two of the key problems that plague this measurement: the limited universe of each team's catching corps and the uncontrolled distribution of the pitchers caught. The first problem is one that never goes away and demands prudent judgment in drawing conclusions from the study of CERAs. Because the comparison is only between catchers on the same team, the presence of a very good catcher (such as Fahey) or a very poor catcher (such as Castillo) can radically skew the CERA for the other catchers. It is crucial to remember that, in the strictest sense, the concept of CERA and matched innings allows for comparisons only between catchers on the same team, not between teams.

It's a lot easier to deal with the problem of controlling the quality of pitchers caught. It's necessary because managers often match catchers to work more with certain pitchers. The catcher working with the best pitchers is obviously going to have an edge in CERA. In 1981–83, Sparky Anderson had a veteran backup in Fahey and a young catcher in Parrish, so he often matched the youngster with the veteran Tigers pitchers, who also tended to be the better pitchers. When Parrish was more experienced and his chief backup was a converted infielder with minimal catching experience, Sparky reversed that trend.

I control this uneven distribution of pitchers by setting up matched innings. If Joe Catcher catches 160 innings from Ace Pitcher and the other catchers have forty innings from Ace Pitcher, then there are forty common innings. On the other catchers' side of the ledger, credit them with the number of earned runs allowed in those forty innings. For Joe Catcher, project his earned runs down from 160 innings to forty innings. For example, if he had allowed sixty earned runs with Ace Pitcher, his matched earned runs would be 15 (40/160 × 60 = 15).

If we do that for every pitcher on the staff, we create a pool of matched innings that, for a starting catcher, will total anywhere from two hundred to seven hundred innings a season, depending on how the catching chores are split up. In that pool of matched innings is a perfect match in the distribution of innings by pitcher. It's as if the catchers were working exactly the same pitcher for those two hundred to seven hundred innings.

In my work with Sports Team Analysis & Tracking Systems, Inc. (STATS), I designed a report that does exactly that. In the sample report on the 1987 Rangers (see page 30), you can see how Geno Petralli had an advantage from being the primary catcher for Charlie Hough, the Rangers' best starter. In raw ERA, Don Slaught's edge in CERA was a slight .15 over Geno's (4.33 to 4.48). But when you look at the comparison of matched innings, Slaught was .41 better than the other Rangers catchers, and Petralli was .07. The difference suggested in raw ERA was less than half the difference found when the quality of pitching was controlled (.15 compared with .34).

This type of report can help eliminate the shameful scapegoating of some catchers for the failures of a pitching staff. Two recent examples are very instructive.

In 1987 Jack Aker was fired in midseason as the pitching coach of the Cleveland Indians. In *The Sporting News,* which is read coast to coast and all over the baseball world, he tore Rick Dempsey's defensive reputation to shreds, claiming that when it came to calling pitches, Rick was "incompetent." He went on to suggest that Dempsey was responsible for the Indians' pitching woes, and thus indirectly responsible for Aker's firing.

I'm here to tell you that as the pitching coach, Aker shouldn't be shy about taking a little responsibility himself. There is nothing in the evidence to suggest he knew what he was talking about. Here is the catcher ERA report for the 1987 Indians. (See page 31.)

Dempsey, who had been traded and was working with a new pitching staff, was actually the most effective catcher the Indians had in 1987. In matched innings he had a .44 edge; Allanson was − .20, and Bando was + .45. Sure, the ERAs were high when Dempsey was in there, but look at who he was catching—Dempsey caught over half of Ken Schrom's innings and had a 5.68 ERA with him, but it was

CATCHER ERA, TEXAS, 1987

MATCHED INNINGS, TO CONTROL FOR QUALITY OF PITCHING

CATCHER	P/9[1]	IP	ERA	H/9	URA[2]	BB/9	K/9	PER 600 PA 2B/3B/HR	CATCHER
Other C	150	504.0	4.55	8.6	.64	4.5	6.8	23/2/18	Other C
Slaught	152	504.0	4.14	8.6	.68	4.2	7.0	22/2/19	Slaught
Other C	153	395.1	4.35	8.1	.73	5.0	7.3	21/2/16	Other C
Petralli	156	395.1	4.42	8.7	.89	5.3	7.6	22/1/17	Petralli
Other C	152	400.2	4.65	8.6	.58	4.9	7.0	23/2/18	Other C
Stanley, M.	147	400.2	5.03	8.2	.45	5.1	6.6	25/2/17	Stanley, M.

RAW TOTALS FOR WHOLE STAFF

CATCHER	P/9[1]	IP	ERA	H/9	URA[2]	BB/9	K/9	PER 600 PA 2B/3B/HR	CATCHER
Slaught	152	554.1	4.33	8.8	.68	4.2	6.9	23/2/20	Slaught
Petralli	157	408.0	4.48	8.7	.88	5.3	7.6	22/2/17	Petralli
Stanley, M.	146	467.0	5.09	8.5	.44	4.9	6.2	26/2/19	Stanley, M.

CATCHING SELECTED PITCHERS

PITCHER	P/9[1]	IP	ERA	H/9	URA[2]	BB/9	K/9	PER 600 PA 2B/3B/HR	CATCHER
Hough	152	90.2	2.98	8.1	1.19	2.9	6.9	20/3/14	Slaught
Hough	149	146.1	3.94	7.3	.98	4.1	7.6	22/2/17	Petralli
Hough	161	48.1	4.84	7.1	2.05	5.4	5.6	17/3/25	Stanley, M.
Guzman	136	89.1	4.63	8.2	.20	4.0	6.2	22/2/22	Slaught
Guzman	151	42.1	5.95	10.8	.64	3.8	7.0	37/0/22	Petralli
Guzman	121	75.2	4.04	7.5	.24	2.9	5.7	26/0/18	Stanley, M.
Williams, Mi.	168	49.2	2.54	5.3	.91	5.8	11.2	6/3/ 9	Slaught
Williams, Mi.	205	24.2	5.84	7.7	1.09	12.0	10.9	10/5/20	Petralli
Williams, Mi.	160	31.2	2.56	3.7	0.00	7.1	9.9	14/0/ 9	Stanley, M.
Witt, B.	198	20.0	5.85	7.7	0.00	10.8	9.4	18/0/12	Slaught
Witt, B.	167	69.2	4.00	7.1	.39	8.1	10.5	15/0/ 9	Petralli
Witt, B.	171	53.1	5.74	7.1	.17	8.9	9.6	24/5/ 7	Stanley, M.
Mohorcic	118	56.2	2.54	7.5	.16	1.3	3.8	8/3/14	Slaught
Mohorcic	132	17.2	4.08	11.7	0.00	3.1	4.6	31/0/38	Petralli
Mohorcic	112	23.2	2.28	5.7	0.00	1.5	5.7	14/0/ 7	Stanley, M.

[1] Pitches per nine innings.
[2] Unearned run average.

CATCHER ERA, CLEVELAND, 1987

MATCHED INNINGS, TO CONTROL FOR QUALITY OF PITCHING

CATCHER	P/9	IP	ERA	H/9	URA	BB/9	K/9	PER 600 PA 2B/3B/HR	CATCHER
Other C	140	325.2	5.47	10.2	.75	3.8	5.4	26/2/21	Other C
Dempsey	145	325.2	5.03	9.4	.97	4.5	5.3	23/3/16	Dempsey
Other C	139	437.1	5.27	9.9	.78	3.8	5.4	25/3/20	Other C
Bando	134	437.1	5.62	10.1	.86	3.5	5.4	26/4/22	Bando
Other C	141	351.2	5.09	9.8	.87	3.9	5.2	24/3/20	Other C
Allanson	144	351.2	4.89	10.1	.67	3.6	5.4	25/2/23	Allanson

RAW TOTALS FOR WHOLE STAFF

CATCHER	P/9	IP	ERA	H/9	URA	BB/9	K/9	PER 600 PA 2B/3B/HR	CATCHER
Dempsey	145	422.1	5.24	9.5	.79	4.4	5.7	24/3/16	Dempsey
Bando	137	565.2	5.62	10.0	.78	3.6	5.3	26/4/22	Bando
Allanson	142	414.0	4.74	10.0	.63	3.5	5.2	25/2/22	Allanson

6.94 with Bando and 6.66 with Allanson. When matched with a decent pitcher like Scott Bailes, he had a 3.14 ERA, while Bando and Allanson were at 4.63 and 6.63.

I even went back and did a separate analysis on the season up to the point where Aker was fired. Bando and Dempsey were basically sharing the catching duties, with Allanson still in the minors. There were nine pitchers that Rick and Chris had each worked with for at least five innings. Dempsey had the better ERA with eight of the nine; in 125 matched innings, Dempsey's CERA was better than a full run lower (-1.07)!

In the spring of 1988 I was in Vero Beach on STATS business when Dempsey was in the Dodgers' camp trying to make the team. In talking with Steve Boros and Fred Claire, I had the opportunity to make the point that Aker's charges couldn't hold water. Dempsey made the club, and because he is catching a quality staff, you don't hear any complaints, even though an argument could be made that he has been less effective than he was with the Indians. As I write this, through the end of July he has a total of 245.2 matched innings. The Dodgers are allowing 3.26 runs with Rick behind the plate as compared with an expectation of 3.19 with the other Dodger catchers. Of course, Dempsey is working with another new staff and a whole new league of opposing hitters, and I count Scioscia as a much better catcher than Bando, who is having another rough year in 1988.

A similar case of scapegoating surfaced in Kansas City. Rookie catcher Mike MacFarlane was shipped to the minors in August of 1988 despite outhitting his competition by 66 points. The Royals had been unhappy with their pitching and claimed MacFarlane's pitch selection was part of the problem. It was a rough blow to the rookie's confidence; he said, "I'm not going to quit or anything, but this is the biggest disappointment of my life."

Given the facts in the case, it is a horrible injustice. In 1987 the Royals gave MacFarlane a September call-up, and in his 56 innings behind the plate the pitchers had a 2.89 ERA. In 1988 he had 347.1 matched innings with a 3.45 CERA compared to an expectation of 3.91. That .46 difference makes it clear that MacFarlane was not the problem.

Actually, the move shouldn't have been so surprising. It wasn't so long ago that the Royals traded a fine-hitting twenty-five-year-old catcher named Don Slaught to get thirty-four-year-old Jim Sundberg, who made twice as much money and was traded after two years for a reserve outfielder (Thad Bosley). Hey, I like Sundberg, but I have a hard time accepting that the Royals wouldn't have done as well or even better hanging on to Slaught.

KC made the trade because it felt Slaught was a defensive liability based on his pitch selection. When he was traded to Texas, one KC executive said, "I hope their pitchers can call their own game." Slaught had been made the scapegoat for KC's pitching problems when the team was making the transition from its ancient staff of 1983 to the baby-boomers of 1984. The truth is that in nearly 1,000 matched innings during those two seasons, Slaught had an edge of .53 in CERA over the other Royals catchers. In both seasons the club had a winning record when Slaught started and a losing record when he did not. And who do you suppose was the other half of the Royals' catching tandem? John Wathan, the same manager who sent MacFarlane out because of his pitch selection.

One guy who was specifically mentioned by Wathan as having been messed up when pitching to MacFarlane was Charlie Leibrandt. It was an interesting charge—illuminating to us about how much of this area really is in the dark. First, Leibrandt himself said that he thought MacFarlane was doing a good job catching him. And second, the numbers show that Mac was doing a much better job than Quirk with Leibrandt.

LEIBRANDT IN 1988 THROUGH MACFARLANE'S DEMOTION

PITCHER	P/9	IP	ERA	H/9	URA	BB/9	K/9	PER 600 PA 2B/3B/HR	CATCHER
Leibrandt	148	47.0	4.79	10.9	.00	3.3	3.8	29/0/20	Quirk
Leibrandt	129	78.2	2.86	8.8	.57	1.8	4.7	25/6/13	MacFarlane

Better than a run per nine innings lower, 3.6 fewer base runners—where's the problem? On the basis of these numbers, MacFarlane didn't deserve a demotion, he deserved a raise.

An interesting study in the difference a catcher can make in a pitcher's style comes from looking at Mark Gubicza's records with Quirk and MacFarlane (see page 34). In September of 1987, MacFarlane caught Gubicza for the first time in the majors; Gubicza pitched eight innings, walked one, and struck out three. That was not your typical Gubicza start; in '87 he usually walked about four and struck out six. But MacFarlane and Gubicza carried that pattern over into 1988—yet when Gubicza worked with the other catchers, he tended to work just as he had for the rest of 1987.

Gubicza looks like two totally different pitchers depending on who is catching him. That raises one of the more interesting questions that CERA may help us to answer: Should a manager attempt to pair off catchers and pitchers according to how well they work together?

For the most part, I'm hesitant to recommend such a strategy.

GUBICZA IN 1988 THROUGH MACFARLANE'S DEMOTION

| | | | | | | | PER 600 PA | |
PITCHER	P/9	IP	ERA	H/9	URA	BB/9	K/9	2B/3B/HR	CATCHER
Gubicza	144	41.2	3.02	8.4	.43	4.1	6.3	10/0/10	Quirk
Gubicza	137	112.0	2.49	8.3	.88	2.8	4.9	21/3/ 6	MacFarlane

First, many of the catcher-pitcher matchups that appear to be significant are really just statistical illusions that will be exposed with time. Second, such a policy becomes an offensive handicap when you have reason to change your catchers based on how they hit the opposing pitcher. If a manager has a strong righty-lefty platoon, there would be a serious offensive loss in going to a defensive platoon.

Third, I suspect that it's a mistake to assume that the more experience a catcher has with a pitcher, the better. This is not the same as a second baseman and shortstop turning the double play better the more years they play together. Turning the double play requires a set of physical skills that can only improve with repetition and experience; consistency is a goal to be pursued. The relationship between the catcher and pitcher in their assault on the hitter is totally different. In many respects, it's a guessing game and consistency is definitely not a virtue.

I've noticed in my studies of CERA that the workhorse receivers who catch 130 to 140 games tend not to do as well in their CERAs as expected from their reputation and past performance. It could be that the steady pairing of catcher and pitcher dulls the mental process to a point that they fail to make adjustments when the need arises. Certainly there is the possibility that they are, unwittingly, laying down a consistent trail of cues and patterns that the hitters may pick up on, consciously or unconsciously.

Still, there are cases when a significant advantage (or disadvantage) does seem to exist in a catcher-pitcher pairing, and it would be foolish not to be aware of it. Bob Boone seems to struggle in getting the best out of Chuck Finley; in 1987 Finley had a 6.34 ERA with Boone, and in 1988 it was 5.13 through the end of July. Lance Parrish seems

to do much better with Shane Rawley than reserve catcher Darren
Daulton does, but Don Carman pitches much better to Daulton than
to Parrish. Both trends were true in 1987 and in 1988.

FROM 1987 THROUGH JULY 1988

PITCHER	P/9	IP	ERA	H/9	URA	BB/9	K/9	PER 600 PA 2B/3B/HR	CATCHER
Finley	155	62.0	2.90	7.8	.87	5.1	6.8	18/0/ 2	Other Cs
Finley	147	136.0	5.62	10.4	.26	3.7	5.8	31/6/12	Boone
Rawley	120	300.0	3.75	9.2	.36	3.1	4.8	33/2/17	Parrish
Rawley	134	74.0	6.81	12.3	1.09	4.4	3.9	30/2/23	Daulton
Carman	132	225.0	4.68	9.0	.40	3.5	5.2	25/4/23	Parrish
Carman	147	105.3	2.99	7.8	.26	2.6	5.0	31/0/17	Daulton

But is the proper solution simply to enforce the best catcher-pitcher
matchup? Think about what is really causing these occasional mis-
matches. This isn't a matter of differences in physical skills; it's a case
of one catcher understanding the strengths and weaknesses of a
pitcher better than another. Looking at the statistical lines on Finley,
it's pretty obvious that Boone has been pushing Finley to be less of
a strikeout pitcher and to show more control. That's a good trade-
off for a lot of pitchers—especially those walking five men every nine
innings—but it isn't working in his case. He appears to be one of
those pitchers whose control of his natural stuff will just have to
develop on its own.

Looking at Rawley and Carman, it's harder to say for sure what
the difference is. I've worked on such cases before, and there are all
kinds of things that one catcher might emphasize over another. Often
it is simply a difference in the confidence in certain pitches: things
like what you call for when behind in the count, and what you use
to punch out the hitter on two strikes. Sometimes there are patterns
that interfere with a pitcher's control. A lot of pitchers can't control
a curveball and a slider at the same time. They need to decide in the
course of a game to drop one to an occasional "show-me" role and
let the other be the breaking pitch they get over for strikes. I remember one case in which a pitcher had trouble keeping his pitches

down when pitching to the left side of the plate. Although neither of them even realized it, the catcher he worked best with had developed a tendency of working him more on the right side of the plate.

If the catcher who struggles with a pitcher learns the approach of a more successful catcher, the benefits should exceed whatever gains would come from a forced matchup. The manager could maneuver his lineup more freely; the team would have better protection against injury or roster changes; and best of all, the catchers would be learning more about how they could help any pitcher. What they learn in one case might help them with other pitchers down the road.

The most powerful lesson I've learned in the study of CERAs is that catching is far more a learned skill than a raw talent. That naturally suggests it is far more coachable than the other defensive positions. You can go only so far in working with an infielder or an outfielder; their physical tools are the center of their defensive prowess. You can't take the worst shortstop in the league and turn him into one of the best, but that may well be possible in the realm of catchers.

It is a fact that rookie catchers generally show a defensive improvement in their matched CERA in their sophomore seasons. They also tend to have more successful rookie seasons if they make the club in spring training. Their transition is also easier if they get to work more with pitchers they have caught in the minor leagues. When a veteran catcher is traded there doesn't seem to be a noticeable effect on his defense with two exceptions: a midseason trade or a switch of leagues. In 1988 Jim Sundberg faced the roughest situation possible, a midseason trade between leagues. After doing a very good job with the Cubs (.32 edge in matched CERA), his first 69.1 innings with Texas produced a CERA of 5.45 when a 3.63 mark was expected.

All of this suggests that a catcher's effectiveness is partially based on his knowledge of the pitchers and opposing hitters. We also see that many catchers show gradual improvement in their CERAs as they increase their catching experience. My analysis of Lance Parrish suggests he was a better catcher in 1986–88 than he was in 1984–85, and much better than in 1981–83 despite the fact that his physical tools have deteriorated. Converted catchers often have very poor CERAs in the early years of their transitions, before making large strides toward respectability. It seems that just developing the basic mechanical skills is such a challenge that they have to put off giving much attention to the finer points of the trade.

Jamie Quirk was a former shortstop/third baseman who never caught an inning until his eighth professional season. He served as Kansas City's backup catcher from 1980 to 1982 with virtually no experience at the position. In 273 matched innings his CERA was nearly a full run higher than that of the other Royals catchers. How would a manager react to a pitcher who had an ERA a full run above the norm in 273 innings? Fortunately for Quirk, no one knew about this aspect of his defense. He is respected now as one of the better-throwing catchers in baseball, and his CERA has improved to a point where it is acceptable, though still a weakness.

There are other cases of players who started out as very poor catchers and made dramatic and lasting improvements in their CERAs. Remember Bill Fahey? Through age twenty-six he was actually one of the worst catchers I have ever seen in CERA. In 1975 Rangers pitchers had a 6.23 ERA throwing to Fahey; just to prove it wasn't a fluke, they had a 6.19 ERA with Fahey the next year for a two-year total of a 6.21 ERA in 236 innings. Then in 1977, Fahey completely turned it around. His CERA was nearly cut in half to 3.32, which was also well below the 4.11 mark put up by the other Rangers catchers. From that point on, Fahey not only had adequate CERAs, they were usually exceptional.

How did he do it? Basically he accepted the fact that he could make a difference and worked at it. The same thing seems to be happening with Texas catcher Mike Stanley. Several newspaper stories in 1988 commented on the tremendous effort Stanley was putting into improving as a catcher. He went around picking the brains of the best catchers in baseball, and religiously kept a book on how to handle opposing hitters with each Rangers pitcher. That notebook goes with him in every pitchers-catchers meeting, and he updates it after each game.

Has it helped? Well, you saw a report that showed Stanley had trouble working with the pitchers in 1987, a +.38 difference in 400.2 matched innings. Through the end of July '88, in 204 matched innings he had a −.49 CERA difference. That turnaround of .87 runs is almost all in his handling of the pitchers. He remains one of the easiest catchers to run on in all of baseball.

The clearest example that such skills are coachable is the career of Jim Sundberg. Sunny was generally perceived to have won his Gold Glove awards through his exceptional quickness as a fielder, his ability to stop the running game, his prevention of passed balls, and his durability. But there were some players, coaches, managers, and scouts who questioned Sunny's ability to call a good game.

The evidence seemed to bear this out. Sundberg's matched-inning analysis gave him the edge in CERA in 1975–76, but remember, that was the period when Bill Fahey was a very poor defensive backup. With Fahey's improvement in 1977, Sundberg went six straight seasons without having a better catcher ERA than the Rangers' reserve catchers.

CATCHER ERA IN MATCHED INNINGS

	SUNDBERG	RESERVES
1977	3.75	2.92
1978	3.52	3.48
1979	3.99	3.51
1980	4.20	4.20
1981	3.36	3.26
1982	4.40	3.65

In Sundberg's defense, I would point out that during this period the Rangers generally went with good defensive backups rather than catchers who were offensive threats. Sunny also caught a huge share of the innings, which may have diminished his effectiveness as measured by CERA. Still, those are not the results one would expect from a catcher honored with the Gold Glove award in five of those six seasons. For all his defensive excellence as a mechanical catcher, his overall defensive contribution was not Gold Glove caliber.

The Rangers entered the 1983 season with a set goal of improving Sundberg's defense under the guidance of coach Glen Ezell. One of the tools used was a pitcher-by-catcher comparison that brought out differences in the ways the catchers worked the pitchers. In 1982 John Butcher worked very well with catcher Bobby Johnson, who had also caught him in the minors. In fact, Butcher didn't allow a single earned run in his 20.1 innings with Johnson. His ERA was over 6.00 in 74 innings with Sundberg.

Looking through the pitch-by-pitch accounts, there were distinct differences in the way Sunny and Johnson handled Butcher. Rather than let Sunny learn Butcher's strengths and weaknesses by trial and error, he was given direct tips based on the success of Butcher and Johnson as a battery. In 1983 Butcher's ERA fell from 4.87 to 3.51; the big improvement was a 3.49 ERA with Sunny as his catcher.

Ezell also worked on a general reshaping of the basic strategies developed by Sunny over the years. One option specifically rejected was calling the game from the bench. Ezell felt strongly that you can coach a catcher off the field, but that he needs to be on his own when he enters the catcher's box. Calling the game from the bench is an automatic handicap for the team; no one is in a better position to evaluate and adjust to a pitcher's present effectiveness than the catcher. The only real hope is for the catcher to learn to do the job himself. Bob Boone is another who is outspoken against the idea of calling pitches from the bench. He considers calling pitches an art form, and learning a creative process simply doesn't happen through rote imitation.

I know that Sundberg cooperated. I knew some of the things he was asked to do; I could see on the pitch-by-pitch charts that he was following through and had broken some of the patterns he had established in the past.

The 1983 season was the most trying year in Sundberg's career. He had several nagging little injuries, a very poor year at the plate, and a number of serious personality clashes with his manager. In the midst of all this, Sunny was the primary catcher for the first Rangers pitching staff ever to lead the league in ERA. His CERA in matched innings came in at 3.37 compared to 3.47 for a group of talented reserves. It was his best showing in seven years and, in context, probably the best of his career.

Some claimed that the effort had been a failure, that the results were a fluke, and that Sundberg simply lacked "baseball smarts." I thought that was a deeply prejudiced opinion, and my written analysis for the Rangers closed with the opinion that "the major factor for the narrowing and seeming erasure of the long-time gap in catcher's ERA between Sundberg and the reserve catchers has got to be Sunny's own improvement."

A lot of time has passed since then, and I am pleased to say the effect has held. If you take his 1988 season through the time of his trade back to Texas, he has over 1,800 matched innings since that 1983 season and has a CERA edge of .12. A change was accomplished, and both Sundberg and Ezell deserve a lot of credit. It's naturally difficult for Sunny to acknowledge that there was a need for the change, but he recognizes the benefit. Speaking in a 1988 interview, he said, "[The criticism of my game calling] was started by a couple of old guys [pitchers] who were struggling at the end of their careers. But because of that, I changed the way I dealt with pitchers, and it's been a change for the better."

CERA offers us another opportunity to improve catcher performance. By identifying the best and worst in CERA, we know where to turn in trying to identify general strategies and techniques that may help a catcher. Without CERA we would simply be chasing the strongest throwing arm we could find. In 1988 a midsummer poll by *Baseball America* said that Ron Karkovice was considered the best defensive catcher in the American League—not so coincidentally, he was also rated the best-throwing catcher. But if we want to learn about catching, we should be more interested in listening to his teammate Carlton Fisk.

MATCHED INNINGS: 1987 THROUGH JULY 1988

CATCHER	P/9	IP	ERA	H/9	URA	BB/9	K/9	PER 600 PA 2B/3B/HR
Other C	139	686.7	4.30	9.2	.45	3.3	4.7	24/4/16
Fisk	137	686.7	3.93	8.5	.41	3.2	4.7	24/3/15
Other C	139	588.3	4.19	9.1	.47	3.3	4.8	24/3/16
Karkovice	140	588.3	4.69	9.9	.40	3.7	4.8	29/5/17

Over the past few seasons I've made it a point to watch carefully the catchers distinctly separated by CERA. Whenever they've been quoted about their catching, my ears have pricked up, and in some cases I've spoken to them about their catching philosophies.

Surprisingly, one of the key differences between the best and the worst is a mechanical factor. A catcher can get more strike calls on borderline pitches by *not* showing the umpire his glove as a target, or at least by drawing it back after the target is given. The best catchers—particularly the ones who call fewer walks in the matched innings—tend to give a full open-faced target to the pitcher and hold the glove closer to their body (watch Boone and Gary Carter). Holding the glove in toward the body is partially a physical reaction. Holding the glove face perpendicular to the ground is a strain on the wrist and forearm; holding the glove closer to the body eases the tension in the arm.

At first, the technique may seem counterproductive, giving a better target to the pitcher, but at the cost of losing the umpire by taking the glove out of his view. It would also seem to hurt your chances of getting a strike call by making you move more to go after bad pitches, particularly the low ones.

But that isn't the way it works. It's easy enough to handle the pitches around the strike zone with the glove held close to the body. The excess movement going after a bad pitch doesn't make a difference, because those are obvious ball calls anyway. It may even help emphasize to the umpire that if the catcher has to move a lot, it's a ball. Now consider the borderline pitch. Along with his natural judgment, the umpire is instinctively looking for clues. If he can't see the glove clearly, he may rely more on the catcher's movement; he didn't move, so it's a strike.

The opposite of this is the glove dropper. Some catchers will give the sign, set the target, and then drop the glove and bring it back up to catch the ball. Some catchers never do it; some do it occasionally, others do it when they are tired, and some do it all the time. Benito Santiago did it a lot in his rookie season, but cut back on it considerably in 1988. The worst I ever saw was Geno Petralli a couple of years ago.

Geno had a horrible CERA in 1985 (in matched innings it was 5.60

with an expected ERA of 3.88), and the big problem was in the walk
column. Even when broken down by pitcher it was maddeningly
consistent that each pitcher would walk more batters with Petralli,
on average, than with the other Rangers catchers. In June of 1986 I
did a quick calculation of Petralli's CERA and found it was again
well over 5.00 with an unusual number of walks. I was pondering this
while watching him catch a game on television during a West Coast
road trip. It suddenly hit me that on every pitch he was giving his
target and then dropping his glove all the way down to where you
could actually see the back of his hand. I was stunned. I had been
watching him for over a year and had never really noticed it before.
The pitcher was losing his target, and Geno's glove was constantly
moving just to catch balls around the strike zone.

Correcting the problem has been more difficult than expected. It
was a deeply ingrained habit. To this day Geno still drops his glove,
but not on every pitch. He doesn't drop it as quickly—which means
a better target for the pitcher—and he doesn't drop it as far. His
CERA and walk rate have shown tremendous improvement, although
I have yet to do a report in which his matched walk rate isn't higher
than the other catchers'. But he's getting closer; it was 5.3 to 5.0 in
1987, and 4.2 to 4.1 at the end of July in 1988.

In the strategy department, Bill Fahey was kind enough to come
into my office and talk at length about the things he emphasized as
a catcher. There were a couple of points you don't hear too often.
One, pitch to the situation as much as the batter. For example, when
you face the leadoff batter, don't worry about pitching to his power.
Concentrate on keeping him off base; throw strikes to set the tone
for the inning and to keep from walking anyone early. If you give
the opposition a base runner and three outs to play with, it'll usually
score him just as easily as if he hit a home run. You totally reverse
the situation with two outs. Stay away from the batter's power even
if it means pitching so fine you may walk him. A man on first with
two outs generally isn't going to come around.

Fahey also made a point of avoiding the big inning when a pitcher
was tiring. Those are the innings that can quickly turn a good outing
into a bad one. Know how your pitcher reacts when he begins to tire.

Don't call the breaking ball that your tired pitcher tends to hang in the batter's eyes. Don't call the fastball inside that might come up short and find too much of the plate. Give the batter the singles but don't risk the big blow. Give your bullpen a chance to save the game.

The most common thread in conversations with the better catchers is *a focus on the pitcher.* Rather than talking about this batter or that batter and a generic pitcher, they tend to talk about a specific pitcher or a style of pitcher and less about the weaknesses and strengths of specific hitters or batting styles. This is not to say they ignore the scouting reports on hitters; many put in a little extra effort to supplement those reports. Bob Boone likes to watch opposing hitters take batting practice, because that's when they'll show you the locations they hit best. But when push comes to shove, the best catchers consistently say something like this: "If my pitcher's strengths can attack their batter's weakness, we'll work him over, but I believe in matching strength to strength before I'll match weakness against weakness."

And there we begin to see the personality found among the best catchers. They tend to be leaders, but not dominating leaders. They want to inspire confidence more than fear; they want to make the pitcher feel involved rather than led around by the nose. If they had a smart pitcher out there who liked to run his own game, that didn't seem to ruffle their feathers.

Among the weaker catchers, there tend to be extremes in personality and depth of strategy with very little middle ground. Some are easygoing, we're-doing-okay types, while others are overly forceful, my-way-or-the-highway goons. Some have flat one-dimensional thinking processes, while others give the impression that catchers rank somewhere ahead of rocket scientists and brain surgeons, and why every team doesn't make their catcher the player-manager is beyond them.

Catchers of both extremes tend to focus more on the hitter. When I asked one of the straight-and-narrow thinkers about this, I got an interesting response: "What gets you second-guessed is when you go against the scouting reports. He [the manager] writes the lineup card. I'm going to keep him happy." In talking with one of the overly complex catchers, I realized that part of his problem was that he worked so hard at being clever that he was forgetting the basics. He tended to blame the pitcher for a lack of execution when it could easily have been his own failure to recognize what the pitcher was capable of doing and making the appropriate adjustments.

Who is the best catcher I have ever seen in CERA? He deserves to be mentioned in this chapter because his unusual reputation was what got me started in digging out the box scores and figuring my matched-inning CERA. He was the first, and I have yet to find better. I'm talking about the legendary Doug "Eye Chart" Gwosdz.

How does a career .144-hitter become a legend? One way is to get promoted to the big leagues after hitting .186 in the Pacific Coast League. Another is to be associated with such fine pitching performances that people can't help noticing. In *The 1984 Baseball Abstract,* Bill James wrote, "The thing about Doug Gwosdz (the Padres always win when he's in the line-up) is getting beyond the stage of a joke. Before last year they were 9–1 with Gwosdz in the line-up, last year 10–3 with a 2.19 ERA."

Terry Kennedy, the Padres' regular catcher during those years, was an All-Star with the bat but had a deserved reputation as a poor handler of pitchers. On his own, Kennedy went to this .144 hitter to ask for help in improving his defense. The next season (1984) the Padres manager and pitchers commented in *The Sporting News* on the improvement in Kennedy's game calling. When Andy Hawkins caught fire in 1985 and went 18–8, he told *Sports Illustrated* that much of the credit should go to his former catcher, now a minor-leaguer, one Doug Gwosdz.

I first became aware of Doug Gwosdz's defensive talents at the end of the 1982 season. In a brief major-league trial he went behind the plate in seven games, and in 44 innings the opposition collected only 27 hits, 12 walks, and six runs (1.23 ERA). That seemed rather remarkable even in such a small sampling. Checking back into 1981, I found 66 more major-league innings caught by Gwosdz. I did a matched-inning analysis of those 110 innings and found he had a CERA of 2.02 when a 3.48 mark was expected.

Looking at his minor-league record, I found that Gwosdz caught as a regular for four minor-league teams: Walla Walla, Reno, Amarillo, and Hawaii. The four seasons before his arrival those teams had a staff ERA 1.2% above the league ERA. In their four seasons with Gwosdz as their number one catcher, they were 8.5% *below* the league ERA, an improvement of about half a run. The four seasons after Gwosdz left, their ERAs rose back 9.2% to .7% above the league ERA.

I looked forward to Gwosdz's 1983 season, and he didn't disappoint me: 153.1 matched innings with a CERA of 2.58 when 3.56 was expected. In 1984, Gwosdz was catching very little and was sent to the minors in late May. He caught only 14 innings with a surprisingly high 3.21 ERA, but he was catching struggling pitchers who had an expected ERA of 4.89 (based on records through May 17, the last sheet of statistics Gwosdz appeared on as a hitter). He has not caught a major-league inning since.

	IP	ERA	H/9	BB/9	K/9
Gwosdz	277.1	2.40	7.2	2.8	5.6
Expected	277.1	3.60	8.7	3.6	5.3

The matched-inning analysis for his major-league career covers 277.1 innings and shows amazing internal consistency. In each season from 1981 to 1984 he had a sizable edge in CERA, and the net result is a difference in ERA of over a run.

And Gwosdz was even better in his 23 major-league starts. Given a chance to prepare in depth for the opposing hitters versus his assigned pitcher, as well as the opportunity to experiment and adjust his pitcher according to what was working that day, Gwosdz put up the following record.

W-L	SHUTOUTS	IP	ERA	H/9	BB/9	K/9
16–3	6	202	2.05	7.1	2.8	5.6

With a little bit of luck he could have been a twenty-game winner. In his four no-decisions, three times he left a low-scoring tie: 3–3

after 10, 2–2 after 12, and 2–2 after 7. In two of his three losses the
scores were 0–2 and 1–2. His six shutouts were thrown by six different
pitchers. Six shutouts in 23 games is a better ratio than any individual
pitcher since Valenzuela had eight shutouts in 25 starts back in 1981.

Personally, I cannot accept that any catcher, or any defensive player
for that matter, can make the difference of a full run a game. I suspect
that better than half that 1.20 run difference is related to (1) the
comparison with a weak defensive catcher in Kennedy, (2) the edge
of a very different backup replacing a frequently used number one
catcher, and (3) normal fluctuation for this sample size.

I also can't accept that Gwosdz is really a .144 hitter. After all, we
are talking about barely 100 at bats spread over four years and with
10% in a pinch-hitting role (yes, they had him pinch-hit 10 times).
A conversion of his minor-league performances from 1980 to 1987
suggests that with more regular use in the major leagues he could hit
.200 with decent power and an above-average walk rate. Let's see:
If a team wanted him to catch 130 games, and if it batted him eighth
or ninth, it would have to give him approximately 450 plate appearances. With that amount of playing time, his run value would be
about 36 runs while expending 326 outs. Give the same number of
outs to the average catcher (based on 1987 catchers), and you would
get about 51 runs. Their batting lines would look something like this:

	AB	BA	2B/3B/HR	SA	BB	OBA	K
Gwosdz	408	.200	21/2/ 9	.327	42	.275	110
Average C	432	.245	19/2/13	.388	36	.304	73

To make up for the 15 runs of offense, Gwosdz would have to
make a defensive improvement of .12 runs per game. That sounds
small, but it's a lot to count on as a predictable difference free of
any other influences. At the same time, we are talking about a catcher
who has shown a 1.20 edge in 277.1 matched innings. If we wrote
off 90% of that as the effect of other influences and unusual statistical
fluctuation, Gwosdz could still match the overall value of your average
catcher.

There are teams out there that could have used Gwosdz as a regular

that just wasn't mentioned when I was pitching. No one ever told me to try to get to know my catchers, and no one told the catchers to go out of their way to get to know their pitchers. I guess they figured all we each had to do was to go between the lines and do our jobs, but it's not nearly that easy. Confidence in your catcher's knowledge of what you can do in each situation is so important. When you're not fighting your catcher and he's in sync with you, it all just flows so easy, and when it doesn't flow, well, that's when you realize just how tough pitching can be.

I mentioned Earl Williams as the worst I ever threw to. I don't mean to knock the guy, and I know a lot of managers wanted him back there because he was such a good hitter, but from a pitcher's standpoint he was a disaster. The complete responsibility for calling the game was on your back; you had no help at all out there. He had no clue what to call when; it was like a random walk with him behind the plate. I suppose he could get away with it for pitchers with those ninety-mile-an-hour fastballs, but for those of us who didn't have that kind of stuff it was impossible. And the worst of it was that when you shook off Earl he took it as a personal affront, so he'd show you up very obviously when you weren't doing what he wanted—and all the time you knew damn well that if you did what he wanted the ball would be over the fence in a hurry. It was a truly frustrating situation for any thinking pitcher when Earl was behind the plate—frustrating for both of us.

But one thing I do believe is that the communication skills needed to be an effective catcher *can* be taught. Craig's observations are right on the money here. Jim Sundberg improved tremendously in calling a game. Don Slaught's learning curve expanded exponentially; Joe Ferguson spent a lot of time working with him while he was here. I saw a world of improvement in just one year with Donnie. It can be taught if the pupil's willing. You don't have to have a high IQ to be perceptive; you just have to avoid getting into set patterns. Sure, experience is crucial; I've always thought that it was ironic that we call the catcher's gear "the tools of ignorance," when its function is to protect him so he can play long enough to be able to *escape* ignorance.

Experience tells the catcher that the best pitch for a pitcher is the one the *pitcher* believes in; the wrong pitch thrown with confidence is better than the "right" pitch thrown with less than 100% commitment. The perceptive catcher can work the pitcher to the pitch that's right for the situation, and also make it the pitch the pitcher wants to throw. That's ideal communication. The best catchers can orchestrate it like a symphony conductor; they can motivate and direct a pitcher without the pitcher even knowing it's happening.

Probably the best example of a guy who can do this is Bob Boone with California these last few years. He's been an incredibly effective catcher for the Angels, even though it's obvious his physical tools aren't what they were a few years ago. One of Booney's tricks that's gotten a lot of attention is this business of "framing" the strike zone. That's kind of a misnomer; what Boone does is actually *extend* the strike zone, and by up to six or eight inches. He'll set up on the corner, but with the heel of his glove in the strike zone. Then, when the pitcher throws the ball into the center of the glove—or sometimes even the webbing—it looks to the umpire as if it's still a strike. So he's added the whole width of the glove to the strike zone; you'd better believe that's a big edge for the pitcher. (Of course, you've got to have a staff that can hit those spots, because if you're jumping all around back there, you'll never get that call.)

That's the other area where a catcher is critical: He's your line of communication with the umpire. No umpire will ever admit this, but *of course* the catcher influences the ball-strike calls. And there are some pretty reliable rules for how to do it:

1. Receive the ball—don't reach or grab for it. This will make it look as though the pitch is right where you wanted it. No pitch you have to reach for will ever look like a strike, even if it is.
2. Move predictably and deliberately; don't jump around.
3. Maintain a tempo. Don't let the game drag with constant trips to the mound or by being slow to set up. (Of course, there are some exceptions. Pudge Fisk, you are one of my best friends, but you are the slowest lug in the game!)
4. If you question a call, do it with your head still and facing the pitcher. Don't drop your head in frustration, turn around to

yell, or hold the ball where you caught it extra long to prove it was a strike. Umps hate to be shown up, and they'll get even if you do it.

5. Frame the strike zone, but don't try to frame obvious balls.
6. Catch the low strike with the glove up, and you'll probably get the call; roll the glove over, and you'll lose it.

And there's one other factor I'm convinced makes a difference, and that's the size of the catcher. Size affects the umpire's ability to see and call a pitch. The larger the body of the catcher, the farther the ump is from the zone. Maybe the stats reflect a bias against bulky catchers: Parrish is big, Dempsey and Gwosdz relatively small. Does this affect their catcher ERAs? Bill Freehan and Earl Williams were big, Yogi Berra relatively small.

So there you have it. If there's one key word, it's *communicate*. The smart catchers do it, the smart pitchers do it, and the rest are making it harder on themselves. Pitching against major-league hitters is tough enough; pitching against your catcher makes your job all but impossible. You can fight with a catcher's personality but in between the lines it's got to be a dance; you've got to get out on the dance floor and do your thing in tandem. It can't be a body-slam.

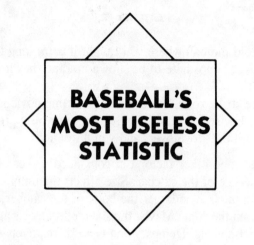

BASEBALL'S MOST USELESS STATISTIC

Baseball has several statistics hardly worth the effort of counting them. One of them, certainly, is the newest official statistic, the game-winning RBI (GW). I can't tell you who led in GW last year or any year, and I don't feel I've missed anything. Yet my least favorite statistic is one of the most respected in the game, a statistic that touches our perception of nearly every aspect of the game. It is older than the RBI or the sacrifice fly and has its own special niche on every scoreboard and in every line score. It is firmly entrenched, and nothing I will ever do or say is going to change it.

Still, given the chance, I will insist that this statistic is not relevant to modern baseball, it is not applied fairly, it misinforms the followers of the game, and it incorrectly shapes our perspective. If allowed to rip only one statistic out of the baseball records of our times, there is no doubt I would immediately turn to the error column.

THE RULE BOOK AND THE OFFICIAL SCORERS

Break out your rule book and turn to Rule 10.13: "An error shall be charged for each misplay (fumble, muff, or wild throw) which prolongs the time at bat of a batter or which prolongs the life of a runner, or which permits a runner to advance one or more bases." Hmm, a wild throw is fairly easy to visualize, and I can understand a "fumble" through its association with football. (Of course, I still haven't seen Rickey Henderson charge down to second base to throw himself on a ball that popped out of the second baseman's glove.) "Muff," though, can be a real conversation stopper when you talk with an official scorer. But there's no need to be embarrassed; even my *Webster's Dictionary* boots that one. It gives a baseball definition that reads: "failure to hold a ball that one has caught." That definition clearly conflicts with Rule 10.13(a): "An error shall be charged against any fielder when he muffs a foul fly to prolong the time at bat of a batter." That situation could never come up under the dictionary definition, because the batter would already be out, since you have to catch it first to muff it.

Are you getting a bit confused? No need to worry. Just do what so many of the official scorers do—rely totally on Rule 10.13, Note (2): "If . . . in the scorer's judgement the fielder could have fielded the ball with ordinary effort, an error shall be charged." (Then, in pencil, it says, "Just give a nasty look to anyone who asks whether that was a fumble or a muff.") At least the language of Rule 10.13 is consistent—vague and unclear all the way through. After "scorer's judgment," "muff," "fumble," and "ordinary effort," you have to admire their restraint that not once does the word *bobble* appear in Rule 10.13.

Even the most precise image, the "wild throw," begins to go haywire as you read 10.13d (2), which demands that an error be charged when a runner advances after a throw takes an unnatural bounce or hits a base or a runner or an umpire "even when it appears to be an injustice to a fielder whose throw was accurate." I remember Al Kaline losing a significant record for most consecutive games without an error when a beautiful, accurate, one-hop throw to third base glanced off the sliding runner, allowing him to advance home. Yet at the same time, the rule book instructs that a wild throw on a double-play relay shall not, under any circumstances, be charged as an error unless there is a base advancement as a result of the throw.

Let me see whether I've got this straight: If Kaline had been a second baseman making a double-play relay, even with all the time in the world and a chance to get the batter by 15 feet, he could throw the ball wild in the dirt, or wide of the first baseman, or even over the first baseman's head, and not be charged with an error as long as the batter continued to race down the line rather than advance to second. In other words, he could make a terrible throw that allowed the opposition a base runner and another out for its offense to play with, but it would not be an error. Meanwhile, when the outfielder Kaline makes a great throw but gets a bad break that results in giving up a single extra base, he is charged with an error. Amazing. *And that's the rare case when the rule is explicit!* It makes you wonder whether they wrote it that way to make us look a little kindlier at the concept of "scorer's judgment," which is the basis for nearly all other error calls.

If so, it doesn't work. The players, the fans, and even the official scorers themselves have a certain conscious awareness that there is no consistent standard of "scorer's judgment." This realization is as old as the game itself, or, as Ty Cobb so frequently complained, "That's a hit in Detroit."

Consider this: According to the official scorers, the Cleveland Indians were the second-best fielding team in the American League for the five-year period from 1976 to 1980. That is what their fielding percentage says. But, to take just one example, shortstop Tom Veryzer never fielded over .969 in five years with Detroit (.962 average), but in his four years in Cleveland he averaged .970, with a high of .974. Traded away in 1982, he fielded .954 for the Mets and Cubs till his release in 1985. A coincidence? Common sense seems to indicate that the official scorer in Cleveland heavily influenced Veryzer's record and that of the Indians with a lenient view toward borderline miscues.

When the Sports Information Service served as official statisticians of the American League, it would publish the errors made by the opposition against each club, a practice that the Elias Sports Bureau began applying to both leagues in 1987. An examination of these records will shake anyone's confidence in the ability of the official scorers to establish a standard for scoring errors.

If you just looked at the error column, you would be convinced that the fielding has gotten much worse in Cleveland since the late seventies. For the five-year period 1983 87, the Indians averaged 144 errors, more than any other American League team. In 1984, the Indians tied Oakland for the most errors in the league (146). A brutal-fielding team, right? If so, then why did Cleveland's opponents make even more errors than the Indians did? Playing before the same tough scorers, Cleveland's opponents made 156 errors, the highest in the league. At the opposite end, the 1984 Baltimore Orioles led the league in fielding percentage, and made 23 fewer errors than the Indians. Yet the Orioles actually made six more errors than their opponents, who checked in with just 117.

If we believe that there is a fairly common standard on which all scorers can base their judgment calls, we should be able to trust the error totals alone to rank fielding consistency. That means that Cleveland with 146 errors should be a worse-fielding team than Baltimore with 123. If this is a reasonable assumption, then the same should be true for the ratio of a team's errors to those of its opponents. The only way to escape this conclusion logically is with the wildly improbable assumption that players who make a lot of miscues in the field happen to be the same people who cause a lot of miscues as batters and runners.

The simple truth is that in 1984 it was Cleveland that made fewer errors than its opponents (-10), not Baltimore ($+6$). In this sense, the Indians' fielders were better by a count of 16 errors rather than trailing Baltimore by 23 errors. That leaves us with a dispute of 39 errors, which is often more than the difference between the teams with the fewest and most errors.

The first column in the following chart gives the ranking of the American League teams according to errors relative to the league average (642) for 1983–87. The second column ranks them by their errors minus their opponents' errors. The third column shows the order of the difference between the two; in other words, which teams have had the most misleading error totals.

The average disagreement between the two methods is 34 errors! That's nearly 90% of the average difference in the first column (38) and roughly 70% of the average in the second measure (50). Differences in the quality of the playing surfaces is a factor in this inconsistency, but the change in Cleveland's error totals from the late seventies suggests that the scorers are the key culprits. If you want to stay with the Baltimore-Cleveland comparison, not only did it not wash out in the larger sample, but the dispute of 39 errors increased

ERROR TOTAL RELATIVE TO LEAGUE AVERAGE		ERRORS MINUS OPPONENTS' ERRORS		ORDER OF DIFFERENCE	
1) TOR	(−71)	1) TOR	(−115)	1) CLE	78
2) MIN	(−67)	2) CHI	(−81)	2) BAL	59
3) CHI	(−57)	3) CAL	(−68)	3) KC	56
4) CAL	(−24)	4) MIN	(−53)	4) BOS	47
5) BAL	(−23)	5) DET	(−19)	5) CAL	44
6) DET	(−17)	6) CLE	(−1)	6) TOR	44
7) NY	(−5)	7) NY	(+2)	7) OAK	33
8) TEX	(+4)	8) BAL	(+36)	8) TEX	33
9) BOS	(+15)	9) TEX	(+37)	9) CHI	24
10) SEA	(+22)	10) SEA	(+39)	10) SEA	17
11) KC	(+35)	11) OAK	(+43)	11) MIN	14
12) MIL	(+39)	12) MIL	(+51)	12) MIL	12
13) OAK	(+76)	13) BOS	(+62)	13) NY	7
14) CLE	(+77)	14) KC	(+91)	14) DET	2

to 137 errors. That is, in the first column, Baltimore appeared to be 100 errors better than Cleveland; yet in the second measure it was Cleveland by 37 errors over Baltimore.

What is happening up there in the press box to create such inconsistencies? I tried to answer that question after the 1985 season by separating my Rangers scoresheets into home and road games and identifying the errors by position and type. This gave me two sets of errors coming in an identical number of games with the same pitchers pitching to the same batters hitting to the same fielding units, but in front of different official scorers. It created a focus on the characteristics of a single scorer against a backdrop of the scorers in the other thirteen cities. Nearly all the 1985 Rangers home games were scored by Burt Hawkins, a man who has watched professional baseball practically every day of every season for over fifty years as a reporter, traveling secretary, media director, and now as an official scorer. If any man would have a feel for the vague standard on which a scorer should hang his hat, Hawk would.

If that standard exists, it eludes even the Hawk. He scored his errors quite differently from his colleagues around the league. It seems there is simply too much leeway to develop any consistency regardless of how experienced the scorer may be. Hawk was much less forgiving of a fielder who was unable to catch a difficult pop fly, or one who failed to catch a tough throw and make a tag; he scored errors on these plays almost three times as often as the official scorers on the road. Hawk was also very tough on first basemen and surprisingly easy on the shortstops; he actually gave more errors to first basemen. There was a distinct pattern in the errors he forgave at shortstop: The number of throwing errors at short was exactly the same home and away, but the number of errors in the initial fielding of ground balls *tripled* for the shortstops when on the road. Hawk seemed to see a lot of bad hops that caused him to forgive fielders trying to pick up balls off the ground. This leniency did not carry over to the outfield, as Hawk charged nearly twice as many outfield errors for failing to pick up a hit cleanly.

If there is a pattern, Hawk's scoring judgment of "ordinary effort" was very tough on what we consider the givens in fielding—picking up a ball cleanly in the outfield, making an accurate throw in the infield, catching a pop-up, catching a thrown ball, and making a tag. He was very lenient in the scoring of the skill plays, how well you initially field the ball off the bat.

It isn't that official scorers lack objectivity in their hearts, but rather that the whole system of scoring errors is heavily centered on very subjective interpretations. I'm not being critical of Hawk; his seems as reasonable an interpretation as any, and in his execution of justice under a poorly designed system he was not swayed by who wore what uniform.

That is not to say that hometown scoring is dead. Under the present system it will always remain a possibility, even if at an unconscious level. Hometown scoring comes when the official scorer begins to identify with the home team and doesn't charge his errors consistently between the two teams. This problem has been with us a long time. Back in Cobb's day, they say the Detroit scorers bent over backward to give Cobb a hit on any questionable call, usually saying that Cobb with his great speed might have beat it out for a hit anyway. Well, the scorers then were reporters, and Cobb as a batting champion was news. And Cobb was not above raising a ruckus or cutting off a reporter who didn't understand the "system." Scoring a possible error as a hit for Cobb helped keep the peace, made things more interesting for your readers, and kept you on speaking terms with the star player of the team on your beat. Hard to resist.

If a similar scoring situation exists today, it is probably going on in Boston, the home of another perennial contender for the batting title, Wade Boggs. The Red Sox were one of the teams with a pretty high discrepancy in the evaluations of its fielders, and home-team scoring favoring the hitters would be one way to explain it.

For a long time I've noticed that Boston's opponents are not given many errors. In 1983 they were charged with 115, second lowest in the league. In 1984 it was 109, lowest in the league. In 1985–86, they were a little high, in the 130s, but in 1987 they were back down to an even 100. That's the fewest errors charged to any AL team's opponents in the 1983–87 period. Now think about the Boston players of that period: Buckner, Barrett, Hoffman, Owen, Boggs, Gedman, Rice, Armas, Evans. Do they strike you as an error-prone lot? During that five-year period, the official scorers charged Boston with 62 more errors than their opponents.

I decided to look through the Boston box scores of 1987 to see whether there was a peculiar pattern when they were separated into home and road games. There was. Boston's opponents made 12 fewer errors in Fenway than they did fielding against the same Boston team in their own home parks (44–56). The number of errors by the Boston fielders followed a more normal pattern by going up a couple on the road. Now why would the Boston fielders do a little worse when they were away from home, while the opposing fielders were doing much better in Boston than in their own home parks? I believe, along with a few other observers, that the three official scorers who serve the Red Sox have established an unwritten policy that you don't take a hit from a Boston batter unless it is absolutely a clear error.

There was something else I noticed in the data that would support this conclusion. Even though I hadn't been specifically looking for this pattern, it jumped out at me that a lot of the errors charged to Boston's opponents in Fenway were outfield errors. I went back and counted them, and 16 of the 44 (36%) were errors charged to out-fielders. There are two things you should know about outfield errors: They generally account for only 16% of all errors, and the vast majority of them are errors for wild throws or a failure to pick up cleanly a ball that's already a hit. Only rarely are they a question of awarding a hit or an error. I would wager that the 28 non-outfield errors charged to Boston's opponents in their 81 games at Fenway is the lowest such total in all of baseball since the 1981 strike season.

The really odd thing about this whole issue is that there is no real need to be making these kinds of decisions. When the rule book instructs the umpires to call a ball or a strike or a runner safe or out, those are the decisions the game has to have to continue—the decisions that become the irreversible facts of the game. It *has* to be a ball or a strike, safe or out. But it does not, in the context of the game, matter whether the batter reached base on a hit or an error. We don't take away the base runner and award an out because Joe Shortstop should have fielded the ball.

We create this record of errors only because we believe it is telling us something significant about how the game was played as well as fine-tuning our evaluation of the performances of the pitchers, hitters, and fielders. What are we assuming when we do this? Do those assumptions reflect the realities of the game? Do we understand the game better because of this information? How does it shape our view of winning performance? These are questions we need to ask in understanding the value of the error column.

ERRORS IN THE CONTEXT OF BATTER-PITCHER PERFORMANCE

Although we have already ripped huge holes in the assumption that the scoring of errors can be done in an objective fashion that produces meaningful differences, let's revive that assumption in order to continue our discussion. For the moment, we'll pretend that errors can be uniformly identified and separated from hits and other forms of advancement. We can now evaluate the central assumption in the category of fielding errors: that errors are totally the province of the fielders and should not be allowed to contaminate our evaluation of the hitters and pitchers.

Is that really true? Can't a hitter significantly influence the frequency of errors? It certainly seems reasonable that if a batter puts the ball in play a lot, he would cause more errors than the player who strikes out 120 times. If he hits a lot of grounders, particularly to the left side, he should produce more errors, since a ground ball allows chances to err on both the initial fielding and the throw. A talented, fast base stealer should also generate more errors on the base paths on extra throws to first and second base, not to mention his superior ability to advance on balls momentarily bobbled in the outfield.

All of this is logical and can be checked against the scoresheets. Researcher Davis Jackson did exactly that with the 1985 season in his book *The Last Word.* Consider the illustrative trio of Willie Wilson, Frank White, and Steve Balboni of Kansas City. As teammates, they played before the same official scorers on the same playing surfaces against basically the same defensive units. Frank White hits the ball hard and often to the left side of the infield, where most errors occur, and in 1985 he led the Royals in reaching base on errors (14), tied for third overall in the league. Wilson is KC's leading base stealer and is generally the leading Royal in drawing combined errors—that is, both reaching base on errors as a batter and advancing as a runner.

And then there is Balboni, a hitter who struck out 166 times in 1985, and hit it in the air when he made contact more than any other Royals regular. On top of that, he spent very little time on base and stole only one base in two attempts. Not surprisingly, White reached base on an error more than twice as often as Balboni (14 to 6). Steve's overall total of errors drawn was nine compared to Willie Wilson's team-leading 19, and that was a *good* showing for Balboni. In 1984, Balboni drew only two total errors compared with Wilson's 20.

These errors do not follow the chance distribution underlying our concept of the error. The pattern is clearly related to the offensive player's skills and style of play. Wilson deserves credit for the extra bases forced by his speed. White deserves credit for reaching base on errors that resulted from his putting the ball in play on the ground to the left side. And Balboni deserves a slight drop in his value for his lack of contact, his fly-ball swing, and his lack of speed, all of which lead to fewer errors.

Does this happen with pitchers? If you match a low strikeout sinkerball pitcher with a fireballing teammate who strikes out twice as many and gives up more flies than grounders, which one would allow a higher percentage of unearned runs? Logic would bet on the sinkerballer; the assumptions behind the error would dictate a coin flip, with the coin landing on its edge.

The best match I can imagine would be Ron Guidry and Tommy John, who pitched as teammates for the Yankees from 1979 to 1982. Guidry did strike out more than twice as many batters as John during this period, and John has a career "ground outs-to-air outs ratio" of 2.50 compared with Guidry's .90 mark. During this span both pitchers threw over 800 innings before the official scorers, in the same parks, and with the same Yankees defense behind them.

Tommy John had 13.7% of his runs classified as unearned, which was above the league average and way above Ron Guidry's 9.8%— nearly a 40% increase going in the direction logically anticipated. And if you think 800-plus innings is not a large enough sample, each has thrown over 2,300 innings in their careers through 1987, and that difference is even wider at the career level: 13.6% for John and 8.3% for Guidry.

Ron Guidry is responsible for reducing the frequency of errors behind him. He deserves to be credited for that difference, which between these two pitchers is an equivalent of more than twenty ERA points. Rather than improving our evaluation of these two pitchers, the concept of the error has blinded us to very real contributions and liabilities of their pitching performance.

THE HISTORY OF DEFENSIVE EVALUATION

While baseball's deep roots and traditions are among the glories of the game, they have also retarded our understanding. The game itself has gone through a number of evolutionary trends these past one hundred years. We left the Dead Ball Era sixty-five years ago, yet we still revere many pre-1920 values that have little relevance to the modern era.

The concept of the error and its corollary, fielding percentage, were born in the Dead Ball Era and received prominent play in the newspapers and baseball guides. In that period, fielding percentage did correlate significantly with run prevention—which is what defensive play is all about.

There are three basic ways that team fielding can help prevent runs: (1) reducing errors; (2) increasing double plays; and (3) converting potential hits into outs. In the Dead Ball Era, the double play was simply not that big a factor due to very aggressive baserunning, a lot of bunting, and inferior gloves that made fielding a slightly slower and more deliberate act. Double plays per base runner are about 60% more common today than in 1900–1919. A fielder with good range has been an asset in any era, but in the early days of baseball just handling the routine chances cleanly was the major challenge in the field.

The early fielders played with small, awkward gloves on poorly kept diamonds, sometimes on all-dirt infields, and with balls that were scarred, sometimes beaten lopsided, and literally spat upon. It is no surprise that the incidence of errors was roughly 225% greater than it is today. In 1911 Joe Tinker, a great defensive shortstop enshrined in the Hall of Fame, made 55 errors and fielded .937, to *lead* the league in fielding percentage.

The ability not to make errors was at a premium. If you were adept at handling bad hops or blessed with large hands, you had a real edge as a fielder. There are a number of stories from the old-timers about how the size of Honus Wagner's hands helped him become a great-fielding shortstop. Does anyone know who has the largest hands among today's infielders? No, of course not, because nobody cares. Glove improvement and better field conditions have made that factor obsolete.

The Live Ball Era brought more homers, more walks, and more extra-base hits—basically, those elements of offense that fielders can't do anything about. These factors figured to substantially lessen the correlation between fielding percentage and run prevention. Further, that drop in correlation should have mirrored the change in batting average's relation to run production, as those same changes (more walks, power hits, and homers) are nearly as separate from the measure of batting average as they are from fielding percentage.

This theory would suggest that fielding percentage should have retained some of its value, just as batting average continues to be significant, though with not nearly the same impact. What actually happened is that the correlation between fielding percentage and run prevention dropped like a rock, and by the 1970s it was practically invisible.

The two other fielding elements—the ability to turn the double play and fielding range—have increased in value while errors diminished to such a point that fielding percentage is like a dinosaur from another age. Who cares whether Carney Lansford fields .980 and Wade Boggs .965? Given the wild subjectivity in the scoring of errors, are we really going to learn anything from a difference of eight errors spread over 162 games?

What have we learned from some of the largest fielding percentage differences of recent years? Take Larry Bowa and Garry Templeton in 1978. That year Bowa won his last Gold Glove, making only 10 errors and leading the league in fielding percentage at .986. Templeton was an erratic twenty-two-year-old shortstop who led the league with 40 errors and fielded only .953. What did we learn from this thirty-three-point difference? Did we learn that Templeton—years away from his later knee trouble—showed spectacular range and fielded 82 more balls *cleanly* than Bowa did, despite playing one fewer game? Did we learn that Templeton led the league's shortstops in double plays with 108 compared with Bowa's 80?

The assumption that there is a strong correlation between the skill reflected in fielding percentage and the other defensive skills is simply wrong. Often the fielder with the better tools—great quickness, a cannon arm—has the ability to make the more difficult plays that also result in a few more errors. The older, more experienced players often have better fielding percentages, but they have also slowed down in the field. And sometimes the player with the soft hands just doesn't have the instinct for where the ball is going.

This idea has slowly seeped into the consciousness of the Gold Glove voters, who more and more reject the fielding percentage leader for glove men with superior range and double-play ability. Ken Reitz used to complain that Mike Schmidt was winning the Gold Glove at third base while making twice as many errors as Reitz did.

Of course, Schmidt was also starting nearly 50% more double plays and fielding cleanly fifty-plus chances per season while playing in the same number of games. No, Ken, those Gold Gloves ended up on the right shelf.

The real tragedy is the fielding performance that we overlook because we won't ignore fielding percentage for anyone less spectacular than an obvious Gold Glover like Mike Schmidt in his prime. Our eyes and minds are not able to assimilate hundreds of separate and fairly anonymous pieces of data scattered over six months. It's far easier to focus on the handful of relatively flamboyant errors, and to let our longtime trust in errors and fielding percentage keep us from developing measures for other fielding talents. And lost in the shuffle is a Darrell Evans, who was a very good third baseman in the seventies though much maligned because his fielding percentage was generally around .955.

Let the record show that Darrell Evans holds the NL season record for double plays by a third baseman (45) and led the league twice in that category. For three consecutive seasons (1973–75) he led all NL third basemen in total chances. In 1976 and 1977, they had him playing mostly in the outfield and first base; it was believed that Evans's statistical range at third base in Atlanta was an illusion created by the makeup of his pitching staff and his home field. In 1978 he returned to third base in a new home park in San Francisco behind a new pitching staff. Guess what? He led the league in total chances, and then did it again in 1979. In case you ever wondered, Darrell, someone did notice.

THE IMPOSSIBLE SOLUTION

Let's get a little crazy here and throw out errors entirely; invite Rule 10.13 to the site of the next atomic bomb test. I am willing to concede that errors are meant to refer to an aspect of fielding skill that does exist. But all the same, we've failed in our attempts to measure that skill. It's barely worth measuring under modern conditions, and our efforts to measure it block us from developing and gaining acceptance for more meaningful measures of defensive contribution. Seriously, who are we trying to kid? Sure, pitchers are helped and hurt according to the quality of the fielder behind them, but do we believe that counting errors is going to separate the pitching from the fielding? If we threw out the errors and the unearned run designation, we might start to look around and see some of the things that really matter— like what pitcher has Ozzie Smith behind him at shortstop and who has Hubie Brooks, who has the second baseman who can't turn a double play and who has the first baseman who couldn't stop a grape-fruit from rolling uphill.

Taking the focus away from the shoddy plays that may cost a pitcher a few runs could also open up a new appreciation for the excellent defensive plays that save a pitcher a few runs. And let's also give the hitter credit for putting the ball in play, and for his speed down to first base and his ability to advance on any bobble by the defense. Let the record reflect the honest confrontation between the offense and defense. The batter goes to the plate knowing that the pitcher and fielders are there to put him out. If the hitter beats them by batting his way to first or beyond, he should get credit for it and the defense should accept fault for it. Isn't it unjust that a batter can be robbed of a hit by a great play, but he never gets any credit when they boot one? Doesn't the booted ball have a value to the offense that the hard-hit out never will? Errorless scoring is tremendously appealing in its consistency, simplicity, and actual relationship to what the game is all about—the battle between scoring and preventing runs.

Still, such a proposal is sure to bring a cry of anguish from the traditionalists, who will also have heart failure at the thought of what this would do to baseball's records. What is interesting is that adopting errorless scoring would not create any statistical standards that haven't already occurred in baseball history. That right there should indicate what an insignificant role errors play in modern times.

Under errorless scoring, baseball records would begin to approach the levels common to the 1920s and 30s, the period remembered as the golden age of baseball. Those were the days when the league batting average was over .270 about 90% of the time, and once even crossed the .300 line. Seven of batting champions hit over .400, a player reached fifty doubles in a season thirty-one times, and another twenty had seasons with twenty or more triples. The league ERAs were very high, reaching 5.04 in the American League in 1938.

Thanks to Davis Jackson's 1985 study, we can get a pretty good feel for the statistical impact of errorless scoring in modern times. Wade Boggs would have led the league with a .387 mark rather than .368. Willie McGee would have led the National League at .371 rather than .353. The biggest gainer in the AL would have been Jim Gantner of Milwaukee, raising his average from .254 to .283; in the NL it would have been another second baseman, Glenn Hubbard of Atlanta, who would have gone from .232 to .269.

Dwight Gooden would have led in ERA, now simply RA or run average. Dr. K would actually have widened his lead over John Tudor, 1.66 to 2.23 instead of 1.53 to 1.93. In the American League, Bret Saberhagen would have jumped from third place to edge Dave Stieb by the narrowest of margins, 3.021 to 3.023. Danny Jackson, Saberhagen's teammate and one who gets more ground balls than most, would have seen his average jump from 3.42 to 4.07. In the NL, Orel Hershiser, who has a career ground-ball percentage similar to Tommy John's, would have seen his 2.03 ERA balloon to a 2.70 run average.

I think we could adapt quite nicely to these kinds of changes in our statistical standards, but sleep easy tonight, baseball purists— errorless scorekeeping is simply not going to happen. Logic cannot argue with the emotions that stand guard over tradition and grow stronger as the years go by. I would gladly trade in my grand dream for just a "base-on-errors" column in the batting summaries.

HOUSE:
THE ERROR OF MY WAYS

Errors, or at least mistakes, are always going to be a part of the game. Mistakes happen; if they don't, then you're probably not playing aggressively enough. Fielding errors are like the bad-debt provision in a business's balance sheet: You don't want a lot, but you get a little nervous if there aren't any.

Players come to accept their fielding limitations and work around them. Steve Garvey knew he had a lousy arm, so he avoided making unnecessary throws. The club helps the adaptation by developing a play in which the second baseman charges the first-base side on a bunt; that was a smart move when Garvey was playing first. Eddie Mathews had marginal hands but would sacrifice any part of his body to stop the ball, and then could scoop it up and make the play. His strong arm allowed him to compensate.

Players on every level know that there are going to be errors given that are deserved. What drives everyone crazy is the errors that aren't. I don't have a problem with the idea of assigning errors, but there's something wrong with how they're assigned. There's no consistency, no certainty that what was an error last night will be one tonight. I agree with Craig that errors are (1) irrelevant; (2) not being applied fairly; (3) misinforming fans; and (4) incorrectly shaping our perspective on the game. But I also agree that they're not going to go away. So I say, let's legitimize the decision-makers.

I propose adding one umpire to every crew and making the job of official scorer be one part of the umpires' rotation around the bases. Home to scorer to third to second to first. Umpires know the game, know the flow, and have a "field" perspective. It's amazing how easy the game looks from the press box; being on the field four days out of five would keep the view realistic. They'd be as impartial as they always (or ever?) are, and the frequent rotation through various cities would keep any individual idiosyncrasies from showing up massively in the stats.

I'd also support the idea of a team error. Why give a catcher an error when a throw hits the bag, but no one was covering? Why punish the outfielder for the perfect throw that hits a sliding runner and bounces away? No individual did anything wrong; charge the extra bases to the team. And why give a hitter a hit when his routine pop fly falls untouched amid four fielders? I say, put all these errorless errors in the team error slot.

But all this talk about errors is really a discussion not about baseball but about statistics. As Craig says, the result is the same no matter how it's scored. I believe that statistics are important for two things: fans and contracts. Sure, ballplayers all pay close attention to the statistics, because they know that at contract time those stats are going to be used to determine their worth. The whole arbitration system has just set this process in stone. And it's also led to all kinds of detailed statistics about how guys hit with runners in scoring position, or how many runners a reliever inherits and strands, and so on. These are the kind of statistics that have something to do with winning and losing, and they're coming about, I think, because you've got agents and general managers and consultants arguing arbitration cases who need all that stuff to make their cases. But the stats are still just stats, and you can't say that because a team has such-and-such statistics it's going to win.

When you talk about errors, I say, let's put aside the physical errors and start talking about the mental ones. I firmly believe that no team has ever lost a pennant because of physical errors, which tend to even out, but any number of them have been lost because of mental errors, the kind of errors that can't be determined or charged by any outsider. I mean missed signs, throws behind a runner or to the wrong base, throws over the cutoff man, improper defensive positioning, throwing a strike on a pitchout, not covering a bag, crossing up a catcher— anything that costs a team and could have easily been avoided with just a little conscious thought. Those errors don't hurt a club's statistics—except the won-lost percentage. Whenever I hear about a team, "They've got a good club, why can't they win?" I think: mental errors.

What can you do to eliminate them? Learn to anticipate. Visualize what might happen before it happens. Know what you're supposed to do and do it without thinking. Every pitcher complains about those endless drills in spring training that have you covering first on grounders to the right side, but that prepares you to anticipate without having to think too much. You see the grounder, you take off toward first. The more situations that become automatic for you, the better you can really think in those rare situations when you need to.

Thinking about anticipation brings up one of the areas in which the pitchers can have an enormous effect on a team's defense, and one that too often reflects another kind of mental error as well: the base on balls. Walks have a direct effect on the chemistry of the team out in the field. Walks dull the defense's senses, and the more balls a pitcher throws, the harder it is for a team to think aggressively on defense. They also deaden the tempo of the game and cut into a fielder's sense of anticipation of the ball in play. It is actually easier for a team to cope with a sequence that goes base hit/pop-up or base hit/double play than one that goes walk/pop-up or walk/double play. When the ball is hit, the defense is involved, and this keeps everyone on their toes.

As a coach, I've established some basic rules of thumb to help combat mental mistakes in pitching. These are practical, concrete solutions to the problems some pitchers face that can lead to too many walks:

1. The best pitch in baseball is strike one.
2. Baseball is statistically in favor of the pitcher—even the best hitters fail seven out of ten times, and .300 hitters hit .300 off mistakes, not off good pitches. Make mistakes down in the strike zone if you make them.
3. A pitcher gets a hitter out with location and/or change of speed. If you can't throw to spots, change speeds. If you can't change speeds, locate. If you do both, you'll win. If you can't do either, pray for rain.
4. A pitcher is always just one good pitch away from getting out of any bad jam. There are only two things better than a double play: a triple play and sex, and probably in that order.
5. Try to get every hitter out in three pitches or less. If you're forced to throw a fastball, throw it away from the hitter's strength. Don't change speed on a first pitch, unless it's the second or third time through the order. A change-up is just that—a change of speed off a fastball. The fastball must be established in the batter's mind first, or the pitch isn't a change-up, it's just slow.
6. The wrong pitch a pitcher believes in is better than the right pitch thrown with less that 100% commitment. If you've got any doubts, step off and reprogram yourself.
7. When you get to a 2–2 count, the next pitch should be the one

you have the most confidence in on that particular day. If you have more than one going for you, great; take your pick. If you throw a ball and go 3–2, throw any pitch, as long as it's a strike. Get it close. All but the most disciplined hitters will offer at anything resembling a strike at 3–2.

Finally, visualize your pitch doing exactly what you want it to do. Play over and over the vision of your pitches working; your body will aspire to your last thought, conscious or unconscious. If you say to yourself, "I don't want to hang this curveball," you're programming a bad pitch into your mental software, and your arm and body, the hardware, will receive the message and deliver that hanger. See, and set in your mind, the exact image of the pitch you want. Feel your body delivering that pitch. By mentally creating a sense of that perfect delivery, you can reprogram your muscles and nerves with positive expectations. Avoiding walks is as much a mental skill as a physical one, and damaging walks are among the most dangerous mental errors in the game.

Tracking errors—physical or mental—with an unbiased consistency will legitimize statistics for fans, management, and players. No change in how errors are assigned—whether we're talking about giving team errors, using umpires, or somehow assigning blame for mental errors—will change how players go about their jobs; there will just be less of a disparity between observation and statistic, between the fact on the field and the numbers in the box score. Craig's idea of errorless scoring has merit, but the umpire/scorer probably has a better chance of being implemented. It will satisfy baseball traditionalists, give extra jobs to the umpire's union, and lend field-level interaction to players and scorekeeping. We're both probably beating our heads against the wall, but can you find error in our attempts to change the system?

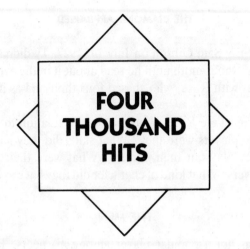

FOUR
THOUSAND
HITS

Four thousand hits. Al Kaline put in twenty-two years, including one final season as a designated hitter, to squeak into the three-thousand-hit club with seven hits to spare. Roberto Clemente got exactly three thousand hits by playing eighteen seasons and barely cheating death's attempt to stop him at age thirty-eight. Sam Rice put in twenty seasons carrying a .322 career batting average but came up thirteen hits shy of three thousand.

We are talking about great ballplayers here. Even when we address the true immortals, they fall out somewhere near thirty-five hundred hits. Tris Speaker stopped at 3,515, Stan Musial at 3,630, and Henry Aaron—who seemed he could play forever—ended up at 3,771. The next star after that is well into the universe of four thousand.

It's simple enough to see why the stellar achievement of four thousand hits has permanently joined Ty Cobb and Pete Rose in baseball's memory. Four thousand hits is their sign, their bond. The next player to achieve this goal is so far off in the distance that we can't truly believe in his existence—comprehend, maybe, but actually believe in our hearts? No.

But taken by itself, four thousand is just a number. And as it links these two vastly different men, it also represents two wildly divergent accomplishments. For Cobb, four thousand hits was just something that happened along the way in his great career. When he smacked a double off Big Sam Gibson on July 19, 1927, Ty didn't even know it was his four thousandth until he read about it in the evening paper. Contrast that with Rose, who chased four thousand as if it were the Holy Grail.

Ty Cobb and Pete Rose. Who are they in relation to each other? What kind of players were they? What skills did they have? In what style did they play out their careers? What were their accomplishments as players? What kind of character did they have as ballplayers?

THE MEN

Ty Cobb was not a popular player among his peers. The harshest assessments of Cobb consistently come from his Tigers teammates. Their most frequent complaint was that Ty responded more to personal challenges than to the task before the team; he was more concerned with showing he was the best than with winning games.

Hall of Fame teammate Sam Crawford remembered Cobb as one of the greatest players ever, but he also pointed out that Ty interfered with the manager, took special privileges, and had a disruptive influence on the team. Crawford once accused Ty of engineering the trades of teammates he disliked.

Davy Jones, who considered himself Cobb's best friend on the Tigers, tells of a time when Cobb was in a rare slump and took himself out of a game against a tough left-handed pitcher he had trouble hitting. But to cover his action, Cobb claimed he left the game in anger over a hit-and-run sign missed by Jones—a sign that Jones claimed was never given.

The opposing players had a bit more respect for Cobb; they only had to see him on the field. But even then, Cobb never garnered the respect one would associate with his skills. In one of the most extreme statements of dislike for an opponent in baseball history, with the batting title of 1910 still up in the air, the St. Louis Browns are said to have lain down for his rival Nap Lajoie in their last two games—not because they wanted Lajoie to win the title, but to keep Cobb from winning it.

The box score does look suspicious, as Lajoie went 8-for-9 in the doubleheader with a triple and at least six bunt hits. This appeared to give Nap the title by one point, and he received a congratulatory telegram signed by *eight Tigers players!* (Cobb had aroused his team-mates' ire by concentrating on winning the new car that was to be awarded for the batting title instead of trying to win games. Among other things, Cobb was accused of failing to follow through on set hit-and-run plays when the pitch was not to his liking. Cobb also chose to sit out the last two games when he felt he had the title wrapped up.)

Cobb's batting title was rescued by the league office, which—probably intentionally—duplicated a 2-for-3 game in figuring the final statistics to give the title back to Cobb. (Incidentally, Cobb's record is also missing the first two games he played in 1906; he went 1-for-8, so correcting the two errors puts his hit total at 4,190 and his career average at .366. And no one knows what to do with Cobb's unofficial hit from 1922. That season the hit total from the official scoresheets shows Cobb at .399. But to give Cobb a record third .400 season, the league statistician, with the backing of President Ban Johnson, ignored the official scoring of an error on a ground ball mishandled way back on May 15. Instead they used the scoring decision of re-spected sportswriter Fred Leib, who had scored the same play as a hit. To his credit, Leib openly denounced the league's action, but the hit went into the books. So Rose either broke the record on hit number 4,190 or 4,191; both were singles given up by Reggie Pat-terson of the Cubs on September 8, 1985, at Wrigley Field.)

What is interesting here is that there are two factions interested in shading our perceptions of Cobb as a player. The people he played with were not too thrilled with his character. The league, and I would add most of the reporters, tended to overlook his shortcomings. The league wanted a star, the papers wanted a hero for their stories, and Cobb was known for courting the press, although it too felt his wrath when he thought he was being slighted.

I would caution most readers of baseball history to be aware of who is speaking in any appraisal of Cobb. There seems to be a decided slant coming from both camps.

One matter that cannot be questioned is that Cobb did take advantage of his stardom in ways that were detrimental to a winning effort. In 1908, Ty scheduled his marriage during the season, much to the chagrin of his manager. In September, in the midst of a pennant race that would be decided by the narrowest of margins, half a game, Ty was gone for *six days*. On other occasions Cobb sat out games in fits of temper, once because his hotel room was too close to some railroad tracks. He frequently missed the bulk of spring training, though he always reported in playing shape. And in 1913 he let a contract dispute keep him out of action till April 30. All these things suggest that his teammates were accurate in characterizing Cobb as being overly concerned with himself at the expense of the team; it's likely that this attitude showed itself in other ways we don't know about today.

Cobb played every game of his team's season just once in twenty-four years, and over the course of his career played just 83% of the schedule.

Some excuse Cobb's sketchy playing pattern as a side effect of his physically demanding style of play, but besides the unnecessary absences already noted, Cobb hurt his team with numerous suspensions for abusing the umpires and other transgressions. One time he earned a three-day suspension for throwing his bat into the stands, and in another case picked up a ten-day vacation for going into the stands and stomping a heckler. And when Cobb did miss games with injuries, they were not always baseball-related. In 1914, Ty missed several games with a thumb fractured in a fight with his butcher.

More to the point, should we even care whether Cobb was suffering more injuries due to his style of play? Doesn't it seem fair that if his style produced extra runs, then it should be held accountable for the offensive loss when Cobb was disabled as a result of that style?

Is there anything in this view of Cobb's career that reminds us of Pete Rose? Emphatically, no. Some of the strongest testimonies to Rose's value come from those he played with and against. In the game itself, Pete was one of the most popular players ever. The old Cincinnati Reds of the 1970s will tell you that he may not have been the best player on their championship teams, but he was without question the heart of the Big Red Machine. When Rose joined the Phillies and helped lead them to their first World Championship ever, the Phillies' best player, Mike Schmidt, publicly said that Pete Rose was the man who taught them how to win.

Pete always wanted to play, always had the enthusiasm to play. He worked hard to keep himself in shape to play every day. You couldn't help but be impressed and admire his durability. Pete played 150 games or more in seventeen seasons, a major-league record. Nine times he played his team's full schedule. He is the only player to have two consecutive-game streaks of 500 or more, the last streak of 678 coming from ages thirty-eight to forty-two.

Everyone seemed to love Pete the player: the fans, the writers, the umpires, the managers, the ground crews, everyone associated with the game. We respected him so much that we sometimes forgot to assess his playing skills accurately. No one ever said that about Cobb. No one said that Cobb was the kind of guy they would have enjoyed playing with, that he brought out the best in you. No one ever said they respected Cobb so much that they forgot how good he was. It seems more likely that his managers and teammates had to reflect constantly on how good a player Ty was just to keep from strangling the guy.

Here, too, is a bias we must watch out for in evaluating these two players. Sometimes there is more emotion than substance in the contributions attributed to Pete Rose. In 1968, the players elected Pete as *The Sporting News* Player of the Year (pitchers are not eligible for this award). They overlooked Willie McCovey, who hit 42 points less (.335 versus .293) with 13 fewer runs scored (94 to 81), but led the league in home runs (36), slugging percentage (.545), and RBIs (105). Rose was nowhere near those numbers, as he hit 10 homers, slugged .470 and had only 49 RBIs. Further, McCovey's team finished second while the Reds were fourth, and Stretch played in a much tougher park for hitters than Rose did.

The baseball writers were even worse when they elected Rose as the National League's Most Valuable Player in 1973. Either his teammate Joe Morgan or San Francisco's Bobby Bonds would have been a far more logical choice. Their stats for the season:

	BA	SA	OBA	R	RBI
Bonds	.283	.530	.372	131	96
Morgan	.290	.493	.408	116	82
Rose	.338	.437	.401	115	64

Morgan played a premium defensive position at second base and played it very well; he fielded .990, led the league in putouts and double plays, and won the Gold Glove Award. The players at least had enough sense to select Bonds over Rose as Player of the Year.

The simple truth is that Pete Rose was never the best player in his league. In a way, that was as much a part of his style as the headfirst slide. Ty Cobb? Well, Cobb was probably the best player in his league at least five times (1907–08, 1911, 1915, and 1916) and just missed in 1909, 1910, and 1912. That is the kind of performance associated with the likes of Honus Wagner or Babe Ruth and no one else. As much as they may have disliked him, none of Cobb's teammates ever said, "We would have won more without him."

I am not inclined to spend much more time than that on the offensive performance of these two players. Offensive statistics are fairly easy to follow, and I don't think anyone is too surprised to hear that Cobb was a greater offensive force than Rose. Those who question it would have little trouble verifying it with a quick run through a decent baseball encyclopedia.

IN THE FIELD

A more interesting topic is how the gray area of defense is often used as a shield behind which one faction seeks to tear down an intensely unpopular player, while another group tries to enhance a beloved one. A classic case of this phenomenon is the popular defensive perception of Cobb and Rose.

Most people will tell you that Rose was the more valuable gloveman. Sportswriters like to cite Rose's versatility: He is the only player to have played over 500 games at five different positions (first base, left field, right field, third base, and second base). Ty Cobb is generally dismissed by his contemporaries as just a run-of-the-mill outfielder. But, as we'll see, Rose's defense was overrated most of his career, and Cobb was an excellent right fielder and a good center fielder for most of his career.

It's not that I'm unimpressed with Rose's versatility as a fielder. In a way it was his greatest defensive asset, and it brings into focus the kind of player he was. When they told Pete they had a better second baseman and Rose was going to left field, he didn't pout or argue that he was better at second than they gave him credit for (which was probably true); he went out to left field and hit. When Sparky Anderson needed Pete to play third base—a position that Rose had never played before in his life—he said something like, "Point me to it," played there the very next day, and finished the year at .317 while leading the league in doubles.

That is vintage Pete Rose, but as much as that tells us about Pete as a team player and about his rare ability to handle being moved around, it tells us very little about his actual defensive skills. If we look closely at the options facing his managers, what do those position changes mean? They indicate that Pete was not a good defensive second baseman; he was a better candidate for right field than Mike Lum, Alex Johnson, Bernie Carbo, or Hal McRae, but not Tommy Harper or Cesar Geronimo; that Rose was a better third baseman than Dan Driessen but not Mike Schmidt; and at age forty-three he was no longer able to play the outfield.

A look at the statistics suggests that Pete was, indeed, a mediocre fielder at second base. It took him two seasons just to bring his range factor (successful chances per game) up to an adequate level, and he was always weak on the double play. As a left fielder and right fielder, Rose was pretty good, but his Gold Glove awards in 1969 and 1970 were based more on admiration for his overall style rather than a thoughtful analysis of his fielding. In 1969 Bobby Tolan led the league's outfielders in putouts and range factor but finished behind Rose in the Gold Glove voting, as did right fielder Bobby Bonds, who led all non–center fielders in putouts and range factor. And in 1970, Rose won his Gold Glove over sterling performances by Willie Davis, Cesar Cedeno, and Bobby Bonds. Oddly enough, there was an outfielder whose defensive record in 1970 was remarkably similar to Rose's. That was Rusty Staub, who was never anyone's idea of a Gold Glover.

Of all the positions that Rose played, he was probably the worst at third base. Pete was adequate only in the sense that he was better than playing Dan Driessen or any other non–third baseman over there; he was good enough to play there, but that is as kind as you can get.

Rose had no range, his ability to start the double play was mediocre at best, and even his fielding percentage—his long suit—was fairly average for someone with an artificial-turf home field. Below are the ten National League third baseman who had at least two seasons of 125 games at third from 1975 to 1978, the years Rose started there. All statistics for those seasons have been projected out to 162 games.

1975–78	PUTOUTS	ASSISTS	FA	DP
Schmidt	128	396	.960	34
Evans	158	380	.944	34
Rader	137	357	.963	29
Cey	135	350	.964	26
Reitz	129	317	.967	28
Cabell	149	301	.955	21
Parrish	127	328	.936	29
Hebner	111	309	.948	21
Madlock	117	292	.951	21
Rose	115	277	.963	23

Clearly, Rose's range at third was very poor—even worse than it looks here. Some of the projections for the others are lowered by their having played partial games at third base, something Rose practically never did. It is interesting to note the other name at the bottom next to Rose. Like Pete, Madlock was a good hitter whose defense was never sufficiently held against him.

We often assume that if you play a position as a regular for a number of years, you have to be a decent fielder. What we forget is that this logic breaks down when we're referring to a great hitter whose bat can make up for his defensive shortcomings. A team committed to playing a Rose or a Madlock at third base is not going to knock his defense, and will probably even attempt to build a false reputation to avoid facing the question, "Can we really afford to play this guy over there?" If you swing the bat like Richie "Hack" Hebner, the commitment is not nearly as strong. When the time comes to do the obvious—like throw him a first baseman's mitt—you *want* to make the point that he is a bad fielder. You tend to exaggerate his shortcomings just as you would ignore those of a Madlock or Rose. So Hebner gets the "iron glove" rap even though he was fielding more balls cleanly per game at third than Rose or Madlock.

When Rose was moved to first base on joining the Phillies, he did very well and was arguably one of the top three defensive first basemen in the league. In his second year at the position he led in fielding percentage (.997) and in assists (123).

So how should we evaluate Rose's defensive credentials? He was a poor third baseman; he struggled to become an adequate second baseman; he was a good outfielder in left or right, but not Gold Glove–quality; and he was a very good first baseman. That's not a bad record, but it certainly doesn't justify the common perception of his defense either during or after his career.

Now consider the case for Ty Cobb. Several of his contemporaries made a point of downplaying his fielding, yet when you examine closely what they actually had to say about it, you get the feeling that they knew they were skirting the truth. Very, very few ever came out and said he was less than a good defensive outfielder. What they usually said were things like, "He wasn't all that special as a center fielder. Tris Speaker was much better." Since Speaker is frequently rated the greatest defensive outfielder of all time, that is hardly a harsh criticism.

We hear this hesitancy best in the voice of Sam Crawford, who liked to point out the fairly obvious truth that Cobb was not nearly as great a defensive contributor as Honus Wagner, a great defensive shortstop. Crawford said, "Cobb could only play the outfield, and even there his arm wasn't anything extra special." It is an awfully backhanded way of saying it, but if you think about it, what Sam actually implied is that Cobb had a good arm, but it was a weakness compared with the rest of his outfield play.

Crawford was only thirty years old in 1910 when the Tigers decided to move him to right field to put Cobb in center. I think Sam knew Cobb was a good outfielder; he just couldn't bring himself to say it clearly and was too honest to lie about it.

Although Ty had a defensive record that fluctuated in quality quite a bit, overall it is strong. He played very well in right field, always above average in range factor, and he led the position in assists three straight seasons (1907–09). As a center fielder in 1910 he caught more fly balls and had more double plays than any outfielder in the league. In 1923, when he was thirty-seven years old, he was second in putouts and led the league in fielding percentage and double plays. Cobb's range factor was above average in over 70% of his seasons of one-hundred-plus games, usually well above average. His performance was definite Gold Glove–caliber in at least four seasons and possibly in as many as eight.

HOW THEY AGED

One of the great myths linking Cobb and Rose is that they aged more gracefully than most superstars. This is very much true for Rose, but it is one of the biggest misconceptions about Ty Cobb's career. The central piece of this illusion is that Cobb's batting average after his thirty-fourth birthday was .360. But Cobb played the twilight of his career in the Live Ball Era, while he spent his prime playing with a relatively dead ball.

For the last eight seasons of Cobb's career, the league batting average was never lower than .281, went as high as .292, and averaged .286. Prior to that he played in seasons when the league average was as low as .239 and averaged .253. To put it another way, Cobb hit about 117 points above the league average before age thirty-four and only 74 points higher thereafter, a 37% drop-off.

Sure, you say, but .360 is still .360. Yes, but in the 1920s Cobb was also stealing fewer bases and hitting with very little power relative to the league. Consider this: If you turn to Cobb's career record in Macmillan's *Baseball Encyclopedia,* you see that through age thirty-two he led the league in fifty-two offensive categories, but after age thirty-two the number is *zero,* regardless of his .360 average.

If anything, Cobb's performance after age thirty-two was abnormally poor for a superstar. Babe Ruth led the league in twenty categories after age thirty-two. Honus Wagner led in seventeen, and both Stan Musial and Ted Williams did it in six. Pete Rose did it in eleven: Five times he led in doubles, three times in runs scored, twice in hits, and once in at bats. Cobb did not age well at all, while Rose was one of the best at maintaining his performance late in his career.

In all fairness, there was a positive development in Cobb's declining years that should be mentioned. When Cobb became the Tigers' playing manager in 1921, his interactions with his teammates began to reflect a more responsible, mature attitude. For the first time, it could be argued that he was making a contribution to the team off the field. In some ways he was still the same old Cobb: He would embarrass a player by criticizing him in front of the team and sometimes in front of the fans, and he was still fiery to a fault as he continued to abuse the umpires, earning too many ejections. Where his old teammate Davy Jones had once said, "Trouble was, he had such a rotten disposition that it was damn hard to be his friend," Charlie Gehringer would now say, "The man had no personality."

But the number of incidents off the field did decline. He wasn't knifing waiters or beating up his butcher. He was getting to spring training on time, did not miss any more games from fits of pique, and proved to be a pretty good manager and excellent batting coach. He took a team with a winning percentage of .396 the season before he arrived and ran off a string of years that went .464, .513, .539, .558, .526, and .513. If he had been a better judge and handler of pitchers, he would have been an excellent manager; his team's real gains were always on the offensive side. The team was next to last in scoring runs before Ty took over, but in Cobb's six seasons they were always third or higher and led in runs scored in 1924–25.

Harry Heilmann and Charlie Gehringer both acknowledge that Cobb helped them become better hitters. Two other future batting champions, Lew Fonseca and Lefty O'Doul, credited much of their batting success to instruction they received from Ty Cobb. In both cases, Cobb went out of his way to work with them even though they were not on his team. Cobb helped them because they asked and were serious about their hitting.

In one area, Cobb proved to be more admirable in character than even Pete Rose. Ty never played himself in front of better players, and Cobb did not take advantage of his name to stay on longer than he deserved. His last year in Detroit he had only 233 at bats, not because he was injured a lot or wasn't hitting (.339 batting average and .511 slugging percentage) but because he felt his other outfielders were even better. In mid-June he benched himself to start an outfield of Heinie Manush (.378), Harry Heilmann (.367), and Fatty Fothergill (.367). Cobb did not play regularly again till he joined the Athletics, where he more than earned his playing time: His .323 average and .431 slugging percentage in his final season were superior to the marks of his eventual replacement, Mule Haas (.280 and .422).

Cobb's personality had continued to mellow in his last couple of seasons, spent with the Philadelphia Athletics. Manager Connie Mack was openly fond of him and stated with great conviction that Cobb had been a good influence on his team. Cobb himself remembered his 1927 season under Mack as one of the most enjoyable of his career. When declining range in the field caused Mack to make the decision to end Cobb's career, Ty was understanding and supportive. If only Rose had accepted the fading of his skills with such equanimity—a subject I will return to at length.

Having fully established the identities and distinct differences between Cobb and Rose as ballplayers, we are probably as ready as we'll ever be to answer the questions about the relative worth of these players.

Who was the more valuable player? If I were a general manager, I would have to go with Cobb. His talent was so awesome that it contributed mightily to winning despite the disruptive nature of his character. His domination of the game for so many seasons is an exceedingly rare and valuable feat. One could conceivably replace Rose's statistical contributions by finding two minor star players and placing their careers back to back. To duplicate Cobb's feats, you would have to find that rare explosive and dominating talent possessed by only a handful of players in baseball history.

As a fan, who would you rather watch play? This has to be a matter of taste, but I know I would rather have watched Cobb. The richness of his talent could come through in a single game, while Rose's gifts of durability and consistency are better appreciated only over time. Equally important to me is that Cobb did things never seen on the diamond before or since. He had such confidence in his ability and such a brazen personality that he would try almost anything and stun you with his success. To be able to sit there and see it done, to see the daring involved, to wonder how much was a unique talent and how much could be taught and incorporated into the game itself—these are things I regret missing.

Ty Cobb was scoring from second on infield outs. He stole second, third, and home on consecutive pitches. One time he stopped the game to tell catcher Lou Criger he was going to steal his way around the bases. Once, to prove he could hit the long ball, he belted three homers in a game and set the league record for total bases. There is no doubt that Cobb had a special presence on the diamond. In Bob Broeg's book, *Super Stars of Baseball,* there is a revealing story of Cobb's first meeting with Bootnose Hoffman, a loudmouthed rookie catcher.

As the scourge of the league for a dozen seasons stepped into the batter's box, Hoffman cracked sarcastically: "So this is the great Georgia Peach?"

Cobb, taken aback, stepped out of the batter's box and surveyed the rookie. "Listen, Busher," he said, coldly, "I'm going to get on and when I do, I'm coming around."

Ty singled, stole, and then tried to score from second on a grounder to deep short. The throw from first had him beaten by so much, however, that Hoffmann determined to retire Cobb with a hard barehanded tag Ty would remember.

Just as Bootnose opened up to let Cobb have it, the fury in flannels took off at him through the air, feet first. One spike caught the catcher's chest protector and ripped it to one side, another cut his thigh and tore one shinguard away. They went down, Cobb one way, Hoffmann another, the ball a third way.

Let Hoffmann tell it as he would over the years:

"Cobb got up, stepped over me onto the plate, brushed his dust off on me, looked down and said, 'Yes, you fresh busher, that WAS the great Georgia Peach.' "

When it comes to which of these two players I admire the most, the answer is just as easy. I have always been attracted to the player who gets the most out of what he has and willingly does what is best for the team over his own interests. Overall, that has to be Rose.

WHOSE RECORD IS IT, ANYWAY?

So what about this all-time hit record? What does it mean in the context of their careers? What is four thousand hits to Ty Cobb, and what is four thousand hits to Pete Rose? When Rose was getting close to Cobb's record, there were a zillion articles trying to compare their different eras. Those building up Cobb pointed out the shorter schedules, the difficulty of hitting the spitball and other foreign-substance pitches, the condensed talent pool of only sixteen teams rather than twenty, twenty-four, and twenty-six as in Rose's time, and the primitive and physically draining conditions of the era—the overnight train rides, no air conditioning, heavy cumbersome flannel uniforms, and a lack of modern medical treatment and rehabilitation.

The response from the Rose defenders centered on the difficulty of hitting modern relievers, the better gloves assisting the fielders, the problem of hitting in night games, and the growth in the country's population as well as the addition to the talent pool of American blacks and Latin American players.

All these arguments have a certain validity to them, without really shedding any light on how best to compare their achievements. Our best bet is to try to control the factors whose impact we understand best. Take the shorter schedule, for example. It is a simple matter to project either player's statistics into the other player's schedule.

Say we want to compare their careers in the context of their ages. In 1918, when Cobb was thirty-one, the Tigers played a schedule reduced to 128 games by the war. Rose was thirty-one in 1972 when a strike got the season off to a late start; the Reds played 154 games rather than the normal 162. If you want to put Rose in Cobb's era, reduce his plate appearances that year by 16.9% (128 is 83.1% of 154).

We will have to give Rose back a handful of at bats each season because the pitchers of Cobb's time were less likely to issue walks than those in Rose's era. It comes out to about 6.7% of his walk total each year. In 1972 Rose drew 73 walks; about five of those would have been at bats in Cobb's time.

I don't see any real need to reduce Rose's durability in sending him back in time. Pete had a fairly lucky career with few injuries, and none required any kind of special care that did not exist in Cobb's day. Pete's playing streaks would not have been out of place, either: some players from Ty's period had streaks much longer than Rose's. Lou Gehrig played under roughly the same conditions as Cobb, and Lou's streak is more than 700 games longer than Rose's two streaks combined. Who knows, maybe Pete would have been known as the "Iron Pony," or something.

We can control a lot of the playing condition arguments by comparing the two to the league averages. Rose hit .301 at age twenty-six when the league average was .249; his average would project to .320 in 1913. That's the year that Cobb was twenty-six, and the league average was .265 [.301 × (.265/.249) = .320].

Another factor to be controlled is the gap between the top batting averages and the rest of the pack in each era. In Cobb's career the top hitters tended to hit much higher relative to the league averages than in Rose's time. The average top contender for the batting title during Ty's career—besides himself—averaged .370. During Rose's career his top competitor for the batting title averaged just .341. That's a rather significant 29-point gap, while the difference between the league averages was only 10 points.

Cobb played in a very special period. If all I knew was baseball history rather than individual hitters, I would predict that the all-time hit leader would have had the fifteen-year period from 1911 to 1925 at the heart of his career. In that time, hitting for average was relatively easy for the top guns. In what is only 18% of baseball's post-1900 period, the game saw 77% of its .400 batting averages. Three of the top eight in career hits covered this period with their careers: Ty Cobb (1905–28), Tris Speaker (1907–28), and Eddie Collins (1906–30).

There are three theories that account for this. The first two arise out of the fact that professional baseball was still in its infancy. The flow of talent to the big leagues was not as consistent and thorough as it would become. Luck was a much bigger factor in determining who made it to the majors. This affected the lesser players far more than the stars; a good pitcher from Humboldt, Kansas, pitching in a semipro league in Idaho might be overlooked—unless he had the talent of a Walter Johnson. This meant that the average and below-average major-leaguers, the bulk of the talent, might not have been as good as players in the independent minors. The top players in Cobb's period were more likely to face a diluted talent base outside their elite group.

The second theory revolves around the fact that instruction in the basic skills had not yet become standardized. Players had very different levels of mastery over their raw skills. A player following a correct technique in those days would derive a greater benefit relative to the rest of the league because the technique itself was not yet widespread. The best example of this is Ruth's early domination in home runs. The Babe's talent was immense, but no one could be that much more powerful than everyone else, and if he were, others would not have been able to catch up to him as quickly as they did in just a few years. Ruth was on the cutting edge of a new style. As long as it remained relatively rare, it gave him a massive advantage that was even greater than his considerable talent.

I lean heavily on a third theory, one based around the style of play common to that period in baseball history. In the Dead Ball Era the threat of the home run was basically nonexistent, and without that threat the base on balls was also relatively rare. Home run crowns were often won with ten or less, and the walk leader would sometimes be in the eighties. The league's most talented hitters were able to give their all to hitting for average; it was the best way to score runs. The live ball eventually changed all that, but the majority of the established stars in 1920 were still going to attack the new ball with the same style they had used all their lives. From 1920 to 1925 the average batting champion for both leagues hit an amazing .398, while the leader in hits averaged 234.

What is the best way to adjust Rose's performance to this condition of Cobb's era? If Rose had been born at the same time as Cobb, his career would have started in 1909 and ended around 1930. The Macmillan *Baseball Encyclopedia* has a section that gives the top five players in several categories for each season. For our comparison, we will combine the averages of the number two through five hitters in batting average. Taking out the number one man removes a lot of the unusual freaky seasons or the influence of a rare dominating player—like Cobb himself, who often took his batting titles with a thirty-point margin of victory. Dividing that average by the league average, we get a figure for this period of 1.317. Repeat this calculation for Rose's era, and the figure for the top two through five in batting average relative to the league mark is 1.254.

The additional factor we will apply to all of Rose's elite seasons is a 5% increase in average (1.317/1.254 = 1.050). This factor will be applied only in those seasons when Rose was among his league's top fifteen hitters (in 87% of such seasons Rose was in the top eight and was never lower than thirteenth).

We are now ready to play Steven Spielberg. On December 18, 1886, Ty Cobb was born in Narrows, Georgia. On that same day, Pete Rose was born in Cincinnati. Ty began his career in 1905 at age eighteen. Pete joined him in the American League at age twenty-two in 1909. Ty had a huge lead in hits due to his earlier start (548 hits through age twenty-one). The gap in career hits continued to widen as Cobb enjoyed his peak years and missed relatively few games. Going into 1913 at age twenty-six, Cobb had an edge of 702 hits, the largest edge he would ever have. The gap would still be 608 hits as they entered the 1919 season at age thirty-two.

It's at this point that Rose would really start to gain on Cobb. While Ty would be missing more games and performing at a reduced level, Rose would relentlessly continue his steady, consistent, durable performance. In 1924 Rose was second in the league with a .363 average, missed only two games, and hit in 44 straight games to break Cobb's league record of 40 straight. In 1925 Rose was again second in batting average and this time did not miss a single game. It's at the end of this season that one can—for the first time—visualize Rose possibly catching Cobb. The gap was down to 332 hits with Rose closing fast.

On July 27, 1928, Cobb played his last game as a regular. His legs could no longer do the job in the outfield. He appeared in only nine games the rest of the year, usually as a pinch-hitter. He retired with 4,191 hits at age forty-one. Pete Rose was still raring to go with his total at 4,111, just 80 hits behind Cobb.

Before continuing this story, we need to ask whether Ty Cobb would have retired with this immediate challenge facing his career hit record. I think there are a number of reasons to indicate that he almost certainly would have.

For one, with Rose's hit total so close to his own, I think Cobb would have been less impressed with the significance of this career record. To be frank, I expect his reaction would have been this: "I have twelve batting titles and a .367 career average. Rose has no batting titles and a .340 average. How important can having the most career hits be if a player like Rose can attain it over a player like myself?"

For the sake of argument, let us pretend that Cobb would have given some thought to going on to defend his career hit record. The verdict was already in that Cobb was through as an outfielder. Even though Cobb had outhit his rookie replacement by 43 points, Connie Mack felt Cobb had become too much of a defensive liability with his bad legs. If Cobb were to continue, he would have had to move to first base, something he studiously tried to avoid throughout his career. Against 2,943 games in the outfield, Cobb had made only 14 appearances at first base, 13 of those way back in 1918 when a shoulder injury made it impossible to throw from the outfield. Ty hadn't played a game at first base in the last 10 years.

Besides, a move to first base would have meant that Cobb would have to leave the Athletics and his favorite manager, Connie Mack. In mid-1928, future Hall of Famer Jimmie Foxx had just put a lock on the A's first-base position.

Now consider how Cobb would view his chances of holding off Pete Rose. *At age forty-one, Pete Rose had just played every one of his team's games!* How much longer would he go on? Cap Anson had played as a regular at first base till age forty-five. No, rather than make the record appear worth fighting over, only to lose out in the end, Cobb would almost certainly have retired.

Now, how should we end Rose's career? The 1928 season had been his worst since 1910 and was right around the replacement level for a first baseman in this era. The most optimistic view has his manager reasoning that it was just a bad year like in 1920 or 1926, and that Rose would bounce back as a regular. Instead, let's be pessimistic and assume this manager recognizes, quite accurately, that Pete is slowing down from old age.

I suggest we model Rose's remaining playing time after the last few years of Eddie Collins's career. Collins was a very similar player to Rose in his consistency, durability, and attitude, and went on as a player-coach much as Rose went on as a player-manager. And, of course, Collins reflects this era as he slipped from being a regular during the period 1925–27.

When Collins quit playing every day in 1925, his at bats fell to 425, then 375, and then 225. We will use those figures for Rose rather than the actual numbers he piled up in modern times. Rose's actual career was artificially prolonged by his pursuit of Cobb, a factor we shouldn't allow to affect these calculations. While this takes several hits from Rose, we will give a few back by basing his 1929 season not on the .245 average he compiled in 1983 while trying to play every day, but rather on his .264 performance in 1985 when his 407 at bats are closer to the 425 we have set for him at age forty-two.

The remaining batting averages for the last two years are based on adjustments of his actual figures at the same age. We will retire Pete at the end of 1931 at age forty-four.

Looking at the career chart of this mythical Pete Rose born in Ty Cobb's time, do we have confidence that this is a reasonable representation? The best measure of the validity of this chart can be found in the column titled "Batting Race," which depicts Rose's placement when his Cobb-era batting average would have placed him in the top ten.

What we have is a very close representation to Rose's place in the batting races of his own time. One career places him in the top ten thirteen times, while the other makes it fifteen. Rose loses his three batting titles from the modern era, but only because Cobb was part of the competition. Without Cobb, Rose would have won batting

PETE ROSE, BORN DECEMBER 18, 1886

YEAR	AGE	BA	BATTING RACE	ROSE'S HIT TOTAL	COBB'S HIT TOTAL
1905	18	—	—	—	36
1906	19	—	—	—	148
1907	20	—	—	—	360
1908	21	—	—	—	548
1909	22	.272	—	162	764
1910	23	.257	—	289	960
1911	24	.360	5th	520	1208
1912	25	.341	7th	733	1435
1913	26	.326	7th	915	1602
1914	27	.360	2nd	1131	1729
1915	28	.364	2nd	1350	1937
1916	29	.320	4th	1549	2138
1917	30	.315	5th	1740	2363
1918	31	.331	4th	1916	2524
1919	32	.376	2nd	2139	2715
1920	33	.315	—	2336	2858
1921	34	.379	3rd	2577	3055
1922	35	.360	4th	2807	3266
1923	36	.353	7th	3028	3455
1924	37	.363	2nd	3256	3666
1925	38	.390	2nd	3491	3823
1926	39	.322	—	3693	3902
1927	40	.383	3rd	3932	4077
1928	41	.295	—	4111	4191
1929	42	.294	—	4236	4191
1930	43	.323	—	4357	4191
1931	44	.288	—	4422	4191

4,422 hits in 13,116 at bats for a career batting average of .337

titles in 1914, 1915, and 1919. His number of second-place finishes for this model is exactly the same as his number of first- and second-place finishes in his actual modern career: five. It would be difficult to fault this analysis by the 232 hits necessary to return the spirit of the record to Ty Cobb.

As a baseball historian, I have always felt that Rose deserved the all-time hit record. He did more to earn what that record represents than Ty Cobb or any other player in history. This record is the perfect one to reflect Pete Rose's career: the steady, relentless drive of a minor star who joined the elite through a combination of durability and consistency unmatched in the history of the game. Ty Cobb was none of these things. He held the record because he was an awesome talent with the fluke of being born in the right time and place where the expression of that talent would come forth in an inflated hit total.

But we can't leave the discussion here. We who analyze these issues can conjure up an ideal baseball world, one set apart from considerations of time or money. But in the real world in which Pete Rose chased Ty Cobb's hit record, something very basic to our understanding of the game and its history went terribly wrong. Let's recall what the history books would like us to forget.

I can remember well when the chance of Rose reaching 4,000 hits was very much touch and go. In 1982 I wrote an article on Rose's chances of getting there and also the odds of his being able to go on to break the career hit record of 4,191. At that time, I felt the in-season settlement of the strike in 1981 had been the key. When the players went out on strike, Pete was forty years old and 370 hits short of 4,000. It was possible that he would not get another hit till after his forty-first birthday.

Fortunately, the strike was settled and Rose collected 67 more hits to enter the 1982 season 303 hits short of 4,000. Among post-1900 ballplayers, only one, Honus Wagner, had managed to collect three-hundred-plus hits after turning forty-one. Still, I wrote that Pete was now favored to break the four-thousand-hit barrier. I argued that he was going to get the at bats and had enough talent left to get so close that he would be allowed to continue for a brief while even if his skills could no longer justify his playing.

Remember, in 1981 Rose hit .325 and played every game. Any kind of decent year in 1982 with his typical 650 at bats—he had not missed a game in four years—would put Pete in position to take a run at 4,000 in 1983. Once he was close enough to do it in a single season, he was in. As I wrote then, "a team would play a .250 hitter for 115 games if he had a shot at 4,000 hits."

Rose's actual 1982 season went for 634 at bats and a .271 batting average, good for 172 hits. He hit only three homers and drove in just 54 runs while playing every day. Only San Diego got less offense out of the first-base position than the Phillies, but it was enough—just enough—to warrant giving Rose a chance to prove it was just an off year. No one wanted to take the chance of unfairly denying him a shot at 4,000; even if Pete cut his at bats back to 525 and hit only .250, he would still reach 4,000.

But Father Time was weighing heavily on Rose's back. In 1983 his performance fell off so much that his team could not afford to give him even 500 at bats. Pete went 121 for 493, a .245 average with no home runs and a slugging percentage reminiscent of Mario Mendoza (.286). That left Rose ten hits short of 4,000.

No problem. The Phillies could afford to play Rose off the bench in 1984 and still cash in on the excitement of his countdown to the historic four thousandth hit. It was not a pretty way to end a career or reach a milestone, but baseball had made such minor allowances before in the pursuit of lesser goals. The closest analogy would be Early Wynn's coming back as a forty-three-year-old who had just gone 7–15 with a 4.45 ERA the previous summer. He was brought back because he had 299 career wins. He went 1–2 and graciously retired with his three-hundred-win milestone.

It was at this point that Rose broke from the script. The Phillies had already invested one sacrificial season of playing him as a weak regular in order to allow him to get his four thousandth hit in a Phillies uniform. Rose rather ungraciously put the Phillies on the spot by informing them that while he did not plan on playing every day, he was set on playing as a regular in 1984.

Forget four thousand hits. The truth was out; Pete was going for the big one. This is where a new game began, an ugly game separate from baseball, a game in which the participant chases a record to the exclusion of all else, while cheered on by fans not so much of baseball but of a queer new game—call it "recordball." It is born of the same impulse that makes people watch a man hop in place for six days because Guinness recognizes such inanity as a "world record." To their credit, the Phillies' response was, "Thanks, but no thanks." Pete was free to try to find such a position in the free-agent market.

At first it looked as if Montreal sold its soul for the pizazz of "Recordball." One could imagine the Expos going with an advertisement that read, "Wanted: Player chasing significant career record. Talent optional." Montreal shamelessly basked in the glory of having the four thousandth hit come in its home opener on April 13. Ironically, it was also the twenty-first anniversary of Pete's first major-league hit, a little reminder that the real value in Rose's accomplishment came as a Cincinnati Red and Philadelphia Phillie, not as a Montreal Expo.

I may be too harsh in my assessment of Montreal's motives. The club did seem genuinely surprised when in August its first baseman–left fielder was hitting .259 with no homers. Maybe Rose had made the sales pitch of his life, and Montreal did not notice he was coming off a .245 season and had not homered since 1982. And maybe Montreal had bought the part of the pitch that said that Rose would make the talented but underachieving Expos into winners, just as he had in Philadelphia. (Never mind the three straight division titles won by the Phils immediately before Rose joined them.)

Whatever the case, Rose was sent home to Cincinnati for Tom Lawless. Lawless was billed as a token payment, but the truth is it was a fairly even player trade. And when you consider that Lawless makes major-league pocket change and fit in well with that quaint old idea that you play as much as your performance deserves, it was a train robbery on Montreal's part.

Rose continued to play in 1985. As a baseball fan, I was greatly disappointed to see it happen, and even more disappointed to see it happen with so little uproar. Where were the media in their watchdog role, helping protect the game against itself? True, Cincinnati was an improved team, but so was Montreal after Pete's exit. In this discussion it doesn't matter whether the Reds won a lot, though it certainly matters why they won a lot. It does not matter whether Rose was overall a good manager, though it matters whether as a manager he was making an appropriate decision regarding his own playing time.

We know that one of Rose's own players, Gary Redus, went so

far as to publicly complain that Rose played himself ahead of far more deserving players. It was surprising how many in the press defended Rose—not by answering the charge, but by asking who Gary Redus was to criticize a baseball immortal like Pete Rose?

One reporter defended Rose by saying that even though he was no longer a .300 hitter, his .264 average was still above the league average. He neatly overlooked the fact that Pete had only two homers and just 16 extra-base hits and 46 RBIs in over 400 at bats. Yeah, it was a good season—for a forty-four-year-old who hadn't had one since 1981. It was an appalling season for a first baseman. It was not a remotely good season relative to the performance of the players who could have played ahead of him.

Remember how Ty Cobb benched himself when he knew he had better players to put in the lineup? Not Pete. The '85 Reds were loaded with excess talent in the outfield and at third base, just the kind of players who are frequently converted to first basemen. When I looked at the club in spring training I came up with five names that I would have preferred to see worked into the lineup ahead of Rose's: Cesar Cedeno, Wayne Krenchicki, Eric Davis, Kal Daniels, and Gary Redus. Of this group, only Daniels did not get the opportunity to play in the majors in 1985. He broke an ankle in midseason in the American Association, when he was hitting .302, slugging .565, and getting on base at a .385 clip. The other four played less than Rose (averaging 190 at bats to Rose's 405), and all ended up being far more productive offensively (as measured by any of the runs-created formulas).

Even if you allow for arguments like "this guy is a righty, and we needed a lefty," or "this guy can't play first," somewhere out of all those options a solution would normally have been found. Look at it this way: With all that talent, would a smart manager have gone with a first baseman who was forty-four years old and in the last two seasons had hit .263 with no home runs in 867 at bats?

Particularly disappointing was Rose's handling of Wayne Krenchicki and Nick Esasky after the Reds acquired Buddy Bell. The two players had been platooning at third base, and both were doing very well. First base was Esasky's best position, and Krenchicki was a fine defensive infielder who had played some first base in 1983 and

1984. The obvious thing would have been to switch the successful third-base platoon to first base.

Nope; Rose stayed at first base while Esasky went to left field. That naturally meant less playing time for Redus, Cedeno, and Davis. And Krenchicki? Well, he got 45 at bats for the rest of the year.

Ironically, it was the handling of the insignificant Krenchicki that left all of Rose's arguments moot. Krenchicki could play first; he was a left-handed hitter, which was the primary need there; and he was not a prospect who would be held back by playing out of position or being used in a haphazard fashion (as if that wasn't happening with Davis, Redus, and Esasky). Krenchicki was also having the best year of his career and outhitting Rose in every way.

1985, PRIOR TO BELL TRADE

	AT BATS	BA	SA	OBA
Krenchicki	128	.305	.445	.403
Rose	229	.262	.323	.396

Equally important is that Krenchicki had better offensive seasons than Rose every year since Pete's performance took a significant dive after 1981.

FROM 1982 TO BELL TRADE IN 1985

	AT BATS	BA	SA	OBA
Krenchicki	706	.289	.395	.356
Rose	1730	.266	.321	.349

During this period Krenchicki also averaged more runs and RBIs per at bat than Rose, and Krenchicki's strongest seasons in this stretch were his last two: In 1984 he had hit .298 and slugged .470.

This did not mean Krenchicki was a star, or even capable of playing as a regular, but it certainly warranted his being given the chance to play a platoon role ahead of a forty-four-year-old player he had outperformed four seasons in a row.

Worse, all of this mess took place during a pennant race as the

Reds finished second, six wins behind the Dodgers. It's worth noting here what happened to Tom Lawless, the man traded for Pete Rose: he ended up in the World Series with the National League champion St. Louis Cardinals. He played exactly as much as his talents deserved, and in that way was far more a winning ballplayer than the 1985 edition of Pete Rose. Lawless was a ballplayer; Rose had become a carnival attraction.

Pete got his all-time hit record in 1985, but he had abused the game in a way that had never been done before. He went far beyond the simple case of letting an older veteran hang on just a moment longer to achieve a major milestone before fading back into whatever role he could earn. Rose passed Cobb by taking advantage of his situation for two, if not three, seasons.

They say one sin leads to another, and I was less surprised when Rose announced he would play again in 1986. Why? Believe it or not, he mentioned Cobb's record for runs scored: "I'm only 95 runs back." I wondered what we should do if he realized he had a shot at the all-time RBI record if he could hang on through age 65.

Well, Rose gave it a try, but a .219 average with no homers in 237 at bats saved Cobb's run record. As it was, Rose still gave himself more at bats than rookie Kal Daniels, who hit .320 and slugged .519 in 181 at bats.

This hasn't been easy to write about. I admired Pete Rose through the vast majority of his career. I was even touched by his reaction to attaining the hit record. Yet what Rose did—what we allowed him to do—was to cheapen every record in the book. The respect we have for baseball records, particularly the career achievements, is based on the assumption, *the trust,* that they are the result of performance and durability in the context of the game. That is, they came out of a winning effort.

Rose betrayed that trust and was allowed to tarnish the special regard held for these records. Future generations may skeptically view all the top career records as they wonder whether the record holder had pulled a "Pete Rose" to attain his mark.

Someone has to say this. Maybe the glitter of the moment blinded us, but I guarantee that sometime in the future, when that glitter has been forgotten, many people will say it. The way this record was attained was a disgrace—a disgrace to Rose, a disgrace to the fans, a disgrace to the media, the game, and all who supported it. It should never have been allowed to happen. It should not be allowed to happen again.

HOUSE:
PETE AND HENRY

You'll have to forgive me if I can't just look at Pete Rose as a series of numbers in a stat line—whatever they add up to. I know Pete. We're not best friends or anything, but he's spent some time at our San Diego School of Baseball's Christmas camps, and I've had some social interactions with him. If you asked Pete about me, he probably wouldn't remember anything about any social gatherings or teaching camps; he'd probably just say, "House? Lefty screwball pitcher with the Braves, early to mid-seventies, I faced him 31 times with five hits, but always hit the ball good. What about him?" Pete lives and breathes the game of baseball, and his obsessiveness, his singularity of purpose—his tunnel vision, if you will—is exactly what made him such a great player for so many years.

I'll never forget a trip to Riverfront Stadium in my rookie year, when the Big Red Machine was in full gear. I came in to face Joe Morgan with two outs and Rose on third. The visitors' bullpen was on the third-base side, and I had to pass by third to get to the mound. I made eye contact with Pete on the way, and I felt my insides just *freeze*. I was nervous as hell anyway, but Pete gave me this look I could only describe as savage. There was no doubt in my mind that he wanted to destroy me, that he could have casually ripped my arms off and not batted an eye. Well! On the third pitch, Morgan laced a triple to right center, and as I was goddamning it back to the mound after backing up third, I made similar eye contact with Morgan. He *winked* at me—not a "hey, I'm cool" wink, but a "hang in there, kid" wink. I'll never forget the contrast between the two.

Rose's genius—and in a baseball context, it *is* a kind of genius—is his absolute ability to adapt mind and body to the baseball environment. He's gotten fame and wealth from it, but it's the competition—with himself, with his opponents on the field, and finally with the record books—that he thrives on. That's just one of the reasons I can't criticize Rose for "hanging on" to try to break Cobb's record.

It bothers me when people talk about how Pete just hung on. There was nothing inevitable about Rose getting the record; Pete just made it look as though it was. I've seen the kind of pressure that comes from approaching that kind of record, because I was with the Braves as Henry Aaron was on the verge of breaking Babe Ruth's home run record. I can't imagine anyone lightly taking on that kind of burden.

The main thing that kept going through my mind around that time was, How can a man play baseball with this zoo going on all around him? I have to think about the statement that the Lord gives broad backs to those who carry the most. The Pete Roses, the Henry Aarons, they can succeed despite the environment. I think the psychological term is *positive denial*—they block out everything but what they need to know and feel to function. And I think some of it served to separate Henry from the rest of the team. Baseball's a fishbowl existence anyway, but it got really out of hand toward the end for Henry. Because, you see, Henry wasn't in the fishbowl with the rest of us, he was out there in a circus that was just about him.

I'm not talking about sportswriters here; sportswriters tend to become just a part of the routine for most of us. But a big media event like Henry's 715th or Pete's 4,192nd brings out the people who aren't all that interested in baseball. They don't understand the environment of baseball, and they do and say the wrong things at the wrong time. People were following Henry into the bathroom, for God's sake. They were asking him political questions because his new wife was active politically, and so he got involved in talking about all sorts of issues that had nothing to do with the game he had to play every day. He was getting death threats—remember, he was a black man trying to break a white man's record—and instead of being able to put them out of his mind, he was surrounded by people asking him what he thought about them. "This guy says he's going to shoot you in the fourth inning, Henry, how do you feel about that?" Well, how in the world are you supposed to go out and play a game with that kind of thing going on around you day after day after day? It can't have been quite as hard on Pete, because there weren't the racial overtones, but I'll tell you that anyone who's been around that kind of circus can have nothing but respect for an Aaron or a Rose who came through and broke the record in spite of it all.

I think it was good for the game, good for the fans to have Pete going for the record. Baseball fans like those kinds of numbers, those milestones. Anything that generates interest in the game and gets that kind of media attention helps support the game. I think it's worthwhile as a reward to a guy like Pete, or Henry, for their long years giving everything they have to the game. I don't have a problem with that.

And there's one other thing about the view that Pete was just hanging on. I'll bet you anything that Pete didn't see it that way. I don't think there's ever been a ballplayer who, on the day he was released, didn't think he could still play. I haven't pitched in the majors for almost ten years now, but until four or five years ago I still had visions of getting back in that saddle and riding. I don't just mean that it's hard for an athlete to have an outside perspective on his own abilities. I mean that there isn't any reason for an athlete to need that kind of perspective. Why should he? There are plenty of coaches and managers out there who won't hesitate to tell you when you're through. If they aren't forcing you out, why leave?

I was very bitter when I was released. I probably hung on a couple of years when I shouldn't have. I was pitching in Seattle for a team on which I was kind of a caretaker, holding a spot on the staff until the young kids came along. I know that now, but there wasn't any way in the world I'd have let anyone tell me that then. That's a part of the denial of reality that every athlete goes through toward the end of his career. You can't be a pro athlete if you don't believe in yourself. And if someone had offered me a chance to keep playing, for any reason, hell, yes, I'd have taken it. And I wasn't chasing anything special but the desire to keep pitching.

So I don't resent Pete Rose staying in the game to try to break a record. And except for a few guys who think they should have had his spot in the lineup, I don't think too many people in the game felt that way either. The sanctity of records? That's for the fans. We just play the games.

WRIGHT:
HENRY, YES; PETE, NO

I find Tom's argument very strange. It begins with "You'll have to forgive me if I can't just look at Pete Rose as a series of numbers in a stat line . . . ," and ends with "The sanctity of records? That's for the fans. We just play the games."

Yeah, right. If Rose had just played the game, we wouldn't be arguing right now. I think it's wildly ironic to begin a defense of Rose by sneering at the use of numbers. Hey, I'm not the guy who wanted 4192 on my license plate. My whole purpose here is to look beyond the numbers; I'm the one who said screw the numbers, the spirit of what 4192 represents belonged to Rose even before he started acting like a blind, selfish fool.

I think Tom feels he's defending his old teammate Henry Aaron by defending Pete Rose. That's ironic, because Henry's record is a classic example of those unjustly cheapened by Rose's drive for the all-time hit record. Because of what Pete did, folks are now inclined to wonder if Aaron did the same thing. Rather than make the point that Aaron and Rose are completely different cases, Tom defends them as one. If I were Aaron, I'd be insulted.

Let me be absolutely crystal clear on this: Henry Aaron's all-time home run record is worthy of admiration both as a remarkable feat and for the way it was accomplished. When Henry was under fire as a player "unworthy" of breaking Babe's record, I took the time to write him a letter from the heart wishing him the best and passing on my hope that he would reach 715. I treasure his reply, and you can bet he is one of the dozen players in the personal Hall of Fame that hangs on my office walls.

There is no doubt that Aaron set that record as a real ballplayer, one who clearly earned his place and his playing time in the context of winning that day's game. When Hammerin' Henry hit number 715, he was coming off a 40-homer season and the best HR ratio of his career. When he broke the record in 1974 he hit 20 homers in just 340 ABs and slugged close to .500 (.491).

I would also defend Aaron's "hanging on" after the record was broken. When people criticize former stars who chose to hang on as mediocre players, I have always jumped to my feet to defend them. It's their life, and it's not our place to tell them how they should live it; as long as they're carrying their weight on the team, it's fair.

When Henry hit .234 as the DH for Milwaukee in 1975, the Brewers also gave 258 ABs to Kurt Bevacqua (.229) and 240 to a young, overmatched Gorman Thomas (.179). Henry had decent power and the best walk rate on the team. He was second in RBIs with 60, which is more than Rose had in any of his last six seasons. Shucks, even when his performance slipped again in 1976, he clearly earned his spot: Both his slugging and on-base averages were above the team average, and his home run rate of one every 27 ABs was the best of any Brewer with more than 150 ABs.

But that's a far cry from Pete Rose's last few seasons. Tom tries to excuse him by making the point that Rose probably felt he could still play, and "There are plenty of coaches and managers out there who won't hesitate to tell you when you're through. If they aren't forcing you out, why leave?" Well, I never tried to portray Rose as the only villain in this mess, but we shouldn't forget that Rose was his own manager those last few years, and so those coaches were working for him.

I also doubt Rose was as completely confident in his ability as Tom would like to believe. I don't doubt the intensity of Rose's desire to play, but he would have to be mentally deranged not to have had some sense of how poorly he was playing; players don't go into five-year slumps. He was one of the most statistics-conscious players in my lifetime; he knew what those measures were saying about his performance. He knew what Philadelphia was thinking after he had two straight bad seasons, and rather than staying and trying to win the starting job, he sought out a contract and a team that would guarantee him one. Where's the confidence there? He also knew what the Expos were thinking when they dumped him in mid-season for Tom Lawless. And you can bet Rose had something to say about the situation he came into in Cincinnati, and that he knew what being a player-manager meant to his chances of catching Cobb.

Yes, Rose had a lot of deplorable help from the media, a segment of fans, the Expos and the Reds, but let's be fair here, Tom—Rose was *not* just reacting as any ballplayer would. They don't all have to be dragged kicking and screaming into the night, and I don't think there's ever been another player who worked harder or more selfishly to dodge the bullet. I cannot find another player-manager in baseball history who handled his own playing time in so unreasonable a manner; I'd say the majority bent over backwards not to favor themselves.

Pete has to take some of the responsibility. He was incredibly selfish in his pursuit of career records: The Phillies stuck by him probably one year longer than they should have, and their reward was a kick in the teeth when they tried to treat him fairly; he sold his 4,000th hit to Montreal; he cashed in his popularity to take over in Cincinnati. Even taking on the mantle of player-manager did not make him stop and clear his head, and he shamelessly applied a double standard where Pete Rose did not have to produce to earn his playing time. It takes a lot of gall to try and turn it around and suggest we should respect him for that.

My respect is for the Pete Rose who played to win. It stopped when he started playing "recordball."

HOUSE:
COMPETITION, NOT COMPUTATION

Craig, we're just going to have to agree to disagree on this one. Analysts and athletes aren't ever going to agree about Pete Rose and the hit record. Records like this happen as a function of competition, not computation.

I'm not going to try to convince anyone that Pete was a good player in those last few years, or even that he wasn't as bad as you say he was. His numbers were awful, and there's no denying that. But you make it sound like it was obvious even to Pete that he had become a bad ballplayer, and I can tell you that Pete *wasn't capable* of seeing himself as a bad ballplayer.

How could he? All his life he'd been surpassing people's expectations. Craig, you yourself refer to Pete elsewhere in this book as having been a marginal prospect when he was signed. How did he get to the point where he could pass a record that had stood for over fifty years? It was his intense drive, his intense determination, his incredible desire to compete that drove him every step of the way. Of course he went after the record with single-minded determination; that's only natural, since it was that determination that made him a major leaguer in the first place. Pete wasn't ever going to accept his limitations along the way to hit number 4,192; if he was the kind of guy who could accept his limitations, he'd never have gotten hit number one in the bigs, much less all the rest.

As far as comparing Pete and Henry Aaron, I certainly can't say that one was any more or less selfish than the other. The analysts can look at the numbers after the fact and say that Henry was productive to the end, while Pete shouldn't have been given the chance. But that's not how these decisions get made. Milwaukee traded for Henry for the gate, just like Montreal and Cincinnati did with Pete. And Henry wasn't still playing because he knew he was going to be productive; he did it because he was promised a beer distributorship and knew he could ensure his financial security by playing. Without that, Henry wouldn't have played; we all knew on the Braves how much his knees were hurting him, and he'd reached the point where playing just wasn't much fun for him anymore. Is that any more or less selfish than Pete? It's just that everything's right out front with Pete; he doesn't hedge, he doesn't hold back anything from the public about his motives.

Look, when it comes to our financial futures, there aren't too many of us in any field who don't look out for number one. Pete and Henry were both lucky to find themselves in positions where clubs were willing to pay them very handsomely to hang on for a few more years.

It's usually just the opposite—teams are only too happy to run your ass off the field before you're ready so they can bring in some younger guy they won't have to pay as much. Ball clubs will only pay a player for as long as he can play, or at least play enough to be economically efficient, and for whatever reason, the Brewers in 1975 and '76 and the Expos and Reds in 1984, '85, and '86 thought it was worth it to pay top dollar for a pair of over-the-hill hitters. You call it "record-ball," but they just called it "gate appeal." I can't see criticizing the player—in either case.

Henry Aaron was a magnificent talent, and his ultimate total of 755 home runs is a tribute to him and to that talent. He fulfilled the responsibilities of that talent, breaking a longstanding baseball record for himself, his teams, and his fans. Pete Rose was not a magnificent talent, but he had an indomitable will, and his record—regardless of what anyone says about what he should or shouldn't have thought about his abilities at the end—was the ultimate expression of that will.

WRIGHT:
THE BITTER END

No, Tom, we will never agree on this one. I don't doubt that it was Rose's intense desire to compete that got him the record. But that competitive instinct turned from winning ballgames to competing for career records. That was wrong, and, yes, I do believe that Rose was aware of what he was doing. There were some folks like the Phillies, and ultimately the Expos, who tried to make him face reality. And certainly the facts were there staring him in the face; he was living them. Certainly as a manager he took on the responsibility to step back and judge himself as a player. Assuming he did that, I can't believe that in the face of the facts around him that he could've acted as he did without letting his desire for career records play a role in his decisions.

It has not been my choice to emphasize Pete's role in this ugly affair. I did and do spread the blame for this among the media, a couple clubs, a new type of fan mentality, and a portion of it to Rose. The player has become the focus here because Tom feels he is blameless, and I consider that perception absurd.

As for Henry Aaron, it doesn't make one whit of difference if the goals of Aaron and the Brewers were exactly as Tom described. Every ballplayer appreciates a big payday; it's his career, how he makes a living and supports his family. And I've never argued that a club should not promote the game or themselves by showing interest in a popular ballplayer. But there is still a huge difference here. Those goals—both those of the player and the club—should be resolved in the context of the game, of whether the player can contribute and improve the chances of winning. Aaron did that. Milwaukee did that. In the case of Rose's final seasons, Cincinnati did not; Rose did not. They perpetrated a fraud, and we let them.

What should be sacred in this game is that you play to win. Until we reached this impasse I never would have thought this could be a point on which "Analysts and athletes aren't ever going to agree."

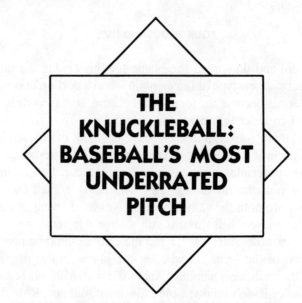

THE KNUCKLEBALL: BASEBALL'S MOST UNDERRATED PITCH

We are, unjustly, in the twilight of an era. We may be witnessing the last days of one of baseball's most baffling, most charming, and most effective pitches. Every fan who has watched a major-league hitter wave ineffectually at a sixty-five-mile-an-hour floater, and remembered his or her own first experience with a ball that broke, will be the poorer for its passing. The knuckleball, this spinless darter with its unpredictable twists and turns, has been a part of the baseball scene throughout this century; it ought to be preserved, not because of its charms, but because of its merits.

Everyone seems to agree that the knuckleball first appeared around 1904 or 1905 in the minor leagues, but no one is exactly sure when or where or even who invented the butterfly pitch. The popular story credits Ed Cicotte and Nap Rucker as co-inventors, developing the pitch while they were teammates on the Augusta club in the Sally League in 1905.

I've always been suspicious of that legend. Rucker and Cicotte were fairly famous pitchers in the Dead Ball Era, and it's always tempting to tie the origin of a pitch to a famous name. I've never come across a reference from Ty Cobb calling Rucker the father of the knuckleball, and that strikes me as odd. Rucker and Cobb were lifelong friends, Rucker was one of only three baseball personalities to show up for Cobb's funeral, and in 1905 Rucker and Cobb were roommates on the Augusta team.

While the New York newspapers made reference to Rucker's "new-fangled knuckle ball" in 1908, they reserved the title of inventor for an out-of-town pitcher. When the Phillies showed up to play the Giants on April 17, 1908, the *New York Daily Press* ran a game story that included this line: "The knuckle ball got a bad advertisement [as] Moren, its inventor, [was] knocked out in the fifth inning."

Lew Howard "Hicks" Moren was an obscure right-hander from Pittsburgh who had pitched briefly for the powerful Pirates teams of 1903–04, but after giving up 16 hits and 10 runs in 10 innings found himself an ex-major-leaguer at age twenty-one. The story goes that in 1904 or 1905, Moren was fooling around trying to throw the ball without putting any spin on it. He discovered it was easier if he shortened his grip by curling his fingers, putting just his knuckles on the ball. When he reduced the spin to less than a full revolution, he was startled to see the ball breaking erratically as it approached the catcher.

Moren knew he had found his ticket back to the big leagues, and by 1907 he was throwing his mystery pitch for the Philadelphia Phillies. He won 11 games, and an unknown writer christened the pitch the knuckleball because Moren's grip reminded him of pig's knuckles. Moren never did gain full command of the pitch, and he was out of baseball four years later at age twenty-seven. Still, the knuckleball had given him four full seasons in the major leagues, and it was responsible for every one of his 48 big-league wins.

Nap Rucker was not a true knuckleballer. He was basically a hard thrower, and a newspaper account makes it clear that he used the knuckleball as a sort of change-up rather than his dominant pitch. Ed Cicotte used an illegal "shine ball" as well as a knuckler, but his nickname of "Knuckles" suggests he was more dedicated to the knuckleball.

There may be a connection between Moren, Rucker, and Cicotte, since all three started off using the difficult knuckle grip. The more popular fingertip grip wasn't far behind, making its debut in 1908 with Detroit Tigers pitcher Ed "Kickapoo" Summers. He was also the first lefty knuckleballer and the first to become a star. Ty Cobb confirms that Summers was throwing the knuckleball in 1908 when he was second in the league with 24 wins and fourth with a 1.64 ERA.

The next year he won 19 and had a 2.24 ERA. His career went downhill after that, and the Tigers released him early in the 1912 season when he was just twenty-eight years old.

There is a story that Cicotte switched to the fingertip grip in 1915 or 1916. This reportedly improved his control of the knuckler and led to his super seasons in his thirties. At thirty-five he led the league in wins (29), winning percentage (.806), and innings pitched (306.2), and the next year he again threw over 300 innings and won 21 games. His career ended that fall as he was banned from baseball for his role in the 1919 Black Sox scandal.

There is no comprehensive list of knuckleballers, but past 1920 I can identify twenty pitchers who threw the knuckleball as their dominant pitch and put in at least four full seasons in the majors. I hope Tom Candiotti will make it twenty-one in 1990.

Gene Bearden	Ken Johnson	Eddie Rommel
Eddie Fisher	Dutch Leonard	Barney Schultz
Freddie	Joe Niekro	Bobby Tiefenauer
Fitzsimmons	Phil Niekro	Jim Tobin
Mickey Haefner	Johnny Niggeling	Hoyt Wilhelm
Jesse Haines	Bob Purkey	Roger Wolff
Charlie Hough	Willie Ramsdell	Wilbur Wood

There's a tremendous amount of quality in that group. Jesse Haines and Hoyt Wilhelm are already in the Hall of Fame, Phil Niekro is virtually guaranteed a Hall of Fame plaque when he's eligible, and Fitzsimmons has borderline Hall of Fame credentials. (Fitzsimmons actually has more wins, fewer losses, and a lower career ERA than Haines.) Four Hall of Fame–caliber pitchers out of twenty; that's about *ten times* the overall rate for pitchers with four years of major-league service.

Consider the knuckleballers on the all-time win list. Among all pitchers who won their two hundredth game after 1920, one out of every eleven has been a knuckleballer (P. Niekro, J. Niekro, Fitzsimmons, and Haines), and two just missed—Dutch Leonard won 191 games working for mostly second-division clubs, and Wilbur

Wood had four consecutive twenty-win seasons and likely would have won over two hundred if he hadn't been a star relief pitcher until age twenty-nine.

But wait, there's more: Nine of the twenty had at least one twenty-win season, and Wilhelm, Wood, Fisher, and Hough all had above-average years as relievers. Thirteen of the nineteen have career winning records, and Johnny Niggeling (64–69) probably would have been a fourteenth had he not thrown 90% of his innings for the St. Louis Browns and Washington Senators. (Niggeling's career ERA is third best in this group.) Only Willie Ramsdell, Barney Schultz, and Bobby Tiefenauer failed to have at least one excellent full season.

BEST FULL YEAR (WAR YEARS 1943–45 EXCLUDED)

	YEAR	W–L	ERA	REMARKS
Bearden	1948	20–7	2.43[1]	
Fisher	1965	15–7	2.40	24 saves
Fitzsimmons	1940	16–2	2.81	
Haefner	1946	14–11	2.85	
Haines	1927	24–10	2.72	
Hough	1987	18–13	3.79	league ERA of 4.46
Johnson	1967	13–9	2.74	
Leonard	1939	20–8	3.54	league ERA of 4.62
J. Niekro	1979	21–11[1]	3.00	
P. Niekro	1969	20–13[1]	2.38	
Niggeling	1942	15–11	2.66	
Purkey	1962	23–5	2.81	
Ramsdell	1950	8–14	3.68	
Rommel	1922	27–13[1]	3.28	
Schultz	1961	7–6	2.70	7 saves
Tiefenauer	1964	4–6	3.21	13 saves
Tobin	1941	12–12	3.10	league ERA of 4.15; team lost 92
Wilhelm	1952	15–3	2.43	11 saves
Wolff	1942	12–15	3.32	team lost 99
Wood	1971	22–13	1.91	

[1]Led league.

And we haven't mentioned any of the pitchers who extended their careers with quality performances as knuckleballers. Hall of Famer Ted Lyons eventually resurrected his career with the knuckleball after his severe shoulder injury in 1931; when he was forty-one years old, he led the league in ERA throwing a knuckleball. Larry French unveiled a brilliant knuckleball in 1942 when he was thirty-four; he ended up having the best year of his career, winning 15 games with a 1.83 ERA and leading the league in winning percentage. He finished the year throwing a one-hit shutout and facing the minimum twenty-seven batters. Ironically, what was the best game of his career proved to be his last; he went into the navy during the war and continued his naval career when the war was over rather than trying a major-league comeback at age thirty-eight.

There has been a tremendous return to those teams who have invested time, money, or player value in knuckleball pitchers. This leads us to a glaring question: Why is the knuckleball being allowed to die out? There are only two active knuckleball pitchers, forty-one-year-old Charlie Hough and Tom Candiotti, hardly a stripling at age thirty-one. And precious few young pitchers are trying to master the pitch anywhere in professional baseball.

I believe there are three key historical periods that helped foster a negative image for the knuckleball. It all seemed to start in the 1940s. Before that the knuckleball was a highly respected pitch, with Cicotte, Rommel, Fitzsimmons, and Haines building up strong records. More important, they all played with very successful teams: Cicotte with the White Sox, Rommel with the Athletics, Fitzsimmons with the Giants, and Haines with the Cardinals. The four pitched on fifteen pennant winners, and you know how baseball loves to imitate a winner.

That all began to change in the 1940s, as literally every knuckle-baller with any ability pitched for some of the worst teams in baseball. In 1942 Niggeling was with the Browns, Leonard was a Senator, and Roger Wolff threw for the last-place Athletics. Mickey Haefner eventually came up to the Senators, and Niggeling and Wolff ended up in Washington via trades.

All four were too old for the military draft and pitched through the war, associating the knuckleball with both losing teams and the inferior talent of the war years. Few noticed or cared that Washington failed to run away with the league only because its offense was so-so and its bullpen lousy. The 1945 Senators led the league in ERA and shutouts while starting four knuckleballers. Together they were 60–43 (.583) with a 2.70 ERA in nearly 900 innings, while the conventional pitchers on their staff barely pitched .500 ball with an ERA over half a run higher.

The knuckleball's next setback occurred in the 1950s, when it was mistakenly put in the relief role. This can be traced directly to the impact of Hoyt Wilhelm's career. Wilhelm had been an effective starter in the minors, but when he finally got his big-league break he was put in the bullpen. Fortunately for Wilhelm, but unfortunately for the future of the knuckleball, he had an excellent year, 15–3, 11 saves, and a league-leading 2.43 ERA. But pitching in relief slowed Wilhelm's development, particularly his control. His excellent command of the butterfly pitch didn't come until 1958–60, when he made 48 of his 52 career starts.

YEARS	WILHELM'S ROLE	BB AVERAGE	ERA
1952–57	Reliever	3.93	3.08
1958–60	Starter/Reliever	2.88	2.55
1961–72	Reliever	2.71	2.37

Conceding that Wilhelm was a great reliever does not mean he wouldn't have been a great and possibly better pitcher as a starter. After all, the only season in which he was primarily a starter may have been his best. In 1959 he completed 13 of 27 starts, threw 226 innings, and led the league with a 2.19 ERA. Of the six knuckleballers who switched from relief to starting roles, all six were successful as starters, and with the exception of Wilhelm, proved to be more valuable in that role. Given more of a chance, I believe Wilhelm would have done the same.

Think about it: The one clear problem for the knuckleballer is his occasional bout of wildness, with the accompanying passed balls and wild pitches. Is this the pitcher you want to bring in with men on base? And what helps to control these bouts of wildness? Steady, consistent, lengthy outings, which allow a knuckleballer to develop his control and to keep it. I've been tracking Charlie Hough's performance for over eight years now, and while his control may go haywire at any time in a game, it's more likely to happen in his early innings, and his control suffers when his workload falls below normal or if he has extra rest between appearances. I can't say this pattern is true for all knuckleballers, but considering the success and development of those converted from relief to starting, I assume these are attributes of the pitch rather than of the individual.

But back in the fifties and sixties, Hoyt Wilhelm was Mr. Knuckleball, and so all the young knuckleballers were typecast as relievers. Phil Niekro, Fisher, Purkey, Johnson, Hough, Schultz, Tiefenauer, and Wood all started off as relievers. Baseball didn't break the knuckleball out of the relief role until Phil Niekro became a starter in 1967 and Wilbur Wood joined him in 1971.

But the change may have come too late. The high attrition rate among knuckleballers trying to develop in the bullpen thinned the ranks and shook baseball's confidence in the pitch. Tiefenauer, Schultz, and a promising minor-league knuckleballer named Al Papai saw their careers die in the relief role. As a reliever, Charlie Hough nearly vanished in 1980 before Eddie Robinson picked him up on waivers and made him a starting pitcher.

And that brings us to our period, when the knuckleball unfortunately is being thrown by pitchers who have an unusually hard time controlling it. Modern observers are surprised to hear that many past knuckleballers have had exceptional control compared with conventional pitchers. From 1958 to 1972, Hoyt Wilhelm averaged fewer than 2.8 walks per nine innings. During Jesse Haines's eight-year-peak, his walk average was as low as 2.06 and never higher than 2.70. Fred Fitzsimmons's career walk average was 2.36, Rommel's was 2.55, and Dutch Leonard was the king of control with a 2.06 average.

In more recent times, Ed Fisher's career walk average was 2.56, and from the time Wilbur Wood became a starter until his knee injury in 1976, his walk average was a brilliant 2.12. It's also easy to overlook that Phil Niekro's control trouble at the end of his career seemed to be age-related; it didn't crop up until he was thirty-eight. We tend to forget this because the rascal turned thirty-eight way back in 1976. In the twelve seasons prior to 1976, Phil had an excellent walk rate of 2.36. Honest, you can look it up. After that he averaged 3.57 walks for the rest of his career—4.21 for the last five seasons at age forty-four to forty-eight.

Back in the late seventies when Phil was first beginning to make this concession to age, we had three other knuckleballers wrestling with control troubles. The first, Wilbur Wood, had his kneecap shattered by a line drive and never regained his fine command of the pitch. In his two comeback seasons he averaged a very uncharacteristic 3.84 walks per nine innings, which forced his retirement after the 1978 season.

The second, Joe Niekro, made the major leagues as a conventional pitcher, and his control was shaky at first when he converted to the pitch he used to throw as a youngster with his brother and father. He didn't gain good control of it until 1980 at age thirty-five. For a while there, 1980–82, he had excellent control of the pitch, a 2.48 walk average and a 2.95 ERA. But at age thirty-eight his control began to slip, just as his brother's had. From age thirty-eight in 1983 to his final release in 1988, his walk average was 3.80.

Finally, Charlie Hough was converted to the knuckleball at a younger age than Joe, but his control of the knuckleball was retarded by his being placed in a relief role. Hough was actually the wildest of the knuckleballers in the late seventies and at the start of the eighties. Until he became a full-time starter in 1982, his career walk rate was 4.63. He did develop much better control as a starter, and from 1982 to 1985 his walk rate was a quite respectable 3.11. But Charlie's control has slipped with age just as the Niekro brothers' had. He turned thirty-eight in 1986, and his walk average for 1986–87 was 3.72.

Yes, things haven't gone well for the knuckleball in the last fifty years. It became associated with losers in the 1940s; it was miscast in relief in the fifties and sixties, and was portrayed as too wild a pitch in the seventies. On top of that, the knuckleball has always had to battle a common baseball prejudice: Knuckleballers simply don't throw hard, and from the lowest scout to the general manager there is an underlying distrust of any pitcher who can't "bring it." If a flamethrower has an off season, his team will stand by him, and other teams will line up to trade for him. If a soft-throwing pitcher has an off year, they'll look to trade him for the nearest warm body.

Hoyt Wilhelm pitched seven years in the minors and didn't reach the majors until he was twenty-eight. One scout who saw him for a number of years filed reports in which he referred to him as "the old washerwoman." Usually it was the "the old washerwoman won another one," but he never recommended him. During his major-league career Wilhelm was released four times, traded four times, sold for cash twice, and once taken in an expansion draft. No other Hall of Famer had to go through stuff like that, people constantly telling him he either wasn't good enough or he was washed up.

I think the key reason that the knuckleball is dying out is that the pitchers today have less and less to do with their own development. If the knuckleball is to be revived, it won't start the traditional way, with some pitcher at the bottom of the chain tackling it on his own. He may try it, but he won't get the support necessary to make a go of it.

Modern pitching instructors just aren't interested in resurrecting the pitch. Most discourage their charges from experimenting with new pitches on their own, and since most of them are unfamiliar with the finer points of knuckleballing, I can't see them being enthusiastic about teaching a pitch they have little to no experience with.

If the knuckleball is going to be saved, the rescue has to start from the top. A general manager will have to see the value of the pitch and decide he is going to raise some knuckleballers one way or another and get a jump on the rest of the league. The scouting director will get the word to start paying attention to any tip-offs about those rare high school or college knuckleballers whom baseball has traditionally ignored. The director of player development will be asked to prepare a list of borderline prospects who might be a good bet for a conversion to the knuckleball. From that list two or three will have to be given the time and encouragement to develop baseball's most underrated pitch.

If there is such a courageous GM out there, I offer the following guidelines for breeding a knuckleballer. All things being equal, stay away from the taller pitchers. Gene Bearden and Ken Johnson were the tallest knuckleballers, and neither was consistently successful with the pitch. Al Papai spent close to twenty professional seasons trying unsuccessfully to master the knuckleball, and he was six foot three.

Joe Niekro, Barney Schultz, and Charlie Hough are six feet two, and all had poorer control of the pitch than most knuckleballers. The real star knuckleballers have either been of normal height or shorter: Phil Niekro (six one), Wood (six feet), Wilhelm (six feet), Leonard (six feet), Fitzsimmons (five eleven), Haines (six feet), Cicotte (five nine). It may be that the fine, consistent mechanics required for the knuckleball are more difficult for the larger pitchers to control.

Near as I can tell, whether the pitcher is lefty or righty or stocky or thin is no factor. Superior control prior to the conversion to the knuckleball helps—it does seem to correlate with how quickly and effectively a pitcher gains command of the knuckler.

There seem to be several common personality traits among the successful knuckleballers. Most were serious craftsmen who progressed through patient, stubborn persistence. They tended not to see themselves as athletes, but rather as baseball pitchers—less concerned with throwing hard and more with getting people out and winning over the long haul. The knuckleball is not for macho personalities overly concerned with their image.

The top knuckleballers were a remarkably unpretentious lot. You don't find many boasters or slapstick comics among them. A couple had reputations as tough-guy loners or crabs, while others had a laid-back, dry wit and gentle, self-deprecating humor. Underneath all this was invariably a deep streak of stubbornness, independence, and diligence. Most showed remarkable staying power, both in lasting out the struggles to get to the big league and then in hanging around when others would have long since retired.

On the more practical side, an early conversion to the knuckleball is preferred. It isn't mastered overnight. The biggest key is to give the aspiring knuckleballer plenty of consistent work in a *starting* role. If he can work on three days' rest without overly upsetting the rest of the rotation, it will speed up his developing control of the pitch.

The future of the knuckleball is pretty much tied to the success or failure of the Cleveland Indians' Tom Candiotti. If that's the way it has to be, he's not a bad choice. Age twenty-seven is pretty late to be making the change, and he is a bit taller than I would like (listed at six-three), but he gets high marks everywhere else. As a conventional pitcher, he had definitely been more a pitcher than a thrower. When he had a good streak for Milwaukee in 1983 (3.23 ERA in 56 innings), I didn't like his stuff but was very impressed that he was getting away with it. He also has a history of good control dating back to his first minor-league season in 1979 when he walked only 16 in 70 innings (2.06).

Best of all, he has the stubborn, battling nature this task requires. After completing his B.S. at St. Mary's College, he was a few months short of his twenty-second birthday and was overlooked in the June draft. Still, he signed as a free agent with Victoria, an independent Class A team. The club released him at the end of the season, but Kansas City signed him as a free agent to fill out its Class A roster at Fort Myers. In 1981 he had elbow surgery and missed all of 1982, but he battled back and bounced around Milwaukee's system for a few years until his release in October 1985, when he signed as a free agent with Cleveland's AAA club. Reminds you a bit of Hoyt Wilhelm, doesn't it—stubbornly ignoring the subtle and not-so-subtle hints that he should pack it in?

I don't know when Candiotti decided to try the knuckleball. He didn't throw it when I saw him in 1984, but I imagine he'd fooled around with it before. Lots of people do. Mickey Mantle loved to throw one; the manager of my softball team throws a dandy knuckler, but that's a long way from making it break consistently, pitch after pitch, and throwing it for strikes. As much as I would praise Candiotti, I think Cleveland deserves a lot of credit for giving him the chance and the support he needed to make the transition successfully. The fact that they signed Phil Niekro in 1986 to serve both as pitcher and knuckleball instructor was a sign of their commitment to giving Candiotti a full shot.

Cleveland! Who would have thought it? And how about the rest of baseball? When you consider how willing teams are to invest millions of dollars and tons of man-hours to sift through mountains of borderline talent in search of a few gold nuggets, it seems ridiculous not to invest about one-thousandth of that effort in a direction proven capable of producing effective pitchers with great longevity, and sometimes even a Hall of Fame talent. It is time to stop sounding the death knell for the knuckleball. It deserves to survive and escape the label of baseball's most underrated pitch.

HOUSE:
THE KNUCKLEBALL—FEAR OF FLUTTERING

Major-league knuckleball pitchers are a treat for fan and player alike, possibly because they're as much a mystery to the players who throw and catch them as they are to the guy who pays three dollars a seat in the bleachers.

"You can't hit good what don't look right," was the way Clint "Scrap Iron" Courtney put it to Ralph Garr after watching Phil Niekro's pitches dance and dip in spring training, 1970. "You can't catch what can't be caught," summed up former catcher Glenn Brummer after watching a Charlie Hough knuckler flit by him in 1985. "Butterflies aren't bullets," Hough said almost poetically when talking about his release point that same season. "You can't aim 'em, you just let 'em go."

Baseball is hitting, catching, and throwing, and knuckleball pitchers uncompromisingly bend all three of these basic absolutes. Everything Craig has said about the knuckleballer as a finished product has merit. A sound case has been made for having a knuckleballer on a pitching staff, and, true to this recommendation, there's a very successful one—Hough—as the ace of our rotation in Texas. I inherited Charlie as a polished pitcher and had nothing to do with the development of his pitch. Charlie will tell you, tongue firmly planted in his cheek, that he alone is responsible for his "awesome physical talent" as he blazes away at American League hitters with a 72 m.p.h. flutterball.

Charlie is most definitely a finished product—a consummate professional with an outstanding feel for the whole game. His success speaks for itself. He, like all knuckleballers, makes it look so damned easy—

when he is on. So does Tom Candiotti at Cleveland, and so did a left-handed pitcher named Mike Anderson in the Pacific Coast League a few years ago—but not easy enough or often enough (and that's why you don't know Mike as a knuckleball pitcher today).

There's an old Yugoslav proverb (surely they're not doing this in Yugoslavia) that says, "Speak the truth and run." From Craig's perspective, nothing is impossible because he and his friends don't have to implement his suggestions. I can't ignore the fact that he has uncovered some remarkable truths. When he first showed me the data about the success of knuckleball pitchers, I too got fired up about "cornering the knuckleball market." However, as I began to formulate practical plans for developing knuckleball pitchers, reality set in—hard. The theoretical validity of Craig's hypothesis is solid, but in looking at implementing it from a management/coaching perspective and a teammate/athlete perspective, "possible" suddenly becomes significantly less "probable."

First, look at it from management's point of view. Financially, the minor leagues are strictly a losing proposition. Depending on the organization, a club loses between one million and two million dollars each year on player development. The attrition rate is exceedingly high. Most general managers would look at me as if I'd been out in the Texas sun too long if I went in with a proposal that took five pitching prospects per year into a four-year knuckleball program when success rates for developing a major-league knuckleballer are, at best, around 1%. Even if I could avoid the issue of cost-effectiveness versus success ratios, I'd have a better chance striking out Wade Boggs than convincing even an enlightened GM that the pitch could be taught up front. Most front offices would rather let the pitch develop itself when a competitive youngster faces reality and has no other way to stay in the game (à la Charlie Hough).

Now let's consider it from the minor-league coach's point of view. Minor-league managers and coaches, like minor-league players, don't want to stay in the minor leagues forever. The Red Sox and Dodgers are the only organizations I know of in which compensation—salary, profit sharing, bonus insurance plans, and promoting from within—keeps a fairly consistent group of minor-league instructors together year after year. Most other clubs experience a pretty high turnover, especially in the lower minor leagues, where rewards can be minimal. The way minor-league managers and instructors get to the big leagues is by winning and/or developing winning talent. This is a bit hypocritical, since coaching staffs are told each year, "Winning is not important in rookie ball; getting players used to a professional baseball environment is. A-ball should be 75% development and 25% winning. AA-ball is a 50–50 split between development and winning. AAA-ball is 25% development and 75% winning." Sounds nice, right? It's only lip service. Every big-league organization would rather win than anything else.

Player development is a bonus, an after-the-fact rationalization. No team goes into a season planning to lose 75% of its games. Don't believe me? Try sitting in on roster-picking sessions during spring training. It can be very cutthroat, because no minor-league manager or coach wants to leave camp with a bunch of projects or stiffs. They fight for a combination of prospects, experience, and filler players who will have a chance at being competitive. With this in mind, I can't imagine a manager choosing to take a pitcher who is working on a knuckleball. Especially when, for reasons I will discuss shortly, this pitcher's losses will mount into double figures. I can't imagine a pitching coach willing to take on a losing proposition—even if he could teach the pitch and its philosophies.

Minor-league managers will always have to tolerate high draft picks who throw hard and lose because they can't throw strikes; that's "baseball's way." This "good stuff" prospect, by virtue of his talent, is not a candidate for the knuckleball. The knuckleballer candidates, therefore, will come from those left after the real prospects have been assigned. With contemporary minor-league development philosophies, it would be tough to convince a manager or coach to carry and use on his staff a low-round draft choice, a marginally talented pitcher who will lose because he is throwing knuckleballs with no command. A novice knuckleballer, struggling to gain command of a pitch he hasn't mastered, has little chance in the current management/coaching system.

Why must a minor-league knuckleballer be a losing pitcher? To answer that question, let's delve into the catcher-pitcher relationship and its effect on a team.

Throwing a knuckleball that breaks is relatively easy. Many pitchers and most regular players can throw pretty good knucklers. They have fun showing off their "uncatchable" knuckleballs during pregame warm-ups, but throwing the knuckleball is only the first step. Throwing it for strikes is the second step, and finding someone who can catch it is a critical third. What a knuckleball pitcher doesn't want is to wind up playing chase with his catcher.

Pitchers who throw knuckleballs need catchers who can catch knuckleballs. Remember Bob Uecker's tip on how to catch a knuckleball? "You wait until it stops rolling." Even the oversized glove developed by Paul Richards for Wilhelm gives only a minimum of help. I can remember a backup catcher with the Braves, Vic Correll, warming up Phil Niekro in a sprinter's stance, with his target held behind his back. He was only half joking. On that particular day, most of Phil's pitches were ending up against the backstop, and Vic's setup revealed his frustration. The flip side of that coin is Bob Didier, a nineteen-year-old catcher who made the Braves' major-league roster out of A-ball in 1969. He was the only catcher in the organization who could catch a knuckleball after Bob Tillman and Walt Hriniak went down with injuries.

Believing their catchers can catch what they throw is a must if a knuckleball pitcher is to have the confidence to win. It's imperative that a knuckleball catcher do just that—catch the knuckleball. His other duties as a receiver become secondary. It's a close-knit relationship, because the two often aren't much without each other. Imagine, then, what this means to a development program in the minor leagues: The problems have just doubled. You can't just put a knuckleballer in Tulsa without also having a catcher there who can hang on to the knuckleball. It's difficult enough to find a young catcher who can catch regular stuff consistently without mixing a flutterball into the equation. Add the subpar lighting conditions of most minor-league parks to the problem, and odds are even a Bob Didier clone would scuffle. There's the possibility that an organization could come up with a veteran catcher or a player-coach who could catch the pitch, but remember, veteran catchers aren't as cheap as rookies. Besides, there aren't that many veteran catchers who are good knuckleball catchers, either.

Could a general manager be convinced that he'll get enough return on his investment? Let's assume for a moment that a front office does agree to put a knuckleball pitcher—and a catcher who can knock it down—on a minor-league team. The kid will still lose most of his games and take over three hours per game to do so. Here's why:

1. The manager who has the foresight to attempt such a task must start the knuckleballer every fifth day and leave him in for at least a hundred pitches, in order for the pitcher to develop his skill with the pitch.
2. Ratios say that 80% of those pitches must be knuckleballs, and that 50% of the knucklers will be out of the strike zone.
3. The umpires are also minor-leaguers, and their strike zones are just as erratic as the pitcher's.
4. Ten percent of the flutterballs will be wild pitches or passed balls, often costing runs.

That means that, for probably twenty or twenty-five starting assignments, the box score for our aspiring knuckleballer will read something like: 3.1 innings, five runs, four earned, three hits, eight walks, three strikeouts.

There's no question that the manager will get very tired of watching and reporting these games, and we haven't even discussed the damage done to the motivation of the other players on the club. Could you play your best every fifth day, knowing you're more than likely not just going to lose but be embarrassed? It's a difficult player-development environment, at best, for all involved.

And now let's look at this from the young pitcher's perspective. Even if all the previous roadblocks to a knuckleball program could be eliminated, what's a young man going to think when he is told that he has to throw a knuckleball to stay in the game? Logic says there will be a mental—if not vocal—rebellion. The candidate will be saying to himself, "This is bull. I won in high school and college with regular stuff and was good enough to get signed. I've been pitching in pro ball for a year and a half, and now they tell me I have to learn a knuckleball or get released. Screw this!" It's a fact that baseball only signs successful athletes. Even nonprospect fillers are players from among the best in their geographical areas.

It's difficult to teach anything new or different to a successful performer. They have to fail, short term, before they become receptive to change. Youngsters will often listen and give token commitment to new information, but when the bell rings, they use the pitches that got them there. Losing—negative feedback when they look at the scoreboard and their record—is what proves to their egos that something different may be required. And remember that, for a good part of the time, they will be losing.

Pitching a baseball professionally requires failing as much as succeeding for all athletes, save the few Dwight Goodens among us. It is tough enough to teach and learn a new "traditional" pitch that can be used between the lines in pressure situations. Forcing a knuckleball on a young man before he truly sees that there is no other choice is a delicate matter. The trick will be selling the kid on the idea.

COACH: Hey, Bubba, I've got a new pitch for you!

ATHLETE: *(Oh shit, here we go again!)* What's the pitch, Coach?

COACH: A knuckleball. It will really take the pressure off your fastball.

ATHLETE: *(What's wrong with my fastball?)* Great! When do we start working?

COACH: Well, before we go to the bullpen, let's talk, Bubba. Listen, I played with Wilhelm and both Niekros, and you've got a chance to be just like them.

ATHLETE: *(Right; old, bald, and ugly.)* How's that, Coach?

COACH: You've got good athletic ability, good work ethic, good mechanics, good game sense, and outstanding durability.

ATHLETE: *(Then why am I 0–7 with a 7.66 ERA?)* You know I'll bust my ass to improve any way I can.

COACH: I know, Bubba, that's why the organization wants you to become a knuckleballer. We feel if anyone can master the pitch, it'll be you.

ATHLETE: *(God, it's already in the books. I'm a knuckleball pitcher!)* Oh, so this decision came from the front office?

COACH: Not entirely, Big Gun, but don't worry about how the decision was made, you just concentrate on learning and mastering a knuckleball down in Sarasota.

ATHLETE: *(F—— A! They're sending me down!)* I can't stay here and learn the pitch with you, Coach?

COACH: Well, I'll get you started today, but the pitching coach in Sarasota is a fine instructor, and there will be less pressure on you in A-ball than in AA-ball.

ATHLETE: *(And I'll be one step closer to getting released. What will my parents think? My girl? Now she can't visit. I wonder if my teammates know. I've got to pack and get my house deposits back. How long a drive is it? I wonder if they'll let me fly. Oh man, don't even think about it now!)* If I go down there and get people out with it, how soon can I get back here, Coach?

COACH: That'll take care of itself, son. Let's go down to the bullpen for a little work.

ATHLETE: *(It's the kiss-off! This is gonna be a tough workout. Just get me out of here, now!)* Super, I'll get a head start.

This mythical exchange is a pretty typical one when a player is "sent out" for special work—like developing a knuckleball. It's not particularly effective in creating the right psychological state for a pitcher to approach this grand experiment. If we're going to try to develop knuckleballers, we must make sure that we do it as positively as possible, to help them develop a full mental and physical commitment toward mastering the pitch. This means that the planning must be done during the off-season; the pitcher must know coming into spring training what his role for the upcoming seasons (note the plural) will be, and it should be made absolutely clear that the decision is not a do-or-die, one-season deal. Fear might make a pitcher throw harder, but it won't help in developing this particular pitch.

Once we've decided on the "how," we should pay careful attention to who is asked to develop the pitch. The knuckler requires a special awareness of the environment—wind, humidity, temperature—since it's the air itself that makes the thing break. A pitcher must be able to read the conditions and adjust to keep throwing a knuckler for strikes. The pitch also demands an unusually large defensive role for the pitcher, since so many of them get nubbed or grounded back in reach of the mound. And since the pitch does travel so slowly, you need a better-than-average pickoff move to give your catchers any hope of cutting off the running game. All of this may explain why knuckleballers bloom so late in life; younger pitchers don't have the overall outlook to master all these subtleties.

Finally, an organization is going to have to really sell the idea of developing knuckleballers internally—to itself, its scouts, its coaches, and its athletes. As we've seen, that isn't going to be easy. And it's going to take a very long-term perspective, because you aren't going to see results overnight. Despite all the reservations I've voiced here, the Texas Rangers took a stab at encouraging some knuckleballers in our organization a couple of years ago. Four pitchers were promised a two-year shot at developing the pitch, so they could just go out there and throw it without worrying about getting released. Of the four, only one, Steve Lankard, is still with our organization. But all four came to us with knuckleballs, and we couldn't fully follow Craig's proposed program with them, using them as starters no matter what, for all the reasons I outlined above.

Nonetheless, we're still looking for the right man with the right stuff to keep the experiment alive. It took about five years for soccer-style kickers to take over in football; they had to be discovered, given the opportunity to perform successfully, and have their success acknowledged on a winner before all teams followed suit. It will take at least that long for baseball to make a real effort to develop knuckleball pitchers, but if just one organization makes it work, others will follow. I wouldn't expect a proliferation of knuckleballers, but we should at least be able to get them off the endangered list.

WRIGHT:
LET'S NOT KNUCKLE UNDER

Although Tom ended on a positive note, the bulk of his comments sound a lot like the second part of Clarke's law quoted in his introduction: "It's possible, but not worth doing."

Tom has made mountains out of molehills here. No one ever said it was going to be easy, and it's always hardest for those leading the way. Let me correct a couple of the misconceptions Tom has left you with.

No one has ever suggested taking "five pitching prospects per year into a four-year knuckleball program." My suggestion has always been to seek out candidates from the pitching "suspects," the guys who don't have the stuff to make it as conventional pitchers. Only 2% of the players who sign minor-league contracts ever reach the majors for even a September cup of coffee. Many of them wash out after just a couple of years. That gives you plenty to choose from, and in that group are some guys who would gladly do anything to keep their careers going.

Tom suggests that ". . . success rates for developing a major-league knuckleball are, at best, around 1%." I feel obligated to point out that is only his guess; I suspect the real figure is much higher. In the last five years I doubt there have been more than eight minor-leaguers who have thrown the knuckleball as their dominant pitch, and that's been a *good* period. I bet there haven't been close to a hundred minor-league knuckleballers going all the way back to World War II. I can't see any reason to estimate that developing a major-league knuckleballer is harder than developing a conventional major-league pitcher, and with the knuckleballer, you are invariably dealing with a player who cost you little to begin with—a low draft pick or possibly a minor-league free agent contract.

Tom's point about the catchers may be the weakest of all. His Vic Correll story is cute, but I defy anyone to name a catcher who was truly unable to learn to catch a knuckleball. Has any catcher ever been traded because he couldn't catch a knuckleball? How about a prospect who couldn't make it to the bigs because he couldn't catch a knuckler? Do you have any idea how many catchers Charlie Hough has worked with in his career? I'd say twenty-five is about right. Some were better than others, some were horrid at first, but I don't know of a single case in which the team just gave up and said he couldn't catch Hough.

Catching the knuckleball is a skill, and I expect any minor-league catcher would be happy to learn it. Heck, they're probably lining up right now after hearing House's story about how nineteen-year-old Bob Didier jumped from A-ball to the majors when Niekro's two knuckleball catchers were injured. I don't recall any problems in finding catchers for Texas's minor-league knuckleballers; they were basically the same guys who caught everyone else.

And it's also stretching the truth to suggest that an organization can't find a place to play a new knuckleballer without hurting the competitiveness of his team. Texas's four minor-league knucklers combined for a 33–34 record in A-ball with a 3.52 ERA in over 500 innings. None was ever the worst pitcher on his team. Some went on to have decent years at higher levels; in 1985 one even had a 2.67 ERA in 105 innings at AAA.

I certainly don't want to throw stones at Texas for their willingness to give chances to knuckleballers, but it would be wrong to leave the reader with an impression that they gave it their best shot. There was no effort to seek out the best candidates or ensure they would get the work they needed. About all the organization did was to take marginal pitchers who could throw a knuckler and encourage them to use it.

Three of the four were real long shots. One had a good knuckler and decent success with it, but he was ambivalent about the change and didn't stay with it. The most enthusiastic was Rick Odekirk, an older convert who already had control trouble before taking up the knuckler (4.59 walks per nine innings), and the third had a knuckler that simply wasn't that good and didn't get any better. He didn't even get the two-year trial; he was signed and released in the same year.

Only Odekirk was put into the starting role that's so important to a knuckleballer's development, and despite what Tom says, it wasn't because the others were so awful. One of the two was a spot starter and reliever before concentrating on the knuckler, and there wasn't any attempt to change his role. The other was never given a single start, although his 3.92 ERA suggests it wouldn't have been a horrible risk. Working with these three was not a costly experiment. They were bottom-of-the-barrel "suspects"; all three had been acquired as minor-league free agents. Odekirk ended up being traded away in a

AA deal, which means he was worth more as a knuckleballer than when Texas acquired him.

As Tom mentioned, the best and most promising was and is Steve Lankard. He was taken very late in the 1985 draft, about the 500th player taken. He was drafted as a submariner; his knuckleball was discovered later. He's a good knuckleball prospect; he has above-average control of his conventional pitches, is comfortable getting people out without being overpowering, and he has that stubborn toughness so appealing in a knuckleballer. Unfortunately, he also had his kneecap broken by a line drive in 1988.

Lankard has yet to become a true knuckleballer and relies more on sinkers and sliders, but I can envision a day when he will have advanced as far as he can with his other pitches and will turn more to his knuckler. Who knows, maybe the chance to reflect on his career—maybe after reading this chapter—will inspire him to make the knuckleball an integral part of his comeback attempt. My best wishes to him, and to the few others who have no fear of fluttering.

HOUSE:
BUTTERFLY COLLECTING

You know, down deep I agree with everything Craig's saying. I don't think the Rangers' organization gave the knuckleball project their best shot; I'd like to have seen it taken further. Craig's right about the long-term value of a knuckleballer, and the long-term advantage to be gained from going out of our way to develop them. But in baseball, it's just so hard to get anyone to look at the long term.

If I were running the organization, I'd have gone for the full treatment. But this is one case where I really can understand why they weren't willing to do it. The key to this program is to take the really marginal talents, the pitchers who were about to wash out of the system, and get them throwing the knuckler on an everyday basis. But those innings have got to come from somewhere, and in all likelihood they're going to be taken away from some guys who might have had a better shot at making the bigs.

Take a pitcher with the talent of a Paul Kilgus—fairly marginal when it comes to the raw tools of pitching, but he knows how to pitch and can get guys out at any level. On stuff alone, though, he might only be a fourth or fifth starter even down on the AA level. This is the kind of pitcher who might get lost if you're going to turn his innings over to someone who was on his way out before he took up the knuckler. And if you remove those wash-out pitchers from the equation, we're doing a lot better than 2% in getting them to the bigs, maybe as well as 10%. That's a lot better than we're going to do with the knuckleballers.

The knuckleball isn't like other pitches. Hell, there are hundreds of guys in baseball who can throw a knuckleball—Larry Parrish probably has the best I've ever seen—but only that small handful who can throw it for strikes. In order to get the knuckler over consistently, your mechanics have to be *perfect,* not just good. The body has to deliver the arm to the proper spot and angle, and the arm's got to get to the release point just right to throw the pitch for strikes. We've done motion studies on most of the pitchers in baseball to determine how close they come to the optimal pitching motion. We couldn't imagine that anyone would come to even 95% of the ideal, but one pitcher hit 99%. Who was it? *Charlie Hough.*

With the fastball or curveball or slider, you can make up in strength for what you haven't done quite right mechanically. With the knuckleball, forget it. You don't have that margin. And how many of the pitchers you were about to release do you think have those perfect mechanics? Right—if they had it, they probably wouldn't be on their way out the door.

By looking at the relatively few knuckleballers who have been successful in the big leagues, and then reasoning backwards to what we should do to develop them, Craig's looking through the wrong end of the telescope. In theory, sure it would be great to have a knuckleballer we could stick in the rotation every fourth day until he's fifty. But in most baseball organizations, even the most progressive ones, long-term thinking doesn't mean twenty years. If you're lucky, it means five.

WRIGHT:
COMING AROUND, BUT NOT FAR ENOUGH

It's nice to see that Tom is relenting a bit, but I think he is still misleading folks with this idea that nurturing a knuckleballer will take away innings from some prospects who have a better chance to make the bigs.

Again, Tom is still guessing at what the success rate is for developing knuckleballers and conventional pitchers. And his example of Paul Kilgus is way out of line. If a pitcher fits the description Tom gave Kilgus, ". . . fairly marginal when it comes to the raw tools of pitching, but he knows how to pitch and can get guys out at any level," he is not going to be one of the pitchers losing innings by introducing four or five knuckleballers into an organization with *six* minor-league teams.

Okay, it's true that room on the minor-league rosters becomes scarcer as they move up to AA and AAA (each organization has only one team at each of those levels), but a knuckleballer can remain in the low minors a lot longer than a conventional pitcher without setting back his progress. While the conventional pitcher needs to advance and test himself against better hitters, the knuckleballer's development is tied more to his own mechanics and control. They don't need to advance to AA or up to AAA until they show they have become a real prospect, with chances as good or better than the conventional pitchers they displace.

Tom's point about proper mechanics being crucial to a knuckleballer is meant to be an argument against my plan, but I see it as exactly the opposite. He suggests that there are no marginal minor-leaguers ready to wash out who possess good pitching mechanics. That's silly. The hundreds of pitchers who hit the bricks every year are dumped for a wide variety of reasons. Some of them are excellent control pitchers with good mechanics, but they simply do not have the velocity to compete at the higher levels.

Teaching what Tom calls "perfect mechanics" can't be easy, but given a pitcher with a sound mechanical base, it's possible—a lot more possible than teaching a guy with an 80 m.p.h. fastball to throw 90. My whole point about the low costs of developing knuckleballers is that the keys to the pitch are more coachable and less dependent on raw talent than producing a conventional pitcher. Tom has only reinforced that idea.

And if my specific plan is wrong, the idea is not. Look, knuckleballers exist; they had to come from somewhere. We have this massive program for the development of conventional pitchers where we seek out their talents and draft them; we create an environment for their growth and we teach them. Knuckleballers are valuable pitchers, no one denies that. So why not put some of those same player development resources into producing knuckleballers?

BET, BET, BET ON THE HOME TEAM

The home-field advantage is as old as the game itself, a heavy presence set in stone. So far in this century there have been only three seasons in which a league failed to win more games at home than on the road: 1917 NL, 1953 AL, 1972 NL. To put it another way, at the league level, there has been a home-field advantage in better than 98% of the seasons played. In any ten-year span in baseball history, the home team's winning percentage will fall between .535 and .555.

Given the strength and consistency of this phenomenon, it's stunning how little we know of its causes. This is not to say we lack reasonable theories: Many believe it's the psychological lift of having the crowd on your side; some claim it's the greater familiarity with the ballpark, or perhaps some subtle tailoring of a team to its home park. Others point to the psychic advantage to the player of sleeping in his own bed and being nurtured by a sense of home. The more cynically minded claim the umpires subconsciously favor the home team in their close calls. And, of course, there is the strategic advantage of batting last that belongs exclusively to the home team.

Of the theories, only the last is so obvious as to need no verification. Managers agonize over strategic choices like the sacrifice bunt or stolen base, weighing the gain of playing for one run versus the possibility of defusing a big inning of three or four runs. They also face decisions about when to pinch-hit for a weak hitter, and what kind of pinch-hitter to use. The best decisions are made by the home team in the bottom of the ninth, because it knows exactly what it must do to win the game. The visiting team, by hitting first, has only the nebulous and possibly nonexistent advantage of drawing first blood by scoring the first run. So far, research into this area has been unable to demonstrate any extra advantage to scoring the first run; a team scoring first wins approximately the same percentage of its games as a team scoring in any randomly chosen inning.

Okay, we know the strategic advantage has to exist, but how big can it really be? Lots of games are pretty much decided by the ninth inning, and the opposition also has a little edge in that it knows exactly what it must do to stop the home team from winning. In a lot of other sports, like basketball and football, there is no strategic edge given to the home team, yet it often has larger home-field advantages than its baseball counterpart.

There is a considerable difference in the run production of base-ball's home teams and the visitors. This must come from something totally separate from the strategic advantage of batting last, since that edge has nothing to do with scoring more runs. I have detailed home-road statistics covering the seasons from 1976 to 1987 (excluding the 1981 strike season because of its unbalanced scheduling). In those eleven seasons, the home team scored 4.54 runs per 25.5 hitless at bats (25.5 is the average for nine innings), and the visitors averaged 4.09.

During those eleven seasons the actual winning percentage for the home team was .544. We don't need any strategic advantage to justify that kind of performance; the expected winning percentage for a team scoring 4.54 runs versus one with 4.09 is around .550. This suggests that the strategic edge is so minimal that it can't be separated out from the effect or effects that make the home-team players more productive. At best, with a generous allowance for error, I estimate that the strategic edge accounts for about 5% of the home-field advantage, certainly less than 10%.

If we want to understand home-field advantage, we have to concentrate on those factors that would enhance the performance of the home team over that of the visitors. All of the five remaining theories have that capability. Unfortunately, they are also very tough relationships to track down. They keep their distance, and often our best view is simply of their shadows. This is never clearer than when trying to deal with the psychic lift of having the crowd on your side. How can we possibly separate this factor out from all the rest for some form of controlled study? It's beyond my vision, but what we can do is try assuming that if this effect exists, then it may fluctuate with the size of the crowd.

If you study how the quality of a team affects its home-field advantage, you begin to see a relationship that looks something like this:

OVERALL W%	HOME W%	ROAD W%	DIFFERENCE (H − R)
.600	.652	.548	.104
.550	.598	.502	.096
.500	.544	.456	.088
.450	.489	.411	.078
.400	.435	.365	.070

One school of thought looks at the difference column and concludes that the crowd factor is the source of home-field advantage, since winning teams generally have better home attendance than losing teams. That's a pretty weak argument, and it won't hold here. In fact, what we have here is a model constructed so that the *proportional difference* (H/R, rather than the *linear difference,* H − R) is the same for all five groups. In each case, the team is doing 19% better at home than on the road; for our purposes, we'll call this a home-field advantage of 1.19.

There's nothing unusual in finding that the relationship is a proportional one rather than a linear one. And this would mean that the linear gap would be bigger for a good team than for a bad team, while the proportions arc held constant. Whenever you see reference to a measure of home-field advantage in this chapter, I mean the proportional difference, the ratio between home and road winning percentage.

I have looked in several places for some indication of a link between home-field attendance and the size of the crowd, but I can't find one. The home-field advantage in the history of the World Series has been normal despite extremely large and enthusiastic crowds. In-season studies of Rangers games with high attendance do not show a rise in the Rangers' home-field edge, even when the quality of the opponent has been controlled.

During the 1971–85 period, several American League clubs experienced significant attendance gains for a variety of reasons. Nine AL clubs had a three-year period in which their attendance per game was better than 40% higher than the previous three-year period. The average gain for the nine clubs was over 8,400 fans per game. How did this affect the home-field advantage? In three cases it went up, in one it stayed the same, and five actually saw their home-field advantage decline with the larger crowds. The average change for the whole group was less than 0.1%.

Again, I caution that a lack of reaction to home-crowd size does not prove there's no advantage to having the crowd on your side. The evidence may just mean that the number of rooters quickly reaches a saturation point at which the size of the crowd makes no difference.

Another theory that is difficult to pin down is the home team's familiarity with its ballpark. If this has real impact, then the home-field advantage in World Series play should be unusually large, as the visiting team would have little to no experience at all in the other's home park. It's true that ever since the leagues began to separate over the artificial turf question, the home-field advantage has been unusually high; from 1971 to 1987 the home team won about 62% of the World Series games. However, in the overall sample of roughly 500 World Series games, the home-field advantage has been a normal .535.

But that is the World Series. In a study reflecting a more normal set of circumstances, I looked at the thirty-four teams since the Korean War that have played in a new home park. That may seem like a lot of teams, but there have been a lot of new parks and plenty of expansion in that time. The thirty-four are listed below. (For anyone surprised by the 1974 Yankees, the Yankees played at Shea Stadium while Yankee Stadium was being remodeled.)

1953 Milwaukee	1966 St. Louis
1954 Baltimore	1968 Oakland
1955 Kansas City	1969 Kansas City
1958 San Francisco	1969 Seattle
1958 Los Angeles	1969 Montreal
1960 San Francisco	1969 San Diego
1961 Los Angeles (A)	1970 Milwaukee
1961 Minnesota	1970 Pittsburgh
1961 Washington	1970 Cincinnati
1962 Los Angeles (N)	1971 Philadelphia
1962 New York (N)	1972 Texas
1962 California (A)	1973 Kansas City
1962 Houston	1974 New York (A)
1964 New York (N)	1977 Seattle
1965 Houston	1977 Toronto
1966 California	1977 Montreal
1966 Atlanta	1982 Minnesota

The disadvantage of playing in a new home park proved to be minimal for these teams. Only nineteen of the thirty-four (56%) had a worse home-field advantage than the league average that year. The average for the whole group was only 1.4% below the league average.

There is one small area where experience with the ballpark does seem to help the home team; that's in preventing the extra base between a double and a triple. In the 1976–87 data, the home-field edge covering nearly 11,000 triples was a huge 26% gain. To put that in perspective, the combined percentage gain in singles, doubles, and home runs was less than half that, only 12%. My guess is that the hometown fielders know the best ways to cut off a long hit, play the balls off the walls, or judge the throws from those key spots where extra-base hits tend to congregate. Still, the overall evidence suggests that familiarity with the home park is a very minor factor in the extra productivity of the home team's players.

A more significant impact can be found in the psychological benefits of being in your home environment away from the park. In the group of thirty-four teams that changed parks, thirteen were playing in a new park located in what was already their home city. Those thirteen had a *higher* home-field advantage than the league despite playing in a strange home park (1.047 relative to the league). The twenty-one teams playing in a new park as well as a new city—an extended road trip, if you will—had a relative home-field advantage of .981.

This might explain why certain individual players have had strong home-field edges even when placed in parks that went against their natural strengths as a player. Some may need that psychological comfort of being at home more than others. On the other side of the psychological coin, some players may feel a lot of pressure from their home life and be glad to get away. And then there is the Pete Rose type, who practically lives at the ballpark when he is on the road and sees every ballpark as his home anyway.

That brings us to the umpires. What role, if any, do they play in making the hometown boys hit and pitch better? Do they subconsciously react to the urging of the crowd and seek to avoid their wrath? Do they respond to the prompting by the bartender, the cabbie, the waitress, the clubhouse attendant, and other representatives of the home city and team? Does the league itself subtly encourage the umpires to favor the home team? There does seem to be a belief, substantiated or not, that home-field advantage is good for attendance, and that more fans come out when they can expect their team to win. Bigger crowds are good for baseball. Certainly, the leagues have never done anything to try to identify and control those umpires who might be more susceptible to the lures of calling for the crowd.

There are episodes in the past that suggest that the leagues have done more than just ignore the danger. When the upstart American League was in open warfare with the established National League back in 1902, AL fans saw the home team win 63% of the time, the all-time high for home-field advantage in baseball history. The magnitude of this mark seems unbelievable without conscious intent by either the umpires or the teams themselves to favor the home team. Given the maverick nature of most expansion leagues, I would suspect the umpires, who were direct employees of the league. After the NL accepted the AL in the treaty of 1903, the home-field advantage in the AL dropped below .600, and by 1904 it was all the way down to .535.

The same thing happened on a lesser scale in 1914–15 when the Federal League was battling for survival. In the three seasons prior to 1914, baseball's home-field advantage was right around .520, but in the next two years it jumped to .542 in the Federal League and .553 in the two established leagues. The same pattern happened during World War I, the depression, and World War II; it seemed that whenever the game had reason to worry about attendance or popularity (spelled m-o-n-e-y), home-field advantage would escalate. I don't mean to imply there were overt instructions in these latter cases, as I suspect happened in 1902. But there may have been subtle encouragement in one form or another, perhaps in an occasional philosophical hint about the need to entertain the troubled masses.

As I sit here blithely casting aspersions on a profession I really do respect, I should hasten to add that the objectivity of the umpires has been relatively good since the end of World War II. At the same time, I have to point out that there is substantial evidence that the umpires do play a role in the home-field advantage. Indeed, they may be the most significant factor of all.

It would be impossible to completely separate the umpire's influence from other factors that may directly affect the players' ability. Fortunately, the effect of the umpires on ball-strike calls would be an influence that would leave distinct and telltale shifts in the data.

Let me make use of a couple of examples to show what kinds of influences are possible. We can use the platoon edge as an example of a performance gain that would have nothing to do with the umpires. I took the twenty-nine right-handed American League batters who had over 600 plate appearances in 1987 and separated their performance by whether the pitcher was a lefty or righty. Because of the bias in issuing intentional walks (roughly 60% of the intentional walks for RHB will come from LHP), I made an adjustment so the walk average reflects the expected nonintentional walk rate.

	BA	POWER % (SA − BA)	BB AVERAGE
Vs. RHP	.278	.187	.088
Vs. LHP	.295	.211	.092
Percentage gain vs. LHP from overall averages	6.0%	4.1%	4.5%

Now let's take a look at what we might expect to see if there was an unusual influence on the calling of borderline balls and strikes. For example, using 1987 data, this is how the average batter performed after reaching the ball-strike counts 0–1 and 1–0. Again, because intentional walks are distributed with a bias in such a split (few intentional walks are issued after an 0–1 count), the walk average reflects the nonintentional rate.

COUNT	BA	POWER % (SA − BA)	BB AVERAGE
0–1	.235	.125	.053
1–0	.277	.172	.107
Percentage gain at 1–0 from overall averages	16%	36%	61%

The smallest effect here is in batting average, increasing substantially as we move to power percentage and then on to walk average.

My 1976–87 home–road data provide a detailed look at the effect of home-field advantage in these three areas. Which category would we expect to be influenced the most if the home plate umpire had a tendency to favor the home team on the borderline ball-strike calls? Obviously, the walk average. Batting average would be the least affected, since a batter's power is more dependent on the ball-strike count than his batting average. And that's exactly what we find.

1976–87 (MINUS 1981 STRIKE SEASON)

	AT BATS	BA	POWER %	BB AVERAGE
Home	764,796	.265	.134	.091
Road	801,016	.256	.125	.083
Gain at home		3.5%	6.7%	9.1%

That points the finger rather strongly at the umpires as a significant factor in home-field advantage. However, it might also be the effect of the home-team pitchers having better control because they are more familiar with the pitching mound than are the visiting pitchers. I can accept the logic of that relationship, but I have trouble accepting it as more than a minimal influence. First, when the pitching mound was lowered in 1969, baseball began to check the mounds more frequently in an effort to keep them uniform (ten inches above the field with an incline of one inch per foot). If the mound theory is right, this extra care should have lowered the home-field advantage, but the home-field edge in 1969–70 was almost exactly the same as in 1967–68. Second, this relationship with the mound would fall under the familiarity-with-the-ballpark idea, and we saw only a minimal impact when we studied that relationship.

After working with the evidence surrounding the home-field advantage, I can't put much stock in the effect of the crowd giving a lift to the players; call it 5%. I'd also give only 5% to the strategic advantage of having the last at bats. I'd allow 10% for familiarity with the ballpark; I'd credit 30% to the psychological benefits of living at home, and I'd charge the umpires with the largest share at 40%.

That leaves only 10% for the shaping of the home team to its home park, although many sportswriters and fans feel it should be far more. I think this comes from our tendency to focus on an extreme park impact on a player or two, forgetting that most of that will be offset by the mixed impact on the rest of the team. We've also developed a knee-jerk reaction equating normal fluctuations in home-field advantage to adaptation or a failure to adapt to a park's idiosyncracies.

To take one example, in 1980 Seattle had a home-field advantage 46% better than the league average, easily the best in the league. A number that large is sure to catch attention, and by the nature of its size, we automatically assume it to be meaningful. We were treated to serious articles about how Seattle had finally adapted to life on artificial turf, sacrificing hitting to play speedy outfielders like Joe Simpson and Juan Benequez and pushing hard-throwing pitchers like Floyd Bannister who don't give up a lot of ground balls. Actually, Seattle wasn't built around its home park at all. At the time it was the best home run park in the league, and Seattle's best home run hitter was Tom Paciorek with 15. The home-field advantage in 1980 was basically a fluke, and in the very next season Seattle had the *worst* home-field advantage in the league.

We also tend to forget that parks can be quite different and still have very few aspects that can be exploited when it comes to winning games. A hitter's park that raises all elements of offense equally will make your batters look better but make your pitchers look worse; it won't help you gain an edge on your opponents. That potential exists only for those parks that significantly favor lefties or righties like Yankee Stadium, affect the elements of offense unevenly like San Diego's Jack Murphy Stadium, or have artificial turf in a predominantly grass league like Royals Stadium.

Yet even when a team has one of these unique parks, the opportunity to build around that edge is a secondary consideration in the context of the ultimate goal. Teams are not out to build a better home-field advantage; they're out to build a winning team. You don't turn your back on a right-handed hitter named Joe DiMaggio just because your park is Yankee Stadium.

When Billy Martin took over the Yankees in 1976, he made substantial changes among his regulars and starting pitchers. Most of those moves were not intended to take advantage of the unique dimensions of Yankee Stadium, which favor lefty hitters and pitchers. Gabe Paul, the Yankees GM, made several trades that confused those who believed in tailoring the team to the ballpark. First, they traded a *lefty pull-hitting catcher* in Ed Herrmann for a bunch of minor-leaguers. Then they traded a *lefty pitcher,* Larry Gura, to get a right-handed backup catcher, Fran Healy, to play behind the right-handed starter, Thurman Munson. The Yankees also traded Doc Medich for Willie Randolph and Dock Ellis, which meant a right-handed batter replaced switch-hitting Sandy Alomar at second base. Then in June of 1976 the Yanks traded *three lefty pitchers* (Tippy Martinez, Scott McGregor, and Rudy May) to acquire Doyle Alexander and Ken Holtzman. Although Holtzman was a former star lefty, the right-handed Alexander was the better pitcher at that stage in their careers.

The Yankees also traded Bobby Bonds, which seemed park-responsive, but what they got in return was hardly a match for Yankee Stadium. They got another right-handed pitcher in Ed Figueroa, plus Mickey Rivers to replace the injured Elliot Maddox in center field. Although Rivers was left-handed, he wasn't seen as a Yankee Stadium hitter. He was a singles-hitting spray hitter, hardly a candidate to pull one into the short right-field seats, and indeed, he didn't hit well at Yankee Stadium during his career.

The one move that matched the ballpark quite nicely was the trade of Pat Dobson for Oscar Gamble. But Martin didn't try to play Gamble every day, platooning him in right field with Lou Piniella. Martin also went the platoon route at DH (Carlos May and Otto Velez) and shortstop (Fred Stanley and Jim Mason) rather than go all left-handed. Overall, with Bonds and Maddox out of the picture, the Yankees had a few more left-handed at bats, but their totals of innings by left-handed pitchers declined 15% and was actually below the league average.

Martin had rebuilt the Yankees by working to fill the club's needs rather than shaping the team around Yankee Stadium. New York had the worst home-field advantage in the league in 1976. They also won the pennant by ten-and-a-half games.

A strong home-field advantage is *not* a feature of winning teams. In a study of American League teams during the fifteen seasons from 1971–85, I separated out the teams with a winning percentage equivalent to over 90 wins in a full season and those equivalent to fewer than 70 wins. The average home-field advantage relative to the league for the 40 winners was a very normal 1.004. Among the 35 losers, the home-field advantage was actually 4% above the league mark (1.041).

Does this mean that a team should *not* build itself around its home park even when it is possible? Well, if it does, baseball teams have been doing it backwards for a hundred years. But more importantly, that is not what those winning teams actually did. Given the opportunity, they were just as willing as the next team to build around their home park. Five of those winners had a home-field advantage at least 15% above the league norm, and all five had home parks that could be exploited more than most: New York (1977), Detroit (1971), Kansas City (1975 and 1978), and Chicago (1972, back when it was one of the toughest home run parks and best pitcher's parks in the league). So why do winning teams in general have such normal home-field advantages?

One of the basic laws of the game is that a winning team will usually have more balance than a losing team. It's a simple case of supply and demand as reflected in the gravity well of .500. The .500 mark is baseball's sign for average, the .500 club that wins just as many as it loses. The further a team moves away from it, in either direction, the harder it is to go in that direction.

It works this way: Say you had a team playing at a .350 clip. Then the kind of players you would need to improve toward .500 would be rather plentiful and easy to acquire. The market is glutted with .450 ballplayers, and there are always some .500 players available at a decent price. Once you are at .500, the effort required to improve becomes more demanding. Joe Average, the .500 player, is not going to help you this time. Now you have to go after the rarer star player. The competition is fierce, and the price may be beyond your means. Imagine how tough it is to improve when you get to be a .575 club.

More often than not, there is virtually no chance to acquire a .600-caliber player, so you start balancing out your roster as much as possible. You replace your average second baseman with a good one. You replace your below-average utility infielder with a player who might be an average starter on another club. You advance by balancing your team; you follow the law of supply and demand.

Remember, your home-field advantage is not an objective reflection of how well you play at home, but how you play relative to your road performance. These winning clubs did very well in their home games. During the 1971–85 period Baltimore had the worst home-field advantage in the league, but its winning percentage at home was still second best at .603. You can only go so high before the gravity well of .500 slows you to a stop, and you naturally turn to other areas where you can still advance. If you're playing .600 at home, you start building your ability to play well in other parks on the road.

We will never understand the origin of the home team's edge as solidly as we have established the simple fact that it exists. The best part of this simple research is the demonstration that we are capable of understanding better even the most nebulous topics through a searching scientific treatment of the available evidence. Look at all we have learned: We found that the home-field advantage is not so much a strategic edge as a basic improvement in the performance of the home team's players. We learned that crowd size and familiarity with the ballpark are minor factors. We got a reasonable glimpse that, yes, the players' productivity is generally heightened by the psychological comfort of living at home. We learned that the umpires are probably a significant contributor to the phenomenon of home-field advantage. We learned that the idea of shaping the home team to the home park is less significant than generally believed, particularly at the league level, and that even in those unique parks where it would seem an advantage, it should be a secondary consideration to meeting the team's needs.

That is a long stretch of miles from the outpost of opinion where we began.

HOUSE:
WHY'S HOME SWEET HOME SO SWEET?

Craig has identified six theories that account for the home-field advantage. He's gone into great detail in showing the evidence for or against the psychological lift of the crowd on your side, the notion of tailoring to a home park, familiarity with the playing conditions, the possible influence on an umpire's calls, and the strategic advantage of batting last. The one I'm going to look more deeply at is the presumed psychic advantage from the sense of being at home.

We have a sign in the clubhouse: "Proper preparation prevents piss-poor performance." If a team has enough talent to compete, then proper preparation can often be the determining factor in the outcome of a game. I believe very strongly that the four elements that enable someone to perform to his potential are physical conditioning, mental conditioning, nutritional conditioning, and mechanical conditioning. *All four of these factors are adversely affected by being on the road.*

Let's look at them one at a time.

Physical conditioning. A player's efforts to maintain a regular program of strength and stamina work are more easily controlled at home. He's comfortable enough to establish a set routine for the day, a routine that will generally involve relatively normal sleeping and waking hours. The basic requirements of daily life—laundry, cleaning, shopping, paying bills, what have you—are all worked into a daily budget of the player's time, and most ballplayers will always include a workout period in that budget.

Players are also more comfortable coming out to the ballpark early at home; the clubhouse, weight room, and field are like a second home. And there is "specificity" in their weight-lifting work—a term that describes the ability to lift more weight when using a familiar machine than when faced with a new apparatus.

Those are just the physical aspects of the workout routine. Then there are the psychological ones. With less reason to get up in the morning, and no wife or family to go home to, the player is more likely to stay out after the game on the road. Body clocks are affected, and the timing needed to get ready for a game is thrown off. Those who like to jog during the day find themselves in a hotel in the middle of a big city and may not want to hassle with taking a cab to where they could run without hitting traffic. And, since ballplayers on the road tend to travel in groups, very few will ever go off to work out on their own.

Mental conditioning. At home, time spent with family and friends helps spread out the impact of last night's successes or failures; there is less solitary time, or time surrounded only with other ballplayers, so the peaks and valleys aren't as extreme. Home is, well, home—it's a nurturing environment where everything around you is familiar and feels as though it's yours. Here, familiarity breeds not contempt but comfort. Competing in psychologically comfortable surroundings increases the chance that performance potential will be reached.

Nutritional conditioning. One of my favorite subjects. It takes a balanced blood chemistry to do your best through a 162-game season. This can be controlled fairly easily at home, where you're eating in your own kitchen for two of the three daily meals (the other being the postgame clubhouse meal), but is very difficult on the road, where meals are so often a room-service cheeseburger or something grabbed in the hotel coffee shop. It's tough to stick to a program of food combining and rotation when choosing meals from even the most complete restaurant menu.

The nutritional habits of ballplayers have long been a physiological nightmare. But baseball players are slowly coming to realize that you can't run a high-powered engine on cut-rate fuel. The home edge, nutritionally, comes because the athlete at home is running on high-octane fuel, while the player on the road is more likely operating on regular.

Mechanical conditioning. You can polish your skills—develop your muscle memory—at home or away with equal efficiency, but it's only logical to assume that such work will be more effective at home because of those three factors cited above. But here, some of the element of tailoring comes into play. A player knows that certain aspects of his skills are emphasized by his home park, so he tends to groove those skills when he's at home. When Wally Moon was with the Dodgers, he didn't stress that inside-out swing when he was on the road, but he sure had it at home. And a road player probably wouldn't want to alter his swing to take advantage of a park peculiarity like the Coliseum's short left-field screen, because why screw up your swing for four games at a time? But for seventy-seven a year. . . .

Finally, there are those players who frankly don't worry too much about familiarity—either because of their own psychological makeup, or because they've been around long enough and played for enough teams that they aren't bothered by the surroundings anymore. Toby Harrah, for example, could handle any park or environment the same way; he'd been conditioned both by his many years in the bigs and by several trades. Also, his base of skills was broad enough that no specific set of circumstances was going to leave him defenseless.

Unfortunately, there are a lot more players who are "homers" than Harrahs. So the bottom line? There really is no place like home.

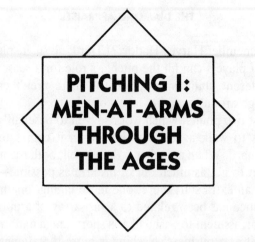

PITCHING I:
MEN-AT-ARMS
THROUGH
THE AGES

Have you ever thought about the importance of the pitcher in keeping every baseball game a mystery? In football they say, "Any team can beat any other team on a given Sunday." Actually, that's not nearly as true in football or the other sports as it is in baseball. The secret is that baseball throws in the wild card of the pitcher.

In what other sport do you have games where a last-place club can be favored to beat a first-place club—even in the home park of the first-place team? It happens all the time in baseball. In 1987, for example, the last-place Cubs would have been favored to win against the first-place Cardinals if they were starting Rick Sutcliffe against Lee Tunnell or Dave LaPoint or Tim Conroy, or even Bob Forsch.

Even when it's the other way around, the outcome of the game is still tremendously up in the air. The star pitcher may be tired or just not able to find his best stuff, while the Lee Tunnells of the world will occasionally find lightning in a bottle, quiet their weaknesses, command their strengths, and beat you not on luck but with great pitching.

This magic works thanks to three factors. First, while each game has its steadying influences in the everyday regulars, the pitcher has an overwhelmingly central role; as he goes, so go the fortunes of the game. Second, pitching is so demanding that it can bring on fatigue before the game is over, capsizing even the most brilliant performance. (Remember Harvey Haddix?) Third, no single player or even a handful of players can fill the pitcher's role for a season; it takes a staff of different abilities and, because there aren't enough good pitchers to go around, varying levels of talent.

Those last two points, which work so well to baseball's advantage, force teams to walk a very fine line when it comes to working a pitcher too hard. When a pitcher is doing well, both the manager and pitcher want to get as much out of his arm as possible—a complete game here, an extra start there, one more inning, one more batter.

This practice has been related to a vast array of arm miseries that are an embarrassment to baseball as a sport, and a matter of practical concern to it as a business. Nothing is more threatening to the stability, planning, and financing of a team than the volatile health of its pitching staff and its pitching prospects in the minor leagues.

Any bit of information on the prevention or rehabilitation of physical impairments among pitchers gives a strategic and financial edge to the clubs that use it. If you examine the dynasties in the history of the game, you'll find in most cases that their consistent excellence was made possible by a pitching staff of surprising durability, with few injuries or sudden drops in effectiveness. This freed them from the burden of spending money or trading away other talent to replace pitchers lost to the normal attrition rate—an important factor in their staying on top.

What's the safest way to train, develop, and utilize a pitcher? That's the general question of the day, and trying to answer it brings up a hundred more specific ones. Why are so many Hall of Fame pitchers relatively late bloomers? In what ways should handling a reliever differ from handling a starting pitcher? Why is it that pitchers often show tremendous productivity early in their careers but vary widely in their later effectiveness? What can a pitcher or manager do to enhance the effectiveness of a "fragile arm"? Why do some pitchers need more rest between starts or fail to bounce back as well as others after a long, strenuous outing? Which is better, a four-man rotation or a five-man rotation?

The biggest problem in answering such broad research questions is: where to begin? One of the great facets of baseball research is the wealth of information on what has gone before us. Track down Old Man Baseball; give a new ear to the winding, twisting tale of the evolution of the game, and you often find your beginning, a direction for more detailed study.

First, we need to overcome our natural hesitancy in listening to tales of pitchers from the early days of baseball. With our minds so anchored by the statistical benchmarks of the present, we feel like Alice through the looking glass when faced with pitchers throwing four hundred innings and tossing thirty-five complete games in a season. But those pitchers of old were human and generally smaller and lighter than the modern player. And their records do have meaning and relevance when taken in proper context.

The careers of Hoss, Cy, Matty, Alexander the Great, and the Hoosier Thunderbolt are part of the history of the game, part of the evolution of the modern pitcher's role. In a sense, they and their contemporaries performed in a laboratory that permitted wild experiments, the likes of which would never be allowed in modern baseball. Rather than rejecting them, we should cherish them for their contributions—not to just their own time, but to our better understanding of the present and the future.

1876–83

The top pitchers of this period pitched in 70% to 98% of their team's games. As the rules prohibited all replacements except in case of injury, they naturally also threw 70% to 98% of their team's innings. However, the schedules had frequent off days and called for fewer than a hundred games, and in the first years as few as sixty. All the pitchers threw underhand, as the rule required that the pitching hand pass below the hip. (The rule was amended in 1883 to limit the delivery to below the shoulder.) The pitchers started out throwing from a box just forty-five feet from the plate, which in 1881 was moved back to fifty feet. Because the game featured few strikeouts, few walks, and numerous fielding errors, we can assume the batters usually put the ball quickly in play and thus reduced the number of pitches per batter and game.

Although throwing underhand or submarine-style is understood to be easier physically, the clubs did recognize that their pitchers needed more rest than this when pitching constantly in a professional schedule. This was especially true as pitching became more difficult and demanding in 1881, when the pitcher's box was moved back five feet.

TOP THREE NL PITCHERS IN INNINGS PITCHED

YEAR	INNINGS PITCHED PER TEAM DECISION	PITCHING APPEARANCES PER TEAM DECISION
1876	8.8	98.5%
1877	8.9	98.3%
1878	8.4	92.8%
1879	7.7	87.6%
1880	7.3	86.9%
1881[1]	6.3	72.1%
1882	6.1	70.0%
1883	6.2	74.1%

[1]Fifty-foot distance.

Two of the era's best pitchers were early casualties to unusually heavy workloads. Al Spalding had been a workhorse in the earlier National Association, but his arm went lame in 1877 at age twenty-five (all ages are as of July 1 of the year in question). In the National League's 1876 inaugural season, Spalding led in wins (47) and started 60 of his club's 65 games, with one relief appearance thrown in as well. Al ended up throwing only 11 more innings in his career.

A similar fate struck Hall of Famer Monte Ward. In 1879 and 1880 Ward averaged 70 games, 591 innings, and 43.5 wins. In 1881, still only twenty-one years old, he experienced arm trouble and became an outfielder/part-time pitcher. Eventually his arm miseries were severe enough to limit him strictly to a position-player's role by age twenty-nine.

1884–92

The 1884 season would firmly link the nineteenth-century pitcher to the modern hurler and his problems. In 1884, the National League removed all restrictions on the pitcher's delivery; they were now free to come over the top and let it fly. Where the submarine style made a pitcher's durability basically a battle against muscle fatigue, the unnatural overhand delivery was much more demanding and opened a seeming Pandora's box of arm injuries.

They didn't have all the fancy names they use today—"painful arch syndrome," "bursitis of the shoulder," "rotator cuff tear," "impingement syndrome," "shoulder tendinitis"—but the symptoms were essentially the same: pain, weakness, stiffness, and sometimes a break in the rhythm of abduction of the arm at the shoulder. On the playing field, sometimes they couldn't throw as hard, sometimes just not as long or as consistently. Sometimes they had trouble bouncing back in their normal rest pattern; sometimes their control wandered or their breaking pitches flattened out.

Making things even harder on the pitchers of this period was an expansion of the schedule to 112 games, and it would continue to escalate to 154 games by 1892. At first the pitchers tried to carry the same workloads they had established as submarine pitchers. The attrition rate among the harder-working pitchers was unusually high. Between the National League, American Association, and 1890 Players League, there were 69 pitchers who threw at least one season of 380 innings or more from 1884 to 1892. Forty-one percent of those pitchers would win their last major-league game within three years of their *first* such season. Only 15 (22%) avoided a significant and lasting decline in their effectiveness within five years, and many of those 15 survivors were established submariners at the time of the change and may have kept their old style despite the new rule. And three of those 15 classified as "survivors" never won a game past age twenty-nine.

History tends to remember those successful survivors. To remind us there was another side, I've included a chart of eighteen of the finer young stars whose arms gave out. It shows their best season at 380-plus innings, the season when it became clear that something was wrong, and the age at which they won their last major-league game.

The fact that most of these fallen stars were cranking out their innings at a very young age is significant: The failure rate in the larger group tended to be more severe among the younger pitchers. Among the pitchers who threw 380-plus innings before age twenty-five, the average age of their last win was twenty-seven. For those who did it after

	AGE	W–L	ERA	AGE	W–L	ERA	AGE AT LAST WIN
Parisian Bob Caruthers	25	40–11	3.13	28	2–10	5.84	28
Pete Conway	21	30–14	2.26	22	2–1	4.91	22
Ed Daily	22	26–23	2.21	24	0–5	7.26	28
Cyclone Jim Duryea	26	32–19	2.56	28	2–10	4.90	30
Bob Emslie	25	32–17	2.75	26	3–14	4.71	26
Hank Gastright	25	30–14	2.94	26	3–14	3.78	29
Pretzels Getzein	22	30–11	3.03	27	4–6	4.22	28
Kid Gleason	23	38–17	2.63	28	2–4	6.97	28
Matches Kilroy	21	46–20	3.07	24	10–15	4.26	32
Phil Knell	26	28–27	2.92	28	7–21	5.49	29
Sadie McMahon	23	34–25	2.81	29	0–5	5.86	28
Cannonball Morris	26	41–20	2.45	27	14–22	4.31	30
Frank Mountain	24	23–17	2.45	25	1–4	4.30	25
Toad Ramsey	21	38–27	2.45	24	4–17	5.22	25
Billy Rhines	21	28–17	1.95	23	4–7	5.06	30
Elmer Smith	19	33–18	2.94	21	9–12	4.88	24
Scott Stratton	20	34–14	2.36	21	6–15	3.92	25
Charlie Sweeney	21	41–15	1.70	22	11–21	3.93	23
Average	23	34–18	2.59	25	5–11	4.99	27

age twenty-five, their last win came at an average age of thirty-two, just a few years short of normal retirement for a regular pitcher in this period. The higher attrition rate among the younger pitchers coincides with present-day observations of impingement syndrome. Players prior to age twenty-five seem more vulnerable, and to the extent that impingement syndrome is seen as a degenerative process, it can often be traced to abuse in the formative years before age twenty-five.

The real pitching star of this period was Charles "Old Hoss" Radbourne. (Radbourne's name is usually spelled without the *e*, but historian Frederick Ivor-Campbell has noted that Radbourne signed his name with an *e*, so that's how we'll spell it here.) Radbourne began his pro career as an outfielder at age twenty-four and didn't pitch his first professional game till age twenty-seven on May 5, 1881. Radbourne pitched as a durable submariner from 1881 to 1883. He was twenty-nine when pitchers were first allowed to throw overhand. The details have become hazy over the years, but Radbourne is believed to have taken advantage of the rule change and threw overhand for at least the first half of the 1884 season.

Old Hoss was also a bit of an innovator in taking advantage of the pitcher's "box," which was six feet by six feet in 1884 and served in place of the modern pitching rubber. The pitcher was required to release the ball from somewhere in the box. Radbourne was said to stand in the right-hand rear corner, turn his back on the batter similar to the way Luis Tiant did it in the 1970s, and then take a hop, skip, and deliver his pitch from the left side of the box. His motion was much like a modern shot-putter's turn. The hitters' complaints that Radbourne's style went against the intent of the pitcher's box—which was to allow the pitcher to deliver the ball from different angles—caused the size of the box to be reduced twice during Radbourne's career.

This charming little fact holds special interest for us, as it demonstrates that Old Hoss had developed a unique way of taking some of the strain off his arm by throwing more with his body. The advantage of the larger pitcher's box in 1884 also helps explain a bit of the amazing durability demonstrated by Radbourne that summer.

On July 16, 1884, Radbourne was suspended by the Providence Grays for cursing his catcher and striking him with the ball after he dropped a third strike. Old Hoss was working in a two-man rotation and already had won 30 games against only 8 losses. Later that month, the other half of the Grays' pitching tandem, Charlie Sweeney, brought about his own expulsion from the league in order to pitch for more money in the Union Association, an outlaw league.

Radbourne was reinstated with a new contract that would pay him to start Sweeney's projected starts as well as his own. Radbourne started and completed 35 of his team's remaining 39 games and tacked on a four-inning relief appearance for good measure. Pitching nearly every day, he won 30 and lost 4. All told he made 73 starts, completed all 73, won 60 games, threw 679 innings, and led the league in ERA. No other pitcher throwing overhand has come even remotely close to such a season.

Before dismissing Radbourne's feat as simply a reflection of a strange era, consider the pregame rituals Radbourne put himself through simply to get his arm loose enough to pitch. The Grays' manager, Frank Bancroft, wrote this as part of a story for *Base Ball Magazine* in 1908:

Morning after morning upon arising he would be unable to raise his arm high enough to use his hair brush. Instead of quitting he stuck all the harder to his task [,] going out to the ball park hours before the rest of the team and beginning to warm up by throwing a few feet and increasing the distance until he could finally throw the ball from the outfield to the home plate. The players, all eagerness to win, would watch "Rad," and when he would succeed in making his customary long distance throw they would look at one another and say the "Old Hoss" is ready and we can't be beat, and this proved to be the case nine times out of ten.

Other sources mention that Radbourne would apply hot towels to his arm and toss an iron ball underhand for several minutes before beginning his pregame throwing ritual. Still, Radbourne ended the season unable to raise his hand to his ear "even if you held a five-dollar bill up there."

It seems remarkable that Radbourne's career did not totally crash after 1884. His ERA relative to the league rose a full run in 1885, and his record fell to 26–20, but he was able to take his regular turn in the rotation and make 49 starts. By 1888, age thirty-three, he was experiencing some trouble bouncing back between starts and averaged only 29 starts in his remaining four seasons. All the same, it was a long-lived and effective career for his era.

Old Hoss deserves to be remembered for his remarkable durability, and we will do well to note the things that stood out in his career: a late start in pitching, a style of delivery that used his whole body, and special attention to his physical conditioning.

1893–1902

In the early 1890s baseball began to worry about the dominance of the "Cyclones," the period term for the hard-throwing "speed-ball' pitchers like Cy Young, Kid Nichols, Brickyard Kennedy, Wild Bill Hutchinson, Ice Box Chamberlain, and the latest arrival, six-one, two-hundred-pound Amos Rusie, "The Hoosier Thunderbolt." The rule seemed to be that the harder you threw, the more colorful your nickname.

Besides a concern for the batters trying to hit these powerful over-hand deliveries, the health of the catcher may also have been an issue. Cy Young remembered, "Chief Zimmer didn't have a padded mitt when he first caught me. He wore an ordinary dress glove with sole-leathered tips sewed on the fingers. You should have seen those amazing callused hands."

Fortunately, these "Cyclones" rarely threw at their top velocity. In this period a pitcher was still concerned with not only pitching effectively but pitching frequently. With the expanded schedule, the top pitchers were expected to pitch in fifty or sixty games and to complete what they started.

Throwing from a pitcher's box just fifty feet away helped these pitchers get away with pacing themselves through the game and the season. At that distance, an 80 m.p.h. fastball reached the batter in the same time that an 89.6 m.p.h. fastball would reach a batter today with the pitching rubber at sixty feet six inches and the pitcher taking roughly a four-and-a-half-foot stride. If a Cy Young just cranked it up to 85 m.p.h., it would be the modern equivalent in reaction time of a 95.1 m.p.h. fastball for the hitter.

That all changed in 1893. The pitcher's box was eliminated, and the pitchers were required to pitch with one foot touching a twelve-by-four-inch rubber slab located sixty feet six inches from home plate. The immediate effect was far greater than anticipated. What once looked like a 90 m.p.h. fastball to the hitters was now coming in at 80 m.p.h. The league batting average jumped from .245 to .280.

The pitchers were all in the same boat and thus felt less pressure to change their style. Cy Young had won 36 games in 1892 with a league-leading ERA of 1.93. With the change in pitching distance, his ERA jumped almost a run and a half (3.36), but it was still among the best (third), and Cy won 32 games. However, there were a lot more tired pitchers by 1894. This meant even easier pickings for the hitters. The league batting average rose another 29 points to .309 in 1894, a season with four .400 hitters. The whole Philadelphia outfield of Sam Thompson, Ed Delehanty, and Billy Hamilton *averaged* over .400 (.404, .400, .399), and the runs scored per game soared to an all-time high of 7.46 per team.

In Baltimore the wheels of evolution were already turning. The Orioles' manager, Ned Hanlon, generally recognized as the game's first great manager, realized that his pitchers were going to have to throw harder at the new pitching distance, and if they were going to throw harder, they could not throw as many innings or appear in as many games.

In 1893 Hanlon's Orioles were 60–70, an eighth-place team. In '94 they improved by 29 wins to take the National League pennant. Much of that gain was made in their pitching staff, which improved from ninth in the league to third. The big change was that the Orioles spread the work around in 1894. No Baltimore pitcher threw over 276 innings, and Hanlon had six different pitchers with at least 100 innings while some of the opposing clubs had only four pitchers on their entire staff.

By 1897 the whole league began to adopt the Hanlon strategy. The four-hundred-inning pitcher was considered obsolete. The few pitchers who tried to throw harder at the new distance while following the old work patterns of the fifty-foot pitchers were not long for the game.

There were four pitchers who threw more than 425 innings in a season during this period. Pink Hawley did it at age twenty-two and had his last winning record at age twenty-five, his last win at age twenty-eight. Lefty Killen also did it at age twenty-two and had his last winning season at age twenty-five and last win at twenty-nine. Also at age twenty-two, Amos Rusie, the most talented pitcher of the period, threw 482 innings to set the record at the modern pitching distance. The Hoosier Thunderbolt had his last winning season and last win at age twenty-seven. Ted Breitenstein was three years older than the others when he tossed 447 innings in 1894 (age twenty-five). By age thirty he was limited to 24 starts and won his last start at age thirty-one.

The last major rule change to shape the relationship between the batter and pitcher involved the status of foul balls not caught on the fly. The rule in the 1890s was that such batted balls did not count as anything; they were simply ignored. This hadn't been a problem in the days when pitchers were firing from the old fifty-foot distance, but now batters found they could just foul off potential strikes they didn't like without losing ground in the count. This not only helped the batter but forced the pitcher to throw a lot more pitches.

Cy Young told a story of how in 1897 Hall of Famer "Slidin' Billy" Hamilton once fouled off 29 consecutive pitches against hard-throwing Sadie McMahon. When Hamilton punched three pitches foul against Young to start off a game, Cy walked up to the plate and said, "Look, Billy, I'm putting the next pitch right over the heart of the plate. If you foul it off, the next one goes right in your ear."

In 1901 the National League ended such confrontations by drafting the modern rule for foul balls: If a foul ball is not caught, it counts as a strike until the batter has two strikes. The effect of this simple rule was remarkable: The league run average fell .66 runs while strikeouts rose 40%. When the American League adopted the rule in 1903, its run average fell .83 runs, and its strikeout rate climbed 31%.

After 1903 we enter one of the more stable periods in pitching history, but before making that jump we should take time to focus on the key figure of durability through this period, Denton True "Cy" Young, the only pitcher whose career spanned the fifty-foot box, the sixty-foot six-inch rubber, the modern foul-strike rule, and the cork-centered ball of 1910.

One of the first things people noticed about the rookie Cyclone was his unusual size and physical condition. At six two, 210 pounds, he was considerably larger than the average player of the period. Old Hoss Radbourne, only thirteen years Young's senior, stood a more normal five nine, 170 pounds. Young's strength came from growing up as a farmer and rail splitter, and his strong legs and endurance came from chasing squirrels as a youngster, a habit of regular running that carried over into his adult years.

Young continued to work the family farm till age twenty-three and threw his first professional pitch in the spring of 1890. By the end of the season he was pitching in the majors for the Cleveland Spiders and making a name for himself with his fastball and his control.

Young was a star pitcher at the fifty-foot distance and kept that status with the change in 1893, but came up with a tired arm in 1894 at age twenty-seven, falling to a 25–22 record with a 3.94 ERA. The next season he followed the lead of Hanlon's Orioles and made seven fewer starts. He lowered his ERA to 3.24 and led the league with 35 wins and four shutouts. Feeling rejuvenated, Young decided to return to his old work level and threw 414 innings in 1896.

The next season Young's fastball lost its zip. His record fell to 21–18, his strikeout average declined more than 20%, and his 3.79 ERA would be his worst relative to the league for his fifteen-year prime (ages twenty-four to thirty-eight). Fortunately his arm bounced back when his workloads again began to reflect the realities of the new age.

Cy finished his career in remarkable fashion. In a time when few pitchers could make it as regulars at age thirty-five, Cy's win totals from ages thirty-five to forty-two were 32, 28, 26, 18, 13, 22, 21, and 19. During those eight seasons only four other major-leaguers won as many as 15 games in a season at age thirty-five-plus, and Young did it more times (seven) than the other four combined (six).

What do we know about this pitching marvel? We know he was fascinated with the mechanics of pitching, that he learned to throw with four different deliveries, and he "wheeled" on the batter both to hide the ball and to get more of his body into the pitch. We know he threw a fastball, overhand curve, sweeping sidearm curve, and a "tobacco" ball similar to the legal spitballs of the day.

Pitching from the fifty-foot box and in the early days of the sixty-foot, six-inch distance, Cy pitched in the style of the day, starting every third day and occasionally every second day, and in an emergency on consecutive days. He credited his durability to his physical conditioning.

"My arm would get weak and tired at times, but never sore," Young said. "I credit it to my legs and my off-season conditioning.

"I ran regularly to keep my legs in shape. In the spring I'd run constantly for three weeks before I ever threw a ball. And I worked hard all winter on my farm, from sunup to sundown, doing chores that not only were good for my legs but also for my arm and back. Swinging an axe hardens the hands and builds up the shoulders and back. I needed only a dozen pitches to warm up for the game."

Cy's belief in heavy conditioning and healthful habits can be seen among his six "Rules for Pitching Success," which appeared in the December 19, 1908, *Sporting Life*. "[Rule 2] Cultivate good habits: Let liquor severely alone, fight shy of cigarettes, and be moderate in indulgence of tobacco, coffee, and tea. . . . A player should try to get along without any stimulants at all: Water, pure, cool water, is good enough for any man. [Rule 3] A man who is not willing to work from dewy morn until weary eve should not think about becoming a pitcher."

If Young had a phobia as a pitcher, it was against wasting pitches. He had excellent control and threw strikes from day one, with a 1.43 walk average in his rookie season and a 1.47 average for his seven-thousand-plus career innings. Besides his twelve-pitch warm-ups and offer to stick the ball in the ear of a batter fouling off too many pitches, Young believed in throwing strikes regardless of the count. In an interview in his later years Cy emphasized that while he did not believe in throwing it over the heart of the plate, "I defend the pitchers who throw the ball into the strike zone at times with a count of two strikes and none." And Young was a willing practitioner of the ancient art of "coasting." Sportswriter Fred Lieb remembers watching Young "protecting a one-run lead, yield a lead-off triple in the last inning against the Athletics and then strike out the side on just nine pitches." Now that's economy!

So what do we have? He had an unusually large physique, he did not throw from the more demanding sixty-foot, six-inch distance till age twenty-six, paid special attention to his pitching mechanics, emphasized low pitch totals, and worked hard on his physical conditioning. Those are the details of the man who threw more innings, more complete games, and won more games than anyone in major-league history, Cy Young.

1903–19

This is the best pitcher's period in the history of the Dead Ball Era (pre-1920). Both leagues were now using the foul-strike rule, and the defense behind the pitcher was improving with the new gloves, better protective equipment for the catchers, and better playing fields.

The pitchers were spreading out the work more and thus were able to throw harder with fewer breakdowns. In addition, a number of new pitches were being adapted to the overhand delivery. Big Ed Walsh established the spitball; Christy Mathewson popularized the screwball, which he called the fadeaway; and an obscure pitcher named Lew "Hicks" Moren discovered the knuckleball. And, of course, the ball remained "dead."

Under the new foul-strike rule, pitchers found they were throwing fewer pitches per game. Getting ahead of the hitter more frequently meant both fewer hits and fewer walks. The very first year the rule was introduced, walk averages fell 12% in the NL, 14% in the AL. Fewer hits, fewer walks, and fewer errors by the fielders all meant fewer batters faced and fewer pitches thrown per game.

To understand the differences between the work levels of pitchers in this era and those of today, we have to keep in mind the different strategies of the periods. In the early part of the century, double-figure home run totals were rare, and most of those were inside-the-park homers. In 1902 Tommy Leach led the National League with just six homers, and all of his career-high seven in 1903 were inside-the-park shots. Without the constant threat of the home run hanging over their heads, the pitchers faced fewer crucial batters to whom they would need to pitch carefully and use setup pitches.

In the modern era, even the average player is capable of hitting a home run, and so he's in scoring position whenever he goes to the plate. And if a modern player reaches first base, he is more of an immediate threat to score because of the higher incidence of extra-base hits with the live ball. The old-time pitchers didn't have to worry as much about runners scoring until they were in scoring position.

The pitchers were also very conscious of the fact that they were expected to complete most of their starts and throw a lot of innings. Some pitchers were just as fanatical about not wasting pitches as was Cy Young. Sad Sam Jones told Lawrence Ritter the following story: "I once heard Eddie Plank say, 'There are only so many pitches in this old arm, and I don't believe in wasting them throwing to first base.' And he rarely did. Made sense to me. . . . You know, I think one reason I pitched so long is that I never wasted my arm throwing over to first to keep the runners close to the bag. There was a time there, for five years, I never *once* threw to first base to chase a runner back. . . . If you stand there like you're ready to pitch, and just stare at him long enough, it'll be too much for him and he'll lean back toward the base. *Then* you pitch."

The fearlessness of these pitchers to throw the ball over the plate can be seen in Stan Coveleski's claim to Ritter that he once went seven full innings in a start without throwing a single called ball. And other pitchers matched Young's meager warm-ups. Tall Tom Sheehan said, "[Grover] Alexander waited until virtually game-time, then walked out, threw a few pitches on the sidelines while conversing with a spectator, then flipped his glove to the mound . . . [and] shut me out." In Alexander's celebrated World Series relief appearance against Tony Lazzeri with the bases loaded, Alexander didn't warm up in the bullpen and threw only five warm-ups from the mound.

The rules of the period also led to further pitching economy; until 1912 the pitchers weren't even guaranteed warm-ups between innings. The pitchers could only sneak in a pitch or two before the first batter would step in the box. One of the oddest homers in history was hit in 1911 when Stuffy McInnis of the Athletics jumped into the box and hit an inside-the-park homer off a pitch intended to be a warm-up.

Given the absence of the long ball, the pitcher's need to pace himself for complete games, and the long haul of the season, the practice of "coasting" became prevalent in this era. Besides Cy Young's noted habit of pitching just well enough to win, Grover Alexander openly admitted he did not bear down until a runner reached base, and Christy Mathewson was notorious for letting up with a lead. This comes through loud and clear in Mathewson's delightful book, *Pitching in a Pinch*. He wrote, "I have always been against a twirler pitching himself out, when there is no necessity for it. . . . Some pitchers will put all that they have on every pitch. This is foolish." Mathewson then related how he lost his first major-league start in the ninth inning because he was tired after "popping" the ball to every batter. The Giants' manager told him, "Never mind, Matty, it was worth it. [That] game ought to teach you not to pitch your head off when you don't need to."

Matty said he never forgot that lesson, and "coasting" played a major part in his famous three-shutout World Series in 1905. Mathewson coasted in his second shutout when he started with a two-run lead and was ahead 7–0 after five innings. This left Matty strong enough to come back on one day's rest to clinch the series on a five-hit whitewash.

It is also worth noting that even though the teams commonly used pitchers rather than coaches to throw batting practice, the team's front-line workhorses didn't have to unless they felt they needed the work. Mathewson showed up late for most games he didn't start, and one can hardly imagine Plank or Jones, who were reluctant to exert themselves throwing to first base in a game, throwing batting practice. Usually the BP chores fell to pitchers like Walt Kinney of the 1918 Red Sox, who got into five games the whole year and whose main task was to throw BP.

How many pitches were being thrown per game during this period? Many years ago I came across a quote I have not been able to relocate for this book. It was a statement by a leading Dead Ball Era pitcher, I believe it was Mathewson, on the stamina required of a professional pitcher. The quote emphasized the need to be able to throw 100 pitches a game. It was phrased to sound like a lot, and I can remember my surprise in that it didn't sound like a lot to me. After working with pitch totals for several years, I know it's ridiculously low by modern standards.

Let's assume it was Mathewson. I have a *1913 Spalding's Official Base Ball Record* in which the National League counted the number of batters faced by each pitcher. For Mathewson it was 1,263 batters in 310 innings. If we assume that Mathewson meant he needed 100 pitches for a complete game, then that would be only 2.73 pitches per batter, about 25% below the modern norm of about 3.6 pitches per batter, or about 130 to 140 pitches per nine innings.

Fortunately we have another source for this kind of estimate. On May 1, 1920, Joe Oeschger and Leon Cadore hooked up for an amazing twenty-six-inning duel. In an interview given in 1980, Joe Oeschger shared several key observations about the game and the era in which it occurred. For one, he gave us yet another concrete example that coasting was a prevalent practice of the day. Oeschger noted he was "a little tired" after the game, "but I was more fatigued in some nine-inning games when I got into many jams. There weren't too many tight situations [he allowed only nine hits in the 26 innings]."

More important, he estimated he threw no more than 250 pitches in that game and didn't identify his estimate as unusually high or low for the feat. An examination of the box score shows 85 at bats and four walks for the opposing team. There were no double plays turned by Oeschger's teammates, and they made two errors, suggesting Oeschger faced 89 to 91 batters. By his high-ceiling guess, Oeschger averaged 2.75 to 2.81 pitches per batter.

Between the Mathewson and Oeschger estimates we have two similar figures to help quantify what we've logically suspected: that the pitchers of this era threw significantly fewer pitches per batter than in modern times. And with fewer batters reaching base than any other time in the Dead Ball Era, pitchers from 1903 to 1919 had the potential for throwing far more innings and far more complete games, while needing less time off between starts.

Immediately after the new foul-strike rule went into effect the innings thrown by the top pitchers began to rise again. In the second year of the rule, Vic Willis gave the National League its first four-hundred-inning season since 1896. In 1903, Joe "Iron Man" McGinnity became the second to top four hundred innings in this century. In 1904, three pitchers threw 390 innings or more; Chesbro, 455; McGinnity, 408; and Powell, 390.

The results in 1905 gave baseball a big scare. Jack Chesbro went from 41–12 to 19–15. Happy Jack's arm gave out in 1907, and he went 14–25 the remainder of his career. In 1904 Jack Powell had his fourth season of 22 wins or more, but in 1905 he slipped from 23–19 to 10–14, and his ERA jumped about a full run. The thirty-year-old veteran continued to pitch several more seasons, but he never won more than 16 and had only one winning record in his last eight seasons.

Vic Willis, the man who broke the four-hundred-inning barrier in 1902, was also struggling. His win total fell from 27 to 12, and he led the league in losses in both 1904 and 1905. But the tremor that shook baseball was when Iron Man McGinnity momentarily buckled under his tremendous workload of 434 innings in 1903 and 408 in 1904.

McGinnity was a legend even in his own time, a rock of durability who had led the league in innings pitched five of his first six seasons. In 1904 he was the league's best as he led in wins (35–8) and ERA (1.61). In 1905 he was 21–15 with an ERA a full run and a quarter higher, right around the league average.

The count for the top five in innings pitched immediately began to fall. It was 403 in 1904, 351 in 1905, and 341 in 1906. But there was one man left to challenge the four-hundred-inning barrier: Big Ed Walsh of the Chicago White Sox. Ed was a big right-hander, six one, 193 pounds. He had been a mediocre pitcher slowly rising through the pro ranks until he developed a tremendous spitball. In the minors he never had a three-hundred-inning season, and his totals in the majors started off with 113, 138, 281. All that changed in 1907, when at age twenty-six he broke loose with 422 innings, 65 more than anyone else in either league. Rather than breaking down in 1908, Big Ed became the last of the forty-game winners and set this century's record for innings with 464. It would be the last four hundred-inning season ever.

In 1909, Walsh began to pay the price as shoulder miseries limited him to 28 starts, 230 innings, and 15 wins. He worked his way back till in 1912 he was again baseball's most durable pitcher. He led in starts and became the last in his league to throw 390 innings (393). That was basically the end for Walsh. Although just thirty-one, he never again threw more than 98 innings in a season and won only 13 more games in his career.

The fall of Big Ed was not unexpected. After Walsh's first collapse, the rest of baseball began to accept that such workloads were dangerous for pitchers. From 1909 till 1920, few pitchers topped 350 innings, and only two reached 390. One was Walsh in 1912, and the other was David "Goliath" Davenport, who led the upstart Federal League with 393 innings in 1915. Davenport was six feet six, 220 pounds. He led in strikeouts and shutouts, won 22 and posted a fine 2.22 ERA. David was quite young at the time (twenty-three or twenty-five, as his birth year has been given as both 1890 and 1892) and paid heavily for his feat. The giant Davenport never won twenty again, never topped 291 innings, and won only three games in his final season at an age no older than twenty-nine.

How astounding was Davenport's 393 innings or Walsh's 464 innings? How does 464 innings in 1908 compare with Mickey Lolich's 376 innings in 1971? Using the Oeschger-Mathewson estimate of 2.8 pitches per batter, we can estimate Walsh averaged about 95 pitches per start in his super year or just under five thousand pitches total— about five hundred *fewer* than Lolich in 1971 even if we use a conservative estimate of 3.5 pitches per batter, an average of 121 per start.

When Walter Johnson threw his career-high 373 innings in 1910, he threw probably 4,060 pitches, or the equivalent of 265 modern innings. Seen in this light, we know the pitchers of this era were not supermen. Three hundred and fifty innings in 1910 was not all that dangerous. Still, 464 innings in 1908 was a little ridiculous, as was Lolich's 376 in 1971, and both paid for those seasons. Kids, don't try this at home.

For this period it's difficult to choose just one significant career to highlight for its durability. Eddie Plank finished his career with amazing strength, and Ed Walsh is an interesting figure even with his eventual failure, but when we speak of unusual durability in the early part of this century we have to turn to Iron Man McGinnity.

Joe was a husky right-hander, one of the more solidly built players of his day at five eleven, 206 pounds. Like Cy Young, McGinnity worked hard year-round. In the off-season he worked in his father-in-law's iron foundry, hence the nickname that fit so nicely with his pitching feats.

Joe began his pro career at age twenty-two and was pitched rather lightly, averaging only 159 innings in 1893 and 1894. His performance didn't warrant a lot of work: His record was 18–29 due to a general lack of control. He retired in 1895 to work in the foundry and support his new bride, but returned to the pro ranks in 1898 at age twenty-seven. A year later he was in the majors and led the NL in wins. McGinnity's crowning achievement as baseball's Iron Man came when he pitched both ends of a doubleheader three times in one month, August 1903, and won all six games. Besides leading the majors numerous times in innings pitched, McGinnity went on to set many minor-league milestones for durability after leaving the majors. Three times he threw four hundred innings in the minors, the last time at age forty-two for Tacoma. His last two-hundred-inning season was in 1923—*at age fifty-two.*

Besides the strong build, extra conditioning, and light workloads in his early years—including no professional workload for ages twenty-four to twenty-six—a key note to the Iron Man's durability was his pitching style. McGinnity was one of the rare submarine, or underhand, pitchers of this century.

One source has suggested that Joe developed this style late in his career after hurting his arm, but this seems highly unlikely. Check Hans Lobert's story of facing McGinnity in his first major-league game: "I came up for the fourth time and McGinnity got two quick strikes on me, both curveballs. That's all he threw, underhand curveballs, one after the other." That was 1903, McGinnity's fifth season in the league, and he began his major-league career with eight straight seasons of 21 victories or more. There is no sign of arm trouble there, and I doubt any pitcher would radically change his delivery during a streak like that. More likely, Joe began his early pro career with an overhand delivery, hurt his arm and came back as a submariner in 1898 *before* he went to the majors.

McGinnity's durability was remarkable even for a submariner and probably was a product of several factors, but more than anything his unusual career confirms the thought that the underhand delivery is easier on the shoulder. Nonetheless, most pitchers chose to trade off the added durability for the greater velocity that came from throwing overhand, as well as the downward break it gave their breaking pitches, making them easier to throw for strikes and tougher to hit.

1920–60

Several factors combined to change the face of the game in 1920. The ball was livened up by winding the yarn tighter around the cork center that had been introduced ten years earlier. The spitball was outlawed that year, except for those pitchers covered by a grandfather clause. The umpires were also ordered to crack down on the shine balls, mud balls, and scuff balls or emery balls. They also began to replace the game ball more frequently.

The result was more hits, more long hits, and then more walks as pitchers tried to work more carefully around the newly engineered power, and the luxury of coasting began to die out in the game.

More pitches per batter, more batters per game, and more pressure situations per game began to make even 350 innings an unhealthy proposition. In 1922 Red Faber had his third straight twenty-win season and led all of baseball with a 2.80 ERA and 353 innings. The next year his wins fell to 14, his ERA rose to 3.41, and in his remaining ten seasons he never had more than 15 wins or threw more than 238 innings in a season.

George "The Bull" Uhle had an even tougher reaction to throwing 358 innings in 1923. Uhle went from 26–16, 3.77 ERA to 9–15, 4.77 ERA. He eventually bounced back for another good year in 1926, but then at age twenty-eight started a string of nine mediocre-to-poor seasons with only two winning records. Again, baseball was paying attention and responded by reducing the ceiling of innings for twenty-one years, until 1944. In 1925 the top five in innings averaged under 300 innings (285) for the first time in baseball history.

The next big scare came after the 1936 season. Baseball's offenses were still booming. The batting average for both leagues was .284, the home run rate was second only to the freak 1930 season, and the walk rate of 3.43 was a new all-time high. The 1936 AL leader in innings pitched crashed in 1937, as did the top two in the NL.

Dizzy Dean led all of baseball with 315 innings in 1936 and went from 24–13 to 13–10 due to a lame arm that limited him to 197 innings. His arm never recovered, and he won only 16 more games in his career, the last coming at age twenty-nine. Dean always blamed his arm trouble on pitching with a broken toe suffered in the 1937 All-Star Game, but it is also true that Dean was one of the hardest-working pitchers of his time. He averaged 306 innings for the five years prior to his arm breakdown, and led the league in innings pitched three times, the first at the young age of twenty-one.

Second to Dean in 1936 was Brooklyn's Van Lingle Mungo, with 312 innings. Mungo had led the league in innings in 1934 at age twenty-three, and his arm caved in after his second three-hundred-inning season in this hitters' era. Although only twenty-six, he never had a double-figure win season or threw more than 161 innings again until the 1945 war season.

Over in the American League, Wes Ferrell had led the league with 322 innings in 1935 and again in 1936 with 301. After winning 25 and 20 those two seasons, he fell to 14 wins with a 4.90 ERA in 1937. Only twenty-nine years old, he had only 33 wins left in his arm and a 6.12 ERA for his remaining 216 innings.

In 1939 Ferrell tried one of the more exotic home remedies to cure his sore arm, which he felt had "arthritis." He took several honeybees and held them against his arm until they stung him, which swelled his arm to twice its normal size. It didn't help.

After these misadventures, the top five in innings averaged only 280 in 1937, a new low for all of baseball history. That figure rose a bit as the offensive explosion finally began to abate, and it took a real jump when World War II pressured baseball to get as many innings as possible out of its remaining pitchers. In 1944 the top five came in at 312, the high-water mark from 1924 to 1968.

Big Bill Voiselle led the NL with 313 innings in 1944, won 21, and had a 3.02 ERA. The next season, still a war year, he won only 14 with a 4.49 ERA; he won his last game at age thirty. In the AL, Dizzy Trout threw 352 innings, the most since Uhle in 1923. Trout went from 27–14, 2.12 ERA to 18–14, 3.14.

The first year after the war Bob Feller astounded baseball by throwing 371 innings, the most since Grover Alexander way back in 1917. Feller, who had spent ages twenty-three to twenty-five and most of age twenty-six in military service, surprisingly suffered only a slight setback in 1947. His win total fell from 26 to 20, and his ERA rose from 2.18 to 2.68. Only his strikeout rate suggested a significant reaction to his 371-inning season; it fell 30% from 8.43 to 5.90 strike-outs per nine innings.

In the 1950s practically no one threw three-hundred-inning seasons with the exception of Robin Roberts, an amazingly strong right-hander, six one, two hundred pounds. He threw his first three-hundred-inning season at age twenty-three in 1950 to start a string of six three-hundred-inning seasons. He led the league in innings and complete games for five straight years. Then at age twenty-nine, his arm began to fail him. His ERA jumped from 3.28 to 4.45, and he led the league in losses. He led in losses again with 22 at age thirty. After seven straight seasons of 20 to 28 wins, Roberts averaged just 11 wins and a 3.78 ERA for the final eleven years in his career.

When Roberts began struggling in 1956, baseball backed off the three-hundred-inning mark completely until the schedule was expanded in the early sixties. In the last season of this period, 1960, the leaders in innings pitched were Larry Jackson with 282 in the NL and Frank Lary with 274 in the AL.

Probably the most interesting career to focus on from this period is that of Bob Feller. He didn't finish it in strong fashion, but he survived what was perhaps the heaviest single-season workload in this century fairly well. In many ways his 371 innings in 1946 was a more difficult feat than Walsh's 464 innings in 1908 or Lolich's 376 in 1971. I have already shown that Lolich probably had to throw more pitches for his 376 innings than Walsh did for his 464. Now consider that Feller faced roughly the same number of batters as Lolich and had considerably more control trouble at that stage of his career than Mickey did (3.71 walks per nine innings, compared with Lolich's 2.20). Added to that, Feller had to crowd his innings into a 154-game schedule by completing seven more starts than Lolich.

Feller started his career in 1936 and proved early that he was a real workhorse. He first led the league in innings pitched at age twenty and did it five times in his career. Besides his 371 season, he also threw 343 innings the season before he entered the war.

After that big 371-inning season he never again led in innings or topped three hundred, but he continued to pitch quite effectively for four more years and led in wins with 22 in 1951. At age thirty-three he ran into some arm trouble and became a spot starter with a record of only 36–30 in his remaining seasons. It was not a very good finish to what was mostly a brilliant career, but it was still an impressive record in light of those who totally broke down under workloads far less severe than what Feller went through.

Feller's durability is linked to two features of his life-style and career. One, Feller was a hard physical worker year-round. He was an avid barnstormer in the off season, remembered especially well for his legendary battles with the top Negro teams of the thirties and forties. He also was considered a bit of a health nut for his generation of players. Bob Broeg wrote of him that "no manager ever found Feller wanting, either in his willingness to work or in his devotion to physical conditioning. From the time he employed arm-and-back-strengthening exercises with a chair in the Feller farm kitchen at Van Meter until he labored alone with stretching exercises in the outfield of major league parks, Rapid Robert was a physical faddist."

Probably just as important to Feller's survival of normally abusive work levels was the time he spent in the military service. He never had to see how his arm would react the next season after throwing 343 innings at age twenty-two. He spent the next three years and most of a fourth in the navy. This sabbatical from the rigors of pitching on a major-league schedule was quite helpful given the current understanding of rotator-cuff impingement syndrome, the modern catch-all diagnosis for shoulder pain and weakness generally related to abuse—usually overwork—of the shoulder joint with the arm at or above shoulder level. Short of a serious rotator-cuff tear, the syndrome is considered totally reversible if dealt with early for those under age twenty-five, and to a lesser extent for those with a more advanced case. According to an article in *The Physician and Sportsmedicine,* "The simplest way and probably one of the most effective treatments is complete rest or modified activity in the shoulder." We don't know whether Feller suffered from impingement syndrome, but we do know that he got the rest.

1961–PRESENT

In the National League's 1962 expansion season, Don Drysdale threw 314 innings to start a run of five three-hundred-inning seasons. By the end of the sixties and in the early seventies, the three-hundred-inning pitcher was a common figure in baseball again. In 1972 the top five in innings averaged 338 innings, the most since 1917. This was the period of Mickey Lolich, the Ed Walsh of the seventies, and of Wilbur Wood, who wanted to see how far you could push the knuckleball (the answer was 376.2—two outs more than Lolich cranked out). Gaylord Perry, Fergie Jenkins, Sam McDowell, Bob Gibson, Juan Marichal, Denny McLain, Mickey Lolich, Claude Osteen, Bill Singer, Vida Blue, Steve Carlton, Wilbur Wood, Nolan Ryan, Jim

Colborn, Bert Blyleven, Phil Niekro, Catfish Hunter, Luis Tiant, Andy Messersmith, and Jim Kaat all threw at least one three-hundred-inning season from 1968 to 1975.

What led to this explosion? For one, the offensive side of the ledger went into a gradual decline after World War II, making life easier on the mound again. The increased use of relievers, improved fielding gloves, and the growing prevalence of night games was a big part of it. The ballparks also went through a big change. From 1954 to 1969 baseball opened eleven new parks, and nine of them favored the pitcher. Abandoned were several offensive parks like Ebbets Field and the Polo Grounds, and two teams left St. Louis's Sportsman's Park.

The most dramatic change came in 1963 when the strike zone was expanded to the top of the shoulders and the bottom of the knees. This alone set off a rise in the number of innings thrown by the top pitchers, much as the foul-strike rule had back at the start of the century. The 1963–68 period belonged to the pitcher.

	BA	BB/9	R/G
1920–45	.277	3.22	4.77
1946–62	.259	3.62	4.47
1963–68	.245	2.96	3.86

While it is true that the strike zone expansion was repealed in 1969 and the height of the mound lowered to ten inches, the pitchers did not immediately revert to their former struggles. The leagues expanded to add four more teams in 1969, which took some of the sting out as 17% of their innings would now be against expansion-level players.

I give even more credit to a subtle change in pitching philosophy that evolved during the 1963–68 period. One of the things that did *not* happen with the reduced strike zone in 1969 was a return to the walk levels common under the strike zone interpretation of 1950–62.

	BB/9
1950–62	3.55
1969–87	3.30

This involves a totally separate area of research, but I have done a study that shows that the American League pitchers quickly adopted a strategy of pitching very carefully in the Live Ball Era; they were willing to walk more batters rather than take the chance of pitching to their power. The National League pitchers resisted this strategy for several years; the difference in walk averages was probably the most distinguishing characteristic between the two leagues from 1920 until World War II. As late as 1938, AL hurlers averaged a full walk per nine innings more than the NL pitchers.

While the NL strategy was probably more correct, the NL went on to adopt the AL trend. But evolution always wins the battle against trends; some trends just last longer than others. Gradually we have returned to a pitching strategy that produces fewer walks, which also means fewer batters, fewer pitches thrown, and fewer pressure situations.

The new theory is that while you can avoid home runs by never giving an inch to the batter, you can win that battle and lose the war. Walks in the Live Ball Era are far deadlier and have more scoring potential than is often realized. If you nag your pitchers into throwing strikes, as Earl Weaver and his pitching coaches used to do, you force them to develop strategies that defuse the home run—or at least the most dangerous ones—without increasing the likelihood of walking the batter. That is the logical line based on sixty years of data from the Live Ball Era, and it has proved to be the evolutionary line.

The 1963–68 period sped up that evolution as it produced and *reinforced* the idea of throwing more strikes and allowing fewer walks. The pitchers were more successful under the larger strike zone, and when it was taken away from them they tried to hang on to the statistical benchmarks associated with that success. They would say, "Hey, I'm walking more guys than I used to and my ERA is higher. I'd better work on throwing more strikes." Because that strategy is basically sound, they gained back some of their success and stayed with throwing strikes.

All these factors combined with the expanded schedule to bring back the three-hundred-inning pitcher. But there were casualties, too. Drysdale's career abruptly ended just after his thirty-third birthday.

Denny McLain and Larry Dierker blew their arms out. Vida Blue and Bert Blyleven had their amazing early careers downshift to a lower level in their late twenties. The three-hundred-inning pitcher began to die again as baseball moved on in the seventies. New pressure was applied to the pitchers through changes favoring the hitter. The AL adopted the Designated Hitter rule in 1973, and the new wave of ballparks favored the hitters. Of the eight new parks opened in the seventies and eighties, five have been hitters' parks, two have been essentially neutral, and only one has favored the pitchers. Further, about half of the existing parks have made changes that significantly altered the park effect, and literally 90% of those changes have favored the hitter.

Overall, baseball has again become very protective of its pitchers. The sudden jump in workloads in the late 1960s and early 1970s has declined steadily since its peak in 1973. Since 1979, the top five in innings pitched have averaged under 300 innings. In 1984 they fell to 263 innings, the lowest in baseball history, excluding the 1981 strike season. Most of this has been accomplished by abandoning the four-man pitching rotation, which was fairly common through 1974 and gradually disappeared, basically vanishing with Earl Weaver's retirement.

The most interesting subject for a tighter focus in this period is the rubber-armed left-hander, Mickey Lolich. If there is one thing that separates Lolich from the other durable stars we have looked at, it would be his general disregard for his physical condition. He was, in a word, fat. Make that with a capital *F*. He could talk about the illusions of wearing a low-slung belt and point to some of the heavies in the stands, but don't let him kid you. He didn't blot out the sun, but he cast a pretty serious shadow.

Mick did not start out like a star. He stayed in the shadows until he won three games in the 1968 World Series. If you weren't a Tigers fan, you probably don't know that was his fifth year as a regular member of the rotation. He was never pushed too hard in those early years, with a high of only 244 innings in 1965 and never more than a dozen complete games in a season. That was peanuts in those days.

There was nothing there to suggest that he was capable of 45 starts,

29 complete games, and 376 innings, or, as if that weren't enough, having a *better* year the very next season. He may have thrown "only" 327 innings in 1972, but he won 22 and actually lowered his ERA from 2.92 to 2.50. After that he was nothing special, 56–70 the rest of his career. His ERA jumped from 2.50 to 3.82 and 4.15 when he led the league with 21 losses in 1974.

Okay, maybe Lolich was helped by not being worked harder when he was younger, but that is not nearly enough to explain the mystery that was Mickey Lolich.

All right, all you Tigers fans, shall we fill them in? Surprise— Mickey Lolich *was not left-handed.* The truth is that Lolich broke his right arm when he was a boy and learned to throw lefty during the healing process. For some reason he never went back to throwing righty. He did everything right-handed except throw a baseball. He even hit right-handed, though he tried switch-hitting for a few years. I guess the limited use of his left arm for anything but pitching helped his durability out on the mound.

So here we are. This is how research often begins, setting up an overview while getting the creative juices flowing. You check some raw hunches and see what else jumps out of the bushes. What have we learned? First, we learned we can significantly expand our laboratory, that we are capable of making sense out of the past and applying it to our understanding of the present and future.

We have seen that "sore" arms and an associated reduction in pitching effectiveness have been a problem throughout baseball history. We have learned that these problems were more common at the upper level of innings pitched for every era. Further, we have seen that what happens to those highly visible pitchers is a matter of concern to the decision makers in the game. We have seen that a consistent response to arm trouble in that group is a reduction in the ceiling of innings that pitchers are allowed to throw.

We focused on individual pitchers of unusual durability because we are looking for factors that may be connected to their odd ability other than just having a unique arm. Some may be bothered that we detailed only five pitchers; six, if you count the brief sketch of Ed

Walsh. Relax. In running through this history of the game my mind automatically flipped through a lot more pitchers than that—basically every pitcher I knew anything about. You will meet a few more of them in the next chapter.

At the same time, I would emphasize that an examination of a few extreme cases is valid in itself for the preliminary study of a topic. Possible cause-and-effect relationships are more likely to be visible in their cases. It is a great way to get started even though in the end those specific cases have very little value. Ultimately, we are looking for relationships that affect large groups of fairly common pitchers, not just what makes five or ten of the most extreme pitchers in history tick.

What Radbourne, Young, McGinnity, Feller, and Lolich have done is to point out possible connections: extra conditioning, a lack of abuse in the younger or formative years, efficient pitching mechanics, a late start or vacation from pitching, a submarine delivery, not throwing with the dominant arm.

Upon further reflection I catch out of the corner of my eye a line running from durability to the ability to throw harder than most. Radbourne, Young, Feller, and Lolich threw about as hard as anyone in their eras. And then there's physique; with the exception of Radbourne, these were basically very "solid" citizens of the diamond.

From there we go to the vague, open-ended questions. Was there something that came up in this story that bothered you? For me, an alarm went off right at the end of the modern era that something was not quite right. The offensive pressure on the pitcher is not as great as in, say, the 1950s. Why are we still having arm problems in the 1980s when we are throwing fewer innings spread out over a longer schedule? What's the best way to limit innings—by decreasing the number of starts or the complete games?

It's time to pack up all this vague knowledge, jump off into the wilderness, and track down the evidence with which we can test out our theories and, we hope, answer our questions. We pick up that trail in the next chapter.

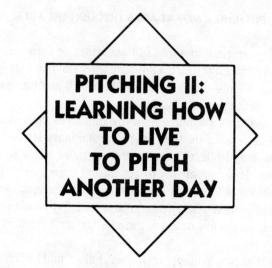

PITCHING II: LEARNING HOW TO LIVE TO PITCH ANOTHER DAY

We're walking in new country now, breaking fresh ground in our investigation of why some pitchers are more durable and enjoy longer careers than others. We hope to uncover knowledge that will be applicable to all pitchers, so we can reduce the number of careers derailed from the simple effort of competitive pitching.

Reaching into the bag of theories we packed from the last chapter, I am especially intrigued with the link between longevity and light workloads in pitchers' formative years, before age twenty-five. Remember that Old Hoss Radbourne was converted to pitching at the age of twenty-seven, Iron Man McGinnity didn't throw very many innings as a young pitcher and was retired for ages twenty-four to twenty-six, Bob Feller spent several of his early years in military service, and Ed Walsh was worked very lightly through age twenty-four, including two seasons of fewer than 140 innings.

There are several other interesting cases that strongly suggest this link. Hall of Famer Eddie Plank, the man who hated to waste throws to first base, was a late starter who reportedly didn't even take up pitching until he was twenty-one. He spent most of his early twenties pitching for Gettysburg College. Plank didn't throw a professional inning until a few months prior to his twenty-sixth birthday. He was such a novice that in his first game the umpire had to stop the game and give him special instruction on how to pitch legally from the stretch position. Despite the late start, Plank went on to win 327 games. Plank and Cy Young were the only Dead Ball Era pitchers to excel past their thirty-fifth birthdays. Plank's best season, 26–6, 2.22 ERA, came at age thirty-six. His last twenty-win season was at age thirty-nine, and his final season at age forty-one included a 1.79 ERA in 131 innings.

World War II and military service in the reserves in the 1950s and 1960s seemed to help a number of pitchers to age well. Early Wynn and Warren Spahn missed several seasons in World War II and still went on to become the first pitchers to notch three hundred wins since Lefty Grove. Whitey Ford and Vern Law spent ages twenty-two and twenty-three in military service and enjoyed exceptional performance after age thirty. At age thirty-five Ford still had the best ERA in the league, and at the same age Law had the best season of his career (17–9, 2.15 ERA). Among today's graybeards, Nolan Ryan at age twenty and Phil Niekro at age twenty-four each gave a season to the military. And a number of others like Bob Gibson, Gaylord Perry, and Steve Carlton were used in a starter-reliever role in an early season, pitching so little it was almost like a year off.

The most amazing pitcher out of this group has to be Warren Spahn, the major-league Methuselah. Spahnie pitched a couple years in the minors before making his major-league debut at the end of the 1942 season. When he entered military service he had pitched only five hundred professional innings spread over three seasons. World War II kept him occupied for the rest of his formative years (ages twenty-two to twenty-four). On his return, Spahn quickly established himself as one of the best lefties in baseball, but our real interest is in what he did after 1956, age thirty-six and beyond.

Despite three serious knee operations during his career, Spahn churned out quality season after quality season and never missed a beat as he hit his late thirties. He holds the following records for pitchers past age thirty-five:

1. most seasons leading league in wins: five
2. most seasons leading league in complete games: six
3. most twenty-win seasons: six

4. most seasons over 250 innings: seven, tied with Young
5. most no-hitters: two
6. oldest twenty-game winner: age forty-two
7. oldest ERA leader with 200 plus IP: age forty

Spahn is the only pitcher in the Live Ball Era to reach 330 career victories, and he finished way past that with 363. Steve Carlton and Tom Seaver were able to match him into their early thirties, but no one has come close to Spahn's finishing kick. Think about it: At age thirty-nine Walter Johnson was in his final season going 5–6, Cy Young led his league in losses, and so did Phil Niekro. At age thirty-nine Warren Spahn led his league with 21 wins, which he did again at age forty while throwing a no-hitter and leading the league in ERA.

At age forty-two Spahn was 23–7 with a 2.60 ERA. At that age even the seemingly immortal Gaylord Perry was just hanging on in his final season with an 8–9 record. Then there is my favorite statistic to capture the uniqueness of Spahnie: He won more games after his thirty-fifth birthday than Sandy Koufax won in his whole career. Holy cow!

How do we account for this? Spahn was not overly large. He is not thought of as a conditioning buff, but he obviously worked hard in his rehabilitation after his knee operations; there is nothing in his career record to even hint at when he had them. He had a reputation as a pitching economist; like Young, Alexander, and Plank, he didn't like to waste pitches. The one thing that really stands out, though, is his absence from competitive pitching in a professional schedule from ages twenty-two to twenty-four.

Because baseball has gone through several changes in the amount of offensive pressure facing the pitcher—as well as changing views of how hard pitchers should be worked—certain periods in baseball history have led to unusually light or heavy workloads for pitchers as a whole. That being true, if there is a link between a young pitcher's workloads and his eventual durability and longevity, there should be corresponding fluctuations in the attrition rates among older pitchers according to the circumstances of the era in which they "grew up" as pitchers.

There weren't a lot of successful older pitchers from 1895 to 1920. The older pitchers of that period spent their youth pitching at a time when the strains of pitching overhand were not even guessed at, or in a time when baseball briefly tried to resurrect the old work patterns.

One ideal period for a young pitcher was 1905–19: Offensive pressure was very low, and baseball had reduced the ceiling for innings as a reaction to the failures of pitchers like Willis, Chesbro, Powell, "Flip-Flap" Jones, and others.

This means that starting in the late 1920s, we should find an unusual number of older pitchers doing quite well. That is exactly what happened. By 1928, you have a record number of pitchers at age thirty-five-plus winning 15 games or more. After the Federal League folded in 1916, the next five seasons (1917–21) had only five pitchers win 15-plus games at age thirty-five or older, and one of those was knuckleballer Ed Cicotte. In 1928 baseball had more than that in a single season: Dazzy Vance won 22, Eppa Rixey won 19, Jack Quinn won 18, Sad Sam Jones had 17 wins, Grover Alexander had 16, and Ray Kremer had 15. All these pitchers spent their formative years in a relatively gentle environment for pitcher workloads. If a pitcher was thirty-five in 1928, he was twenty to twenty-four from 1913 to 1917.

The oddity of one season seeing six pitchers thirty-five or older reaching 15 wins remained unmatched for the next fifty years. In 1938, the oldest pitcher in baseball with 15 wins was Red Ruffing at age thirty-four; the thirty-five-year-olds had been blitzed by the offensive explosion of the Live Ball Era. If you were thirty-five in 1938, you had spent your formative years pitching from 1923 to 1927.

The over-the-hill gang would ride again in the late 1970s and early 1980s.

PITCHERS 35 + YEARS OLD WITH AT LEAST 15 WINS

YEAR	NUMBER	TOTAL WINS	
1978	5	72	
1979	4	78	
1980	7	131	
1981	4	72	(projected)
1982	6	106	

Essentially the same thing had happened. Most of these old-timers had their formative years after 1962, when baseball's offense was at its lowest for the Live Ball Era and the ceiling for innings, particularly in the first half of the decade, reflected the concerns of the 1950s when Robin Roberts's arm blew out after several seasons of heavy use. A pitcher who was thirty-five in 1978 would have been twenty in 1963, twenty-four in 1967.

In defending this analysis of what happened in the late 1920s and 1978–82, I must point out another theory that also accounts for this phenomenon through a totally different approach. In his *The 1983 Baseball Abstract,* Bill James came up with a fascinating economic theory that fit quite nicely.

A year ago, concerning Gaylord Perry, I commented on the fact that we have a basketful of pitchers around with 200, 250 or more career victories, whereas in 1968 there was only one active pitcher with 200 wins (Don Drysdale with 204), and the tenth man on the list of leading pitchers in career wins had the preposterously unprepossessing figure of 123. There are now around 30 active pitchers with more than 123 wins. Pitchers who were 35 years or older accounted for only 84 major league wins in 1967; in 1980 they accounted for 266. . . . The question before the house is, why has this happened?

. . . The same thing—the same sudden (in historical terms) forceful shift toward older pitchers—has occurred once before in baseball. . . . Between 1917 and 1932 . . . the number of wins posted by pitchers 35 or older increased from 7 (!) to about 150.

. . . Do you remember Waite Hoyt's quote, "Wives of ballplayers, when they teach their children their prayers, should instruct them to say: 'God bless Mommy, God bless Daddy, God bless Babe Ruth.' Babe has upped Daddy's paycheck by 15 to 40 percent!" The common thread between the two periods 1917–1932 and 1967–1982 is a dramatic upsurge in player salaries. Suppose that you are Gaylord Perry, and for years you were one of the best pitchers in the game, and for this you were paid—oh, I don't know, $40,000 to $75,000 a year, I suppose, which is a good living wage, but by the time the government takes its share it won't buy very much farm land, and then all of a sudden at age 40 people are throwing whole counties at

you if you can just hang around and pitch .500 baseball for another
year. Are you going to retire, or are you going to hang in there for
as long as you can?

A related matter here is that I have always believed that many
pitchers pass through a crisis about the age of 30 when they lose
their good fastball, and that causes many of them—far too many of
them—simply to give up, walk away from the game, when if they
would stay around and try to learn to work with what they have left,
they could become just as effective as they were. . . . Jerry Koosman, Jerry Reuss, Luis Tiant, Jim Kaat. . . . A large percentage of
all pitchers who will put their heads down and bull their way
through the crisis, it has always seemed to me, would come out of it
better pitchers than they ever were. But most, like Drysdale, don't
want to do it; either they walk away, or they try pitching the way
they have always pitched, getting gradually less effective until they
are released at 33.

Anyway, this notion dove-tails nicely with the economic interpretation of the phenomenon. . . . You don't walk away from the
chance to earn five times as much as you were earning two years
ago. But the economic incentive is not relevant unless it is, indeed,
possible to make the transition.

The last line is the essential difference between the two theories.
My theory—call it the formative environment theory—identifies these
periods as ones when more pitchers were physically able to make
such a transition; all they were battling was a natural aging pattern
that eroded their fastballs and dulled their durability. In other periods
the older pitchers were also more likely to be battling escalating
impingement syndrome as well as an occasional serious rotator cuff
tear. Incidentally, I followed Don Drysdale as guest on a radio show
in Arlington in 1984, and during his interview he mentioned that it
was a rotator cuff tear that ended his career so early, not a lack of
interest or incentive to adjust.

Bill's economic theory—which I essentially endorse as a very real
factor—tries to account for why a Gaylord Perry at age forty would
"hang around and pitch .500 baseball for another year." But Perry
did not need an economic incentive to push him to pitch at age forty;

the man's arm was giving him all the push he needed. Do you retire at age forty right after winning the Cy Young award (1978, age thirty-nine)? Do you retire when you have won at least 15 games for thirteen straight years, including a streak of 11 consecutive winning seasons?

One way to separate the formative environment theory from the economic theory is by watching the number of at bats given to hitters age thirty-five or older. The economic theory should work equally well on the older hitters, driving them to hang on for the money just as much as the pitchers. The formative environment theory grows out of the unique nature of pitching, so it doesn't link the two groups at all; we would expect their peaks to occur more independently.

If we study the period between World War I and World War II, we get an excellent view of the economic theory at work—for the older hitters. During the 1920s we see baseball salaries increasing to a point where more and more older batters were willing to make the sacrifices and adjustments necessary to extend their careers.

AVERAGE INNINGS AND AT BATS, PER TEAM, BY PLAYERS 35 + YEARS OLD

	INNINGS	AT BATS
1919–24	64.9	282
1925–29	162.5	424
1930–35	154.4	286
1936–41	126.4	301

After the stock market crash in October of 1929, there was a dramatic drop-off in the next four years. The older batters had already cashed in on paydays they had never expected—possibly paid off the house and saved enough to buy into a business or a farm. They weren't going to hang around when management started handing out pay cuts.

There was a slight resurgence later in the 1930s. Baseball attendance began to rebound a bit, so the money may have been better. More likely, it looked a lot better. The new batch of older players probably hadn't paid off the house or saved much money, and they may have been supporting a raft of relatives. The country's economy was improving, but I doubt many folks, including ballplayers, were ready to trust it. Baseball was a security blanket to cling to.

Yet this impressive symmetry goes right out the window when you look at the distribution of the older pitchers. As they moved along in the 1920s they made far bigger gains than the older hitters. Then when the Great Depression hit and the veteran batters started to opt for retirement with a 33% decline in playing time, the veteran pitchers kept going with a meager 5% cut. In fact, to the best of my knowledge, the 1930–35 period had the largest ratio of veteran innings to at bats (.540) of any six-year period in baseball history. Then in the late thirties the two groups actually started going in opposite directions.

Yet this all makes sense if we realize that the economic factor is only a secondary influence on the veteran pitchers, who were responding more to the factors embodied in the formative environment theory. The veteran pitchers were too good to retire when the depression struck. In 1930 you've got thirty-seven-year-old Ray Kremer leading the NL with 20 wins; thirty-nine-year-old Dazzy Vance is fourth with 17. In the AL, Jack Quinn posts a 9–7 record with six saves despite being forty-six years old.

In 1931, the Dodgers got nearly 30% of their wins from three pitchers who were all at least forty years old (Vance, Quinn, and Dolph Luque). All of these veteran stars came out of an excellent formative environment, the 1905–19 period.

The veteran pitching presence begins to vanish as we move past 1935. Suddenly we start getting a lot of burned-out veterans who had spent their formative years in the 1920s before the pitching workloads adjusted to the much heavier demands of the developing Live Ball Era. It's interesting to note that the best veteran pitcher in the late thirties was Coonskin Davis. He won 22 games at age thirty-five in 1939, and later won 15 at age thirty-eight in 1942. Davis was a unique case in that he didn't even start pitching professionally until he was already out of his formative years at age twenty-five.

If we apply the same analysis in the modern era, we again find support for the formative environment theory as a separate effect from the economic theory.

This time let's begin with 1975, the season an arbitrator made Catfish Hunter a free agent and baseball salaries were still in their pre–free-agent days.

AVERAGE INNINGS AND AT BATS, PER TEAM, BY PLAYERS 35+ YEARS OLD

	INNINGS	AT BATS	RATIO
1975–79	95.0	266	.357
1980–83	164.4	382	.430
1984–87	133.4	632	.211

You can see the veteran batters hanging on in increasing numbers as the salaries escalated. In fact, baseball has only just recently turned the corner on salary escalation, and it's interesting to note that 1987 was the first year the number of veteran at bats per team hadn't increased since 1980.

AVERAGE AT BATS, PER TEAM, BY PLAYERS 35+ YEARS OLD

1979—325	1982—459	1985—645
1980—247	1983—502	1986—756
1981—320	1984—603	1987—524

But not so for the veteran pitchers. While the older hitters were still riding a steep escalator, the older pitchers slipped into a clear decline. After a rapid peaking in 1980–83, when they averaged over 164 veteran innings per team, no season since has reached 140, and the average is 133. Look at the change in ratio between veteran innings and at bats. In the last four seasons it has been less than half that of the four years before, and less than the ratio of the 1975–79 period.

Why? Because in 1980–83 you had a large number of veteran pitchers who had spent their formative years pitching in the gentle environment of the 1960s. Most of those had finally retired by the time you get into the 1984–87 period, and the new batch of veteran pitchers had been raised in a much harsher pitching environment.

The pitchers who are now thirty-five or forty years old pitched in the early seventies. The 1969 four-team expansion thinned the pitching ranks and forced many of these pitchers into dominant roles before they were ready. Conditions were tougher with the shrunken strike zone, lower mound, better hitters' parks being built and the DH rule coming to the American League in 1973. There were more batters faced per game, more pitches thrown, and more pitches thrown in pressure situations. And you had a carryover of the practice of throwing three hundred innings, which was revived in the easier sixties.

The young pitchers of the seventies would normally show up as the veteran pitching stars of the mid-eighties. Yet for 1984–87, almost all the thirty-five-plus pitchers winning 15 games or more were either knuckleballers or ancient dinosaurs like Carlton, Sutton, and Seaver. Excluding knuckleballer Charlie Hough, Bert Blyleven is the only pitching child of the early seventies thus far to win 15 games in a season past age thirty-four.

Between the last chapter and this one, we have identified several factors that may be tied to a pitcher's longevity. Some, such as Mickey Lolich's throwing with his nondominant arm, are dead ends. I don't believe there is another such pitcher we can study, it's not practical to tell a pitcher to throw with his other arm, and we aren't going to break the arms of a lot of little kids just to test Lolich's experience. One or two kids would probably be enough.

Just kidding.

Another factor that's difficult to evaluate is the pitching mechanics of a hurler. We simply do not have that kind of information for much of baseball's past. However, it is reasonable to assume that if a proper motion allows the legs and back to do more of the work in the acceleration and deceleration of the arm, there should be less strain on the arm. There were notations in the careers of Radbourne and Young that established them as being among the pioneers in developing styles that tried to use the body more and the arm less.

Mechanical strain on the arm is, incidentally, a factor in the negative impact of pitching in a hitter's era. Why do pitchers work from a windup with the bases empty rather than always throwing from the set position, the motion used with men on base? Studies show they generally don't throw any harder from the windup, and sometimes pitchers find it easier to control their pitches from the set position. The reason pitchers work with the two deliveries is that the windup uses the body more and puts less strain on the arm. So if a pitcher works in a heavy offensive environment that produces more base runners than usual, that also means more pitches are being thrown from the stretch position.

Putting the "Lolich factor" and pitching mechanics aside, that leaves the following connections for further investigation:

1. age at start of professional career
2. noninjury interruption early in career
3. baseball environment in the formative years (prior to age twenty-five)
4. pitching workloads in the formative years
5. pitching delivery (conventional, sidearm, submarine, or involving less arm speed as with the knuckleball)
6. physical conditioning
7. stockiness of frame as measured in pounds per inch of height
8. quality of fastball

The following chart (page 188) is a general investigation of all eight factors for the forty-one pitchers in this century (through 1987) who twice won 15 or more games past age thirty-four.

In judging their formative workloads, I used my knowledge of baseball history to put in relative terms the workload of their professional seasons, both minor- and major-league, before age twenty-five. I used a five-level scale from very light to very heavy.

A determination of whether they gave special attention to their physical conditioning was based simply on whether the stories of their careers indicated such an interest. Anecdotal evidence is all we have to go on.

In determining the quality of their fastball, I concentrated on their strikeout rates, which generally correspond with speed. This is stated as the ratio of each pitcher's strikeout average to the league average for their three major-league seasons with the most innings.

Clearly, this group has a lot of late entries into the professional ranks. It is quite rare for a pitcher to make his minor-league debut at age twenty-four or older, yet in this group nearly one out of five got an unusually late start in their pro career. We have seven clear cases of this and a probable eighth in Long Bob Ewing, whose minor-league record—if he had one—has not survived. Working with the staff of the Baseball Hall of Fame Library, all I could determine is that he was a late bloomer who has no known record of pitching professionally before age twenty-nine. I placed him on the chart as starting his pro career at age "25?"

Among the eleven who started their careers as teenagers, four had their careers sidetracked for a year or more in the early going. Ford, Spahn, and Wynn were in the military, and an antiquated rule forced the Cardinals to carry Steve Carlton on their major-league roster at age twenty. Although perfectly healthy, Carlton threw only 25 innings the whole year. Phil Niekro and McGinnity did not start as teenagers but also had interruptions early in their careers.

There is an unusually large representation of hurlers whose formative years came in the two periods most favorable to the pitcher. From the Dead Ball Era after the foul-strike rule went into effect (1901 in the NL, 1903 in the AL) we have Adams, Alexander, Cicotte, Grimes, Johnson, Jones, Kremer, Meinie, Quinn, Shocker, and Vance. The brief period of the expanded strike zone in 1963–68 produced Carlton, John, Koosman, Joe Niekro, Seaver, and Sutton. Forty-one percent of the total pitchers came from two periods, which account for only 26% of the total span.

Probably the strongest connection among these pitchers is the lightness of their workloads in their formative years. Nearly two-thirds of the group had a formative workload easier than the historical average. We've got four pitchers who never threw a single professional inning in their formative years. There are nine more whose formative workloads have to be characterized as "very light." There are only four pitchers in the whole group who had unusually heavy workloads prior to age twenty-five.

In regard to unusual deliveries, there is an abundance of knuckleballers (five), as well as a pure submariner and two sidearmers. There was not much chance for a recent submariner to make this list. Since the reliever became a part of the diamond scene, the few submariners have been channeled in that direction to take advantage of their ability to bounce back on short rest. Obviously, a study covering this breadth of baseball history has to involve starting pitchers only.

Is there a special commitment to extra physical conditioning in this

PITCHERS WITH TWO SEASONS OF 15+ WINS AT AGE 35+ (1900–87)

NAME	AGE OF FIRST PRO SEASON	EARLY CAREER INTERRUPTION	YEARS AGE 20–24
Babe Adams	23	—	1902–06
Grover Alexander	22	—	1907–11
Three-Finger Brown	24	—	1897–1901
Bert Blyleven	18	—	1971–75
Steve Carlton	19	Age 20	1965–69
Spud Chandler	24	—	1928–32
Ed Cicotte	21	—	1904–08
Mike Cuellar	20	—	1957–61
Coonskin Davis	25	—	1924–28
Long Bob Ewing	25?	—	1893–97
Whitey Ford	18	Ages 22–23	1948–52
Bob Gibson	21	—	1956–60
Burleigh Grimes	20	—	1914–18
Lefty Grove	20	—	1920–24
Charlie Hough	18	—	1968–72
Tommy John	18	—	1963–67
Walter Johnson	19	—	1908–12
Sad Sam Jones	20	—	1912–16
Jim Kaat	18	—	1958–62
Jerry Koosman	22	—	1963–67
Wiz Kremer	21	—	1913–17
Dutch Leonard	20	—	1920–24
Iron Man McGinnity	22	Ages 24–26	1891–95
Heinie Meinie	26	—	1906–10
Joe Niekro	21	—	1965–69
Phil Niekro	20	Age 24	1959–63
Claude Passeau	23	—	1929–33
Gaylord Perry	19	—	1959–63
Eddie Plank	25	—	1896–1900
Jack Quinn	22	—	1904–08
Chief Reynolds	24	—	1935–39
Preacher Roe	23	—	1935–39
Red Ruffing	19	—	1924–28
Tom Seaver	21	—	1965–69
Rip Sewell	24	—	1927–32
Urban Shocker	22	—	1911–15
Warren Spahn	19	Ages 22–24	1941–45
Don Sutton	20	—	1965–69
Dazzy Vance	21	—	1911–15
Early Wynn	17	Age 25	1940–44
Cy Young	23	—	1887–91

WORKLOAD IN FORMATIVE YEARS	DELIVERY	SPECIAL CONDITIONING	POUNDS PER INCH OF HEIGHT	STRIKEOUTS VS. LEAGUE
Very light	Normal	—	2.6	.96
Normal	Normal	—	2.5	1.24
Light	Normal	—	2.5	1.16
Very heavy	Normal	—	2.7	1.31
Normal	Normal	Yes	2.8	1.62
Very light	Normal	Yes	2.5	1.17
Very light	Knuckler	—	2.5	1.03
Normal	Normal	—	2.3	.89
None	Sidearm	—	2.5	.83
None?	Normal	—	2.3	1.11
Light	Normal	—	2.6	1.15
Light	Normal	Yes	2.6	1.30
Light	Normal	—	2.6	1.18
Very heavy	Normal	—	2.7	1.79
Normal	Knuckler	—	2.6	1.07
Light	Normal	—	2.5	.71
Heavy	Sidearm	—	2.7	1.50
Very light	Normal	—	2.4	.95
Very heavy	Normal	Yes	2.8	.93
Light	Normal	Yes	2.9	1.13
Light	Normal	—	2.6	.80
Light	Knuckler	—	2.6	.92
Very light	Submarine	Yes	2.9	.80
None	Normal	—	2.5	.62
Light	Knuckler	—	2.6	.90
Light	Knuckler	—	2.6	1.30
Very light	Normal	—	2.6	1.18
Light	Normal	—	2.8	1.12
None	Normal	—	2.5	1.27
Very light	Normal	—	2.7	1.09
Very light	Normal	—	2.8	1.31
Very light	Normal	—	2.3	1.27
Very heavy	Normal	Yes	2.8	1.54
Heavy	Normal	Yes	2.9	1.55
Very light	Normal	—	2.5	.75
Normal	Normal	—	2.4	1.22
Light	Normal	—	2.5	1.33
Heavy	Normal	Yes	2.6	1.15
Light	Normal	—	2.7	2.47
Heavy	Normal	—	2.8	1.13
Heavy	Normal	Yes	2.8	1.32

group? It's hard to say, since only ten received recognition for such an emphasis. Still, that strikes me as a goodly portion considering that it isn't the kind of information that usually survives about a player unless it really stands out, as it did in the cases of Young, McGinnity, and Ruffing.

A much clearer bias comes through on the pitchers' physiques. There are only a handful of light-framed pitchers (Cuellar, Ewing, Jones, Roe, and Shocker), but you have three times as many with unusually solid physiques: Blyleven, Carlton, Grove, Johnson, Kaat, Koosman, McGinnity, Perry, Quinn, Reynolds, Ruffing, Seaver, Vance, Wynn, and Young. (A ratio of 2.7 pounds/inch was required for inclusion in the latter group—about 195 pounds for a pitcher standing six feet.)

Judging by their relative strikeout rates, most of the group belonged to the power-pitching club. Over 70% were above the league average for their three busiest seasons. Eighteen of the forty-one led a major league in strikeouts at least once.

The most logical theory for why high-strikeout pitchers have longer careers centers on the common association between high strikeouts and superior fastballs. If a pitcher has a great fastball, then he has the option to develop an extra pitch or improve his control to compensate for a fastball that declined from good to adequate. It's a lot harder for the pitcher who starts out with an average fastball. Even a nonpower pitcher throws fastballs roughly 65% of the time. What can he do if that basic pitch slips with age to an inadequate level? Usually he retires.

This makes perfect sense and is consistent with the evidence. A few years ago I did a study of the strikeout levels for the forty-seven active pitchers who were thirty-three or older in 1984. The study did show that strikeout levels fell by 8.5% for ages thirty-one to thirty-three relative to their levels at ages twenty-eight to thirty. Also, the pitchers with the higher strikeout rates (at least .70 per inning) actually had a larger decline, 13%, than the overall group. It seems that power pitchers do not lose less off their fastballs; their edge comes in their ability to adjust and handle the loss better than those starting out with less velocity. At first glance, our group of forty-one ancient winners seemed to contradict this finding. Their strikeout rates declined only 5% from ages twenty-eight to thirty to thirty-one to thirty-three. However, an uncommon result for an uncommon group is not all that surprising. The whole idea of this group is their unusual ability to stave off the decline associated with advancing age.

Another way to look at this issue would be to break the forty-one down into two groups according to their workloads in their formative years. First, we have to cut out four pitchers—Vance, Sewell, Meinie, and Kremer—as none of the four had more than 33 major-league innings through age thirty. Splitting the remaining thirty-seven pitchers produces a clearer difference in their aging strikeout levels.

FORMATIVE WORKLOADS	K/9, AGES 28–30	K/9, AGES 31–33	DIFFERENCE
None, very light and light (22)	4.56	4.43	3%
Normal and heavy (11)	5.42	5.03	7%
Very heavy (4)	6.07	5.06	17%

When viewed from this perspective, we can see that the unusual retention level of their fastballs—as reflected in their strikeout rates—is due to so many of our forty-one having easy workloads in their formative years.

Seen in this light, Nolan Ryan's career is a very interesting case history. He just missed joining these forty-one pitchers as he won 16 games at age thirty-five, and only a series of bad breaks have kept him from getting a second fifteen-plus season past age thirty-four. At age thirty-six he won 14 despite missing over a month with nonpitching-related injuries (inflamed prostate gland in the spring and pulled hamstring in September). In 1987, at age forty, he led the league with a 2.76 ERA in over 200 innings, but the Astros gave him such poor run support that he won only eight games. With more normal support, by my calculations he would have had at least 17 wins.

One of the great stories in recent seasons has been the velocity retained by Ryan's fastball after he passed age thirty-five. I saw radar readings on him in 1984 when he was thirty-seven, and he was throwing consistently in the low- to mid- nineties. In 1985, age thirty-eight, he registered his tenth season of over 200 strikeouts. He made it eleven at age forty when he not only led all of baseball with 270 strikeouts, but he set the all-time record for strikeouts per nine innings, 11.48. Going into 1988, he has averaged 9.33 strikeouts per nine innings since his thirty-fifth birthday. Know what his career average is? It's 9.46—a difference of 1%.

Ryan has a solid physique at six two, 195. He is known for his dedication and hard work in the Astros' conditioning program, and he stays physically active year-round thanks to his working ranch. But what really stands out about Nolan's career is the light workload of his early years. He turned pro at a young age, but after throwing 78 innings at age eighteen and 205 at nineteen, he spent almost all of age twenty fulfilling military obligations, pitching only 11 innings. Then at age twenty-one he was rushed to the majors, where he played a very limited role; his innings pitched totals were 134, 89, 132, and 152 from ages twenty-one to twenty-four. He totaled only 801 innings spread out over seven years prior to age twenty-five.

Do you see what I am getting at? Our forty-one pitchers were durable for all sorts of reasons. Some lasted because they were blessed with an outstanding arm. Others had exceptional pitching ability that could fade considerably and still leave them good enough to get people out. And some pulled it off by an unusual set of circumstances that helped preserve their arms. It's those circumstances that we are most interested in, and light work in the formative years keeps coming to the fore as one of the manageable factors.

MEASURING PITCHER WORKLOADS IN THE MODERN ERA

The way pitching strategy has evolved—and is still evolving—has made it very difficult to judge when a modern pitcher is being pushed too hard. That difficulty has increased as the number of complete games has decreased. And complete games have declined steadily ever since the Live Ball Era began. They went into an even steeper dive after World War II, and that decline continues today.

It doesn't take a rocket scientist to understand what's happening.

It wasn't hard for Grover Alexander to throw 38 complete games in 1916 when he was probably averaging about 92 pitches per start. It's a lot more difficult in the 1980s when the average number of pitches per nine innings is up around 135. And every year I'll score at least a half-dozen games in which one side uses over 200 pitches to get through a game.

Okay, things have changed since Alexander's day. Some of those extra pitches come from facing a couple extra batters per game. Some come from the threat of the lively ball forcing the pitcher to work more carefully to each batter. But the big factor is the change in strategy brought about by the development of the modern bullpen. No one worries about pacing himself anymore; the job of finishing the game belongs to the bullpen. The modern pitcher is expected to battle every hitter, and there is no shyness about working deep into the count by nibbling at the corners or setting up a hitter with a waste pitch.

Our failure to see the significance of this change has kept us from controlling the rash of arm troubles that afflicts the modern game. The modern hurler is bigger, stronger, better conditioned, has better mechanics through better coaching, better medical support, throws fewer innings, and generally has more rest between appearances, yet still we are facing a crisis in pitching depth in both leagues. Pitching careers are shortening up, and the number of disabling pitching injuries is at an all-time high.

The problem is that by institutionalizing the high-pitch game, we have eliminated a major safeguard that used to protect the best and hardest-working pitchers—call it the "easy complete game." Back when there were fewer pitches per batter, fewer pitches per game, and less pressure to constantly give it your all, there were lots of days a pitcher could throw a complete game without nearing his fatigue level. Such a game was an oasis in the demanding desert of professional pitching. That day, there would be no competitive temptation to do more; no manager asking for another inning, no worry about letting your teammates down, no glory to seek. That game was done, the feat accomplished.

Those frequent breathers were once a natural part of the season, but for the modern starter such games come few and far between. We have created a situation in which it takes a major effort to get through even the most routine game. Nearly every time out is a test to see how much the starter can get out of his arm. Over and over, he is pushed right to the edge and sometimes beyond.

The idea of the bullpen as a buffer against such abuse goes right out the window when it comes to the pitchers who need it the most. Bullpen justice is not blind; it does not protect all pitchers equally. A good pitcher—or even a mediocre pitcher having a good day—is always under the gun to give another inning or two, to try to give the much-used bullpen a night of rest.

Most managers believe that even a tired Star Starter (call him Mark Fidrych) is better than a rested Joe Reliever (call him Steve Grilli). And Ace Reliever (try John Hiller) can be saved to pick up the rest of your starters (oh, just call them Dave Roberts, Joe Coleman, Vern Ruhle, and Ray Bare).

It doesn't matter so much that we reduce the Star Starter's innings by having him pitch in a five-man rotation, or that we pull him when he's too tired to go on. The point is that as long as he appears effective, the competitive pressure of the game pushes him to the limit every time he takes the field. The only exceptions would be the easy complete game—a vanishing breed.

Mark "The Bird" Fidrych was an extremely talented young pitcher who rose quickly through the professional ranks. After a little more than one full season in the minors he was enthusiastically starring for the Detroit Tigers as one of the most popular pitchers to ever play this game. He was twenty-one years old, a tall, skinny kid at six three, 175 pounds. He had fine control and a fastball with exceptional movement if not exceptional speed. His strikeout rate was well below the league average.

Manager Ralph Houk felt he was sufficiently protecting Fidrych's arm by pitching him in a five-man rotation. The Bird wasn't one of those three-hundred-inning youngsters; he tossed only 250, but to get them he went deep into every start. Fidrych led the league with 24 complete games, rather remarkable in that he had only 29 starts (plus two relief appearances). The results proved to be disastrous, as Fidrych went from 19–9 with a league-leading 2.34 ERA to a pitcher with only 162 major-league innings left in his arm. He won only 10 more games and had a 4.28 ERA.

I grew up as a Tigers fan. What happened to Fidrych made a strong impression on me. It made me realize that in trying to protect the modern pitcher we can no longer rely on innings pitched as our sole measure of a pitcher's workload. We also have to consider how often he's pushed past his endurance level within his starts. I began studying the workloads of starting pitchers as a combination of their innings pitched and an estimate of their batters faced per start. The simple formula for the latter is:

$$\frac{\text{Estimated Batters Faced}}{\text{Per Start (BFS)}} = \frac{(\text{Innings} \times 3) + \text{Hits} + \text{Walks}}{\text{Starts} + (\text{Relief App.} \times .5)}$$

Obviously the measure is meant for comparison of starting pitchers only. The .5 figure for relief appearances applies only to the old work pattern, in which a starter would make an occasional relief appearance, sometimes as a substitution for a start when he was skipped over in the rotation. That happened a lot to the number three and four starters back when the four-man rotation was in vogue. When dealing with the more modern role of a true starter-reliever, who intersperses several relief appearances among his starts, thus getting fewer days of rest, that work pattern is more of a strain, and this formula becomes inadequate.

My favorite study using BFS is an examination of modern pitchers who had an exceptional season at a young age but were unable to achieve even moderate success in their late twenties. In setting the guidelines, I wanted the star season to be truly exceptional in order to rule out as many lucky flukes as possible. I settled on an ERA better than 20% below the league average in at least 210 innings, which is 30% more than the requirement to qualify for the ERA title. The measure of their decline would be that they would not have a winning season (over .500) with 10 wins or more after age twenty-eight. For the fifteen-year period 1966–80 there were fifteen pitchers who met those guidelines.

STAR PITCHERS BURNED OUT AT A YOUNG AGE, 1966–80

	AGE	ERA	IP	K	LAST "WINNING" AGE
Bahnsen	23	2.05	267.1	162	27
Dierker	22	2.33	305	232	27
Fidrych	21	2.34	250	97	21
Gullett	20	2.64	218	107	26
Haas	24	3.11	252	146	27
Keough	24	2.92	250	121	25
Kline	24	2.40	236	58	24
Matlack	22	2.32	244	169	28
McGlothen	24	2.70	237	142	25
McLain	24	1.96	336	280	25
Merritt	23	2.53	227.2	161	26
Nash	23	2.28	228.2	169	25
Nolan	19	2.58	227	206	28
Rozema	20	3.09	218.1	92	20
Travers	23	2.81	240	120	27
Average	22	2.54	249	151	25

They make a pretty impressive composite pitcher, one who at age twenty-two lit up the sports pages with a 2.54 ERA in 249 innings, yet never had a winning season in double figures past age twenty-five.

Before examining their formative years, I created a similar group from the same era but from the opposite end of the career spectrum. I used the same criteria, except the super season had to come *after* age thirty, and their last winning season had to be age thirty-four or later.

There were sixteen pitchers who qualified for the second group, but before continuing the analysis, I thought it wise to take out Phil Niekro, who was the only knuckleballer in either group. He also created a problem as the only pitcher in either group who worked primarily as a reliever throughout his formative years.

(Even so, it's worthwhile to take a quick look at Phil's formative years, since his longevity stands out even among the class of knuckleballers. His workload as a young reliever was very mild. His biggest season was only 51 appearances and 110 innings. And, as noted earlier, he spent all of age twenty-four in military service. In light of

EXCEPTIONAL PITCHERS AFTER AGE 30, 1966–80

	AGE	ERA	IP	K	LAST "WINNING" AGE
Bunning	35	2.41	302.1	253	37
Carlton	35	2.34	304	286	39[1]
Cuellar	32	2.38	290.2	182	38
Gibson	32	1.12	304.2	268	37
Gura	32	2.96	283	113	36
John	34	2.78	220	123	44[1]
Koosman	33	2.70	247	200	40
Palmer	32	2.46	296	138	36
Perry, G.	33	1.92	343	234	40
Perry, J.	32	2.82	261.2	153	37
Reuss	31	2.52	229	111	36[1]
Rooker	32	2.77	263	139	35
Ryan	34	1.69	219.1[2]	206	39[1]
Seaver	36	2.55	249[2]	130	40
Sutton	35	2.21	212	128	41[1]
Average	33	2.38	268.1	178	38

[1]Still active in 1988
[2]The 1981 strike season has been projected for Ryan and Seaver

all the surrounding evidence, it seems reasonable to link his unusual staying power to his light workload in his formative years.)

Excluding Niekro leaves us with two groups of fifteen pitchers each. Call the group of star pitchers burned out at a young age The Flashes. The exceptional pitchers after age thirty will be The Veterans. It's interesting to note the repetition of characteristics from our old group of forty-one. You have a lot more power pitchers among Veterans than in Flashes. You also have a bunch of mooses in the Veterans, with the lone exception of the slightly built Cuellar. I also count no fewer than seven pitchers in among the Veterans who were noted for their special attention to physical conditioning (Carlton, Gibson, Gura, Koosman, Palmer, Seaver, and Sutton).

But the real differences between the groups can be found in the chart detailing their workloads in their formative years. These charts give their innings in each year from ages eighteen to twenty-four as well as the BFS measure for each season of 170 or more innings. It's interesting to see that the highest BFS in either group is Fidrych's 34.0 in his big season at age twenty-one.

FORMATIVE YEARS OF FLASHES AND VETERANS

(BFS GIVEN FOR SEASONS OF 170+ INNINGS)

FLASHES	AGE 18		AGE 19		AGE 20		AGE 21		AGE 22	
	IP	BFS	IP	BFS	IP	BFS	IP	BFS	IP	BFS
Bahnsen					53		193	27.6	138	
Dierker	147		187	27.3	99		234	31.1	305	32.3
Fidrych			34		171	29.0	250	34.0	81	
Gullett	78		78		218	27.7	135		228	25.4
Haas	96		171	29.0	172	27.9	198	27.3	31	
Keough					2		218	29.0	197	26.7
Kline	85		71		132		69		178	28.2
Matlack	173	29.9	176	29.6	183	31.0	189	28.4	244	30.8
McGlothen	46		179	27.3	229	31.5	179	29.5	253	29.9
McLain	109		239	32.3	159		220	28.9	264	29.0
Merritt	223	31.1	159		85	27.5	267	29.6	144	
Nash			189	30.4	195	31.2	228	30.1	222	26.9
Nolan	104		227	28.8	155	25.7	140		251	29.1
Rozema	164		126		218	32.5	209	31.2	97	
Travers	137		89		3		76		197	24.8

VETERANS	AGE 18		AGE 19		AGE 20		AGE 21		AGE 22	
	IP	BFS	IP	BFS	IP	BFS	IP	BFS	IP	BFS
Bunning	123		150		129		163		193	27.9
Carlton			178	28.5	25		180	27.8	193	28.1
Cuellar					155		221	27.2	216	30.2
Gibson							85		190	30.2
Gura							88		99	
John	88		162		217	30.1	168		184	23.4
Koosman									119	
Palmer	129		92		208	29.7	83		37	
Perry, G.			128		191	25.7	189	29.8	219	29.4
Perry, J.			120		231	29.6	200	29.2	153	
Reuss	66		112		193	29.2	212	29.5	211	27.3
Rooker					10		0		63	
Ryan	78		205	27.5	11		134		89	
Seaver							210	26.7	251	30.6
Sutton					249	32.3	226	25.6	233	27.6

AGE 23		AGE 24		TOTAL IP THROUGH AGE 24	AGE 18–19 IP	
IP	BFS	IP	BFS			
267	30.6	221	26.7	872	0	Bahnsen
270	31.6	159		1448	334	Dierker
35		15		586	34	Fidrych
243	28.7	160		1140	156	Gullett
185	28.5	252	32.1	1105	149	Haas
177	28.6	250	32.2	850	0	Keough
222	29.8	236	30.1	993	85	Kline
242	30.4	265	32.1	1477	349	Matlack
76		237	32.6	1199	225	McGlothen
235	26.7	326	31.3	1553	348	McLain
228	28.0	238	27.1	1444	382	Merritt
229	27.6	115		1178	189	Nash
245	28.6	176	28.2	1298	331	Nolan
145		156		1064	290	Rozema
240	30.2	122		911	226	Travers

AGE 23		AGE 24		TOTAL IP THROUGH AGE 24	AGE 18–19 IP	
IP	BFS	IP	BFS			
180	27.9	163		1154	273	Bunning
232	29.0	236	31.8	1044	178	Carlton
148		118		858	0	Cuellar
211	29.6	128		614	0	Gibson
193	28.7	142		522	0	Gura
223	27.5	178	24.1	1220	250	John
170	30.8	200	30.5	489	0	Koosman
181	30.1	305	32.8	1035	221	Palmer
199	27.8	85		1011	128	Perry, G.
261	29.4	224	28.5	1189	120	Perry, J.
192	26.5	279	30.3	1265	178	Reuss
115		152		340	0	Rooker
132		152		801	283	Ryan
278	31.2	273	31.1	1012	0	Seaver
224	28.1	293	30.2	1225	0	Sutton

This is also our first opportunity to see whether there are differences by age within the formative years. That is, should we handle a pitcher age twenty to twenty-two with greater care than one twenty-three or twenty-four, and if so, how much more should we ease up with a teenager? This chart makes it perfectly clear that age demands such differences as well as cementing the expected conclusion that the Flashes were worked much harder in their formative years than the Veterans.

1. Flash pitchers started their careers earlier than Veterans: A full 73% of Flashes were pitching professionally by age eighteen, as opposed to only 33% of Veterans.
2. Veterans averaged 919 innings in their formative years, or about 20% less than the 1,141 average of Flashes. This is true even though nearly half the Flashes were already pitching less late in their formative years due to arm trouble.
3. Veterans averaged far fewer professional innings as a teenager and only gradually closed the gap with the Flashes as the two groups matured.

AVERAGE INNINGS BY AGE

	18	19	20	21	22	23	24
Flashes	91	128	145	187	189	203	195
Veterans	32	76	108	144	163	196	195
Ratio	2.84	1.68	1.34	1.30	1.16	1.04	1.00

4. When throwing a 170-inning season, the average BFS for Flashes indicates they were being pushed harder in their starts than the Veterans at nearly every age, but especially in the younger years.

AVERAGE BFS BY AGE (170 + IP SEASONS ONLY)

	18	19	20	21	22	23	24
Flashes	30.0	29.2	29.8	29.7	28.3	29.1	30.3
Veterans	None	28.0	29.4	28.0	28.3	28.9	29.9

5. The Flashes averaged nearly two-thirds more seasons of 30.0-plus BFS than the Veterans (23 to 14); they did it at an earlier age (21.7 to 22.8) and with higher BFS (31.4 average versus 30.9).
6. Flashes had more than three times (16 to five) as many BFS of 31.0-plus than did Veterans, and at an average age about a year and a half younger (21.6 to 23.0).
7. Among the Flashes, over half (eight) had at least one season of 31.0-plus BFS in a season before age twenty-four. Among Veterans, only two pitchers did this.

There are several points of instruction that can be taken from this little study. First, starting as a teenager and throwing a lot of innings in your formative years is not automatically a point of concern. Tommy John, Jerry Reuss, and Jim Bunning were all pitching at age eighteen and ran up over 1,150 innings in their formative years. Reuss led all Veterans with 1,265 formative innings. The key is that they had mild use during that period. None threw more than 123 innings at age eighteen, or more than 162 at age nineteen. Bunning never had a two-hundred-inning season in his formative years, and John and Reuss had very reasonable combinations of innings and BFS. Reuss did have one season of 279 innings with a 30.3 BFS, but not until he was twenty-four years old, and he had worked up to it well by throwing 192 to 212 innings in each of the four previous seasons.

Gary Nolan gives us the best indication that a teenage pitcher should be handled with unusual care. The only thing out of the ordinary about Nolan's formative years is his season at age nineteen: 227 innings and a 28.8 BFS. The most innings by a Veteran teenager was 205 by Nolan Ryan, and he had a low BFS of 27.5.

Looking at some of the soft-tossers like Bill Travers and Steve Kline suggests that finesse pitchers are a bit more vulnerable and should be held to lower BFS. They blew out their arms even though they weren't pushed any harder than five or six of the Veteran pitchers.

In some cases there are no solid indicators to explain why one pitcher develops problems and not another. Stan Bahnsen had borderline abuse for his build and ability, but I've seen dozens of similar pitchers who did not develop a fragile arm. And Don Gullett appeared to have been used in a very reasonable manner but won his last major-league game at age twenty-seven. Actually, this happens frequently in the larger general class of professional pitchers.

It's important to remember that we are looking at a group of exceptional pitchers who have already passed several tests of their pitching arms. They survived the minor-league culling process; they all were good enough to pitch several years in the major leagues; and they were good enough to star in the major leagues, even if for a short while. This selection process was helpful in proving that the declines of the flashes were unexpected, and it helped make clear that even the most talented pitchers can benefit from careful handling. But it doesn't bring out a fact that surfaces in other research: that there are many who simply don't have what it takes to work year after year in the steady competitive work pattern of a professional pitcher.

There is another factor to be considered here. One thing that doesn't appear in total innings and seasonal BFS are cases of heavy in-season abuse. There are two kinds of managers whose sense of strategy routinely abuses pitchers. Some are sensitive to their pitchers in that they will try to identify who can and cannot be pushed, and they will try to space out their workload, but they overestimate each pitcher's propensity for work over a long haul, and when they identify a workhorse, they'll dangerously test his limits. Billy Martin and Chuck Tanner have been like that.

Then there are others like Ralph Houk, Harvey Kuenn, and Joe Altobelli, who don't look for workhorses or worry much about spacing out a pitcher's load. They look for the hot hand and ride it; they manage solely from a standpoint of winning that day's game. Even though they might not consistently work a pitcher as hard as the other group, they would do some crazy things to follow their strategy of winning in the short term. They might refuse to make concessions for a pitcher with a fragile arm, have a starter throw 175 pitches in a game, or let him make several high-pitch games in a row. Sometimes a pitcher's problems can be traced to this type of abuse that won't show in seasonal measures.

There are exceptions that go the other way, too—pitchers who seem to be abused yet enjoy long careers. Three pitchers among the Veterans crossed into a danger zone that has propelled other pitchers into careers closer to those of the Flashes. One was Jim Palmer, who had the highest formative BFS among our Veterans, 32.8, and he did it in a season of 305 innings! Probably the strongest mitigating factor was that he did it at age twenty-four and hadn't come close to anything like it in his earlier years.

The other two pitchers were Seaver and Sutton, the only two Veterans who had a BFS over 31.0 before age twenty-four. Sutton may have gotten off lightly because it was his first season with no professional workloads preceding him, and his remaining formative BFS were quite reasonable. Seaver may have avoided trouble through a number of factors. First, his season was right on the borderline, 31.2 at age twenty-three. He had a strong, stocky physique and picture-perfect mechanics; he was a power pitcher; he threw in a good pitching environment as a young pitcher; the season was 1968 with Shea Stadium as his home park. That covers just about every compensating factor that might excuse his heavy workload as a youngster.

This is not to say that these three were not affected. All three made a more difficult transition into their thirties than did the others in the group.

CHANGE IN ERA AND K/BB RATIO,
RELATIVE TO THE LEAGUE
FROM AGES 28–30 TO 31–33

	ERA	K/BB RATIO
Palmer	+ 4%	−13%
Seaver	+ 5%	−12%
Sutton	+14%	−22%
Other 12 Veterans	− 7%	+13%

In fact, these three were the only ones in the group to get worse in both categories as they moved into their thirties. They did adjust, and all three are going to the Hall of Fame, but it probably cost Palmer a place on our historical list of forty-one veteran winners; it may have cost Sutton the superstar seasons missing from his Hall of

Fame credentials; and is it so strange to suggest that Seaver might have had a better career?

Were Warren Spahn's best seasons as good as Seaver's? No, they weren't. So why should Spahn win about fifty more games despite missing three seasons at ages when Seaver was racking up 57 wins? Who knows, maybe if Palmer, Sutton, and Seaver had been handled a little more gently in their early years, Palmer would have won three hundred games, Sutton could have nabbed his three hundredth before age forty-one, and Seaver could have closed in on four hundred wins.

There are several other Veteran pitchers worth profiling. Gaylord Perry is a fascinating figure when discussing the durability of pitchers. He threw over three hundred innings six times, and that is the uncontested record for the Live Ball Era. He was a good but not great pitcher in his twenties who went on to have his best season at age thirty-three and won a Cy Young Award at age thirty-nine. Check out this comparison with Tom Seaver's career:

AGE 22–28	WINS	INNINGS	ERA
Seaver	135	1,931	2.38
Perry	60	1,070	3.22

AGE 29–41	WINS	INNINGS	ERA
Seaver	176	2,851	3.19
Perry	229	3,727	2.88

Now, how the heck did Perry do that? He had efficient mechanics, a stocky physique, and off-season activity (farming) that kept him physically active year-round. But Seaver could match all that and throw in a few more. Tom had a superior fastball, always worked in a five-man rotation, and started out as a significantly better pitcher.

The one big difference was in their formative workloads. Gaylord was a bit of a late bloomer and wasn't pushed hard as a young pitcher. In his formative years he had only one two-hundred-inning season (219 at age twenty-two). The next year he actually had a 31.0 BFS for 156 innings at Tacoma, but fate stepped in at that point, and Gaylord was promoted to the Giants, where he threw another 43 innings but in a very light workload as a starter-reliever. To make things even easier, he was practically given a year off the next year at age twenty-four; he threw one complete game at Tacoma and was again promoted to the majors, where he was used sparingly out of the bullpen: 76 innings, only four starts (none completed), and 27 relief appearances. Truth is, other than that 156-inning stretch at Tacoma, Gaylord never had a BFS over 30.3 until he was twenty-eight years old.

Perry did go on to register a number of extremely high BFS seasons. However, it is typical that pitchers with light workloads in their formative years can handle remarkably high BFS seasons later in their careers. Sometimes there will be a drop in effectiveness for a single season, but it generally isn't a lasting effect unless the workload was extremely abusive.

How much can a pitcher take later in his career if he's handled carefully as a youngster? That's a difficult question even when we assume the pitcher has a sound arm capable of withstanding professional use. The modern pitcher isn't coming out of the sixties anymore; the number of pitches per batter is gradually but steadily rising, which means the safety BFS zones have to be lowered slightly.

From the examples of ten or fifteen years ago, I believe such a pitcher could safely throw 325 innings in a four-man rotation with a BFS as high as 33.5. Above that, and even this rare pitcher takes a chance on a short-term negative reaction and possibly one that could endanger his career. Catfish Hunter was never pushed too hard in his formative years, but his arm decided on an early retirement after BFS of 33.7 and 34.2 at age twenty-nine to thirty. Thank you, Billy Martin. Before that, Hunter looked like a breeze for 300 wins, with maybe a shot at 350. For any who wonder, Catfish was not the most abused pitcher under Martin. Working Rick Langford in a five-man rotation, Billy ruined what appeared to be an iron arm with back-to-back BFS of 35.6 and 34.7.

There are two other Veteran pitchers worth examining in detail. In many ways Bob Gibson's story is a cross between Nolan Ryan's and Gaylord Perry's. Bob started off with 85 innings at age twenty-one. The closest he came to being overpitched was a 30.2 BFS in 190 innings at age twenty-two. Like Ryan, Gibson had control troubles that kept his managers from pushing him in attempts to win games, but his fastball was so outstanding it kept advancing him to the higher leagues. Like Perry, he got to the majors at age twenty-four and was lightly used in a starter-reliever role: 87 innings in 12 starts and 15 relief appearances. He totaled only 614 professional innings in his formative years.

Like Perry, Gibson went on to have his best season after age thirty (1968: age thirty-two). Like Ryan, Bullet Bob was celebrated for the long life of his fastball. His best strikeout year came at age thirty-four, and he last topped two hundred strikeouts at age thirty-six.

And then there is Jim Rooker, the no-name hurler with barely 100 wins (103) who somehow snuck into this group to rub elbows with a Hall of Fame crowd. Rooker began his career as an outfielder and didn't fully turn to pitching till age twenty-three. Prior to age twenty-five, he threw fewer than 350 innings total and never more than 152 in a single season. He was not very talented and lost about twice as many as he won through age thirty (21–44). But his arm stayed strong, giving him the chance to keep improving at an age when most pitchers start slowing down. From ages thirty-one to thirty-five he was 22 games over .500 with a 3.00 ERA. In 1974, at age thirty-two, he had a season to qualify as a Veteran, and he clinched it with a 14–9 season at age thirty-five.

Palmer, Sutton, and Seaver overcame long odds to pitch their way among the Veterans. There were two pitchers who beat even longer odds in pitching their way *out* of the Flashes. Dennis Eckersley and Frank Tanana worked a lot harder as youngsters than most Flashes. Both turned pro out of high school, had a two-hundred-inning season as a teenager (202 for Eckersley at eighteen, 246 for Tanana at nineteen), and threw over 350 innings at ages eighteen to nineteen (369 for Eckersley and 375 for Tanana). Both threw over 1,500 innings in their formative years (1,592 for Eckersley, 1,669 for Tanana). Both turned in numerous seasons of high BFS in two-hundred-inning chunks. Eckersley had a 32.4 BFS in 268 innings at age twenty-three; Tanana had a 33.8 in 288 innings at age twenty-two.

It would be amazingly shortsighted to say they avoided paying for this abuse simply because they escaped our grouping. Eckersley was a Rookie of the Year, only the eighth major-league pitcher since 1900 to fan two hundred batters in a season before age twenty-two. When he finally reached that ripe old age of twenty-two, he threw a no-hitter and made the All-Star team. Prior to Clemens, he was Boston's last twenty-game winner and the last Red Sox starter to have back-to-back ERAs under 3.00.

But that was it for his Hall of Fame path. The next year, at age twenty-five, his ERA jumped to 4.28, and it looked as if he might never have another winning season. From ages twenty-five to twenty-eight his ERA was 4.42 with a 43–48 record. His strikeout averages fell from the 6.70 of his early years to a mediocre 4.83. Through a special conditioning program designed by Dr. Arthur Pappas, Eckersley regained enough of his old form so that, handled carefully, he was able to go 11–7 for the Cubs in 1985. That eliminated him from our qualifications by the narrowest of margins. His arm still lacked the durability to make it as a starter, but he has experienced a resurrection of his career as a relief pitcher. Yet even in this role, his manager, Tony LaRussa, makes a point of handling him with more care than most relievers. In 1987 Dennis made only 54 appearances with 116 innings; in 1988 he had four more appearances (60) but fewer innings (72.2).

Frank Tanana was probably the most talented pitcher in my memory to be damaged by abusive workloads at a young age. There are only a handful of pitchers in baseball history who had a season averaging twice as many strikeouts as the league average. Tanana nearly joined that group when he was just twenty-one years old. In 1975 he averaged 9.4 strikeouts per nine innings compared with the league average of 4.9. From ages twenty-one to twenty-three he had a sparkling major-league ERA of 2.53 over a span of 786 innings.

But Tanana's fastball suddenly vanished into the void at age twenty-four.

Like Eckersley, Tanana started off as such a talented pitcher that he was left with enough talent to regroup and come back with the help of a strenuous conditioning program. But like Eckersley, he has

TANANA	ERA	STRIKEOUT AVERAGE
Ages 21–23	2.53	8.4
Ages 24–29	3.85	5.0

done well only when handled with special care and is only a shadow of the pitcher he was, and probably could have remained.

It's also enlightening to use a BFS analysis on the six modern pitchers who threw a three-hundred-inning season in their formative years. As you can see on the accompanying chart, none of the six was abused more as a teenager than Denny McLain. When he was just nineteen years old, he had a 32.3 BFS in 239 innings. Later, at age twenty-four, he threw 326 innings with a 31.3 BFS. He had a great fastball, a solid physical frame, and, in my eyes, near-perfect mechanics. Of all the pitchers in my generation, I believe McLain came the closest to perfect form. Denny also had the edge of pitching his formative years in a great pitching environment, 1964–68. He seemed a perfect candidate for a long-lived career except for his being worked incredibly hard in his early years. He went on to throw another 325 innings and win a second Cy Young award at age twenty-five, and then it all went up in smoke. He threw only 384 innings the rest of his career, with a 4.78 ERA and a 17–34 record.

A similar fate struck Larry Dierker, who, at age twenty-one, threw 234 innings with a 31.1 BFS. Then at twenty-two he chucked 305 innings with a 32.3 BFS. That year he was 20–13 with a 2.33 ERA. The next year he won just 16 as his ERA jumped a run and a half to 3.87. He won only 68 more games in his career, with the last coming at age thirty.

	AGE 18		AGE 19		AGE 20		AGE 21		AGE 22	
	IP	BFS	IP	BFS	IP	BFS	IP	BFS	IP	BFS
Blue	152		146		172	30.0	312	31.6	151	
Blyleven	69		218	27.0	278	30.6	287	30.6	325	33.5
Dierker	147		187	27.3	99		234	31.1	305	32.3
Jenkins	78		150		196	27.1	134		184	20.7
McLain	109		239	32.3	159		220	28.9	264	29.0
Palmer	129		92		208	29.7	83		37	

Vida Blue was worked about as hard as Dierker, and Bert Blyleven was worked harder than anyone in this era other than McLain and Tanana. Blue and Blyleven managed to keep their careers going despite a significant drop in their effectiveness just as they entered what should have been their physical prime at ages twenty-seven to thirty.

BLUE	ERA	INNINGS PER FULL SEASON	K/BB
Through age 26	2.80	287	2.2 to 1
Age 27–30	3.65	250	1.8 to 1
Age 31–36	3.83	164	1.3 to 1

BLYLEVEN	ERA	INNINGS PER FULL SEASON	K/BB
Through age 26	2.79	283	3.1 to 1
Age 27–30	3.36	234	2.2 to 1
Age 31–36 ('87)	3.59	247	2.6 to 1

The other two who threw three hundred innings before age twenty-five went on to have more normal aging patterns, but both Fergie Jenkins and Jim Palmer struggled more after age thirty than most had expected. After averaging 21 wins and 304 innings for eight years, Jenkins averaged only 14 wins and 230 innings at ages thirty-one to thirty-six. Palmer did a little better, winning 20 games as late as age thirty-two, but thereafter his performance dropped dramatically. After five straight 20-win, sub-3.00 ERA seasons, he averaged only 12 wins and a 3.53 ERA the next four. He won only five more games after age thirty-six (5–7, 5.15).

AGE 23		AGE 24		TOTAL IP THROUGH AGE 24	AGE 18–19 IP	
IP	BFS	IP	BFS			
264	30.0	282	29.8	1479	298	Blue
281	31.5	276	32.3	1734	287	Blyleven
270	31.6	159		1448	334	Dierker
289	31.1	308	31.1	1339	228	Jenkins
235	26.7	326	31.3	1553	348	McLain
181	30.1	305	32.8	1035	221	Palmer

JENKINS	ERA	INNINGS PER FULL SEASON	K/BB
Through age 26	3.07	281	3.6 to 1
Age 27–30	3.14	303	4.2 to 1
Age 31–36	3.64	230	2.8 to 1

PALMER	ERA	INNINGS PER FULL SEASON	K/BB
Through age 26	2.72	250	1.8 to 1
Age 27–30	2.48	278	1.7 to 1
Age 31–36	3.15	235	1.5 to 1

There's no doubt that Palmer and Jenkins aged the best of this select little group, and there is also no doubt they were the least abused of the three-hundred-inning youngsters. Compared with the other four, they threw fewer innings in their formative years and fewer innings as teenagers. They were the only ones of the six not to have a 31.0-plus BFS before age twenty-three, and both had their three-hundred-inning season at age twenty-four.

PROTECTING OUR YOUNG PITCHERS

It's important to remember that the strongest statement we can draw out of all this evidence is that there is a link between some degree of eventual arm trouble and a history of heavy workloads in the formative years. Although we have established certain guidelines for evaluating such workloads, there is nothing set in stone that X work level will lead to Y reaction.

There are numerous crossovers from one group to another. Although Blyleven did show an effect in his career, many pitchers would have quickly folded after his very heavy formative workloads. Certainly, if we blindly laid his formative years next to those of, say, Don Gullett, there is no doubt that Gullett's line is the one we would associate with a pitcher still going at age thirty-seven, and Blyleven's line would be the one we would tie to a career ended at age twenty-seven.

The idea of establishing rigid measurements for cause and effect is unrealistic, and that is not the goal here. Given a young pitcher who could make an impact on a major-league race, the evidence is not there to justify firmly shackling the manager's use of that pitcher. For that situation, the goal is simply to make the manager aware of the potential effect on that pitcher's career if he is consistently pushed to his endurance limits.

In the minor leagues, where the goal is player development, cautious guidelines are more than acceptable. Some recommendations from this research are:

1. As a teenager, a pitcher should not be allowed to throw two-hundred-inning seasons or have a BFS over 28.5 in any significant span (150-plus innings). This does not include instructional league or winter-ball innings if there is a reasonable amount of time off between the leagues.
2. A teenage pitcher should not start on three days' rest, which generally means no four-man rotations in A-ball.
3. For ages twenty to twenty-two, they should average no more than 105 pitches per start for the season (105 pitches is the rough equivalent of a 30.0 BFS). A single-game ceiling should be set at 130 pitches.
4. For age twenty-three to twenty-four, the restraints can be eased up, but their season average should stay under 110 pitches in most cases. The single-game ceiling can be jumped to 140 as long as the pitcher is still strong.
5. When it's time to pull a tiring youngster, don't wait to take advantage of a strategic short-term edge such as a platoon advantage on the next hitter.
6. Minor-league pitchers should be pushed to throw more strikes per batter. It is better that they start out aiming for this goal and later ease into learning the art of teasing and setting up a hitter.
7. Proper physical conditioning should be emphasized from the introductory level until it becomes second nature.
8. An organization should be willing to advance a minor-league pitcher with good stuff a step ahead of his effectiveness. The

logic is that if the pitcher is less likely to be a dominant factor in winning, his manager is less likely to try to push him to win a single game.

9. When possible, a young rookie starter should be introduced to the major leagues in a long-relief role before he goes into the rotation.

The study, evaluation, and control of workloads for young pitchers is becoming more complicated due to more and more highly competitive leagues that overlap with the seasons that make up a pitcher's career in the *Baseball Register*. In the 1960s you didn't see many pitchers reacting to high BFS in their first pro season. Generally, they couldn't get enough innings after the June draft to do much lasting damage. They still don't get a lot of professional innings in that first season, but a high BFS tends to mean more because of a possible overlap with their final amateur season. This is particularly true with the college players.

It wasn't so long ago that I preferred to see a pitcher get drafted out of college rather than high school. A pitcher out of high school generally had a greater chance of abuse in a professional league than in a college league. That is definitely changing. Baseball has learned to treat its younger pitching prospects with more care, while the college programs have become increasingly dangerous. The college seasons, particularly at the big baseball schools that produce so many prospects, are constantly growing longer and becoming more competitive. Many a college pitcher's first pro season is simply an extension of his college season, with little or no time off.

Craig Swan's college workload probably played a major role in his premature demise from an ERA leader at age twenty-seven to one with chronic shoulder stiffness from age twenty-nine on and a final career record of 59–72 (.450). Swan pitched in a very active baseball program at Arizona State University, where he still holds the school record for wins (47) and innings (457). In his senior year he pitched his team into the College World Series, which was played in mid-June. He had already been drafted by the Mets when he played his last college game, and he went right from the College World Series to pitching for Memphis in the Southern League. On the surface it looks as if he had a 32.3 BFS but in only a 108-inning season. Actually, he played a continuous season of 251.2 innings with a 31.4 BFS.

The same kind of problem can occur with pitchers in the winter leagues in Latin America and Mexico. Probably the worst combined abuse is the case of Alan Fowlkes, a former star prospect of the San Francisco Giants whose strong point was supposed to be his durability. In college he set NCAA records for most complete games and innings in a season, completing 19 of 23 starts and throwing 206 innings. I estimate his BFS had to be close to 35.0. In his second year as a professional he was Pitcher of the Year in the Texas League and led in innings and complete games. He then went down to Mexicali and pitched another 210 innings in winter ball, giving him well over 400 innings for the year. He was twenty-two years old. That was way back in 1981. He ended up winning just four major-league games with a 5.19 ERA, and today you are left wondering, "Who the hell is Alan Fowlkes?"

To further protect the future of its pitchers, a major-league organization needs to be aware of the past workloads that a college pitcher is bringing to a rookie league. It also needs to negotiate a work program and monitoring system with the Latin clubs using their pitchers in winter ball.

SPECIAL CONDITIONING AND TREATMENT

In general this topic is definitely out of my league, but it is appropriate to note what special programs have been associated with the prevention and rehabilitation of these general arm problems. There are several different approaches that appear to help. Ironically, the proponents of one are often the harshest critics of the others, even when the results don't appreciably differ.

A good example is the debate over whether the arm should be treated with ice or heat after pitching. For a long time heat was the accepted treatment, but now icing the arm is fully in vogue. By suggesting anything else, I am sure to get a dozen letters explaining why ice is better. Don't bother; it isn't my business to endorse either one, but simply to point out what folks have done that they associate with their success. I think it is fair to note that two of baseball's most durable pitchers, Satchel Paige and Gaylord Perry, placed a very strong emphasis on applying heat to their throwing arms after pitching. When Perry was with the Rangers, he used to have a ridiculously hot salve applied from his shoulder to his elbow. The salve was so hot that the trainer actually had to wear gloves to apply it. And despite the continual disputes between medical doctors and chiropractors, some pitchers feel their arms bounce back better after each outing if they have regular chiropractic adjustments to their upper necks. Storm Davis attributes his recent comeback to a year-round chiropractic program.

A lot of successful programs advocate throwing year round, usually every third or fourth day in the off season. Earl Weaver's Orioles threw even more frequently, about three times a week. On the surface this may seem questionable, but there is a radical difference between light throwing and pitching competitively. Remember that everything we have looked at suggests that throwing is not the culprit as much as throwing past one's fatigue level.

Throwing year-round is supposed to be good for muscle memory and avoids the forming of adhesions as well as the danger of straining the arm while building it up after a long layoff. Light throwing is also recommended as a good way to stretch out the shoulder muscles. George Bamberger, former pitching coach and manager, believes the best thing a pitcher can do for his arm is to throw every day for twenty minutes, both in and out of season. Jerry Koosman and Tom Seaver were two pitchers who felt they aged better because they made it a point to throw regularly in the off season.

The new wave of conditioning programs focuses more on freeing up the shoulder joint by increasing the flexibility of the shoulder while building up and balancing the strength of the muscles involved in acceleration and deceleration. They also frequently work out the back and legs for better shock absorption during deceleration.

As with the throwing theorists, they advocate year-round conditioning with a minimal layoff at the end of the season, then a building program in the off season followed by a maintenance program heavy on flexibility during the season. As mentioned, Dennis Eckersley and Frank Tanana are two pitchers who feel they regained some of their effectiveness and durability through special conditioning programs. However, the real leader in this field was Steve Carlton.

As a youngster, Carlton had a fairly normal level of use. No heavy use as a teenager (178 innings), about 1,000 innings in his formative years with a single-season high of only 236. He did have one high formative BFS (31.8), but at the later age of twenty-four. Carlton was later worked extremely hard at age twenty-seven, a 33.7 BFS in 346 innings, and had a very strong negative reaction the very next year. The slump continued over a three-year span.

CARLTON	W–L	ERA	K/BB
1972	27–10	1.97	3.56
1973	13–20	3.90	1.97
1967–72	101–69	2.86	2.38
1973–75	44–47	3.56	1.85

There were other signs that his arm had become "fragile," such as his having trouble bouncing back after a series of high-pitch games or a heavy season of work. In the 1975 season, he wasn't pushed as hard and had his first BFS under 30.0 in seven years. His next season (1976: 20–7, 3.13 ERA) was his best since his Cy Young award in 1972.

Then in 1977 Carlton began doing the strength-and-flexibility program designed by Gus Hoefling. Almost immediately, Steve began to react less to high-pitch games and remained more effective throughout the season. He increased his complete games by four, threw 30 more innings, won 23 games, and dropped his ERA to 2.64.

By his third year in Hoefling's program, Carlton's strikeout average actually began to rise. At age thirty-five he set a career high in strikeout average with an 8.47 mark. He raised that to 8.48 at age thirty-six, 8.71 at age thirty-seven, and at age thirty-eight it was 8.72, enabling Carlton to pass Early Wynn as the oldest player to register a career high in strikeouts (Carlton's record was broken by Ryan, age forty, in 1987).

In his first eight years in the Hoefling program, ages thirty-two to thirty-nine, Carlton's record was 145–81 (.642) with a 2.95 ERA and a strikeout average of 7.61. All three measures are superior to those of his career through age thirty. Yet I would not suggest that Hoefling's program would achieve such strong results with other pitchers. Hoefling himself concedes that Carlton worked harder in the program than seemed humanly possible. It's also important to remember that this was a case of enhancement, not rehabilitation of a serious problem.

There has been criticism of Hoefling's program as being too severe and dangerously stressful on several body joints. But many pitchers do modified versions of it, including Tanana, and, of course, others have made improvements in programs totally separate from Hoefling's.

In recent years there has been a growing respect for the benefits of extended rest, a little patience before weighing results, and then controlled light use. This has helped when dealing with pitchers with fragile arms as well as the more serious shoulder problems. Pascual Perez was disabled three times in 1985 with "severe tendinitis of the rotator cuff." He was 1–13 with a 6.14 ERA in 95 innings. The problem seemed so severe that the Braves released him in spring training the next year. Perez took the whole regular season off and pitched just 67 innings in winter ball, averaging barely six innings a start.

In two years Perez had first thrown 95 innings spread around three stints on the DL, then took off a year and threw 67 very light innings in winter ball. That seemed to make all the difference in the world, as he was quickly back in the big leagues in 1987 and pitching great. As I write this in 1988, Perez has made 20 starts in his comeback and has a 1.98 ERA.

It wasn't so long ago that no one ever seemed to make a successful comeback from rotator cuff surgery. This may have been because the surgery was commonly used only in the severest cases, but there also wasn't as much patience with the pitcher's recovery. Don Gullett had his rotator cuff surgery in the fall of 1978 and was in spring training five months later. He was instructed to throw every other day on the sidelines and developed a persistent pain that caused him to be disabled the rest of the year. From there, either Gullett or the Yankees, or both, gave up on his arm. He never pitched professionally again.

In 1987–88, we have seen four pitchers—Rick Reuschel, Atlee Hammaker, Charlie Lea, and Bruce Sutter—make successful major-league comebacks after rotator cuff tears that required surgical correction. This is totally unprecedented, and the clearest similarity among these cases is an unusually long recuperation period. Reuschel had his surgery in March '82. He did not begin pitching competitively again until late June of the next year. Starting off in the minors, he was worked very lightly in 21 appearances, averaging only 5.1 innings a start.

The next year he was disabled with some shoulder soreness both in the spring and fall, and pitched only 92 innings. Finally, in 1985, more than three years after his surgery, he began to pitch effectively and with reasonable durability. In fact, Reuschel threw 248 innings that year, the fourth-highest total of his professional career. He followed that up with 216 innings in 1986 and 227 innings in 1987.

Atlee Hammaker had a long history of shoulder trouble before he underwent surgery for a torn rotator cuff prior to the 1984 season. He was back in action by June, but threw only 41 innings before bone spurs in his elbow disabled him and required surgery. With that extended rest, his shoulder ended up making a nice recovery. The next season he made a career-high 29 starts. Atlee then missed all of 1986 with knee surgery and a second operation on his shoulder. This time, though, the rotator cuff was not torn, and it was a minor arthroscopic procedure to just shave the muscle.

In 1987, more than three years after his surgery for his torn rotator cuff, Hammaker set new career highs in appearances (35), starts (31), and innings (192.7), and, in a big hitters' year, he had the second-lowest ERA of his major-league career.

Charlie Lea suffered a double tear in his rotator cuff, surgically repaired in May of 1985. He did not pitch competitively in 1985 or 1986, and in 1987 he threw less than 100 innings in 23 starts. In 1988, nearly three years after his surgery, he stunned everybody by making the Twins' staff out of spring training. After a rough start, he has settled down, and at this writing in midseason he is a regular member of their rotation and has a winning record.

In August of 1986 Bruce Sutter had an incomplete tear of the rotator cuff repaired through arthroscopic surgery rather than a more radical form. With that procedure there were expectations that he would be able to pitch in 1987. However, in February '87 he underwent shoulder surgery again to remove scar tissue, causing him to miss the entire season. In 1988, almost two years after his rotator cuff repair and with virtually no competitive pitching during that time, Sutter is working effectively out of the Braves' bullpen again. The extra time to recover and ease back into the saddle seems to have done the trick in all four cases.

Of course, all of these pitchers are being handled with unusual care. There is a lot of evidence that suggests similar care helps pitchers whose arm trouble is less dramatic or disabling. If a pitcher's arm develops signs of "premature aging"—an unusual drop in effectiveness, failure to bounce back in normal rest patterns—it doesn't necessarily mean he is on his way out as an effective pitcher. In many cases his career can be salvaged by a little time off and then adjusting his workload downward.

Dennis Martinez was worked very hard in his formative years. He was already beginning to report some shoulder soreness at age twenty-four and was disabled by it for much of the next season. Because of that disablement he threw only 112 innings that year, the fewest of his seven professional seasons. He bounced back the next year to have his best season ever, but it also signaled his return to a heavy workload with a 31.5 BFS while leading the team in innings.

He pitched much worse the next year as his ERA jumped nearly a full run from 3.32 to 4.21. As he continued to pitch, he put up three straight years of ERAs over 5.00. In 1986 he was again disabled with a sore shoulder after throwing just 6.2 innings. Dennis threw only 19.1 innings in a minor-league rehabilitation assignment before the Orioles gave up on him and traded him for a player to be named later. He ended up throwing 98 more innings that season for a total of only 124 innings with only one complete game in 19 starts and a BFS of 23.6.

The next year he began very lightly with 10 minor-league starts, slowly building up to a complete-game one-hitter in which he faced only 28 batters. Along the way he threw only 57.1 innings and had a BFS of 24.1. On July 7, he was ready to return to the majors, where he was carefully handled by manager Buck Rodgers and performed very well. In 22 starts he threw only two complete games and had a BFS of 27.6. He averaged just 95 pitches per start, and had only nine games over 100 pitches, with a high of 130. More important, he also had a 3.30 ERA. Martinez has flourished under a similar program in 1988. Going into the All-Star break he had a BFS of 27.3, the same 95-pitch average, and a 2.76 ERA.

When a pitcher gets older, many managers are willing to use pitch ceilings to make sure they will bounce back in normal rest pattern. Gene Mauch used to do it with Don Sutton; Hal Lanier did it with forty-year-old Nolan Ryan and helped him win an ERA title. I expect the wave of the future to be similar pitch ceilings for any pitcher of any age who shows signs of what is sometimes termed a "premature aging of the arm."

Such pitchers have always been with us and are very difficult to manage. They often can pitch strongly through a high-pitch game and invariably still have a reaction that lingers and builds on itself. Usually they start to falter in midseason. Early in the year the manager is not pushing anyone other than his best pitchers. As the schedule thickens, the front-liners need a bit more relief help, the bullpen gets thin, and the number four or five starter with the weak arm gets pushed to give an extra inning. He has a little trouble after a high-pitch game and faces a few extra batters the next time out because he gives up an extra hit here, a walk there. He ends up with a streak of three relatively high-pitch games, totally begins to lose it, and struggles the rest of the second half.

An excellent case history would be Rick Honeycutt. He developed a fragile arm very early in his career and had a natural pitch ceiling that was so low it made it difficult for him to work effectively through a season. Fortunately, Honeycutt developed into a sinkerballer who threw very few pitches per batter.

When he was traded to Texas he was already following a common trend of such pitchers—pitching very poorly in the second half after a good start. I do not have his performance with Seattle broken down by innings and earned runs, but the Elias Sports Bureau has the data in the form of the opposing hitters for 1979–80.

OPPOSING HITTERS VERSUS HONEYCUTT

1979	BA	SA	ERA
Before All-Star Break	.244	.394	3.60
After All-Star Break	.295	.449	4.69
1980			
Before All-Star Break	.256	.399	2.82
After All-Star Break	.307	.490	4.60

When Honeycutt was traded to Texas in the strike year of 1981, he turned in a career-low ERA of 3.30 in 128 innings. Things just worked out by chance that, regardless of the strike, Honeycutt had a very, very soft workload that season. He did not have a hundred-pitch game till June 3. In his 18 starts he had only five hundred-pitch games, and his season high was only 113 pitches. In one start he threw a complete game on only 83 pitches.

In 1982 Honeycutt had his worst ERA (5.27) as exactly the opposite happened. Rick started off with three straight hundred-pitch games, including his Rangers career high of 130 pitches. Honeycutt was a total disaster for the next month: 40 hits in 26.1 innings with an ERA over 6.00.

Forty-two days after the 130-pitch game, Rick began to pitch well again. He had been so bad in the intervening six starts that early bombings kept him below a hundred pitches in every outing. He got back on the beam, and in his next four starts he threw three complete games with a 1.54 ERA. But Rick threw 97 pitches the first game, 112 the second, and 117 the third. In the fourth game he threw a complete-game shutout on 119 pitches, his third straight game over 110. That was the end of Honeycutt's effectiveness for 1982. In his remaining 78.1 innings, he allowed 110 hits and had a 6.66 ERA.

In 1983 Honeycutt led the AL in ERA by getting off to a brilliant start that coincided with a very light workload. In his first seven starts he never topped 96 pitches and averaged only 87. That streak ended in his eighth start, when he threw a complete-game victory using 121 pitches. In those first eight starts, he had an ERA of 1.33 in 61 innings.

After his 121-pitch game, Detroit bombed him (four runs in six innings). He rebounded from that loss, but three starts later he began his first streak of three straight starts over one hundred pitches. His next start was his worst of the year: 4.2 innings, seven hits, four walks, four runs. That was the beginning of a tumbling collapse from what had begun as a brilliant season.

HONEYCUTT 1983	IP	ERA	BB AVG.
Through June 25	118	1.45	1.60
After June 25	95.2	4.99	2.73

Along the way, Honeycutt was traded to the Dodgers, so I can only guess at his pitch totals for '84. Again, he got off to a fast start, but his season began to falter in early June after throwing back-to-back complete games.

HONEYCUTT 1984	IP	ERA	BB AVG.
Through June 6	91	1.88	1.68
After June 6	92.2	3.79	3.30

Some blamed his second-half problems on his hurting his shoulder in a fall while jogging. But Rick's ineffectiveness began three and a half weeks before his fall. In the four starts prior to his injury he had allowed 29 hits and 20 runs in just 22 innings. If anything, Honeycutt's performance initially picked back up after missing two starts during his recovery period.

Honeycutt's pattern of fast starts and slow finishes continued in '85 and '86.

1985 2.11 ERA on June 9, 4.22 ERA thereafter
1986 1.93 ERA on June 30, 4.52 ERA thereafter

In 1987 I again got access to his pitch totals through the STATS data base. The results were amazingly similar to what I found during his Texas tenure. Rick got off to a great start while averaging just 80 pitches per start, only once going over a hundred with a 114-pitch effort. Then on May 12 he threw a 128-pitch complete game against the Cubs. That would be his high-pitch game of the season and also the turning point in his effectiveness. He lost his next 13 decisions.

HONEYCUTT 1987	W–L	IP	ERA	BB AVG.
Through May 12	2–1	35.2	1.51	1.51
After May 12	1–15	103.2	5.82	4.17

In nine seasons (1979–87), only once did Honeycutt fail to get off to a fast start, and that was the one season when he started off with what were, for him, three high-pitch games. Only once has he finished the season as an effective pitcher, and we know that was the one time when he had a consistently light workload throughout the season.

Would Honeycutt, and other pitchers like him, pitch more effectively through a whole season if appropriate pitch ceilings were set and strongly followed? Because firmly following such guidelines is a rarity, there really aren't sufficient data for study, but I am inclined to believe the answer is yes. Certainly it seems worth finding out. And if it's too hard to work around a starting pitcher with such a low pitch ceiling—and Honeycutt's is unusually low—it might be best to bite the bullet and do what LaRussa did in 1988: As he had done with Eckersley, he turned Honeycutt into a reliever.

Incidentally, that's where all the old relievers used to come from; they were burned-out starters who couldn't hack the starting grind anymore. The idea of putting a young quality arm into the relief role is a fairly recent development, one that's less than twenty years old. It hasn't been a bad idea given the importance of the bullpen in the modern game, but it cuts down the options for the Honeycutts of the world. Besides, even in this role, the manager could still help the fragile pitcher by handling him with care. Honeycutt was doing fine as a reliever in 1988 until he was called on to pitch in three consecutive games for the first time (June 15–17). At that point he had a 3.09 ERA in 24 appearances covering 35 innings. He then struggled in his next 14 appearances, with a 5.56 ERA in 22.2 innings.

There is no escaping it. At every level and with every pitcher, there is something to be gained from a better understanding of what the pitcher can handle at that point in his career. And if the long-term ramifications were better understood, it might help us control the competitive pressures that frequently push a pitcher down a path of abuse.

Fernando Valenzuela was one of our pitching treasures in the 1980s. He was that rare combination of a golden talent with an iron arm. Because we believed so much in the iron, we destroyed the gold, and now even the iron is threatened. Fernando was worked very hard as a teenager, particularly at age eighteen, when he threw 205 innings with a 30.2 BFS. When he was just twenty years old he led the NL in innings and had a BFS of 31.1. At age twenty-one, it was 285 innings and a 32.0 BFS. In his remaining formative years he never threw fewer than 257 innings, and his BFS went 31.9, 32.6, and 32.3.

Without missing a beat, he continued to pour it on, with 269 innings and a BFS of 32.9, and then in 1987 he ran up a 33.3 BFS in 251 innings. That year he *averaged* 126 pitches per start. That's a long way from the days of Christy Mathewson and Grover Cleveland Alexander, who rarely threw a hundred pitches even when they tossed a complete game. In Valenzuela's 12 complete games he averaged 148 pitches. In one three-week span he made six starts that averaged 157 pitches!

But there was a price. Valenzuela was worked so hard in his career that we don't have to look to his late twenties for a reaction. Like Vida Blue, who never repeated the brilliance of his big year at age twenty-one, Valenzuela has never been able to match his season at age twenty. Rather than improving as he moved toward what would normally be his physical prime, his performance declined.

YEARS	INNINGS	HIT AVG.	BB AVG.	K AVG.	RUN AVG.	ERA
Through 1982 (age 21)	495.0	7.2	2.7	7.2	2.95	2.62
1983–1985 (age 24)	790.1	7.7	3.5	7.3	3.68	3.06
1986–1988 (age 27)[1]	662.2	8.4	3.9	6.7	4.01	3.69

It was only a couple of years ago, after the 1986 season, that folks were assessing Fernando's chances for three hundred career victories, pointing out that he was already a dozen career wins ahead of Seaver at the same age. Since then, he has gone 19–22 with an ERA over 4.00 in nearly four hundred innings before going on the disabled list with a serious shoulder injury that may affect his future. Despite all that talent and the amazing durability he demonstrated for so many years, it has now become painfully obvious that even the iron arm of Valenzuela had a need to be monitored and handled with care. And if it is true for the exceptional pitcher, how much more important is it for the average pitcher?

We have the ability to monitor, to study, and to better understand the needs of each pitcher from eighteen-year-old Joe Prospect to a Fernando Valenzuela on the comeback trail. We know that in the modern era it takes more than monitoring a pitcher's innings to gauge a starter's workload; we also have to hold in check the magnitude and frequency with which he is pushed past his normal endurance level, start by start. We know that the younger pitchers in their formative years need to be handled with exceptional care that eases to a general monitoring in the prime seasons.

We have a feel for the special treatments and programs that pitchers are successfully using to prevent or rehabilitate injuries associated with the heavy demands placed on a professional pitcher's arm. We have learned that careful monitoring and special handling, such as the use of pitch ceilings, can enhance the performance of those with a history of abuse or advance the recovery of those battling back from actual arm trouble. We've come a long way from the uncharted wilderness we faced two chapters ago. Now it is time to tackle one of the major innovations of the modern game intended to help the pitchers, yet one that is woefully wrongheaded. But that's a chapter in itself.

PITCHING III: BRING BACK THE FOUR-MAN ROTATION

Relying heavily on a fifth starting pitcher is nothing new in the history of baseball. Back in the early days of this century, it was common for a team to mix and match its rotation past the top two or three starters. But until this decade, most teams were willing to use their best starting pitchers in a pattern in which they frequently worked every fourth day.

The first manager to use a distinct five-man rotation on a regular basis was Frank Chance, way back in 1906. In his first full season as a playing manager, he took over a highly talented and deep pitching staff that had just led the league in ERA. Chance decided to spread the work around by going with a five-man rotation that he used for both 1906 and 1907. Despite the presence of stars like Three-Finger Brown and Big Ed Reulbach, no Cub made more than 32 starts in the 154-game schedule. When his staff was thinned out by injuries in 1908 and 1909, Chance returned to the four-man rotation but continued to experiment with a rotation of five whenever he felt he had five quality pitchers.

It's easy enough to see why Chance liked the idea. It coincided with his immediate success as a manager. The Cubs won the pennant in both 1906 and '07 and led in ERA with marks of 1.76 and 1.73. But don't get carried away with those numbers; the balance of the game was tilted heavily toward the pitcher at that time, and the Cubs'

home field was a superb pitchers' park. (This is back before Wrigley
Field was even a gleam in an architect's eye.) Chance's Cubs played
in a mammoth park that had huge foul areas and a wide-open outfield
that stretched to 560 feet in straightaway center field.

The Cubs of that era routinely led in ERA with or without Chance
and his five-man rotation. Relative to the league ERA, they were
almost as good the year before, and one of the most impressive ERA
titles under Chance occurred in 1909, when he was using the standard
four-man rotation.

CUBS' ERA RELATIVE TO LEAGUE

1905	.682
1906	.669
1907	.703
1908	.911
1909	.676

Very few teams had the option to follow Chance's logic, which was
based on having five good starters. Others experimented with the
five-man rotation because they felt it helped their pitchers perform
better over the long haul of the season. Yet the four-man rotation
ruled this century. As late as 1974, at least two-thirds of the major-
league teams were still using four-man rotations. After the 1981 strike
season only Earl Weaver still used it, and when he retired it vanished
completely.

One theory holds that the famous 1969 Mets killed the four-man
rotation. When we hit the late seventies, there were a lot of young
pitchers running into arm trouble, and folks noticed that Seaver,
Koosman, and Ryan were still stars despite being in their mid-thirties.
All three had pitched in their early years with the Mets, who had a
firm policy against any starter working with less than four days' rest.
They say Seaver went through his whole career without a single start
on three days' rest. I doubt that's true, but I get the point.

Of course, the Mets weren't protecting them by just using a five-
man rotation. They brought their pitchers along slowly and kept their
BFS down. We've already seen that Ryan and Koosman could have

been pitching in a four-man rotation and still qualified as having light formative workloads. And we have also shown that Seaver was slightly affected by his heavy formative workload despite pitching in a five-man rotation. He clearly did not age as well as the other two, relative to his own ability.

The shift to the five-man rotation was also the method baseball used in the late seventies to follow the typical knee-jerk reaction of lowering the ceiling for innings pitched. The new rotations eliminated starts and thus reduced each starter's innings.

It had been a long time since Frank Chance had brought out that strategy. In the interim, when baseball wanted to reduce the ceiling of innings they turned to a combination of approaches. The most popular one before World War II was to occasionally substitute a long relief appearance for a start. In the old 154-game schedules a workhorse starter could, in theory, start every fourth day and make around 42 starts. What they often had him do instead was something like 35 starts and seven relief appearances. They kept their top starters working on a regular basis, didn't widely alter their rest pattern, and ensured that some easy appearances were sprinkled throughout the season.

Another practice, and the one that became especially prevalent after World War II, was simply to reduce the number of complete games. Both strategies were geared to make a major impact on the problem of pitchers constantly being pushed into a potential danger zone over an extended period of time.

The same cannot be said about this modern answer of reducing innings by eliminating starts through a five-man rotation. That does little to relieve the constant pressure that the modern hurler works under. I have yet to see a single study that convincingly shows its benefit. Logically, I can accept that it must help to some degree, but just as logically the impact is minimal. If all that mattered were just reducing innings or increasing rest, then BFS would not work as an indicator of a pitcher's workload.

We have seen a lot of young pitching stars whose careers have broken down or gone into a premature decline despite the fact they worked in five-man rotations in which they stayed away from the massive inning totals associated with the four-man rotation. Ralph Houk burned out Mark Fidrych and then Dave Rozema despite the fact he used a five-man rotation and held Fidrych to 250 innings and Rozema to 218. And many of our veteran pitching stars like Carlton, Gibson, and Perry spent the bulk of their careers working in four-man rotations.

WHY GO BACK?

That is a very fair question. Returning to four-man rotations, in itself, doesn't relieve the pressure either. Yet a return to four-man rotations might help baseball more productively address the larger problem and learn to bring it into check.

First, it would put our focus back on ways to eliminate dangerous innings rather than just any innings. Our previous studies have indicated that it's not the number of innings thrown that's dangerous, but the number of innings thrown past the pitcher's endurance level. Implicit in the argument for the five-man rotation is that the pitcher will be helped by the longer rest, which will also reduce his total innings. If we accept this logic, then the next alarm over pitcher blowouts will send us to six-man rotations rather than asking why the five-man rotations didn't work as expected.

Second, five-man rotations put a strain on our pitching resources. It's hard to come up with five starters, and often we need six because our fourth and fifth starters aren't good enough to have our full confidence. Too often clubs are forced to rush young pitchers into demanding roles they aren't ready to handle, or into unusual roles that hamper the development of their full skills.

But I expect the real reason baseball will eventually return to the four-man rotation will be the simplest of all: It helps win games. The five-man rotation is not on that evolutionary path; it's a digression, a dead-end alley. Just as baseball once believed that walking a lot of batters was better than throwing a home-run pitch, we are now chasing an illusion that our pitchers work better on four days' rest and that the five-man rotation significantly improves their future.

Naturally, there are pitchers who work better on four days' rest, but no one has shown that the differences are so large that they couldn't perform well enough in a four-man rotation. And there is evidence that suggests there are just as many pitchers who work better on three days' rest. In my own studies and others', it has been noted that there are classes of pitchers whose control improves considerably on three days' rest, leading to better performance. All indications are that in a large group the differences end up washing out, and you are left with the natural advantages of the four-man rotation.

The nagging argument against bringing back the four-man rotation in modern times is that the demands on a starting pitcher have become too great for him to work effectively on three days' rest. Although the four-man rotation has died out as a general rule, circumstances still lead starters to work on three days' rest from time to time. In the present era about 9% to 10% of starts still occur on three days' rest. The most recent published study on starts by rest pattern was based on the 1986 season. Researcher Geoff Beckman discovered that, overall, there were not significant differences in effectiveness by days of rest.

ERA RELATIVE TO LEAGUE AVERAGE
FOR STARTING PITCHERS (1986)

3 Days' Rest	.975
4 Days' Rest	.991
5 Days' Rest	1.023

Now, it's true that may be slightly skewed by the fact that a club would be more likely to push a good pitcher to pitch on short rest. Beckman left a way to check that by giving an individual breakdown on each club's main starting pitchers. Out of 109 listed starters who worked on both three and four days' rest, 51% did better on three days' rest.

Beckman went on to note that it was the National League pitchers who were doing better on three days' rest, and that their AL counterparts actually did worse. From that he made a conclusion that there is "evidence to suggest that some National League teams can go with four starters and make it pay off. But there is no evidence to suggest that using four starters helped any American League team. There is clear evidence that some were hurt by it. . . . I can't help but think that any AL manager who consistently uses a four-man rotation (without having definitive proof that it benefits each and every starter) is grossly mishandling his staff."

That would seem to fit the standard theory of why we have abandoned the four-man rotation. The modern game, particularly in the offensive-minded DH league, has become too demanding for starters to work on three days' rest. But when I looked closely at Beckman's analysis, his conclusions were clearly overreaching the data.

First of all, it wasn't true that "there is no evidence to suggest that using four starters helped any American League team." In both leagues, the teams that had the most experience starting on three days' rest tended to be the ones who did better at it. Of the six AL teams whose starters made more than ten starts on three days' rest, four performed better when working on three days' rest. All of Oakland's top five starters worked better on three days' rest. One reason the NL starters may have performed better on three days' rest was they did it more often—12% of the time, compared with 7% for the AL starters.

Second, splitting the data by leagues reduced the sample size to a point that comparisons between the two sets would have to result in very large differences to be sure they wouldn't wash out in a larger sampling. The differences Beckman noted did not carry that kind of significance. The overall split of AL pitchers showed 25 of 56 doing better on three days' rest. Granted, that isn't 50%, but it also isn't justification for thinking that without perfect supportive evidence, an AL manager would be "grossly mishandling his staff" by adopting a four-man rotation.

I repeated the study with a 1987 data base, and again, the overall results showed little difference between the ERAs by the number of days' rest.

ERA RELATIVE TO LEAGUE AVERAGE
FOR STARTING PITCHERS (1987)

3 Days' Rest	.998
4 Days' Rest	.988
5 Days' Rest	1.002

The percentage of individuals doing better on three days' rest was 49%, but this time it was 55% in the American League and 41% in the NL. In fact, the edge held by the American League starters was about the same as the National League held in 1986. When you combine the two seasons the leagues were remarkably similar and showed no general change in effectiveness by days' rest.

ERA RELATIVE TO LEAGUE AVERAGE
FOR STARTING PITCHERS (1986–87)

	NL	AL
3 Days' Rest	.991	.987
4 Days' Rest	.994	.987
5 Days' Rest	1.018	1.005

There are still occasional experiments where a team will decide to go with a four-man rotation for a portion of the season. The most recent was under the direction of Royals manager John Wathan in 1988. He stayed with it through May 10 and then added Ted Power to the rotation. For those first 32 starts, Saberhagen, Leibrandt, Gubicza, and Bannister never missed a turn, and they were called on to pitch with three days' rest 14 times. That right there is more than most modern clubs will have in a full season.

They had their rough moments, but they also had an ERA of 3.13 versus 3.78 in their other starts. And they surprisingly went farther in their starts on three days' rest, an average of 7.0 innings as opposed to 6.2. When they switched over to the five-man rotation their staff ERA was 3.66. The Royals reached the All-Star break in 1988 with an identical 3.66 ERA. It would be hard to make a case that they did not pitch as well in their four-man rotation or that doing so took anything out of their arms in the short-term future.

If there were an unusual number of blowouts during the last heydays of the four-man rotation—something that still has not been shown—they may have resulted from the difference in orientation between managers as they began to split over the four-man versus five-man issue. In my research of that period I noticed that there was a tendency to find higher BFS on teams that worked with four-man rotations.

There's a certain logic to that. A manager who leans toward the four-man rotation generally wants his best pitchers out on the mound as often as possible. That same approach would lead him to push his top dogs for an extra inning whenever possible.

The managers who were early converts to the five-man rotation were doing it either to protect their pitchers' futures or enhance their effectiveness for the long season. That protective attitude of disciplined restraint doesn't jibe with the profile of a manager with a habit of pushing his pitchers hard in individual starts.

In giving consideration to bringing back the four-man rotation, it would be a good idea to call up the example of the manager who worked the four-man rotation with the greatest restraint—and success. Earl Weaver took a lot of ignorant, jealous abuse about his handling of pitchers. On one hand he was criticized for not having confidence in young pitchers and holding them back. Then he was chastised for overworking his pitchers and refusing to give up the "archaic" four-man rotation.

Folks, Earl was a hell of a lot deeper than the simple pundit who stated, "It's easier to find four good starters than five." When I look at Weaver's handling of pitchers, I see a manager who was concerned with getting the most out of his staff, but who also had a unique sensitivity to the durability of a pitcher's arm. I also discovered in his book *Weaver on Strategy* that he had established a set of personal guidelines that seemed geared, intentionally or not, to promoting the durability and consistency of his pitching staff.

First, Earl had a policy of staying in rotation early in the year rather than sneaking in extra starts for his best pitchers by sending them out there literally every fourth day.

If a team wants to get off to a fast start they can go with three starting pitchers in April. That's all you need with an early-season schedule that features so many off days. But I was never really concerned about getting that fast start. I learned a long time ago that it's a long

season, and I wanted everyone strong. Say I decided to start Palmer
and Dennis Martinez [all I could] in April. Then Scott McGregor
and Mike Flanagan wouldn't be getting the work they needed to be
prepared for the heavier schedule in late May and thereafter.

One of the side effects of this policy was that his top starters were
able to make an easier transition from the lighter work of spring
training. They would essentially work on four days' rest through most
of April, then go to three days' rest only when the schedule had filled
out. It also meant fewer starts and innings for the pitchers Earl would
work the hardest during the season. During Earl's long career, there
were thirteen other managers who used four-man rotations and gave
a pitcher more than 40 starts in a season. They did it 27 times with
15 different pitchers. Despite Weaver's dedication to the four-man
rotation, *no Oriole pitcher ever made more than 40.*
 'Weaver was *very* conscious of when a pitcher was tiring, and he
used this as his main criterion in switching pitchers, rather than reacting to platoon differences. His book downplays the importance of
having a righty and lefty coming out of the bullpen, and then dedicates
a couple of pages to pulling pitchers who are tired, including seven
rules titled "How to Tell If a Pitcher Is Losing His Edge." He concludes the passage with an example of a pitcher who has shown no
signs of tiring but has suddenly given up some hard-hit balls. Rather
than take any unnecessary risks, Weaver pulled him.
 During Weaver's career, there were over fifty three-hundred-inning
seasons thrown, and eleven different pitchers topped 325 in a season—some of them two or three or even four times. How many
pitchers ever threw a three-hundred-inning season under Earl? Just
one, and Jim Palmer's high was 323 innings. How many of Earl's
pitchers had a BFS of 33.0-plus at any age? Well, there was Palmer—
did I mention Palmer? But Earl's real caution came in his handling
of young pitchers, something that began after he had a bad experience
with a young prospect in the minor leagues.
 When Earl was managing in AA at Elmira in 1966, he was given
a twenty-three-year-old prospect who topped the scales at just 165
pounds but had led the Northern League with 16 wins while losing

only four. His name was Dave Leonhard, and under Earl he led the Eastern League with 20 wins against only five losses. He also threw 230 innings with a 32.4 BFS.

Weaver and Leonhard were promoted together to AAA the next year. Weaver watched Dave struggle to a 9–7 record. Going into that season, Leonhard had a 2.51 ERA for his three professional seasons. His Elmira ERA of 2.27 jumped to 3.88 in Rochester, and his strike-out-to-walk ratio was literally cut in half from an excellent 2.86 to 1.43. Leonhard was never the same pitcher, although he did adapt and rose with Weaver to the majors, where he had a brief career as a long reliever–spot starter.

Did that experience make an impact on Weaver? He never again came even close to working a younster that hard. From AAA to the majors, a total of nineteen seasons, how many pitchers do you think Earl had with a BFS over 30.0 before age twenty-three? Would you believe just two? And both were just barely over that level: Palmer at 30.1 and Dennis Martinez at 30.2, both doing it at age twenty-three. In all that time Earl let only one pitcher (Martinez) throw more than two hundred innings in a season before age twenty-four.

One way Earl accomplished that was by "Weaver's Eighth Law: The best place for a rookie pitcher is in long relief." This firm rule created a light use pattern for one season that invariably came during the pitcher's formative years. We have seen the positive effects of that same pattern in the careers of durable stars like Bob Gibson, Gaylord Perry, and Nolan Ryan.

This is not to say the Orioles organization was routinely protective of its pitchers. As with most organizations, several of its minor-leaguers were pushed hard, and they were delivered to Weaver with questionable durability. Weaver made it a point to notice and handle them with care.

Mike Flanagan had a 30.2 BFS at the young age of twenty-two, and when he got to the majors Weaver noted, "Flanagan threw a little harder when he was in a five-man rotation—that extra day of rest helped him. But Flanagan still had enough stuff to win every fourth day." If you check, you will see that early in Mike's career

Earl gave him that extra day's rest or substituted a relief appearance when he could. It wasn't until he was twenty-six that Earl let him make more than 33 starts in his four-man rotation, and no matter how successful Flanagan became, he never had a BFS higher than 29.8 for Earl.

Weaver did exactly the same thing with Scott McGregor. Few people remember that McGregor was a hard thrower when he started off in the Yankees organization. BFS of 31.5 and 34.3 at ages nineteen and twenty preceded his being disabled at age twenty-one. His fastball vanished, but McGregor successfully changed his style and made it to the big leagues, although he, too, had an arm that couldn't be pushed. Like Flanagan, McGregor's BFS for Weaver were always under 30.0. Even more amazing is that Weaver was already acting on this knowledge in their first full seasons.

> You have to be careful not to overuse a pitcher. But a manager learns about his pitchers' arms. Tippy Martinez can throw a lot without it bothering him, so I used him often. That was not the case with some others. . . . Mike Flanagan could never go out and pitch in seventy or eighty games a year like Tippy. Neither could Scott McGregor. Physically, their arms couldn't stand the wear. When I used them in the bullpen during their rookie seasons, I made sure they had three days between appearances.

Weaver was not shy about pushing Jim Palmer because he felt Jim had one of those exceptional arms and kept himself in great shape. And the whole organization thought it had another "Palmer-Arm" in Dennis Martinez. Dennis was so good so young and seemed so durable that the Orioles pushed him from his first day as a professional. By the time he was twenty-one, he was throwing complete games 70% of the time in Rochester.

For the time that Weaver had Martinez, he treated him in almost exactly the same pattern he had used with Jim Palmer. The big difference between Palmer's and Martinez's eventual futures was not simply Dennis's drinking problem, but that he had been worked much, much harder in his formative years. His formative workloads

MARTINEZ	AGE	IP	BFS	CLUB
1974	19	179	30.8	Miami
1975	20	195	30.0	Miami
1976	21	208	31.6	Rochester
1977	22	167	26.7	Baltimore
1978	23	276	30.2	Baltimore
1979	24	292	31.2	Baltimore

fall somewhere between the levels of Vida Blue's and Bert Blyleven's, and like them he suffered a severe drop in his effectiveness in his late twenties and is just now beginning to recover from it over five years later.

Weaver probably contributed to the decline of another pitcher when he pushed Ross Grimsley to a BFS of 31.2 at age twenty-four in 1974. But a manager who contributes to the demise of only two pitchers in sixteen major-league seasons is doing a heck of a job. The Orioles made at least that many errors in the two seasons after Earl's 1982 retirement.

What happened in Baltimore? Weaver turned over what looked like an up-and-coming team. In his last significant managerial move he shifted rookie Cal Ripken, Jr. to shortstop. Going into the last game of the season, he had led the team to a tie for the best record in baseball. And he did it with a pitching staff in transition, one on which no one won more than sixteen games.

The new manager would not only have twenty-two-year-old Ripken established at shortstop (remember, he played half his rookie year at third base, and Earl stuck with him when Cal was hitting .117 on May 1), but Eddie Murray was still only twenty-seven. More important, the Orioles' pitching was poised to rejuvenate with Storm Davis and Mike Boddicker ready to take on major roles and bolster the staff. This is how the Orioles staff looked going into spring training, 1983 (see top of next page).

With Ripken and Murray running one-two in the MVP voting, and with the pitching improved, the 1983 Orioles cruised to a pennant and World championship. But then the mighty ship began to sink like a rock, led by the disintegration of that talented staff and ending an era unique in baseball history.

CAREER MARKS

	AGE	INNINGS	ERA
Mike Flanagan	31	1480.0	3.81
Scott McGregor	29	1175.3	3.68
Dennis Martinez	28	1474.0	3.29
Mike Boddicker	25	38.7	4.19
Storm Davis	21	100.7	3.49
Tippy Martinez	33	552.0	3.16
Sammy Stewart	28	499.0	3.43

There have been a few managers who could build a staff better than Earl Weaver, but I believe he was the game's absolute best for keeping a quality staff going. During Weaver's tenure, the Orioles had at least one twenty-game winner for 13 consecutive seasons, a major-league record for this century. Nine different pitchers took part in that record, and several did it more than once. They combined to put 22 twenty-win seasons on the board. Project the 1981 strike season, and you could have made it 14 consecutive seasons, 10 different pitchers, and 24 twenty-win seasons.

The skill reflected in that record is rarely appreciated. It's so easy to sit back and say, "Look, he had all these great pitchers." Well, it's hard to get there, but it's even harder to stay there. You learn to value that skill a little more when you see how fourteen seasons of excellence can totally fall apart in just a couple years.

And that's exactly what happened when the Orioles hired Joe Altobelli. He's an excellent manager in many regards, but when it comes to pitching, Joe is a poor man's Billy Martin. He's a fine tactical manager who often gets dramatic pitching improvements in his first couple seasons. His judgment of pitching ability and who has the hot hand is a laudable skill, but it isn't the sole source of his early effectiveness with pitchers. A large part actually comes out of his poor feel for what it takes to keep a pitcher going. Rather than responding to the needs of each individual pitcher, Altobelli blindly uses them according to what will win today. That strategy carries steep long-term costs in damaged starters and relievers. It's the kind of approach that earns you kudos as a manager one year and gets you fired the next. That's what happened to him when he managed San Francisco, and it happened again in Baltimore—*despite an immediate shift to a five-man rotation!*

ERA RELATIVE TO THE LEAGUE

SF			BAL		
1977	1.009	Before Altobelli	1982	.980	Before Altobelli
1978	.959	First year	1983	.894	First year
1979	.922	Second year	1984	.930	Second year
1980	1.115	Fired in midseason	1985	1.055	Fired in midseason

In 1983, the fragile arm of Scott McGregor was suddenly pushed to the limit by Altobelli. Despite the five-man rotation, Scott threw a career-high 260 innings and had a 30.4 BFS, his highest since his fastball vanished back in 1975. That winter I wrote a report predicting that McGregor's career would likely take a turn for the worse, an observation I also shared in a letter to Bill James in April '84. Scott was only twenty-nine when he went 18–7 with a 3.18 ERA in 1983, but thereafter his ERAs went 3.94, 4.81, 4.52, 6.64, and 8.83 before his release in 1988.

When McGregor faltered in 1984, Mike Boddicker became Altobelli's new workhorse. Boddicker had turned in a 30.2 BFS at age twenty-two and had a bad reaction the next year as his ERA rose from 2.18 to 4.20 and his strikeout-walk ratio fell from 3.11 to 1.65. He got it back together and made it to the big leagues, but he was exactly the kind of pitcher Weaver would handle carefully, keeping his BFS under 30.0, as he did with McGregor and Flanagan.

That wasn't Altobelli's game plan. Although Mike had never before thrown more than 197 innings in a season, he ended up with 261 crammed into a five-man rotation by putting up a 31.9 BFS. Boddicker left that season as a twenty-seven-year-old carrying a career ERA of 2.89 in 479 innings. The next season his ERA jumped to 4.07, followed by 4.70 and 4.18 the next two years.

Storm Davis was the Orioles' star pitching prospect, the next Jim Palmer, but he was worked much harder than Palmer as a teenager. Davis had a 30.0 BFS in 187 innings when he was just nineteen and tossed 338 professional innings in his teens. In the fall of 1983 I was asked to write a report on Davis, and I cautioned that he might have a mild impingement case that could worsen. I noted, too, how insensitive Altobelli was about using Davis. I wrote:

> Davis ran into arm problems after a streak of excessively long appearances. In one 5-start stretch he faced 36–39–27–35–38 batters. The four mid- to high 30's are the four highest for his whole season. After that stretch his effectiveness dropped and Baltimore took him out of the rotation, at one time giving him 11 days off.
>
> Davis's season through that stretch showed a 3.11 ERA (136 IP) and an average of 7.7 hits and 6.4 K's. In eight starts since then Davis has had a 3.99 ERA with an 8.2 hit average and only a 4.2 K average.

So, after two years under Altobelli that saw several in-season bouts with arm trouble, Davis's career shifted into reverse. Although he was just twenty-three and had a career ERA of 3.37 in over 500 innings, his ERA jumped to 4.53 in 1985 and averaged 4.35 for the next three years.

We haven't talked about measures of abuse for relievers, but you don't have to look too hard to see that Altobelli used both Tippy Martinez and Sammy Stewart in different, more demanding roles than Weaver did, and their careers folded after the initial success. Dennis Martinez struggled under Altobelli with ERAs of 5.53 and 5.02. This was more a result of abuse that happened before Joe took over the Orioles, but ironically his hands still weren't clean in this case: When Dennis was only twenty-one years old and completing 70% of his starts for Rochester, guess who his manager was? Joe Altobelli.

All this mayhem ended up dumping a battered and broken pitching staff at the feet of the returning Earl of Baltimore. And no, he wasn't able to put Humpty Dumpty back together again. In 1986, the full season of Earl's short return, both Dennis and Tippy Martinez had shoulder trouble and were limited to a total of 23 innings for the season. McGregor, Boddicker, and Davis were all still struggling from the abuse under Altobelli's handling. The only new arm belonged to Ken Dixon, a youngster who had been badly abused in the minor leagues at age twenty-three when he completed 20 of 29 starts and put up a BFS of 33.2 in 240 innings. This staff couldn't be saved; it was destined to crash and leave the Orioles to start from scratch. The best Earl could do was try to slow down the disintegration, which he did.

ORIOLE ERA RELATIVE TO THE LEAGUE

1985	1.055	Altobelli-Weaver
1986	1.029	Weaver
1987	1.123	Ripken

The difference between the four-man and five-man rotations was no factor at all in what happened to the Orioles. Although Altobelli had used a four-man rotation when he managed San Francisco in the late seventies, he had the Orioles join the rest of the baseball world once he took over there. The Oriole staffs, which had survived so well under the four-man rotation, crashed under the five-man rotation. The difference was in who was managing the pitchers, how much care was being exercised. That's what really matters, not whether it's a rotation of five instead of four.

Yet there is still a chance that I am overstating the case of the four man rotation. Maybe with the heavy demands of the modern game we really have edged past the point where it is safe to work through a whole season in a four-man rotation. Maybe we snuck by that barrier right at the end of Earl's career. That wall has to be out there somewhere, just as it was in that long-ago day when baseball stopped working pitchers in three-man rotations.

But if we've entered that new land, we can't have gone that far past the gate, and that's why I left one of Earl's little eccentricities for last. If I were going to bring back the four-man rotation, I'd make a point of turning back the slowly escalating pitch totals of the modern game. One thing that Weaver was an absolute fiend about was having his pitchers throw strikes. He loved the base on balls on offense and hated it on defense. In *Weaver on Strategy* he tells how he and pitching coach George Bamberger "harped on it from the time they came to the park until the moment they left."

In 1967 the Orioles issued more walks than any team in the league. Midway through '68 they hired Weaver, and they rose to fifth in fewest walks allowed. In his first full season as a manager the Orioles led the league in fewest walks allowed. Not once did he ever manage a staff that walked more than the league average.

Yet Weaver's approach went deeper than that in pitch conservation. Although he appreciated a good fastball as much as any manager, the Orioles emphasized putting the ball in play over big strikeout totals. Despite all those great pitching staffs, they never led the league in strikeouts. In Earl's fifteen full seasons they finished as high as third in strikeouts only once. Nine times they were in the bottom half in Ks. In 1975 they led the league in ERA and finished eleventh in strikeouts.

When it came to individual pitching stars, no Oriole pitcher ever led the league in strikeouts or strikeout average. No Oriole ever finished second. And only one, Mike Flanagan in 1979, even finished third.

While baseball was growing into a game that nibbled at the corners and pressed the pitchers to throw more perfect strikes, the Orioles routinely took big bites of the plate. If there is one thing that sticks in my mind after closely watching over a decade of Weaver pitchers, it is that every single starter and nearly every long reliever could throw a breaking ball for a strike when he was down in the count. I don't believe Weaver would allow a pitcher in his rotation who couldn't command a breaking pitch. Mixing pitches and speeds, throwing strikes; that was the Orioles' way.

> Some pitchers get into a frame of mind in which they believe they must throw a perfect pitch. That isn't true. You can't just lob the ball down the middle, but you don't have to make a great pitch, or the perfect pitch every time. The key to pitching is throwing the pitch the hitter isn't looking for. If you can do that, it doesn't have to be on the corners.

If reviving the four-man rotation would lead us to exercise more care in handling our pitchers and trying to reduce the number of pitches per batter, it would do far more to protect our pitchers' futures than the false sense of freedom we feel in five-man rotations. Which of these two seasons is more valuable, and which is more dangerous if thrown by a twenty-three-year-old?

W-L	ERA	INNINGS	HITS	K	W
18–10	3.36	257	246	163	53
20–11	3.36	265	254	168	55

The first line is Bret Saberhagen's from 1987 when he made 33 starts in a five-man rotation. The second line is a projection of the same season, in a four-man rotation that remains intact early in the season even if it means pitching on four days' rest, à la Earl Weaver. To be on the safe side, we also cut back his average innings per start from 7.8 to 7.0. In return for those slight concessions Kansas City would get five more starts from its best pitcher instead of from its fifth-best starter.

Now which is safer? Banking on the protection provided by the extra rest in the five-man rotation, Saberhagen ran up a BFS of 32.4. In the plan of our four-man rotation we reduced his BFS to 29.1. I don't know what Saberhagen's future is going to be like, but given a choice, I think everyone's purpose would be better served by our sample four-man rotation line.

What did we do here? Although we added eight innings to his total, we also cut out twenty-six of the most dangerous innings a young pitcher can throw, the ones when he is pushing past his endurance level (7.8 − 7.0 = .8; .8 × 33 = 26.4). Cutting the right 26 innings isn't as easy as it sounds; usually those are innings in which the pitcher doesn't want to come out, the manager doesn't really want to take him out, and the crowd is not going to be too thrilled, either.

There is no easy way. If a manager is going to do it, he has to face up to those pressures with vision and courage. But the rewards are great. Your fifth starter becomes a long reliever/spot starter—a much easier role to fill—and the careful handling of your pitchers, especially the young ones, will increase the consistency and quality of your future pitching staffs. In the end, the four-man rotation can still pay off in the modern game.

HOUSE:
ANOTHER PATH TO PREVENTION

Baseball is a great game, but without question it ages and abuses pitchers' arms. Every club tries to watch its pitchers carefully, but often this attention is based on a lot of misinformation and a heavy dose of tradition. And that's sad, because there has been more than enough research from fields outside baseball—athletic and other-wise—to significantly reduce the number of injuries if only ball clubs would just open their eyes. Other sports take state-of-the-art infor-mation and techniques and run with them; baseball warily eyes any-thing new, spitting tobacco juice at it to see whether it'll go away. But arm injuries won't.

Craig's research is certainly impressive. But that's what it is—research. One of the problems for me about sabermetrics is that it's all about the past. Craig makes a pretty persuasive case, but it assumes that things will be done the way they've always been done. It can't anticipate different ways of doing things that, I believe, are going to change the rules of what a pitcher can and can't do. In Craig's world, you accept the way things are and try to accommodate yourself to them. I think we can do better.

Craig and I agree that there are three main areas that determine how long and how strong a pitcher can go: mileage, mechanics, and conditioning base. Where I think he's dead wrong is in treating the last two as subsidiary factors and focusing all his attention on the first. Craig calls for pitch limits, which would address the issue of mileage, but it ignores the other two pieces of the pie. The biggest drawback to pitch limits is that they homogenize: They treat all pitch-ers the same because of the dictates of history. This approach will slow down the development of pitching prospects who *don't* have a propensity for sore arms—and there are such people, and we can identify them.

A better idea is to watch carefully and pull a pitcher if, without any obvious flaw in his mechanics, his speed on the radar gun drops three miles an hour for three straight pitches. That's a sign of muscle fatigue, and that's what we're all trying to prevent—pitching through muscle fatigue. But this method is more flexible, and isn't going to retard a pitcher's development, since it lets him find his own appropriate level.

Incidentally, I agree with Craig about the four-man rotation. I've never seen anything that led me to believe that three days of rest wasn't enough; the key question is what you're doing to get your staff ready to handle a particular workload. A pitcher's physical ability to pitch is a function of his workload, his mechanics, and his conditioning. It's only in the last few years that we've made strides in improving the third area.

We've only begun to scratch the surface when it comes to finding ways to train and prepare pitchers. I firmly believe you can develop a program that will help create the twenty-year pitchers that have been the exceptions to the rule. My proposal is for a program I've termed "prehabilitation." Prehabilitation is more than just standard preparation; it involves testing for mental, physical, and nutritional problems *before* starting on a developmental program so that the program can be tailored to the individual. Then specific problem areas can be addressed, precareer and preseason, before the damage that would follow from a traditional workload can happen.

A prehabilitation program should diagnose, prescribe, and direct remedial action in any individual's fitness regimen. The components of such a testing program would be as follows:

1. *Psychological testing and interpretation.* Baseball is a very high-stress occupation. Some people, regardless of their physical tools, are not going to be successful in that kind of environment. Proper psychological testing will help a club identify those players who are cut out for the life or identify those areas where counseling can help an individual overcome the problems that could stifle a promising talent.
2. *The psychophysiology of baseball as a vocational choice.* This means the motivational and biomechanical matching of an individual's conditioning level with the daily requirements of his

sport as an occupation. It requires determining those strength and stamina components required for the individual to maximize productivity. You build for a season the way you would train for a decathlon. The skills required for baseball are every bit as varied as those for the decathlon, and so the training regimen has got to take this into account. You start with general strength building, then work on range-of-motion exercise, and finally turn to skill-specific resistance exercises. Any shortfall in one area can be addressed and remedial action taken before physical breakdown occurs.

3. *Nutrition for achievement.* What does this player need to eat to balance his blood chemistry in an optimal fashion? Studying this will bridge the metabolic gap between the variables of mental and physical conditioning. This will ensure a complementary relationship among mind, body, diet, and the sport, completing the prehab "loop" and meeting its goal of maximizing potential for performance.

4. *Biomechanical optimization.* Computer studies have shown that there is a precise optimal motion for such throwing actions as the javelin, the hammer throw, and the discus—a best way of converting a body's strength and energy into a powerful throw. Why not the pitching motion? Pitching is a function of balance, direction, and weight transfer; each pitcher's motion can be studied and analyzed, and improved. Repetition will cause muscle memory to "groove" that optimal motion into the brain's software, so it will become as natural and unconscious as the pitcher's original and faulty mechanics.

We can train and develop pitchers who will go beyond the limits of the past. Is baseball the only stressful area of athletics? Hardly. In every single sport, proper training has expanded the bounds of strength and endurance. Why shouldn't this be true for pitchers? Look, we know the weight of a baseball, we can measure the amount of arm speed a pitcher generates, we can determine how close to the ideal motion he comes, and we can figure out how many pitches a week we expect him to be able to throw. When all these variables have been nailed down, we can make a precise calculation of the amount of stress placed on a pitcher's body—not just his arm—and we can develop a weight-lifting program that will prepare him to withstand it.

Proper weight training would have to involve the muscles of the back and legs as well as the shoulder and arm. Everyone concentrates on the stress caused by a pitcher's arm acceleration, but most overlook the problem of deceleration; the arm has to go from top speed to zero in about half the time it took to get to top speed in the first place. That puts enormous stress on the muscles of the legs and back to absorb all that extra energy. Through our motion analysis, we can measure this stress and insure that a pitcher's program takes it all into account.

Let's get specific. We know that in the shoulder capsule there are three anterior (front) muscle groups involved in the acceleration of the arm, and two posterior (rear) muscle groups that are involved in its deceleration. Impingement syndrome is, functionally, a strength imbalance between the anterior and posterior groups. In all pitchers we've tested, we've discovered that the posterior muscle groups are weaker, largely as a result of conditioning that aimed to increase arm speed without worrying about the arm's need to slow down. By proper understanding of the physiological process of throwing a baseball—taking it not just up to the release point, but all the way through the motion—we can produce that proper balance that will keep pitchers from developing arm problems in the first place. It requires rigorous weight training and constant attention to the program, but it can be done.

Baseball's 90% attrition rate can be reduced with proper application of a prehabilitation program. I believe this totally. Neuromuscular functions (strength, speed, power, skill) can be related to psychological components (motivation, experience, and emotion) and energy output (aerobic and anaerobic stamina work) to create a foundation that will help a pitcher maximize his performance—young or old, four-man rotation or five. Egos and ignorance aside, the economics of today's game is forcing a different approach on even the most die-hard traditionalists in an effort to improve the return rate on their investments in signings. Prehabilitation, properly applied, will lead to injury-free careers, a major advance from the too-frequent cycle of great years followed by pain, stints on the disabled list, a return to the same old habits, and then the specter of surgery and a lengthy rehab. We're using prehabilitation on the Rangers, and the arm problems that have come up in my time with the club have come from either pitchers who came to us from other organizations with the damage already under way or from guys who didn't follow the program properly. I know I'm way, way out on a limb on this subject, and if I go into the tank, you'll probably never hear of me again, but I'm absolutely convinced that this program is going to revolutionize how pitchers are trained. (Incidentally, we've also instituted pitch limits for those pitchers who have already had arm trouble in the past; prehab requires a clean slate.) Prehabilitation works; watch us.

WRIGHT:
A FINAL PITCH

It's true that evidence comes only from things that have already happened, but it is wrong to suggest that an examination of the evidence locks our perspective on the past. There are times—several right here in this book—where my vision of the possible future is as bold, radical, and challenging as anything that has passed Tom's lips. But I don't think this is an appropriate subject for flights of fancy. In this area I want to be practical and realistic in anticipating how things are likely to be changed.

Perhaps the difference between my perspective and Tom's comes from the position of influence he occupies. It's easy for Tom to get enthused about his new ideas coming into practice because he can make them happen in his world of Texas pitchers. He can say, "Throw footballs because it will help your mechanics," and footballs get thrown.

To meet my goal from my position, I have to take a more conservative stance. I've pointed out the relationship between superior mechanics and the more durable pitchers, but if you ask me if baseball is going to get heavily into "biomechanical optimization," I have to realistically say no. Same for nutrition and psychology. An emphasis on improved physical conditioning seems far more likely.

But when it comes to selecting a central area to emphasize, it strikes me as most realistic to focus on the way pitchers are used in the game. Baseball has shown a tremendous willingness to make adjustments in this area; they tinker with rest patterns, reduce the number of innings thrown, develop new relief roles, and cut back on the complete games. This approach has given them a certain amount of control over the problem. By these efforts and results I think we know a lot more about how the process might be refined. For me, this is the central path, and I don't think it is a mistake to choose it.

I think there is another element that should not be overlooked in emphasizing this path. Obviously, we are looking for an approach that can affect a wide range of pitchers. When the solution is a part of the game, you influence all pitchers. Tom's prehabilitation plan steps out of the game and into the larger life of the player. In that regard, it becomes a personal solution, or at least it should be. When it goes beyond being a personal option, I think we are treading on dangerous ground. I don't know that leading these horses to water is going to make them drink, and I'm not sure we have the right to try to make them. They didn't sign up for prehabilitation, they signed up for baseball, and I think the central solution ought to be based in the game.

Finally, let me address Tom's criticism of my idea of setting cautious pitch limits in the player development program, that my approach "will slow down the development of pitching prospects who *don't* have a propensity for sore arms—and there are such people, and we can identify them." I don't doubt that there are such people, though I don't believe we can identify them with the certainty that Tom suggests. But even if we had a confidence level of 90%, I'd still make the same recommendations.

The ceilings I suggest for a minor-leaguer in his early twenties are not going to hold back anyone's development. Those levels can produce a very normal season of work. I think the evidence is pretty clear that even those with the iron arms can benefit from lighter use in their formative years. The workload of a minor-league pitcher should give him enough innings to develop naturally and test himself against a professional use pattern. I've allowed for that. Why take the risk of going beyond that in the most vulnerable years of his career?

And I would point out that Tom's suggestion of waiting for a drop in velocity on three straight pitches isn't adequate. For one, not all pitchers will show fatigue in that manner. They can be gassed without any drop in velocity; their pitch location may start jumping around erratically instead. Second, I don't want my young pitchers constantly reaching an obvious fatigue level.

HOUSE:
ABOUT THOSE HORSES . . .

Craig, if we can't get those horses to drink we're the only professional sport that can't. Baseball's the only sport where this kind of program isn't being used. If when we sign a player we make it absolutely clear to him what we expect of him if he wants to stay in our organization, we've got every right to expect him to follow the program. And if we don't do this, we'll be following the same backwards path as everyone else in the game.

WRIGHT:
TURNING HORSES INTO MACHINES

I wasn't going to get into this topic, but here goes. I don't like the idea in any sport of building a superathlete in a way that unnaturally rules a person's life. I think it's dehumanizing, an unhealthy image for the fans, and ultimately hurts the sport's appeal. It doesn't bother me if a player *wants* to give his life over to such a program, but I don't think he should be forced to just because he wants to be a professional player.

And it isn't enough of a choice to say, "If you sign, this is how it's going to be." I don't think you'd lose any prospects, but if their heart wasn't in it, you would be exerting a pressure that might drive them out of the game down the road—and I'm talking about real players meant to play this game. Certainly I could see them retiring early out of a desire to regain control of their lives.

Such a comprehensive program for baseball players would be especially hard and abusive to their individuality. We're talking about a sport with very long careers and with many players already committed to year-round involvement, besides a demanding day-by-day season that can stretch from mid-February to mid-October. I could see such a path producing a lot of burn-outs and unhappy, shallow people.

Yes, it is fair to ask a professional player to condition and prepare himself to play, but there is a point out there where you cross a line morally and may even see it backfire in the results. I don't think Tom's broadest view of prehabilitation will ever come to life in baseball—which is the central reason I don't turn to it as a solution—and its possibility is disturbing to me.

IF IT AIN'T BROKE, DON'T FIX IT— IMPROVE IT

I'm basically a traditionalist at heart. I don't like change for the sake of change. I shudder when I hear a reasonable baseball person respond to a problem by saying, "We have to do *something!*" Too often, that means that he'll act on the first appealing idea that crosses his desk. This approach has sabotaged a lot of teams and whole organizations, and it's dangerous when it's applied to the game itself. The wisdom of "if it ain't broke, don't fix it" seems obvious.

But there is a world of difference between panicking and fixing something that isn't really broken and calmly, coolly, and carefully looking for ways to improve it. A lot of successful teams take their first step down when they become satisfied with their success rather than constantly moving forward. When they forget how they got to the top they lose what it takes to stay there.

The sport of baseball is much more stable than any one team, but it would be a mistake to think the game remains static. Nothing stays the same. The world around baseball changes, and the game itself can't help making subtle unplanned alterations with the passage of time. New pitches are discovered. Ballpark designs change. Fielding gloves are improved. New pitching roles are developed. But these evolutionary changes aren't necessarily positive. No one intended for baseball games to last three hours while providing the same action they used to cram into two hours. No one told the pitchers to become .140 hitters with no power.

The game of baseball has never stood still. Once no substitutions, except for injury, were allowed. Pitchers threw underhand. A walk first required nine balls, then eight, six, seven, five, and then four. At one time a batter was allowed a fourth strike if the third strike was called rather than swung on. The resiliency of the ball has changed several times, and the purpose of the fielding gloves has moved from protecting the fielder to helping field the ball.

The game often finds itself being remodeled by new developments in baseball strategy. Such maladaptations as overly long ballgames and increasing specialization of player roles seem to irritate many fans, but if these strategic changes don't always enhance our enjoyment of the game, there isn't any reason they should. The driving force behind new strategies has nothing to do with the welfare of the game. That isn't the concern of strategy; its purpose is to win ballgames. It is our mistake if we blindly give those forces complete responsibility for shaping the game.

Rather than relying on the luck of mutation, we can take direct responsibility for the future of the game. If we understand the appeal of the game, we can establish guidelines for measuring potential beneficial changes. Whenever I'm struck by an idea for improving the game, I look for its contributions to one or more of the following goals:

1. *Keep the offense going.* Follow the rise and fall of baseball's popularity through the years and the message is clear: The fans want offense. Bill James said it best: "Offense is making things happen. Defense is keeping things from happening. People would rather watch things happen."

2. *Eliminate the dead time in the modern game.* All the talk about the reflective pace of baseball has little to do with the way the modern game now drags on. This is not the pace that made people wax poetic about the lovely pauses built into the game. In fact, we passed the proper length about thirty-five years ago. In 1952, they were complaining because the average game was taking two hours and twenty-five minutes and only 147 games were played in less than two hours. Shoot, that would be flying

today. The average game is about 15% longer, and I can't remember the last game I saw come in under two hours. I am not necessarily looking for shorter games. You can do that by giving the pitcher the upper hand again and kill attendance at the same time. What we need is to just get the games moving again.

3. *Keep the game human and natural.* Sport is an expressive art form, a release of our archetypal feelings. What makes a sport successful is its ability to express or even meet the needs of that society's collective unconscious. Baseball gives us a moment's respite from our ties to a larger, complex society that runs our lives more than we do. Man in nature in small tribes where everyone knows the other; physical, thoughtful, complete, self-sufficient, strengths and weaknesses exposed and dealt with; a ball, a wooden bat, a leather glove, the grass below, the sun above, and man. This is a part of baseball's appeal, and we should be concerned with preserving it.

4. *Guard against specialization.* The longer a game exists, the more sophisticated it gets. The competition is so fierce that anything that works is likely to be repeated throughout the sport. This causes a leveling off of performance, and the impact of even a truly great player is reduced. There is a dulling of extremes that in turn places a new emphasis on smaller edges. The pressure to win generates specialized pitching roles, a greater emphasis on platoon matchups, and one-dimensional bench players.

    While specialization helps create new winning edges, it dehumanizes the game and returns us to an unpleasant aspect of the larger society from which we are trying to escape. Rather than honoring the individual who learns to cope with his weaknesses while living off his strengths, we move toward a game in which the best player is not an individual at all but a composite of players—one hitting righties, another hitting lefties, one hitting for power, another doing the baserunning, and yet another wearing the glove.

5. *Support variety in the place of specialization.* Trite but true, va-

riety is the spice of life and the spice of modern baseball. One of the blessings of the dulling pressure of sophistication is that while it rounds off specific performances, it also provides pressure to develop new styles or mixtures of styles to create new edges. The fact that the power hitter, high-average hitter, and the base-stealer co-exist in modern baseball is partially a response to this pressure. The more ways a player or team has to express winning value, the more we preserve the mystery that makes a baseball game so fascinating. We need to support that variety.

If we eliminate specialization as a solution to the pressure of sophistication, we will enhance the variety in the game. Forcing a player or team to play with weaknesses rather than just avoid them creates the space for greater extremes in performance. This larger differentiation in player skills would also open up the strategic options as both player and team learn how best to play around their weaknesses.

Before going on to my own pet ideas, let us first examine the most recent tinkerings with the game.

THE DESIGNATED HITTER

When I call for more variety in the game, I don't mean that we should allow the leagues to separate by the rules they play under. That doesn't put variety *in* the game, it simply adds differences that drive us apart. The mystique of two leagues doesn't come from their playing different games; if it did, we'd invite the NFL to send a team to the World Series. What makes the rivalry between the National and American Leagues so fascinating is that they play the same game, but only rarely face each other. It's one thing for the leagues to differ in style or strategy, but it is quite another to assault a central principle of the relationship: that they play the same game under the same rules.

I think Commissioner Ueberroth really missed the boat on this one. His real responsibility was to undo the error of his predecessor, which was to allow one league to play under different rules from the other. What baseball really needed from Peter the First was a laying down of the law that baseball will be played under one set of rules. Give the clubs one year to convince each other whether to DH or not to DH, then require a binding vote.

Personally, I've come to like the DH, but my main concern is for a resolution that would get us all playing the same game again. At the same time I don't think we can afford to let the "death before DH" crowd bully the decision. Dinosaurs may be nice to remember, but they are hell to live with.

I opposed the designated-hitter rule when it was first proposed. I didn't like the reasoning, which seemed to be a knee-jerk reaction to a momentary swing favoring the pitchers over the hitters. I also was repulsed by the idea of a player being allowed to hit without any defensive responsibilities. But the more I actually watched games under the DH rule, the more I began to like it. Then I began to understand why I liked it and why it was a legitimate improvement.

Certainly the added offense is a part of it. I like hitting, and I enjoy the pitching more when presented against a more threatening back-drop. It naturally follows that I don't particularly enjoy watching pitchers hit, although I know a few National League fans who like to lie about their delight in watching Nolan Ryan hit (1983–87: 28-for-317, .088, one home run, 107 strikeouts, and 17 "excuse-me" RBIs). Funny how they never used to mention this special delight before the DH controversy.

I still have trouble respecting designated hitters as real players, but they haven't irritated me as much as I thought they would. Some are aging stars who have hung onto their swings while age has knocked their legs out from under them. Some are key players recovering from an injury that momentarily keeps them out of the field. Some are regulars just getting a rest. And some are refugees from the artificial-turf speed explosion that took away their defensive jobs in right or left field. While none of these justifications really strikes my fancy, I prefer any of them to seeing a bunch of pitchers hitting .140 and being collectively outhomered by a Don Baylor having a bad year.

Most of the arguments against the DH have trouble holding water when you stop and think them through. I used to think the DH would be the death knell for the "complete player." Now I realize that is nonsense. The DH rule is not the problem but simply a reaction to the already existing problem. The modern pitcher is not a complete player, and he is not going to be one; his value as a pitcher is so central to his role that it overrides his other contributions, no matter how bad a hitter he may be.

This has to be obvious even to the "dump the DH" fans. Do they really believe that the National League is letting the pitcher hit? The constant bunting and pinch-hitting in the pitcher's slot is all an attempt to get around the fact that the pitcher is *not* a complete player.

The average number of at bats each National League team gives its pitchers is aboout 355. The rest go to a bunch of mini-DHs, players like Greg Gross, Lee Mazzilli, or Danny Heep. In 1985–87, Gross had only 172 chances in the field while playing in 294 games with 403 at bats. Is he a complete player? No; his real role is to hit for the pitcher late in a close game when a real batter is needed. He is essentially a mini-DH.

The designated-hitter rule just goes one step further in dealing with a reality and a need that cannot be legislated away. It does not follow that the DH rule will lead to defensive-offensive platooning as in football. Baseball's problem with the pitcher is unique. There is no other position at which a player can concentrate so much of his value into preventing runs that no one cares what he hits. Oh, some managers like to talk that way about some light-hitting shortstops with good gloves, but they certainly don't act on it. You don't see any .140 hitters at shortstop. Ray Oyler was an absolutely brilliant shortstop, but the only way he could get more than 255 at bats in a season was to hit a career high of .207. When he bottomed out at .083 as a late-inning defender at age thirty-one, he was history. How much thought would the Mets give to releasing Dwight Gooden if he hit .083 one season?

Another complaint about the DH rule is that it takes strategy out of the game, with the evidence being that the American League teams don't sacrifice or pinch-hit as much as the National League. But I question the claim that those differences really reflect what we mean by strategy. Strategy is more than just moves made by a manager;

true strategy requires choices, options, room for differences of opinion. Doing the obvious is not strategy. Batting the pitcher ninth is not strategy. Bunting with a .140 hitter in a potential sacrifice situation is not strategy. Pinch-hitting for the pitcher when you clearly need a hitter late in a game is not strategy.

The choices, the real decisions, the real differences of opinion between managers are *heightened*, not dulled, by the DH rule. You have to decide what kind of offensive player you want in that slot. With nine hitters you have strengths and weaknesses that change from day to day, bringing variety and new strategy to the making of lineups. Think about it: In the National League, even the best-hitting pitcher is considered such a weakness that he is *always* relegated to the ninth spot.

You want real bunting strategy? Watch the American League. When a Steve Buechele or Frank White lays down a sacrifice, you get a lot of folks looking at each other, asking, "Would you have done that?" Do you know which league has the most nonpitchers bunting? The American League. Do you know which league has the greatest variety between its teams in sacrifice totals? Bill James points out that the standard deviation is much higher for this category in the American League under the DH rule, another indication of the differences of opinion that are the signposts of real strategy.

The same thing can be said about pinch-hitting. The American League pinch-hits more for nonpitchers than the National League does, and there is greater variety in those decisions from team to team. By cutting down the use of automatic pinch-hitters for the pitcher in certain situations, you're saving more options for the true strategic decisions that may arise later in the game.

I like the DH rule because it adds to the offense without any dangerous tinkering with the relationship between the pitcher and batter. I like the DH rule because I don't have to watch the pitcher bat or see his ineptitude paralyze the strategic options of his team. Both those benefits would exist under a rule that would preserve the idea that a regular batter must have some defensive responsibility: Simply go with an eight-man lineup without including the pitcher.

What are the disadvantages to this rule? Well, it means a break from the traditionally sacred baseball number of nine, although it doesn't change the idea of nine against nine in the larger sense. It means more at bats for each player, which will mess up the significance of some records just as the move from the 154-game to 162-game schedule did. It also means that the slugger with bad hands or bad wheels is in trouble, but that is probably more an asset than a problem. The eight-man lineup would surely set a strong precedent against defensive-offensive platooning, as well as delighting fans like myself opposed to the specialization embodied in the designated hitter.

The problem with the records can also be turned into a plus. Despite the inevitable financial arguments against it, a shorter regular-season schedule would clearly be in the best interests of the game itself. Our most important games, the games that decide pennants and world championships, are being played in weather that has little to do with the game of baseball. With the eight-man lineup we could shorten the season back to 154 games and still have more plate appearances per lineup slot than in 162 games.

All in all, I prefer the eight-man lineup to the DH rule, which I prefer to letting the pitchers hit. I like the prospect of seeing the best hitters get an extra at bat in most games. I like the emphasis on the complete player.

THE TWENTY-FOUR-MAN ROSTER

Well, if you like complete players, you have to like this idea. The twenty-fifth man is generally a specialist just like the designated hitter, usually a pinch-hitter or a light-hitting late-inning defender who might also do some pinch-running. The only difference is that the DH meets a real need in the game while the twenty-fifth man doesn't. Eliminating that extra man does not go against baseball history; rosters used to be much smaller, as low as seventeen men early in this century. Players were expected to be more versatile, and it worked better than you might suspect.

The twenty-four-man roster has brought back some of this emphasis on versatility. Rangers third baseman Steve Buechele used to play second base and played it pretty well. With the smaller rosters that skill now means something. I like that; I think the fans like it. We can certainly identify with it. Versatility and small rosters are a big part of our own experience from the sandlots on up. Reducing specialization even a little by dismissing the twenty-fifth man has made some managers grumble and upset the player's union, but I don't notice many fans complaining. It still looks like baseball, and the minor leagues get by with even smaller rosters: twenty-three at AAA and twenty-two in AA. Twenty-four is also a more natural number for baseball, which seems to revolve around multiples of three. For me, the question is not whether twenty-four is better than twenty-five, but whether we could get by with twenty-one.

SMALLER GLOVES

Fielding gloves really began to grow after the introduction of the Edge-U-Cated Heel in 1959. This new design eliminated the old open heel, which caused the glove to sit loosely on the hand. By providing a closing flex at the outer heel of the glove, it allowed the sides of the glove to more closely follow the contours and action of the hand and wrist. The hand could now reasonably control a much larger glove.

I have no beef with the Edge-U-Cated heel; it isn't the culprit here. It's a real blessing in its ability to make the glove work more as part of the hand. It's a delight to field with and pleasing to watch as it brings out more of the fielder's dexterity. But it has allowed the development of gloves so big that they take over the play, substituting in some ways for a fielder's skill and certainly dehumanizing it.

The game was originally designed to be played bare-handed. Gloves were introduced to protect the hand and allow the defender to field hard smashes rather than prudently letting them go by. I believe that somewhere between those and the monster gloves of the present is the ideal fielding tool. Whenever I've used my little brother's Little League glove, or on the two occasions I've had to field with an old pre-1920 glove, I've enjoyed the challenge and come away feeling more involved and confident as a fielder. It's difficult to explain, but I've found a lot of players, both amateur and professional, who have had similar experiences. Fielding with small gloves is not that hard, and it's oddly satisfying for the fielder. How it would look from the stands, I don't know.

I do know that with the Edge-U-Cated heel, the fielding artistry we love so much would remain even with much smaller gloves. What we would give up would be the consistency with which certain plays are made and the "netting" action of so many catches with the larger gloves. Overall, I believe the concept of smaller gloves would go over pretty well with the fans.

The smaller gloves would create three distinct improvements in the game. One, they would help the offense a bit. Two, they would provide a new emphasis on the human element in the game. Three, they would provide more variety by strengthening an option for the hitter—that of putting the ball in play and on the ground. I am also pretty sure it would create clearer differences in fielding skills among the individual fielders.

The rule book already controls the size of the gloves, so the precedent for the change is already in place. The glove should still provide protection, but otherwise I say let the hand in the glove play as big a role as possible. I propose we drastically reduce the size of fielding gloves so they barely extend beyond the fingers of a large hand, with a webbing barely wider than the ball itself. I have no objections to the first-base mitt being a couple inches longer with a wider web, and the catcher's mitt could remain as is, perhaps with a reduction in the maximum circumference from thirty-eight inches to thirty-two.

FOUR BALLS/THREE STRIKES?

One thing I will not propose is tampering with the ball-strike count. The idea of fiddling with the number of balls and strikes is a fairly common one. Charlie Finley often mentioned the possibility, citing a motive close to my heart: speeding up the game. Back when the DH rule was first being considered, some thought was given to changing the number of balls and strikes to favor the hitter. Proponents correctly pointed out that baseball fooled around with the number of balls and strikes several times in the nineteenth century. Most of the time it involved reducing the number of balls required for a walk. The change most commonly advocated is three balls/three strikes, which may seem symmetrical, but baseball has never had an era when a walk did not require more balls than the number of strikes allowed a batter. This leads some to propose the even more disastrous three balls/two strikes system.

The three ball/two strikes rule would be absolutely deadly to our carefully balanced and beautiful game. The problem is that a "three-two" rule makes the batter-pitcher confrontation a first-pitch battle. The batter could be immediately facing a strikeout if he did not hit a first-pitch strike or potential strike. This would turn everyone into contact-conscious first-ball hitters, making hitting more talent-based than skill-oriented. It would destroy the strategy of hitting and signal the extinction of the power hitter, whose game is often built on discipline and pitch anticipation. Under this rule he could no longer afford to guess and take a tough or unanticipated strike.

The tendency for more first-ball hitting under a "three-two" rule would also mean far fewer pitches per game—so few that the top pitchers would probably be throwing complete games practically every time out while working in four-man rotations, possibly three-man rotations. The four-hundred-inning pitcher would be reborn, and baseball offense would probably reach a new low in the Live Ball Era.

The game might be able to survive under the three ball/three strike proposal. It would push the pitcher to throw strikes early and keep him from wasting pitches when he does get ahead in the count. The offense would be improved; the games would be quicker, or at least have more action. Why, then, do I oppose it?

My opposition centers on two points. First, it would drive a lot of talented pitchers away from the game who simply do not have the control to survive in a situation in which three balls is a free pass to the batter. Far more important, it would destroy the variety and balance in the game by changing over to an offense built on power and walks. We know that starting a modern hitter with a 1–0 count— which is exactly what this rule does—improves power more than batting average and drives the walk rate sky-high—about a 69%

increase. It would create a game in which fielding ability just doesn't matter that much. It is difficult to defend against power hits and impossible to catch a walk or a ball in the seats. The high-average hitter, the glove man, the base stealer, any nonpower player, all of them would diminish in importance, and many would be run right out of the game. No Vince Colemans or Alfredo Griffins in this game. And the pitchers would be dominated by control artists with no place for a young Nolan Ryan or a Phil Niekro.

For me, the four ball/three strike rule is a crucial point of balance in the game. I may be underestimating the ability of the players to adjust to the pressure inherent in the "three-three" proposal, but why take the chance? The unstated wisdom behind "if it ain't broke, don't fix it" is to avoid taking the chance of breaking something that is already working. We cannot afford to take such a chance with this beautiful sport. There are too many other, less risky options that would speed up the game and give a boost to the offense without threatening the delicate balance that makes the game work so well.

IMPROVING THE RUNNING GAME

We are living in a very special time in the Live Ball Era. This is the first time in baseball history that speed and power have flourished at the same time. The key is that the modern base-stealer has a much higher success rate than in past eras, which justifies the gamble even in a big-bang offense. It is in the game's interest to protect that success rate, and perhaps even to raise it.

Some of the gains we have made come from improved stealing techniques, the ability to run faster on artificial turf, and pitchers using slower deliveries that put more of the body into the pitch. I believe those advantages have pretty much peaked, and we are now entering an era when baseball is trying to legislate a healthy atmosphere for the stolen base.

This has been particularly true in the National League, where the umpires are very stringent in enforcing the balk rule. The number of balks per steal attempt is much, much higher in the NL than the AL, sometimes 90% higher and rarely below 30%. The pitchers and base-stealers traded between the leagues often say the NL umpires are much tougher in what they allow the pitchers to do in holding runners on first.

And, of course, in 1988 baseball issued a specific directive to the umpires calling for a discernible stop before the pitcher could come out of the set position. A lot of different reasons have been given for this change, but stated or not, there was an obvious assumption that it would enhance the running game by making it harder for the pitcher to rush his delivery and fool the runner. As I write this, we are about two-thirds through the season, and it's hard to see where it has helped the running game, except possibly to set off more balk calls. The success rates on steals in both leagues are about the same as in '87.

The biggest assist the umpires have given the running game actually took place the year before the new balk rule was ordered. In 1987, the success rate jumped dramatically to set all-time highs in both leagues. That seems a bit too much of a coincidence. I'm convinced that in some way it was indicated to the umpires that they were to crack down on the "phantom tags" on stolen-base attempts.

For years the umpires had been hurting the running game with a strong penchant for calling base-stealers out if the play was close. Some seemed to call it by when the ball got there rather than by the tag. Some seemed to dislike the headfirst slide; they assumed that if you had to go in headfirst, you must be in trouble, so you're out.

In 1983–85 I scored approximately four hundred games and noted any call in the field when a replay showed the umpire was obviously wrong. The play botched most often, by far, was the call on steal attempts. Hey, I know this is a tough call to make: It's easy to get screened; you have to call a tag in what is usually a bang-bang play; and the position you really want is going to put the back of your head right in line with the catcher's throw. Still, none of this explains why, when the umpires missed the call, they called the runner out almost six times as often as they called him safe.

This looks a lot like umpiring by the path of least resistance. When you call a base-stealer out on a close play, you are surrounded by four players (pitcher, center fielder, second baseman, and shortstop) who will say, "Nice call," and there is only one runner who is going to jump up and yell, "What?!" before leaving you on the field with your four good buddies. And, of course, the crowd can't see the tag, but they can follow the throw, so why not play it safe and call it more by the throw than the tag?

One reason is that blowing calls against the base-stealer puts a tremendous crimp in the running game. To come out ahead, a base-stealer generally needs to steal two bases for every one caught stealing. That's hard to do when you never get the benefit of the doubt on a close call. Well, that started to change in 1987. I no longer keep track of the blown calls in the field, but it was very noticeable to me that the umpires were sticking their noses into that play and more frequently calling the actual tag rather than how fast the ball reached the fielder. It was the only thing I saw that could account for the record-setting success rates.

There are other legislative suggestions that crop up from time to time to assist the running game. We could make the fake pickoff moves to second and third base illegal. There's no reason that this should be a balk only for a runner on first base. And Bill James has suggested that we allow the pitcher only three throws to first base per batter. If he doesn't get him the third time, the runner goes to second and is credited with a stolen base.

Bill's suggestion is especially intriguing. The crowd hates all those throws to first base. I once saw Charlie Hough throw over to first base nineteen times in one inning. His own home crowd started booing him after the first five. What bothers me about the three pickoff proposal is that we can't really predict how it will affect the game. Its proponents assume that the pitcher would usually throw over to first base just once. He won't want to take the chance of missing on a second attempt, which would put the base runner in the driver's seat, knowing that the pitcher couldn't throw over unless he was sure he had him picked off. That would be the ideal result. Things would be pretty much the same; the game would move a little quicker, and the leads would be a little bigger.

What I am afraid will happen is that the base runners will push the situation to a point where pickoff battles would become inevitable.

Getting back to first base would become as big a goal as stealing second. Pitchers would be just as slow or slower in working with men on base; they just wouldn't actually throw the ball to first. They would keep backing off the rubber, taking more time between pitches, and pausing longer in the set position to try to freeze the runner or waiting for the right moment to throw over, usually causing the batter to step out of the box so the whole process could start all over again. All of this is going to distract from the more interesting battle between pitcher and hitter. And accenting the importance of each pickoff throw will pressure pitchers to try to circumvent the balk rule as much as possible, adding to the importance of a vague rule that is incapable of uniform enforcement.

I would like to *totally* reshape the rules of the running game. I want to eliminate the whole idea of holding the runners. It's boring, it slows down the game, and it sets off such a complexity in rules and interpretations that the fans can't follow it. The vast majority of fans don't understand the balk rule. I'm a real student of the game, and I don't understand everything that can be called a balk.

But I don't want to throw out the baby with the bath water. I want to keep the advantages of speed and the strategic options of putting a man in motion for either a steal or a hit-and-run. What I propose is that we go with a set leadoff position, whatever number of feet off the bag seems to give the game proper balance. It would work this way:

1. Once the pitcher steps on the rubber, he cannot throw over to first base, the runners must stand square to the diamond (as they presently do), and they can't lead off any farther than the "leadoff marker."
2. After taking the set position, when the pitcher raises his front leg, the runners can take off if they wish. If we get a smart-aleck pitcher who tries to throw without raising his leg, then the runner can take off when the ball leaves his hand. If the runner leaves early, he's out.

It's simple, clear, and relatively easy to enforce. Instead of looking for twenty different things, the base umpires only need to line up their runners with a view of the pitcher's front leg. Heck, amateur umpires are called on to make similar calls all the time in softball. Think what would still be left in the game: Speed would still count; we'd still have base stealing and hit-and-runs. The pitchers would still vary in their ability to stop the running game—the pitcher with the high leg kick and big breaking ball would still get run on a lot. Shucks, I bet the base-stealers would still differ in their ability to get a "jump" by developing a rhythm that coincides with a reading of a pitcher's motion prior to lifting that front leg.

The game would move along faster, the officiating would be more uniform, and the fans would follow the game better. It also has the beauty of giving us an easy control over the running game. If things get out of whack, we can simply change the allowable leadoff distance. The baseball diamond is even a natural for setting the leadoff marker. The cutout of grass near the bases could be modified to correspond with the leadoff boundary. It may be too radical an idea to get much serious consideration, but don't tell me it wouldn't work.

PURE HALF-INNINGS: A BATTLE AGAINST SPECIALIZATION

Players have specific strengths and weaknesses. Those differences are a major part of what in-game strategy is built on. Unfortunately, the strategies we have developed rely heavily on a solution that works against the appeal of the game. We simply play around those weaknesses by pulling players and inserting others. It wasn't always like that. For the first fourteen years of the National League, no substitutions were allowed except in the case of injury or with permission of the opposing team. I don't think we have to go back that far. I suggest that we eliminate substitutions on a half-inning basis.

Consider the way baseball works right now. Say my name is George Brett. I am a feared hitter, especially against right-handed pitchers. I am the player the opposing manager is going to try to neutralize by making specialized substitutions. If the starting pitcher is tiring and puts men on in front of me, the opposing manager is not going to let him face me. He is going to try to stop me by substituting his most effective relief pitcher. He is certainly going to make the move if he can stack the deck by replacing a tiring right-handed starter with a lefty relief ace. His whole strategy will be aimed at stopping a ballplayer who is capable of giving baseball a unique and extreme performance.

Pretend I am Dwight Gooden, a power pitcher who eats up right-handers. I am cruising in a brilliant game when I start to tire just a mite, lose my concentration, and give up a double. Now the opposing manager pinch-hits for a right-handed second baseman who has trouble with my hard stuff. Instead, I have to face a lefty who hangs in well against righties and sees the fastball real well. That ain't gonna help my ERA, my win totals, my strikeouts, or my shutouts.

The same thing is true for a lesser player having a great day. If I am Joe Pitcher going for a shutout or a no-hitter in a close game, the opposing manager is going to make whatever specialized substitutions might neutralize my day in the sun. If I am Joe Hitter and find myself with four hits or three homers, in the eighth or ninth inning I am unlikely to get a chance to face the starter I hammered for seven innings. If anything, the opposition is looking for every edge it can find to cool my hot bat.

Well, some folks may start crying, "Why are you babying these guys? We want to see the best against the best." Fine. Go with your nine best fielders and nine designated hitters. Switch your pitchers anytime you want so Brett never faces a righty. I'll just go across the street and play racquetball, and don't get any ideas about coming on the court and hitting my backhands for me.

Look, the idea of baseball is that the hitter and pitcher go against nine guys. Aren't those odds steep enough already? That is the way the game was designed. The least we can do is honor that intent on an inning-by-inning basis. This "best against best" noise is a joke. Best against best would be Brett against Gooden, strength against strength. What specialization is really about is not matching player against player but pitting a player against his own weakness.

Now stop and think about that. Is that really what you want?

Rather than batter-by-batter substitutions, allow them only by the half-inning. You want to pinch-hit in the inning? You will have to anticipate and give your lineup changes to the umpire before your first batter steps in for the inning. You want a reliever? You will have to make your move while the teams switch sides. Instead of focusing on a single batter, the specialist strategy now has to deal with groups of batters.

What are the problems here? Some might complain that it eliminates too much strategy. Not so at all. Such a rule won't knock out the edges that make specialists possible; it just changes the way the manager can exploit them. Platoon factors will still play a role in the original lineup and cause potential lineup changes between innings when a new pitcher takes the mound. The bullpen will still have a lefty specialist to take on an inning when two of the first three batters are left-handed-hitting regulars. The relievers will still separate into middle relievers, short relievers, and stoppers. The real beauty is that the managers will have to think ahead and take visionary gambles with a great deal at stake, especially in making their pitching changes. And remember, gambling, the difference of opinion, is the essence of strategy.

One of my initial concerns for such a rule change was that the manager would occasionally be forced to stay with a tired pitcher too long, a dangerous practice for the health of the pitcher's arm. But on further reflection I became convinced that such a rule would ultimately help prevent such abuse. Under the present rules, managers are constantly pushing successful pitchers to get by just another batter or two, staying with an obviously tiring pitcher until a man reaches first base. Under my proposed rule the managers are going to be extremely leery of sending a tiring pitcher out there for another inning.

Baseball is a big-inning game. In about two-thirds of all games the winning team will score as many or more runs in a single inning than the losing team will in the whole game. Avoiding the big inning is what pitching and defensive managing is all about. The managers are not going to take a chance of being locked into an explosive big inning with a tiring pitcher. What the research really indicates is that it is the constant pushing of a pitcher past his endurance level over a long period of time that hurts him. That is far more of a problem under the present rules than under my proposal. There also is no question that this rule change would benefit the relievers by cutting down the number of times they have to warm up without getting in the game. Of course, we could always offer some protection from letting an inning get totally out of hand by allowing a pitcher to be removed if he faces the whole batting order in an inning

The difficult part in this proposal is how to guard against teams faking injuries to sneak in a strategic substitution. I believe this problem can be whipped by employing a three-fold defense. First, the injury replacement should require the umpire's approval. Second, the umpire will have the option to require the replacement to bat or throw from the same side as the "injured" player. (I think it needs to be optional for that rare situation when the injury is obvious and his team would be at a tremendous disadvantage if the option was invoked and the club did not have another rested left-handed pitcher or a natural left-handed hitter.) The third and best defense would be that if an umpire has to remove an injured or ill player in midinning, that player will be disqualified from future play for a certain number of games. I would suggest three games for a hitter, five for a reliever, and nine games for a starting pitcher to guarantee he misses a start.

This very simple rule against substitutions during an inning is loaded with benefits to the game. It works against the specialization that creates one-dimensional players. It gives more variety to player values. It creates a broader range of performance by treating our best players more fairly. Although the rule favors hitter and pitcher equally, overall it will favor the offense by taking away the batter-by-batter pitching changes that can defuse a potential big inning. And it will add to the excitement of the late innings since a potential big inning is more likely to happen late in a game when a manager might err in judging his pitcher's endurance.

A powerful side benefit to this rule is its potential to cut chunks of dead time out of the game. Managers won't be slowing down the game during the inning to make substitutions, and they won't have to play cat-and-mouse games that try to get the other side to show its hand first. Pinch-hitters will be in place, ready to go when the inning starts.

But this is all peanuts compared with the savings by eliminating pitching changes during the inning. No more stalling by the pitcher, catcher, and manager to ensure the relievers have had a chance to get loose. None of that breathless entertainment of watching the manager slowly trudge out to the mound, signal for a reliever, and then watch the reliever walk, trot, or drive in from the bullpen, followed by the riveting excitement of the reliever's warm-ups from the mound.

More and more these days, we see two or more pitching changes in the same half-inning. I recently attended a Rangers game in which the two teams combined for four pitching changes in one inning. What makes it particularly irritating for the fans is this generally happens just when the game is getting interesting, and usually toward the end of it. This may explain why so many fans leave games, even relatively close ones, before the ninth inning. I suspect the fans set themselves for the pace of the game in the first six innings, not realizing that the last two or three innings rarely follow that early pace. The fans start getting antsy as the game rolls past their estimate and into their postgame plans. Before you know it, they talk themselves into leaving a game they had really planned to see through its conclusion.

It is a beautiful rule; so logical and simple that it already feels like a part of baseball. Sometimes I think there is a ghost page in the rule book. It contains all the really good rules we have somehow overlooked. I believe at the top of the page you would find the simple instruction: "No substitutions are allowed during a half-inning except in the case of injury or illness."

IMPROVE THE UMPIRE, IMPROVE THE GAME

In recent years I've been sharing my view that the quality of umpiring has slowly been declining from the relatively lofty level of the 1960s. A number of longtime baseball observers have quietly agreed with that observation. One sportswriter in disagreeing suggested that this might be an illusion based on seeing a lot of Rangers games when the team was out of the race, the outcome meant little, and the umpires were less on their toes. My response: I rest my case.

No, that's not fair, since the umpiring in lackluster games could have been just as bad in the past. But I don't buy it. I also watched the Tigers play through some lean years in the seventies, and, yes, in my memory, the umpiring was better. Even when I look at World Series films I am impressed by the superior umpiring in the 1960s. They made more of an effort to get the call right rather than cruising and making the easy call, the one that looks right to the most people. It's worth trying to understand why things have changed.

Umpires are not machines, they are not totally neutral, and they have characters and distinct trends that can affect how ballgames are played and how they come out. For several years I used to have a section on my scoresheets that I reserved for comments on the umpires. From those notes, I began to realize there were distinct patterns in their calls.

I discovered one trend I had never really noticed before. A lot of umpires—a little more than a third of them—had a pattern of calling "eveners." It works this way: You call the close pitches according to whether the pitcher or hitter is behind in the count. If it is 2-1, the close pitch is a strike. If it is 1-2, it's a ball. Simple, but just one of many trends I never would have picked up without the notes.

Besides telling me who played eveners, they tended to point out who had trouble calling the breaking ball, who was inconsistent on location, who called high strikes, low strikes, wide strikes, strikes close to the batter. I saw who favored the veteran stars of the game, who called the balks, who rang up the false double plays, who called the tag plays by when the ball got there rather than by the tag. I saw who held grudges, who called for the home team, who got lazy in a boring game, who would avoid calling a third strike, and who was out of position in the field.

Take Larry McCoy. A sampling of some of my notations on him reads: "pitcher's umpire," "gives pitcher big plate with three balls," "not afraid to ring up called Ks," "calls strike on big breaking ball," "waits to call late break on knuckleball," "homer," "likes veterans." By "homer" I was indicating that he, on that day, seemed to be treating the home team a little better than the visitors. "Likes veterans" means I felt I caught him giving a break to either a veteran pitcher or batter. In his case, I can distinctly remember that when Carl Yastrzemski was in his final tour, the first pitch was a ball with McCoy behind the plate—even if it were right down the middle. The other comments, which come from several different scoresheets, all reflect his tendency to go with a larger strike zone, especially on the big breaking balls.

His opposite number would be Dan Morrison, who has a consistently tight, small strike zone and misses a lot of breaking-ball strikes. Still, he became a favorite of mine because he was consistent, fair, and seemed to really care about getting it right. You never saw "favors veterans" or "homer" in his notes.

Steve Palermo is generally cited as the best AL umpire, and my notes pick up a lot of that. He hustles for calls in the outfield. He calls the balks. He practically never plays eveners when behind the plate and has no qualms about calling the third strike. His strike zone is very consistent, though maybe a little low and wide. He is very firm about not calling the high strike. He also is one of the few umpires who really checks the time between innings to make sure the radio and TV people get their full two minutes (this is the second-base umpire's job).

Oddly enough, as meticulous as Palermo is in all his other duties, he is rather nonchalant on his calls of stolen bases. I have caught him nailing three runners who were actually safe, and in all three cases he seemed incredibly blasé and perhaps not in the best position— totally at odds with his overall style. When I took these notes in 1983–85, this seemed to be a common weakness among the veteran umpires and crew chiefs. The ones who hustled and got on top of the steal plays were from the younger set, like John Shulock, Mark Johnson, and Dan Morrison.

Everyone asks about Ken Kaiser, baseball's most visible umpire. My notes characterized him as an umpire who rises to the challenge. He'll call a great game when it's needed and be quite sloppy in a nothing game. A lot of nights I caught him calling flagrant "eveners." In the field he tends to ring up outs on anything reasonably close. He ends up nailing some safe base runners and gets a few false double plays, while rarely missing the other way except to bug Eddie Murray.

I don't know what Murray ever did, but he starts off in the hole when Kaiser is behind the plate. I once saw Kaiser eject Murray because he didn't like the way Eddie was looking at him. Seriously. However, I don't want to suggest that Kaiser has a long "hit list" for an umpire. He has a kind and forgiving nature next to that of Vic Voltaggio, who is consistently nominated as the champion grudge holder in the AL.

But I'd better stop this name-by-name analysis before I really get into trouble. Kaiser is also a good place to stop in that he is an excellent example of the kind of umpire we can help. I will say it again: Kaiser's a good umpire when he wants to be. I have seen him work beautiful games when he tries. Then he runs the game well and calls an accurate game behind the plate. He needs a little push, a little incentive to curb his laxness. A Palermo, who is a perfectionist at heart, just needs a critical reminder—which he will probably resent, but which I'd guarantee he'll work to erase.

Feedback. That would be the heart of my umpiring improvement program. If you want to successfully modify seemingly nebulous, almost surely unconscious behavior patterns, you have to have feedback. We have virtually everything we need to give our umpires quality feedback, thanks to our improved record-keeping and access to videotapes for practically every game played. If an umpire tends to favor the home team or the pitchers or the hitters, it will show statistically in a reasonable sample after you control the home-field advantage, the park effect, and pitchers involved. If an umpire misses one type of play over another, a video record of his missed calls should pick it up and possibly show why. If there are complaints that an umpire plays eveners or has an odd strike zone or has trouble on breaking pitches, that can be studied and documented.

The analysis of an umpire's work behind the plate is particularly tricky, but I am confident that even my primitive limited study chased very few ghosts. The study of umpires is not a total vacuum. Dave Driscoll has done statistical studies on home-plate umpires in Blue Jays games, beginning with his *1985 Blue Book: A Statistical Analysis of the Toronto Blue Jays* and repeated for 1986 in his book *Jays Jazz*. And Richard Kitchin from the Society for American Baseball Research did a study of the game totals with each umpire behind the plate for 1986 and 1987. *The 1988 Elias Baseball Analyst* included a brief statistical analysis on the umpires. Their data consistently tend to back up many of the observations in my notes.

For example, Dan Morrison's unusually small strike zone was picked up in all four studies. Driscoll ranked him among the five best "hitters' umpires" in his 1985 study. Kitchin's data noted that walks are up and strikeouts are down when Morrison is behind the plate, and Elias pointed out his strikeout-to-walk ratio was the second worst among the thirty-two umpires who worked home plate at least ten times in 1987. The only one lower was Derryl Cousins, an umpire both Driscoll and I had noted as a hitters' umpire before the 1987 season.

I was particularly fascinated with Driscoll's 1985 data that noted the number of pitches per batter for each umpire. It turned out that eight of the nine umpires I tabbed as calling "eveners" had also called more pitches per batter than the average umpire in Blue Jays games. When you think about it, that makes perfect sense. With the average around 3.65, the nine averaged 3.83 pitches per batter. Between the two teams, they averaged 91 batters per game. That comes to an extra twenty pitches per game without involving any extra batters. We might also look at it as twenty pitches that were missed due to a trend that is probably controllable.

Kitchin's data were unique for their attention to balk calls. In 1986 the NL crew of Froemming-Davidson-Kibler-Marsh called 34 balks per 100 games umpired, while the crew of Brocklander-DeMuth-Montague-Rennert-Weyer called about *80%* fewer balks per game (six per 100). In the AL the crew of Clark-McKean-Morrison-Shulock called the balk more the way your average NL crew did, which gave them nearly five times as many as the AL crew of Barnett-Bremigan-Hirschbeck-Roe (a paltry three per 100 games).

Okay, if we have established that these differences exist and if we assume they could be corrected, what would it mean to the game? It could speed up the game a bit; eliminate "eveners" and you have fewer pitches, which means less fatigue and fewer pitching changes. Better calls on the bases and consistent enforcement of the balk rules would help cultivate the running game. And, of course, this would help the offense—always a plus for the fan's enjoyment of the game. A clearer, more consistent and definitive strike zone would also add more variety to the expression of pitching and hitting strategies. Remember, all the strategy that comes out of the four ball/three strike format is based on the assumption that a strike is a strike and a ball is a ball.

We rely on the umpires for this; they do a good job, and we can help them do a better one. I also can't help adding my personal belief that good umpiring adds class and integrity to the game and may help hold down the circus atmosphere that seems to be more and more a part of big ballgames. Let the umpires lead the way in concentrating on the game. We need them to ignore the crowd, ignore the drama of a no-hitter or a veteran seeking a record career accomplishment. We rely on their integrity to give real meaning to greatness.

Where do we start this reform movement? First, let's dump this outrageous practice of having two separate staffs of umpires. Consolidate the rules and the umpires and promote major-league baseball rather than American League or National League baseball. At least it will make travel easier on the umpires; there could be longer stays in double-team cities, and less distance to travel to the next city.

Second, we need to create a statistical bank to assist in the study of the appropriate forms of evidence. Third, we need to create a video review system for missed calls in the field. We could add to the duties of the official scorer the job of noting each play in the field that according to the replay was obviously incorrect. That list would be used by the home team to make up a videotape of those errors which would be sent to the "umpire review office," or whatever we call it.

Fourth, we need to encourage the individual teams to make their complaints about the officiating to the same office. We should guarantee anonymity and require a complete videotape of the game for complaints about ball-strike calls. I would also suggest sending a spot-checker out into the field to do evaluations and to interview managers and catchers to see whether their complaints form a pattern worth investigating.

Fifth, put some teeth in the review process by allowing the assessments to determine postseason assignments, and give the review board the power in extreme cases to remove an incompetent umpire who is making no progress.

While this is being done, we should try to improve the officiating by removing some of the pressures that lead to poor officiating patterns. I'm absolutely convinced that the average umpire feels real pressure to follow the path of least resistance. Consider these trends:

1. As covered in the chapter on home-field advantage, the evidence suggests that the umpire's ball-strike calls subtly favor the home team. That is the path of least resistance; more cheers, fewer jeers.

2. In the field, the majority of missed calls favor the defense. Again, the path of least resistance. The defense gets to remain on the field and complain about a close call. The runner who is called out has to leave you in peace eventually.

3. The highest incidence of missed calls in the field are at second base, where the umpire does not even have a base coach to rag him about a close out call.

4. Many umpires call tag plays at all bases according to when the ball got there rather than by the tag itself. Path of least resistance? You bet. Everyone can see when the ball got there. They can't always see the runner's leg sneaking by the glove and leading to a high tag on the thigh. Call him safe, which he is, and everyone who wants him out is screaming. Call him out based on the ball beating him, and there is a touch of doubt in the minds of those who saw him as safe.

5. The fairly common practice of calling eveners at the plate is a path of least resistance. They are calling the borderline pitch in favor of the batter or pitcher by a pattern designed to keep the intensity of their complaints at a minimum. The player in position to be least damaged by the call gets the call.

6. The same thing goes for those who don't call eveners throughout the count but resist calling the third strike on a hitter. A hitter may forgive a bad strike call for the first or second strike,

but if he thinks you missed a called third strike on him, you know he is going to howl.

Does this mean a manager should try to outcomplain the opposing manager? Well, in one sense, yeah, sure, but you have to realize this general trend doesn't apply to all umpires. Some like to be abused. It gives them a reason to show their authority and give you a hard time. Incidentally, I think that type of personality makes an absolutely horrible umpire.

Overall, I think most umpires will not respond to constant complaining unless there is some doubt in their own minds. Loud complaints over a legitimate beef may actually help a team—but it hurts baseball. It delays the game, undermines the respect of the umpire, hinders his own sense of judgment, and creates a confrontational atmosphere between umpires and managers and players.

If I'm correct in my contention that the quality of umpiring has slipped in the last twenty years, it is probably due to a combination of factors including their increased job security and unionized protection. However, I don't consider that the chief factor by a long shot. If we have trouble here in River City, it is because we have done too little to support and enforce respect for the umpires. Having failed to do this, we only increase the pressures that drive them down that path of least resistance.

How did we let it get so far away from us? I believe it started when the players started getting the big money and became bolder and more vocal with management. Would anyone disagree that the modern player has an inflated view of his place in the game and less respect for authority compared with just twenty years ago? I think that carries over onto the field and to their relations with their umpires. And because the players are the ones the fans identify with, the problem runs like electricity up into the stands. The bolder and more disrespectful the players are to the umpires, the more the crowd picks it up, and then the two groups just seem to feed off each other's ire.

In this sense, it isn't the baseball of the 1940s to the 1960s, and it's foolish to expect the umpires to control the game with only the same support system used in those very different times. The game needs to reshape the image of the umpire and what he is expected to take in the course of the game. I favor a crackdown through the traditional channels, but I think it has to come down so hard that it stands out from anything that has happened in the past. I say we sit the teams down and tell them in the clearest terms possible that a new era has dawned. Treat the umpires with respect on the field or expect to take a hike. I am talking about sitting down the umpires and saying don't hesitate to tell a disrespectful player, coach, or manager to go have a seat in the clubhouse. If you wait until you're angry to give someone the heave-ho, you have waited too long. If you think a player or manager is overdemonstrative in his argument in such a way that it incites the crowd, toss him no matter how strong his point or how clean his language. I want the umpires to know that even if they feel they missed the call, they don't have to let anyone go berserk and delay the game. Tell the offender that you called it as you saw it, and if he isn't off the field in five seconds, he can keep going when he hits the dugout.

I am calling for swift and immediate ejections without regard for the value of the player being tossed. I think the umpires should have the authority to add a one-game disqualification or suspension at their discretion on any ejection. This would help quiet the complainers who really let it fly late in the game when an ejection will only cost them an inning or two. An ejection should also carry an automatic fine of one or two days' pay. A one-minute deadline to vacate the field after an ejection is also long overdue. It certainly doesn't help the situation to allow a player or manager to stay on the field screaming at an umpire for a couple of minutes after he's been tossed. If he can't find his way off the field in that reasonable time, let him miss the next game or two. I also think we need to aggressively fine managers, coaches, and players who make derogatory comments about the umpires in the media.

I'm not interested in letting the umpires off scot-free here. There should be fines and suspensions for umpires who have taken to arguing and baiting players and managers. If an umpire has to turn to say something to the dugout, it had better be because he is sending someone to an early shower. And any umpire who even jokes in the media that he has one strike zone for one player and another for all the rest should consider himself lucky if he is ever allowed to take the field again.

To really make this work, we have to provide the players, coaches, and managers an alternate way to vent their frustrations. When they grumble to the umpire, they should be able to spit out, "You can count on that one going to the league office!" Any player, not just managers and coaches, should have the right to file whatever kind of report he wants and be assured of anonymity. The umpires should be assured that if a complaint is not backed up solidly by a review of the evidence, it goes absolutely nowhere—not to their feedback file and not to any evaluation file.

Eventually the dust will settle, and we can start counting the bodies. I trust one of them won't be the well-being and popularity of the game. I don't expect to see the players or managers bowing respectfully to the umpires after a close call, as they do in Japan. I do believe we could realize a goal of quality umpiring, the likes of which have never been seen before; that the managers and players will treat umpires with the respect the position deserves even in times of badly blown calls; and the fans, following the players' lead, will let the umpires fade into the background where quality umpiring should be. I may be dreaming here, but I don't see the danger of trying, and I do see a number of positive side benefits that would emerge even if we fall far short of that goal.

From smaller gloves to nine-on-nine innings to umpire feedback. Who would guess that such a beautiful game would have room for so many improvements? The appropriate way to look at it is to remember that baseball has made hundreds and hundreds of changes as it evolved and can be counted on to make many more in the future, far more than the number I have proposed here. It's just a question of time. Evolution is a slow process. Sabermetrics in this case is simply trying to speed up that process and avoid the dead ends. These ideas for improvement should not be judged by their number but for their quality. If they favor the game, they deserve consideration.

HOUSE:
CHANGES FOR THE BETTER

It may have dawned on you by now that I'm not your basic good ol' boy pitching coach. I think baseball's a wonderful game, with time-honored traditions and rituals, and I know that part of its charm is that the game is so much like it was back when Babe Ruth and Cy Young were playing. I'm definitely a baseball traditionalist, but only when it comes to those traditions that enhance the game.

Like everyone else, I can find a few things to tinker with here and there. I agree completely with Craig's comments about the umpiring. Job security for the umpires is one of the worst things to happen to baseball in a long, long time. I think the attitude, the work ethic, the whole image of umpires in the American League—I can't speak for the NL—is a lot worse than when I was playing. It's like the tenure system in our schools—when the umps know their jobs are secure, they've got no reason to try to do them well. We're just promoting mediocrity. There's about 10% of the umpires who have no business working in the majors—I'd make sure that they get the right kind of feedback, and if they don't improve, I'd ship them right out.

We took a real step backwards this past year with the new interpretation of the balk rule. The rule calls for a discernible stop, right? Well, what's discernible to an umpire can depend on the pitcher, the manager, the time of day, what he had to drink last night, etcetera. Even with the strike zone, which varies from umpire to umpire, you get to know what someone's calling. There is nobody, and I mean *nobody*, who's consistent about calling the discernible stop. What we did was to change the way we were interpreting a rule and changed it in a way that really emphasized the presence of the umpires, the men who, when they do their jobs best, are supposed to be invisible.

Okay, we can hope that was just the 1988 freak show. Here's one that can last a little longer: *Put away the radar gun!* Oh, it's got its uses, but most of the time we try to judge a pitcher purely on his raw gas, and not so much on how he pitches. Maybe I'm a little biased, because my best fastball was clocked at 82 m.p.h. on a "quick" gun, but I believe the gun should be used as an indicator, not a decision maker. It can tell us when a pitcher's getting arm-weary— the speed on both his fastball and curveball will drop significantly and consistently—so the manager can bring in a fresh arm, and maybe not make a young pitcher throw past what Craig calls his fatigue level. But I wouldn't use it to judge someone in the sense of good or bad. The gun can't tell you about movement, it can't tell you about location, and it can't tell you about a pitcher's ability to deceive the hitters. We shouldn't preclude the variables in favor of raw gas.

Though it isn't my field, I have one suggestion for the hitters: Make the clear plastic face mask a part of the helmet. A baseball coming at a hitter at 90 m.p.h. is a fearsome thing. Don Slaught went to the face mask after his nose and cheekbone were shattered by Oil Can Boyd, and it helped him come back. But it would be even better for preventing serious injuries in the first place. It sure would have helped Tony Conigliaro and Dickie Thon to have been wearing helmets with face masks.

The progression in baseball has been from the hat, to the hat with a hard liner, to the hard hat, to the helmet and ear flap. Protecting the face would be the logical next step. Although Slaught had some problems with the mask, others who have tried it talk about the "cone of concentration" it gave them. Art Howe, who wore one after a beaning, said, "It's like the pitcher was in a tunnel. Just him and me and the ball." And that's the way it should be.

These are small changes, little things that wouldn't really change the game all that much. But there's a really big change I'd like to make that wouldn't change the game on the field but would sure help change the players, and for the better. My biggest criticism of baseball is how incredibly backward we are about player development. Even the best organizations in baseball have an 85% to 90% attrition rate. It's time for us to act, not just react, and change the way we identify, train, and support our athletes.

Professional baseball is a unique subset of life. It's almost a culture of its own. No matter how physically or mentally gifted an athlete may be, when he signs a contract he is being reborn into an unusual and potentially threatening environment. His survival will be a function of how he adapts to the demands of this unfamiliar setting. The baseball life is a vagabond existence, it's played out in a fishbowl, and it's loaded with stressful situations both on and off the field. Stress on the field can help fuel an athlete's competitive fires; whether it does nor not, its effects will show up in his performance. But stress from just living the baseball life is only now being recognized.

We thrust mere babies into an environment in which they're surrounded by strangers of varying intelligence levels, ethnic backgrounds, and communications skills, and we ask them all to live and work together seven days a week for seven and a half months. Ballplayers spend more time with some truly incompatible teammates than they do with their wives and children. And the game, by necessity, gets top priority if they are going to survive. All things that other people consider "normal" are of secondary importance. And if someone isn't able to adjust to this weirdly skewed set of values, he gets thrown by the wayside. Talk about a stressful situation! And we expect the young player to find order and meaning in this with no particular help or guidance. It wouldn't work in the business world, and it doesn't work in baseball.

We need to use psychological testing, as I've proposed elsewhere in discussing prehabilitation, to find those athletes who are best suited to this particular grind. And we need to work with those we do sign to counsel them on how to cope with this unusual way of life. We can't keep throwing players into the deep end of the pool and asking them to swim.

WRIGHT:
SOUNDS GOOD, BUT . . .

I'd like to make a couple of quick comments on two of Tom's suggestions. I'm ambivalent about the clear plastic face mask. Don Slaught is a friend of mine, and I felt that blow more personally than others I've witnessed. As a fan, I was appalled to see Dickie Thon struck down when I believed he was the most valuable talent in the whole National League. But there is definitely a downside to this kind of idea that is often overlooked. As we provide the batter with more protection, whether by equipment or in the rules, he becomes more daring in putting his body on the line—and perhaps the pitchers become more willing to throw dangerous pitches.

It's a fact that more batters are hit by pitches right now than in any other era in this century. I would also bet that more players are hit in the head than at any other time. I believe strongly in the batting helmet, and even in the ear flap, but I wonder if there isn't a point at which we do more harm than good. The rules aimed at punishing the beanball, combined with the improved equipment, have made batters more and more willing to dig in at the plate and lean in. When that pitch up and in comes, the one they think the pitcher "can't" throw, they're just not as ready for it as they were when beanball wars were a part of the game. Maybe preserving a little fear is the best protection we can offer. I'm not saying that's true in this case, but it's worth thinking about.

Tom's comments about reducing the minor-league attrition rate disturb me. I'm all in favor of anything that can help these youngsters adjust better to the peculiar life-style of the professional ballplayer, but I'm suspicious of any attempt that reduces the number of minor-league jobs. Although that may not be Tom's intention, that's going to be the inevitable consequence. You have to remember that the minor-league attrition rate is essentially a manufactured level. There are only so many major-league jobs, and they are held for x number of years. Beyond those two factors the minor-league attrition rate is solely determined by how many minor-leaguers you have.

Tom believes that with careful testing and a better selection process we could eliminate a lot of those minor-leaguers who ultimately aren't going to make it anyway. That is a dangerous assumption. A common characteristic of the most productive farm systems is that they have more minor-league teams than the other organizations—in other words, they have more players to choose from in the first place. That's not a guess or a theory—that's a fact. I'd have to be pretty thoroughly convinced that my testing program worked before I'd fly in the face of that fact by reducing my artificially high "attrition rate."

There are a lot of productive major-leaguers who were originally signed as minor-league filler talent rather than as clear prospects. Glenn Hubbard was signed not because he had major-league tools but because he was a hustling son of a gun who would be a good guy to fill out an A-ball team. Luis Polonia of Oakland got his first pro contract primarily because he was bilingual and could serve as an interpreter on a rookie league team with a lot of Latin American players. Pete Rose was borderline when he signed; so was Joe Morgan. The more room we have in the minors, the more room we have for the development of these types of players. Now Tom may argue that proper testing wouldn't overlook guys like Hubbard, Polonia, Rose, and Morgan, and it would cut some of the other dead weight. Maybe, maybe not. I'd rather combine the two: Refine the selection process, but hold open the number of minor-league jobs for the "I-may-be-mistaken" ballplayers.

HOUSE:
WINNING THE WAR OF ATTRITION

I'll get to Craig's point about the attrition rate in a moment, but I just want to add one thing about the face mask. One reason we see so many hit batsmen these days—and we'd see an awful lot more if the umps weren't throwing guys out of the game so quick—is the Charlie Lau/Walt Hriniak school of hitting. Lau directed hitters to throw themselves into the pitch with their weight shift, and if you're setting up to do that on an outside pitch, it's real tough to react to that ball that busts you inside. No matter what we do with the equipment, I don't think we'll ever take fear completely out of the game. No one's more padded and protected than a hockey goalie, and I'd bet the fear level, if there was some way to measure it, is no less today when a puck comes at your face than it was back before anyone wore masks.

Now to the attrition rate. Did I say anywhere that I wanted to reduce the number of minor-league jobs? I don't—absolutely do not. I just want to see our organization get more out of the people it has signed.

Baseball has pretty much left everything to genetics; we'll do some training, but for the most part players are on their own. We can do better, and if we do it will be to our advantage, even without reducing the number of minor-league teams. If an organization is better able to produce major-league talent, that gives it more options when it comes to picking players, making deals, even just having qualified backups in case of injury. That's the goal of improving our methods of identifying and developing players.

In the early days of the farm system, Branch Rickey had an enormous advantage over everyone else because he had so many more teams, and thus more potential major-leaguers in his system. In today's game, you can't stockpile players the way Rickey could, but if you can do a better job of developing the talent you've got, you'll have all the same advantages. You'll have veterans being pushed to keep their jobs by the extra players you're bringing through the system, you'll have surplus to deal to fill your holes, and you'll even have the economic luxury of knowing you've got a lower-priced youngster to take the place of a higher-priced vet you're trading away. Since you can't have more players in the system, I say let's try to get more out of the players in the system.

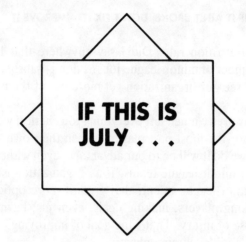

IF THIS IS JULY . . .

It wasn't so long ago that we could joke that few things in life were certain: death and taxes, the sun rising in the east, summer following spring, and some time in July the National League beating the American League in the All-Star game. From 1950 to 1982 the National League went 30–5 in All-Star competition (they played two All-Star games from 1959 to '62) for a winning percentage of .857.

Do you know how hard it is to play .857 ball, even for just 35 games? The 1986 Milwaukee Brewers got off to the hottest start in baseball history with 13 straight wins, but by game 35 they were down to a more realistic .571 figure. The closest match to the NL's domination of the All-Star game was the 1984 Detroit Tigers; on their way to winning 104 games, they started the season with an identical 30–5 record.

Consider this: .857 is the expected outcome when a .710 team (115 wins in a full schedule) plays a .260 team (42 wins). Okay, 35 games is a small enough sample that it could produce a large variation just by chance. For example, it became apparent over the whole 1984 season that the Tigers were really a .642 club and their opposition during the streak was .469 caliber. It's also true that the Tigers played a bit over their heads, as the normal expectation from their season's runs scored and runs allowed shows they were more like a .612 team. The expected outcome from a .612 team playing a .469 club would center around .630, not .857.

That still doesn't mean that, by comparison, the AL All-Stars were roughly a .470 team and the NL was a .630 team. If we use the Tigers as a model of what kind of team can play .857 ball over 35 games, we have to acknowledge a key difference between the scores in the Tigers games and in these All-Star games. The Tigers were much more dominant, outscoring their opponents 215 to 109; the NL squeaked by in several tight games in that thirty-three-year period, outscoring the AL by just 187 to 122. This suggests the two leagues were not as far apart in ability as the Tigers and their opponents were.

I won't bore you with all the complex calculations, but if a .612 team can go 30–5 against a .469 club while outscoring it 215–109, then the same record with a scoring differential of 187 to 122 could come from the meeting of clubs playing .528 (86 wins) and .472 (76 wins). So was this the approximate difference between the two leagues, or at least the disparity in the quality of their top stars? Possibly, but it's still tremendously difficult to call. The All-Star game is far from a typical game. Besides being an exhibition game, it's not even played by the same rules as regular-season games. You must use at least three pitchers, and none for longer than three innings. Your starting lineup is based on a vote that often reflects sentiment and popularity rather than performance. The rosters are overly large, and there's an agreement to use as many of them as possible.

The real debate over the All-Star results is whether they indicate a superiority of the talent of one league over the other. I would say yes, this was probably true through about 1965. It would be ridiculously naive to suggest that the leagues have always been equal in talent. It is also quite likely that when disparities exist, they show up in the meetings between the leagues in both World Series competition and in All-Star games.

Historically, it's reasonable to assume that the National League was superior as the more established league in the early part of this century, say, through 1909. You can see a hint of that in World Series play; the National League won two-thirds of the Series, with a .600 winning percentage in the individual games. The law of competitive balance turned on the National League from 1910–20; the American League was hustling to improve while the National League was becalmed by its success as the dominant league since 1876. The American League won nine of the 11 series, .625 for the individual games.

The National League jumped back into it in the twenties. It won four of the first six Series, but then ran into Ed Barrow's juggernaut Yankees. The strength of the Yankees kept the rest of the American League on its toes and helped make it the better league for over twenty years. From 1927 to 1949 the American League won 70% of the Series and 63% of the individual games. It also won 75% of the All-Star games.

The seeds of change were planted in 1947 when Jackie Robinson became a Brooklyn Dodger. The National League got a big boost when it became the first league to pursue black players actively. Because the National League was not yet signing the less talented black players, the first sign of their impact came at the All-Star level. In 1950, the National League All-Star team had two black starters in the lineup, Jackie Robinson and Roy Campanella, and the second pitcher to go into the game was Don Newcombe. The American League had Larry Doby starting in center field. He would be the only American-born black starter for the American League All Star team until Leon Wagner in 1962.

During that time the National League team was adding Henry Aaron, Willie Mays, Frank Robinson, Ernie Banks, Junior Gilliam, Johnny Roseboro, Maury Wills, and Bill White to its All-Star lineup. The National League, which had won only four All-Star games prior to 1950, won four straight from 1950 to 1953.

The National League would ride its edge in black stars for some twenty seasons. The free-agent draft would not come into existence until 1965, and given a choice, the young black stars wanted to sign with "Jackie Robinson's league." After all these years, it's difficult to fully remember how important Jackie Robinson was to the black community during his playing career. Willie Mays wore number twenty-four because it was the reverse of Robinson's forty-two. Henry Aaron asked to switch from the "honor" of a single-digit uniform number because he wanted to wear a double number as Robinson did, and went with his now-famous forty-four. Even today, you find a lot of double numbers worn by young black players who emulate the black stars who were originally honoring Jackie.

But there was more than just player preference operating here. The National League teams felt pressure to keep up with the Dodgers by scouting and signing their own black players. There was a time when the American League privately billed itself as the "white league," except for that irrepressible rascal, Bill Veeck, up in Cleveland. American League clubs looked to the Yankees as trend-setters, and they didn't let Stengel have a black major-leaguer until eight years after Robinson's breakthrough. Other AL teams shamelessly dragged their heels in signing black players. Neither the Tigers nor Red Sox played blacks in the ten years after Robinson's debut; the Red Sox continued to hold out till 1959.

By 1954 the edge was more leaguewide than just at the star level, and it could be seen in the World Series as well as in the All-Star game. From 1954 to 1965 the Yankees were the only American League club to win a World Series, and they still lost five of the nine they appeared in. The National League won two-thirds of the fall classics and had a .560 winning percentage in the individual games. This was no small feat, as the lack of parity in the AL put a large concentration of the league's talent into one team, the Yankees. The NL did even better when able to group its stars: During this period, it won 69% of the All-Star games.

The leagues began to even up in the late 1960s. The American League was freely signing black talent, working harder in the Latin American market, and hustling to stay competitive with the NL. The World Series records since then suggest that the leagues have never been closer. From 1966 to 1982 the NL was 9–8 in winning the World Championships, while the AL led 52–51 in individual World Series games.

Despite this new age of parity, the NL was still clobbering the AL in the All-Star game. In those seventeen seasons the AL was 1–16 in All-Star competition. It's true that there were some great battles in those games; in about half of them the game was tied or the NL was trailing into the seventh inning, and seven of its wins were by a single run. All the same, even a normal expectation from the runs scored and allowed would give the NL a distinct advantage of 13–4.

A key factor during the first half of this era was that the NL still had a clear edge in the depth of *star* talent. This was the residue of the National League's edge in signing the best black talent before the draft was instituted in 1965. Even when the American League was pushing hard to be competitive in scouting and signing black players, those with a real choice—the ones with the kind of star potential that guaranteed serious suitors in both leagues—tended to sign with the National League.

Look at the distribution of black All-Stars coming into baseball before the draft. Joining Robinson, Campanella, Irvin, Aaron, Banks, and Mays as a new generation of black NL superstars: Fergie Jenkins, Willie McCovey, Bob Gibson, Billy Williams, Lou Brock, Willie Stargell, and Dick Allen. The American League had to settle for the lesser stars like Willie Horton, Mudcat Grant, Reggie Smith, Tommie Agee, Carlos May, Rod Carew, Blue Moon Odom, Roy White, George Scott, Al Downing, and Paul Blair. That group had trouble competing with just the second level of the NL's black stars, players like Bobby Bonds, Jimmy Wynn, Curt Flood, Alex Johnson, Vada Pinson, Tommy Davis, Willie Davis, Dock Ellis, Don Wilson, and Al Oliver.

Primarily because of the free-agent draft, this effect began to fade around 1972. And even though Lou Brock made his last All-Star appearance in 1979, and Al Oliver's was in 1982, this influence was pretty much dead by 1976. Indeed, if you look at the All-Star rosters of the American League in 1976–77 you have seven black stars who were signed through the draft process: Jim Rice, Reggie Jackson, Vida Blue, Willie Randolph, Chris Chambliss, Mickey Rivers, and Ruppert Jones. On the NL rosters, there wasn't a single black player left from the star talent it had accumulated before the 1965 draft.

So why did the National League continue to beat the American League like a drum in the All-Star game, winning seven straight from 1976 to 1982? There were a number of factors contributing to that slaughter that have nothing to do with the relative quality of the leagues or their top talent—at least in regard to winning baseball games. What the National League had is a winning edge in the special context of the All-Star game.

THE DH RULE

The designated-hitter rule has handicapped the American League in All-Star competition since its inception in 1973. The most obvious problem has been that designated hitters are being selected to play in a game that until 1989 totally ignored the DH rule. As recently as 1988, the fans elected Paul Molitor to start at second base even though he had been a DH most of the first half and played only one game at second. The DH rule also keeps older players on the scene long past their prime and often leads to their appointment to the team for sentimental reasons.

The DH rule put a forty-one-year-old Henry Aaron on the 1975 AL All-Star team; he hit .234 that year and was 0-for-1 in the game. Reggie Jackson was elected to the starting lineup in 1984 despite being thirty-eight years old, coming off a very poor year, and having played only 47 games in the outfield in 1983 and just one game there that season. He was 0-for-2 as an All-Star.

From 1973 to 1988, there have been twenty-one AL All-Stars who made the team while playing primarily as a DH. About a third of those selections have been sentimental DHs—older former stars with questionable All-Star qualifications:

	AGE	BA	HR	RUNS	RBI
1974 F. Robinson	38	.245	22	81	68
1975 Kaline	39	.262	13	71	64
1975 Aaron	41	.234	12	45	60
1979 Yastrzemski	39	.270	21	69	87
1982 Yastrzemski	42	.275	16	53	72
1983 Yastrzemski	43	.266	10	38	56
1984 R. Jackson	38	.223	25	67	81

The Don Baylors, Andre Thorntons, Richie Zisks, Carl Yastrzemskis, Larry Parrishes, and Hal McRaes also limit the roster's mobility with their lack of a position, and the AL manager is pressured to pinch-hit more frequently to make sure they get a chance to play. Then there are the pitchers who don't know what to do with a bat. Neither side lets its pitchers hit much in All-Star competition, but at least the NL manager has more of a choice. If his pitcher is throwing well, he's more comfortable leaving him in to hit or bunt. The AL manager meanwhile is wondering whether his pitcher knows which end of the bat to grip. I've heard one story of an AL All-Star pitcher who was so concerned with not embarrassing himself that he specifically asked the manager not to use him if he would have to hit. In 1987, NL reliever Lee Smith won a tight 2–0 game while throwing three strong innings, something that required his taking a trip to the plate. You'd never see that happen with the AL squad. Since the DH rule, no AL pitcher has taken an at bat in the last four innings of an All-Star game.

The DH rule may also hamper the effectiveness of the AL All-Star pitchers. It leads to more batters faced and more pitches thrown per inning, tougher lineups, and more pitches thrown from the stretch position. We've seen in the chapters on pitcher workloads that pitching under the DH rule can be more dangerous for the top starters and relievers. That's exactly who makes up the All-Star staff. The AL pitchers may be a bit more tired come July than the NL hurlers, and they are less likely to maintain All-Star performances in the future. The American League did not get a lot of repeat use out of pitchers like Steve Busby, Mark Fidrych, Frank Tanana, Dennis Eckersley, Matt Keough, Lary Sorensen, Steve Stone, Mike Norris, or Matt Young.

THE 1977 EXPANSION EFFECT

Since 1977 the American League has had fourteen teams to the National League's twelve. This has a tremendous impact on the All-Star game, where roster depth takes on a new meaning with so many players getting into the game. Every year deserving players are left off the squad because of the rule requiring at least one representative from each team. The problem is further complicated by an understanding that if a team has only one representative, an extra effort will be made to get him into the game.

If your talent is spread over more teams, it increases your chances of having teams without a legitimate All-Star, particularly if two of them are fairly new expansion teams. In 1977 the two representatives of the AL expansion teams were Ron Fairly and Ruppert Jones. Their 1977 statistics are given below, with those of fifteen stars who could not find a spot on the All-Star team.

	POS	AB	H	2B/3B/HR	SB	BB	R	RBI	BA	SA	OBA
Fairly	DH-1B	458	128	24/ 2/19	0	58	60	64	.279	.465	.360
Jones	OF	597	157	26/ 8/24	13	55	85	76	.263	.454	.325
Bonds	OF	592	156	23/ 8/37	41	74	103	115	.264	.520	.345
Bostock	OF	593	199	36/12/14	16	51	104	90	.336	.508	.388
Cooper	1B	643	193	31/ 7/20	13	28	86	78	.300	.461	.329
Cowens	OF	606	189	32/14/23	16	41	98	112	.312	.525	.355
Gamble	DH-OF	408	121	22/ 2/31	1	54	75	83	.297	.588	.379
Harrah	3B	539	142	25/ 5/27	27	109	90	87	.263	.479	.387
Lemon	1B	553	151	38/ 4/19	8	52	99	67	.273	.459	.336
McRae	DH	641	191	54/11/21	18	59	104	92	.298	.515	.357
Murray	DH-1B	611	173	29/ 2/27	0	48	81	88	.283	.470	.335
Porter	C	425	117	21/ 3/16	1	53	61	60	.275	.452	.356
Soderholm	3B	460	129	20/ 3/25	2	47	77	67	.280	.500	.347
Sundberg	C	453	132	20/ 3/ 6	2	53	61	65	.291	.389	.366

	W–L	INNINGS	ERA
Goltz	20–11	303	3.36
Guidry	16–7	211	2.82
Leonard	20–12	293	3.04

Both Fairly and Jones got into the game as pinch-hitters (strikeout and fly out), while All-Star teammate Jason Thompson (.270, 31 homers, 105 RBIs) did not. The American League lost 7–5. Here are some other weak selections who were their team's only All-Star representative since the expansion to fourteen teams:

YEAR	TEAM	PLAYER	POS	AB	H	2B/3B/HR	SB	BB	R	RBI	BA	SA	OBA
1978	TOR	Howell	3B	551	149	28/ 3/ 8	5	44	67	61	.270	.375	.324
1979	OAK	Newman	C	516	119	17/ 2/22	2	27	53	71	.231	.399	.269
1977	OAK	Gross	3B	485	113	21/ 1/22	5	86	66	63	.233	.416	.349
1980	MIN	Landreaux	OF	484	136	23/11/ 7	8	39	56	62	.281	.417	.335
1984	MIN	Engle	C	391	104	20/ 1/ 4	0	26	56	43	.266	.353	.312
1985	TEX	Ward	OF	593	170	28/ 7/15	26	39	77	70	.287	.433	.329
1987	CLE	Tabler	1B	553	170	34/ 3/11	5	51	66	86	.307	.439	.366

1979	TOR	Lemanczyk	8–10	143	3.71
1980	TOR	Stieb	12–15	243	3.70
1980	SEA	Honeycutt	10–17	203	3.95
1982	TOR	Clancy	16–14	267	3.71
1982	SEA	Bannister	12–13	247	3.43
1983	SEA	M. Young	11–15	204	3.27
1987	CAL	M. Witt	16–14	247	4.01

In each and every case there were several more deserving players who had to be left off the team, players who might have made the difference late in the game when so many of the All-Star games have been lost by the American League.

THE ARTIFICIAL TURF FACTOR

The National League has also had an edge as the "artificial turf league." By the time the American League had its first artificial surface, half the NL had turf fields. It was another four years before the AL got its second turf surface, and even today it still plays less than 29% of its games on artificial fields.

The NL has shaped its teams around this turf influence, selecting players with a greater emphasis on speed and quickness on defense. They have also adopted a pitching style that moved away from control and breaking pitches to hard stuff and trick pitches.

Since 1971, the National League's first year as a 50% turf league, you could pretty well predict the outcome of the World Series by the playing surfaces involved. If both teams had grass fields, the American League would win—true in '73, '74, '77, '78, and '84; not true in '81 or '86. If the National League had a turf home field and the American League team had grass, the National League won. That was the case in '71, '75, '76, '79, and '82. It missed in '72 and '83. Still, ten correct out of fourteen (71%) would be a gambler's dream. (All-turf series have been rare, with no apparent edge; the AL is ahead 2–1, but it's totally even for the individual games at 10–10).

There has been a lot of artificial turf in recent All-Star games. The tendency has been to showcase the newer stadiums, and they are the ones most likely to have the synthetic sod. From 1973 to 1988, half the All-Star games were played on turf, though only ten of twenty-six teams have home carpets. In those games the National League out-scored the American League 41–17, compared with 37–31 on grass.

The NL's turf-influenced pitching style is uniquely suited to All-Star pitching. You see, on a grass field the batter needs really solid contact to get a hit. The idea on grass is less to overwhelm the hitter and more to keep him from ripping a pitch. The turf approach is to avoid giving up the cheap turf-singles. The American League style is to set up the batter to make contact but not good contact; the National League style is to come right at the hitter and be as unhittable as possible.

What we end up with is an American League pitching style that is closer to that of a starting pitcher; he's going to pace himself while establishing his control and the command of his off-speed pitches. The National League style is more that of a reliever. Well, heck, everyone is a relief pitcher in the All-Star game, since nobody can pitch longer than three innings. By the time your conventional starting pitcher has his game going, he is out of the contest, particularly on the American League squad, on which the manager is less likely to let the pitcher hit. It's a fact that from 1973 to 1988, American League pitchers have gone three innings eight times compared with thirteen for the NL. From 1973 to 1988, the American League pitchers who were starters during the regular season have done exceptionally poorly in the All-Star game, with an ERA of 4.65 in 102.2 innings compared with 3.17 in 113.2 innings for NL starters.

The All-Star game also favors any pitcher throwing a freak pitch. In this once-a-year matchup he gets to initiate total novices to the mystery of his special pitch. Remember how Carl Hubbell's screwball struck out Babe Ruth, Lou Gehrig, Jimmie Foxx, All Simmons, and Joe Cronin in succession in 1934? It seems that the artificial-turf explosion in the National League not only began to highlight the power pitcher, but encouraged those pitchers who could come up with something unusual, something like the screwballs of a Tug McGraw, Mike Marshall, or Fernando Valenzuela, the super split-fingered fastball of Bruce Sutter, or the knuckleballs of the Niekro brothers. Through 1988, this group of trick pitchers has shut out the AL in 19.2 All-Star innings. And fate made one of these pitchers the most significant All-Star performer in the final heyday of the NL All-Stars.

THE BRUCE SUTTER STORY

In the late seventies, just when it seemed the AL was pulling even with the NL's All-Star talent, it ran into the Bruce Sutter factor. This is a story of luck as much as anything. In the last five years of the NL's domination (1978–82), the American League always went into the seventh inning with a decent chance to win. Four of those five times the NL was able to call on a pitcher who threw a nearly untouchable hard sinking pitch, the likes of which could not be found in the AL.

In 1978, the game was tied 3–3 after seven. Sutter came on in the eighth and retired the side in order. The NL scored in the bottom of the eighth; Sutter retired the first two in the ninth and left the last batter for Phil Niekro. Winning pitcher: Bruce Sutter.

In 1979, Sutter came into the game in the seventh with the NL losing 6–5. He shut down the American League again while the National League pushed across single runs in the eighth and ninth. Winning pitcher: Bruce Sutter.

In 1980, the American League was down 4–2 as the game entered the eighth. Sutter held the AL hitless for the last two innings. Save: Bruce Sutter.

In 1981, Sutter got the call in the ninth after the NL scored two in the eighth to take a 5–4 lead. Sutter threw a perfect inning to seal the victory. Save: Bruce Sutter.

Four All-Star appearances, two wins, two saves, 6.2 scoreless innings with seven strikeouts and only two hits allowed. Sometimes it really is just a case of having the right player in the right place at the right time.

THE FUTURE

As I write this, the leagues have split the last six All-Star games (1983–88) with the AL outscoring the NL 20–17. I see no reason under the present conditions that one league should pull far ahead of the other in either World Series or All-Star competition. There is no gigantic factor as there once was with the star black players. The NL still has a slight edge in certain All-Star factors, but they are minimal and getting smaller. There is still pressure to unify the leagues on the DH question, and they are going to start alternating the DH rule according to which league is hosting the All-Star game. We will be entering a cycle of more grass parks getting the All-Star game. When expansion comes, the NL will likely take on more cities to restore a balance between the leagues. The American League is playing more games on artificial turf and will have more future All-Stars coming from those teams with artificial home fields. As these things balance out, we can count on the equality of talent—which is probably as well balanced as at any time in history—to continue to show up in the All-Star game as much as it does in the World Series.

HOUSE:
LEAGUES APART

The All-Star game is for the fans, mostly. I'm sure everyone's really honored to be elected to the All-Star team, and they play the game to win, but if you asked most ballplayers, they'd just as soon have the three days off to be home with their families. By July, you've been going at it for about five months, and the wear starts to show. There aren't all that many holes in the schedule, and that three-day break looks awfully inviting.

That doesn't mean the game isn't played seriously. You don't get to be an All-Star without being an intense competitor, and for all the talk you sometimes hear about people just going through the motions, well, don't you believe it for a minute.

So what accounts for the National League's dominance in the All-Star game? I played in both leagues during the seventies, and certainly at that time the National League was a much faster league: The players were faster, the game was faster, and the pitchers were a lot faster. You heard a lot then, and still do to some extent, about how the National League is a fastball league while the American relies more on breaking stuff. But I don't think anyone's looked at one of the reasons for that, and that's the umpires.

Because of the inside chest protector, which the AL umps didn't wear in those days, the NL umps were much better at getting close to the strike zone and calling a pitch by location. You could get the low strike in the NL but not in the AL, so the pitchers who lived on fastballs down thrived in the NL. The AL umps just weren't that good at calling location, so you had no choice but to rely on change of speed; you didn't know whether you'd get the calls you needed to get hitters out on location alone.

The hitters in the American League were guess hitters, and thrived on hitting mistakes—those off-speed pitches that hung or the change-ups they could sit on. "Cookies," we call them, and if you throw one to a good hitter, you're gonna get crushed. But you don't make those kinds of mistakes too often with your fastball. So the AL All-Star hitters were looking for pitches they just weren't going to get from NL pitchers. And the NL hitters were used to seeing fastballs all the time, so the ones the AL pitchers were throwing to set up their breaking balls looked just fine to them.

It's a subtle thing, and an easy one to miss, but I really believe that the better ability the NL umps had to call location on a pitch had enough of a ripple effect to show up in these kinds of results. And I should also say that since the AL umps have started using the inside protector, they've gotten better at giving you location, and you're seeing more fastball pitchers in the American League than you used to. Baseball's a constant process of evolution, and the abilities of the umpires is one of those things, like the size of the park and the speed of the turf, that you've got to adjust to to survive.

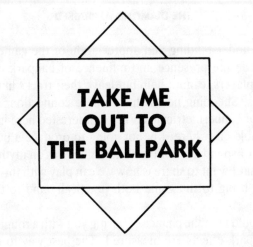

TAKE ME OUT TO THE BALLPARK

Believe it or not, there are some fans who actually complain about the fact that baseball's playing fields aren't all the same. Fortunately, there aren't many who feel this way; the very nature of the game seems to discourage this approach. But should the sad day ever come when all ballparks are shaped by a cookie cutter, they will still imprint their character on the game through their differences in hitting background, lighting, smog levels, elevation of the park relative to sea level, local winds and weather, etcetera, etcetera. In this area, the variations in the game and its conditions are too great to be bounded by mere dimensions.

Let us praise the unique beauty of baseball, where each park is different, an individual home for its team. Let the other sports look on in envy; if you've seen one football field or basketball court, you've seen 'em all. When was the last time you heard of a football fan making a pilgrimage to all the NFL stadiums, or a basketball fan bragging about which NBA arenas he's been in?

The playing fields of baseball hold a special magic. The players are familiar characters in a popular play; the parks are the different settings, allowing new perceptions of the strengths and weaknesses of the players. Let the other sports support the unisex image of society; in baseball, let it be *vive la difference*. We will celebrate our idiosyncrasies, not apologize for them.

A better understanding and appreciation of the game of baseball has to include the presence and influence of ballpark effects. Ballparks, like players, cannot help but leave their tracks in the numbers of the game. Shedding new light on these connections is a popular subject among sabermetricians. I'm not interested here in duplicating work available elsewhere; I'm not going to produce a bunch of ballpark charts or spend a lot of time with influences on mythical average players. What I want to share is how we can play with this knowledge, what it can bring to the game both practically and to the fan's enjoyment.

Still, I should take the chance of boring you with a rough description of how ballpark effects are measured. The best way to measure the general influence of a park is to compare performances by both teams in all games played in a park with those in that team's road games. That way, you have essentially the same hitters hitting against the same pitchers and against the same defensive units; the only two major changes are who gets to bat last and the ballpark itself.

For example, the batting average for both teams in Red Sox home games for 1983–87 was .2841 versus .2653 in road games. Because there are fourteen teams in the American League and we want to compare Fenway Park to the average park in the league—which would include Fenway—multiply .2653 by thirteen, add .2841, divide by fourteen, and you have the norm for those performers spread fairly evenly over the fourteen ballparks. That result is .2666, which is divided into .2841, producing 1.066. So Fenway Park in 1983–87 seemed to raise batting averages by about 6.6%.

Short fences, an excellent hitting background, good lighting, extra day games, small foul areas—all these things combine to make Fenway Park a haven for hitters, especially for high batting averages. It is no accident that through 1987, a Red Sox player has won sixteen of the forty-two batting titles since the end of World War II (Williams, 4; Boggs 4; Yastrzemski, 3; Runnels, 2; Goodman, 1; Lynn, 1; and Lansford, 1). And it is no surprise that a meeting of the batting champions from Baltimore, Seattle, Oakland, Houston, Milwaukee, San Francisco, San Diego, and the New York Mets provides for very little conversation: Frank Robinson, meet Frank Robinson.

Familiarity with park influences can give us a special perspective on the careers of certain players. Ron Guidry is one of my real favorites, but I have to admit that his talents have been uniquely suited to take advantage of Yankee Stadium. The deep left-field area protected him against right-handed power hitters. The lefties who would normally get a boost from the short right-field porch are held in check by Guidry's ability to keep his fastball low and away, and his slider breaks away from lefties.

Guidry has played his whole career with Yankee Stadium as his home park. It's only natural that he would adapt his pitching style more and more to that ballpark as the years went by. That gave him a distinct edge to exploit in his later seasons when his raw talents were declining. I have innings and earned run data on Guidry in Yankee Stadium that dates back to 1980. His home-field advantage really took off in 1983–87, ages thirty-two to thirty-six.

GUIDRY, 1980–82			GUIDRY, 1983–87	
INNINGS	ERA		INNINGS	ERA
296.1	3.37	Home	555.1	3.03
262.2	3.73	Road	459.2	4.56

Ballpark influences can create illusions in a player's career when he gets traded from one team and one ballpark to another. When Rod Carew was traded from a friendly hitters' park in Minnesota, old Metropolitan Stadium, to the poor hitting background in California's then-unenclosed Anaheim Stadium, his steady stream of batting titles went dry. It was not his road batting average that suffered, nor was it just advancing age that ended his monopoly on the title:

CAREW'S CAREER	BA, HOME	BA, ROAD
1967–78 Minnesota	.341	.328
1979–81 California	.312	.327

By the same logic, Reggie Jackson deserves a bit more respect for his eight years in Oakland, his year in Baltimore, and his five years in New York. Through age thirty-five, Jackson played in home parks that hid his offensive contributions as measured by the Triple Crown statistics. The knock on Reggie was always for his relatively low batting averages, but during those seasons Jackson's road batting average was sixteen points better than that of eventual Hall of Famer Carl Yastrzemski in his whole career. Reggie's road average through age thirty-five is also higher than Jim Rice's road average through 1987, and Rice has an overall career average of .302. If Jackson had been with the Red Sox his whole career, his lifetime average would probably be in the .290s. If Rice had played in the home parks from Reggie's career, he would be remembered as just a decent-hitting outfielder in the high .260s with 20-to-25-homer power and a reputation for grounding into a ton of double plays. But then again, without his .300 average and 100 RBIs to protect him, Rice might have done something about those GIDP records.

It is not my intent to rip Jim Rice. Put him in a neutral park rather than those Reggie labored in, and he would be seen as more than just a decent hitter. My point is that the luck of the draw and a haziness about park influences cause most fans to see a great hitter (Jackson) as a good one and a good one (Rice) as a great one. I am not saying that Jackson was as good an offensive player as Rice. It is not even close. *Jackson was by far the better player.*

It's important to stress here that while we talk about a park's general influence on the average player, the actual influence on specific individuals will vary greatly. Sticking with Fenway Park, we know that left-handed hitters derive an extra edge from the steady diet of right-handed pitching used to combat the cheap home runs by righty hitters to left field. That helped Fred Lynn more than it helped Yastrzemski, and it helped Yaz more than it helped Ted Williams. That is the order of their platoon differentials, and also the order of their offensive gains at Fenway.

If you're a right-handed pull hitter, the short left-field wall can change a few fly balls that are outs in other parks to hits and homers at Fenway. But if you're a right-handed hitter who doesn't hit fly balls but hits the ball back up the middle, all you get out of Fenway is a good hitting background, an advantage that can be offset by having to face a lot of right-handed pitching. That's why Rice, Carlton Fisk, and Butch Hobson hit about forty points higher at Fenway, while Rick Burleson hit only ten points higher. That's why Bill James prior to the 1981 season made the rather farsighted and accurate prediction that Burleson would make a better and faster adjustment to his new home park than his fellow escapees, Fisk and Lynn.

	1980 BOSTON		1981 NEW TEAM	
	BA	SA	BA	SA
Burleson	.278	.366	.293	.372
Fisk	.289	.467	.263	.361
Lynn	.301	.480	.219	.316

Returning to Reggie, which home park helped him the most statistically? That would be Anaheim Stadium. The Angels' home park went from being a pitchers' park to a neutral park when it was completely enclosed in 1980. This improved the hitting background and blocked the wind that held back some long hits, especially off the bat of a straightaway power hitter like Reggie. The Big A is the only home park that Jackson has had with a home-field edge in home runs. His homers as an Angel were about 30% more frequent at home than on the road, well above the average 5% home-field advantage for homers.

In which home park was Jackson most valuable? Without question it was Oakland-Alameda County Coliseum. Oakland has the toughest hitters' park in the league, especially for batting average. This hurt Reggie statistically, as he hit 18 points higher on the road in his eight years in Oakland, but this factor also made the "short-sequence offense" of his home runs more valuable. If a park reduces all elements by 10%, an offense that requires only one event to score, as with a home run, will still be 90% as effective. But one that requires three events—say, three singles—is going to be 73% as effective ($.9 \times .9 \times .9$). Jackson also had the advantage of "big park" power—he hit them so far that the dimensions or "carry" of the park was not as much a factor. Indeed, Jackson's power in his home games as an Oakland A was only slightly worse than his road performance.

Baltimore's Memorial Stadium was the next-best home park for Reggie. Before some changes in 1986, Baltimore's park effect was similar to Oakland's in that while it didn't increase home run frequency, it did heighten the value of the home run relative to the other offensive elements. But Memorial Stadium has shorter corners, which favors home run hitters who pull the ball. This wasn't true in Oakland, where Jackson had developed a straightaway power stroke. What made Jackson's power unusual was his ability to drive the ball deep to left center. This was an important edge in Oakland, far less so in Baltimore.

Probably the worst home park for Reggie's value to his team was Yankee Stadium. This may seem rather startling at first. Most fans are very aware that Yankee Stadium's dimensions favor left-handed home run hitters, and Jackson had some of his best seasons there, including his top two seasons in batting average, .300 and .297. There are two factors that must be considered here. One, Jackson received some excellent hitting instruction from Charlie Lau during his years in New York. Lau always worked best with straightaway hitters like Jackson and made some changes that helped Reggie stand in better against left-handed pitching. Most of his improvement as a hitter came against southpaws. In fact, over one two-year span Reggie was actually a better hitter for average versus lefties than versus right-handers. The other factor to remember is that Jackson's numbers would look better just by the change in ballpark. Yankee Stadium reduces batting average, but not to the degree of Jackson's prior home parks. When Jackson hit .293 for Oakland in 1973, it was a more difficult feat than his .300 mark in New York.

Remember, too, that Jackson's extra power was to left center, which is the deepest part of Yankee Stadium—the deepest left-center field in all of baseball. Graig Nettles, a lefty pull hitter with decent home run power, was made for Yankee Stadium, not Reggie Jackson. Nettles's performance at Yankee Stadium was amazingly similar to Jackson's; it was on the road that their talent separated.

With the possible exception of Bill Dickey in the late 1930s, I doubt you could find a lefty hitter better suited to Yankee Stadium than Graig Nettles. And it would be hard to find one worse suited to the

1976–81, JACKSON'S YEARS AS A YANKEE

	BA	2B AND 3B/AB	HR/AB
Jackson-Home	.276	1 every 24.8	1 every 17.3
Nettles-Home	.276	1 every 24.6	1 every 17.3
Jackson-Road	.286	1 every 12.5	1 every 13.0
Nettles-Road	.238	1 every 28.2	1 every 25.2

park than Jackson. Reggie not only lost several homers to the death valley in left-center field, but he also misplaced a ton of doubles. In his last two seasons as a Yankee he hit 35 doubles on the road and only *four* at home.

If Jackson had spent his first nine years as a Yankee, he most likely would have developed a Yankee swing just as he developed an Oakland swing. It's easy to overlook this factor when we inflate or deflate individual performances according to generalized park factors. A player's style and talent base must be considered when we speak of park influences on an individual. In the 1976 *Baseball Research Journal*, John Tattersall noted that Elston Howard set the Yankees' home run record for home park futility. Elston hit only 32% of his career homers as a Yankee in Yankee Stadium. Joe DiMaggio, another right-handed hitter, hit 41% of his homers at home. There is a very good scientific reason for this: Joe DiMaggio could hit the ball a lot farther than Elston Howard.

It is points like this that must be remembered in such debates as, Who was the better hitter: Joe DiMaggio or Ted Williams? Joe's fans tend to overstate the effects of both Yankee Stadium and Fenway Park on these two. Williams's career was not as greatly aided by Fenway Park nor was DiMaggio's as badly scarred by Yankee Stadium as they claim. Ted Williams had a smaller percentage gain in batting average at Fenway than his teammates Doerr, Stephens, Foxx, or Cronin, and smaller than modern Red Sox like Rice, Lynn, Boggs, or Yastrzemski. It is also a fact that Williams hit 25 more homers on the road than he did at home.

It doesn't matter that Williams hit only .296 at Yankee Stadium while DiMaggio hit .334 at Boston. Besides the difference in ballparks, that also compares Ted's hitting against the superior pitching of the Yankees with Joe's battering of the Boston staff. The more reasonable comparison is to take their road performances and add the equivalent of one-seventh of their home performance. That gives them equal percentages in the eight parks, although DiMaggio is still slightly favored in facing Boston pitchers in place of the New York staff for one-seventh of his appearances. The results are close, but Williams still comes out on top—near identical batting averages, but more power and a lot more walks.

	BA	SA	OBA	HR/AB
Williams	.332	.620	.469	1 per 14.2 AB
DiMaggio	.331	.602	.400	1 per 16.8 AB

Put away the ballparks, DiMaggio fans, start working on explaining away the fact that over two thousand of Williams's at bats (28% of his career total) came after an age when DiMaggio was already retired, or why it shouldn't matter that during DiMaggio's career the league offense was 14% higher than during Williams's. The ballpark question can be pretty much laid to rest.

My favorite ballpark story is how, in our historical hindsight, we missed the true beginning of the Live Ball Era. Traditionally we mark the beginning of the Live Ball Era in 1920. It's generally understood that today's offensive styles didn't spring forth in full form in 1920; that would take fifty or sixty years of evolution. It's equally true that the game didn't suddenly jump to the style of the near future, say 1925. The process was a slow one built on several factors: the livelier ball, the outlawing of the spitball and other "foreign-substance" pitches in 1920, the practice of replacing the game ball more frequently, and the adaptation of batting styles to the new long-ball potential, something discovered by a former Boston pitcher never instructed in the finer points of "correct" batting form.

As historians, we felt the need to draw the line somewhere, and 1920 seemed like such a nice, round number. And, of course, Babe Ruth hit 54 homers, which tends to catch your eye when the previous high was 29. The apparent magnitude of this feat convinced us that this is when the livelier ball was introduced. It is probably also the source of our erroneous belief that the new era being ushered in was chiefly the result of a livelier ball. If the Babe had hit 54 homers in 1919, we might be calling that the start of the livelier ball. If that were the case, we would have seen more clearly the other factors—the new rules and practices—that caused baseball's offense to continue to accelerate during the 1920–25 period. Maybe we would be calling it "The Rule 8.02 Era" (rule 8.02 outlawed the foreign-substance pitches), or maybe "The White Ball Era" or simply "The Home Run Era."

The study of park factors has brought out the truth that the ball was livened up in 1919, not 1920, and that Babe Ruth was just as capable of hitting fifty homers in 1919 as in 1920. I believe the Spalding Sporting Goods Company was sincere when it denied any change in the design of the ball in 1920. I believe Spalding because it openly mentioned the factor that could account for a suddenly livelier ball: After World War I, it began using a higher grade of woolen yarn from Australia that wound tighter, and this may have been the change that put the rabbit in the ball.

I believe it because it fits so well. The first season after the war is 1919, and that's the season when the homers first began to pick up. The number of homers per game in 1918 was .023; in 1919, it jumped 70% to .039, the largest percentage jump between seasons in the history of the game. Babe Ruth set a new record with 29 homers in the 140-game schedule; if they had played the more traditional 154-game schedule, baseball would likely have seen a new record for most players with ten or more homers.

But the Babe put his fifty-homer stamp on 1920, and the true beginning of the live ball has been overlooked ever since. Yet the only reason Ruth hit fifty-plus homers in 1920 rather than 1919 was simply where he played his home games. Thanks to historical research by John Tattersall and park analysis by Pete Palmer, we can quickly see that Ruth's 1920 home run explosion could have been easily anticipated. Old Fenway Park was very large, and few homers were ever hit there. When Babe hit his 29 homers in 1919, only nine were hit at home; his Boston teammates hit only *one* homer at old Fenway, and Boston's opponents hit a total of three.

When Ruth was traded to the Yankees, their home park was the

Polo Grounds, the best home run park in either league in 1919. Compared with the average park, it increased home runs by a factor of 1.68, a tremendous gain over old Fenway's .39 factor. If we assume the general home-field advantage in home runs was roughly the same 5% as today, then if Ruth had played in a neutral home park in 1919, his 20 road homers suggest he would have hit 41 overall. If his home had been the Polo Grounds, he would have been expected to hit 55.

So in 1920, Ruth actually moved into the Polo Grounds and hit 54 home runs while playing in 142 games. He hit only five more homers on the road than he did in 1919; the key was the change in his home park, which jumped his homers at home from nine to 29. In fact, Ruth continued that pace as long as the Polo Grounds was his home park, averaging 55 homers per 150 games. The basis of our belief that the Live Ball Era began in 1920 had nothing to do with the state of the ball, but rather with the differences between two ballparks.

The idea of Fenway Park ever having been a pitchers' park is not as outlandish as it seems. Baseball's playing fields are always changing, and the final effect can be a total reversal for a ballpark. The real Dr. Jekyll and Mr. Hyde of ballparks was Braves Field in Boston, home of the Boston Braves from 1915 to 1952. The original dimensions were 402 feet down each foul line and 550 feet to center field. There has never been anything like it, before or since. In 1921, 34 of the 38 homers hit at Braves Field were inside-the-park home runs. For 1923–27, the park's home run factor was .37, and the overall run factor was .88. With the average National League park as the norm of 1.00, it was almost three times easier to hit a home run elsewhere in the NL than in Braves Field. The park could knock twenty-five points off a pitcher's ERA if he remembered to show up for the home games, fifty points if he missed the train for the road games.

Then in 1928 they decided to build bleachers *within* the old walls, cutting down the distances by seventy feet or so. This resulted in such a barrage of homers that they changed things back a bit in midseason. The park home run factor for 1928 was 1.25, not outlandish for other parks in baseball history, but a little stunning when your park was at .37 the year before. The second set of changes kept the park at a more reasonable .76 level from 1929 to 1935.

Babe Ruth retired in a Boston Braves uniform in 1935. To mark the Babe's retirement from the game, they decided to bury the home run again at Braves Field. In 1936 they again made it the roomiest park in baseball, as they moved home plate back fifteen feet. From 1936 to 1941 they played with a park homer adjustment of .52, the equivalent of the Astrodome on a bad day. With home runs a bigger part of the game in the 1930s than the 1920s, this made Braves Field even more of a pitcher's paradise than its original days.

In 1935, Deacon Danny MacFayden was traded from the Reds to the Boston Braves. When the park was restored to roughly its original dimensions in 1936 he was thirty-one years old; his career record was 72–103, and his career ERA was 4.40. No one was mistaking him for Dizzy Dean, but in 1936 MacFayden was second in the league with a 2.87 ERA, with old Diz himself third at 3.17. The next season MacFayden came up with another good ERA of 2.93, but it was only the third-best ERA on the Braves' staff. The Braves' Jim Turner led the league in ERA, and Lou Fette, another name to forget, was fifth.

The pitching party ended in 1942 as they continued to move around home plate and to play with the fences. By 1944 Braves Field was rivaling the Polo Grounds as the *best* home run park in the big leagues. Remember Danny MacFayden? Well, the Deacon tried to come back and help the Braves out during the war years. A 5.91 ERA convinced him the park was not quite as friendly as he remembered it. In 1945 there were 131 homers hit at Braves Field, compared with only 69 in the Braves' road games. The park had come full circle from the worst hitters' park to the best. It was a roller coaster of change that would not stop till the Braves left town in 1953.

The magnitude of changes inflicted on Braves Field don't happen today, but the frequency of significant changes is just as great or greater. We've already mentioned the changes related to the double-decked enclosure of Anaheim Stadium, home of the California Angels. Prior to that change it was one of the best pitchers' parks in baseball with an .895 run level. Now it has a neutral overall run value. The strikeout adjustment fell from an unusually high 1.07 to a normal rate. This suggests that the hitting background was greatly enhanced by the changes. Nolan Ryan's record 383-strikeout performance as an Angel in 1973 would have been far less likely in the renovated Anaheim Stadium.

A couple of parks have undergone some subtle changes simply through lighting improvements. The Mariners adjusted their lights and raised their batting average adjustment a couple of points while lowering their strikeout factor from 1.085 to 1.005. The New York Mets improved their lights in 1982, which also helped batting averages while cutting down the strikeouts.

In 1984 the Texas Rangers kept their fences the same but cut off the prevailing prairie wind that constantly blew in from right center. They also replaced their convex outfield pads, which caught a bit of glare along the top and hurt the hitting background. The net result was a tremendous offensive gain, going from an extreme pitchers' park to one clearly favoring the hitters.

San Diego started fooling with its fences and its hitting background and totally revamped the image of its park. In the 1970s the park had a run adjustment second only to the old Astrodome as a pitchers' heaven. Home runs were as rare as bad weather—then *shazam*! It's still a tough park for batting average, but it's up to a .96 run level now that it's the best bomb factory this side of Wrigley Field. Since Atlanta raised its fences prior to the 1984 season, San Diego has actually been the better home run park in the 1985–87 data. Just six years ago I could never have imagined writing that as anything but a joke.

The good folks at Wrigley Field gave us another valuable lesson on the importance of the hitting background. In 1982 they did away with most of it, treating us to *Sporting News* stories of Cubbies crying that someone might get killed, though I suspect most were concerned for a death in the family whose first initial is a decimal point. What happened is that a very good hitters' park in the 1.24 range fell with a thud to a normal 1.01. Because the hitters had better press agents than the pitchers, the hitting background was mostly restored in 1983. Appropriately, they got back most of what they lost, as the present run value is somewhere in the neighborhood of 1.17. Sabermetricians will be eagerly watching the effect of the Wrigley lights. I would guess the lights will lower the high batting average factor of the park.

Some park changes are so subtle that we often don't expect them to affect the way the park plays at all. When Baltimore put up its new scoreboard in 1986, it was such a small change compared with the Texas wraparound billboard-scoreboard, that no one expected it to change anything. Yet it greatly influenced the wind currents that carry fly balls to center field, turning it significantly from a negative to a positive home run park. In Fenway, the erection of new scoreboards and placing of luxury boxes along the roof line on both sides of the field have adversely affected the way the ball carries there. It's still a great batting average and doubles park, but its impact on home runs has declined significantly. In fact, the yearly home run factor has been below average three years in a row (1985–87).

All of these intentional and accidental tinkerings have happened in the last few years. There are several others that could be mentioned. Comiskey Park became a much better hitters' park in this decade by playing with the center field area, moving home plate, and improving the hitting background. Cleveland moved its fences in around the late 1970s. San Francisco did the same in 1982. Cincinnati lowered its fences in 1984. Both the Yankees and Astros have played with their fences several times since 1985, almost always bringing them in. Milwaukee took down its mascot Bernie Brewer's summer palace, which towered above the stands in left-center field. This seemed to set off a significant offensive rise in the park factor. Seattle raised its outfield wall in left field in 1988. And when Montreal's Olympic Stadium finally began using its roof in 1987, there was a significant offensive explosion. The early indications are that it is one of the most significant park changes of the last twenty years.

You may have noticed that most of these changes have been geared to help the offense. That has been a distinct trend of late. Forget the rumors of juicing up the baseball; what we are really doing is juicing up the ballparks. It is no exaggeration to say that 90% of the park changes since 1976 have favored the offense. By studying the parks that have changed the least we can get a feel for what's happening at the league level. Just since the start of this decade, the difference between the stable parks and the league average has jumped about 6% to 7% in both leagues. The neutral park of 1980 has become the pitchers' park of 1987 by simply staying the same. The offensive gain in American League parks has been across the board, with both batting average and power getting boosts. In the National League it has been mostly a jump in home run potential.

WHERE DO PARK FACTORS COME FROM?

Understanding how a park plays is often simply a matter of the obvious: Short fences means more home runs. Artificial turf, with its faster bounce and roll, means more balls scooting past the outfielders for doubles and triples. The ball carries farther at higher altitudes, meaning more homers; Atlanta's park has fairly normal dimensions but sees a lot of homers because Atlanta is the highest major-league city. (Look for some interesting home run totals when Denver joins the majors.) And then there are a lot of park influences we are just beginning to understand.

Take the base on balls. Ballparks influence the frequency of walks; that is a fact. The "why" does not come as easily. Perhaps our own general blindness to this statistic hides the source. Many fans could name in three guesses the best and worst parks for batting average or home runs or runs in general. There are probably only a dozen in the whole country who could identify the best and worst parks for drawing walks. On the off chance it comes up, you might be interested to know it is Montreal's Olympic Stadium and Dodger Stadium in Los Angeles, respectively.

Both parks have been remarkably consistent in their effects; both had the same type of park factors before and after the strike season, which was excluded because of unbalanced scheduling and an unequal number of home versus road games. The unanswered question remains, "Why?"

We know it's partly the weather. A seasonal thermal map of North America can isolate seven major-league cities that play in significantly warmer weather than the other nineteen teams. As a group, these seven parks show a significant reduction in both walks and strikeouts. This fits rather well with what we know about baseball when played in warmer weather. A month-by-month study of the leagues through

1978–87 (1981 STRIKE SEASON EXCLUDED)

	AT BATS	BB	BB AVG.
Montreal-Home	49,055	4,648	.0866
Montreal-Road	49,725	4,190	.0777
Percentage difference at home			+11%

	AT BATS	BB	BB AVG.
Los Angeles-Home	49,481	4,289	.0798
Los Angeles-Road	49,539	4,851	.0892
Percentage difference at home			−11%

three full seasons (1979–80, 1982) showed a significant though small reduction in walks and strikeouts for the two hottest months of the season, July and August. Okay, that fits; Montreal is a lot colder than Los Angeles. But the effect didn't change any when the Expos began using their roof in 1987; the walk rate was still 12% higher in their home games.

We also know that parks that accent power hitting also tend to produce more walks. It appears to be less of a factor than the weather, but a legitimate one all the same. When San Diego and Texas became better home run parks, they also became far more conducive to the base on balls. It only makes sense that the pitchers would tend to pitch more carefully when there is a greater threat of a home run.

This, however, does not fit for Montreal. Neither the Dodgers nor the Expos have home run parks—in fact, before the Expos began using their roof, they had the worse home run adjustment of the two. The Expos also had a poorer power park than the Blue Jays' stadium in Toronto, and that park seems to have a minimal effect on walks despite the cold weather.

At one time I thought I had the answer: Both Toronto and Montreal are football parks in the Canadian league, which means a significant overlap in the schedules of the two sports. Toronto's pitching mound is not on the football field, and thus wouldn't have to be removed and rebuilt several times during the season, which might perhaps create an inconsistent mound, which might throw off the pitchers' control. In Montreal, the pitcher's mound has to be removed for the football games. The only problem with my little theory is that I recently found out that Montreal has a retractable platform under the mound to avoid having to change it constantly. I still think there is a connection between the mound and the unusual park walk adjustment. Maybe we'll find out that the whole damn mound is slightly tilted sideways on its mechanical lift.

Another common area of confusion in park adjustments involves how a park affects right-handed hitters versus left-handed hitters. Some believe that Fenway Park favors righties over lefties. Actually, it's about even, with the lefties getting more in batting average and the righties getting a few more homers. Yankee Stadium is a far better park for lefties than righties, but it is also commonly believed to be a good park for all lefties, when it actually helps only the small class of left-handed pull hitters like Dickey, Nettles, and Mantle from the left side.

Tony Kubek believes Toronto's Exhibition Stadium favors lefty home runs because the ball carries better to right center. I don't doubt the last part is true; Kubek has a good eye, and I think he has seen more than enough Blue Jays games to pick out whether the ball carries better in a particular direction. But I have tried a number of times to establish that the park significantly favors left-handed homers, and the results keep coming out damnably neutral. Time may still prove Kubek's deduction to be correct, but it doesn't always follow that the obvious connection is the true one.

The clearest ballpark contradiction between common observation and actual research involved a very similar case with the prairie wind at Arlington Stadium in Texas. Before the Rangers erected the present scoreboard and advertising boards that wrap around the outfield area, the prevailing wind blew in over right center and held up any long balls hit in that direction that were higher than the outfield fence. This was extremely visible; thousands noticed it, hundreds of thousands commented on it. Everyone down to the last player, fan, and reporter believed that Arlington Stadium was tougher on left-handed homer hitters than right-handed homer hitters.

I believed it and set out to discover the magnitude of this effect.

Surprise! Over a seven-year period covering 615 home runs, more left-handed homers were hit in Rangers *home* games—appropriately counting both teams—than were hit in Rangers road games. And there were 75 fewer home runs hit by *righties* at Rangers home games than in road games. Sacrilege and pass the straitjackets! Many responsible people in the press and even in the Rangers' organization itself refused to believe the evidence.

	LEFT-HANDED BATTERS HR/AT BATS	RIGHT-HANDED BATTERS HR/AT BATS
Arlington Stadium, 1976–82	308 / 15,438 (.0200)	441 / 21,470 (.0205)
Ranger road games, 1976–82	307 / 15,299 (.0201)	516 / 21,241 (.0243)
Percentage difference at home	−00.5%	−15.6%

Interestingly, among these seven seasons were three when the Rangers were outhomered at home but managed to outhomer their opponents on the road. This odd phenomenon fit in well with the realization that Arlington Stadium actually favored left-handed homers over righty homers. You see, in those three seasons the Rangers had 32% fewer left-handed at bats than their opponents. In the other four seasons, when the Rangers had a normal home field edge in homers, they also had the edge in left-handed at bats (+11%).

Coming up with a realistic theory to account for this unexpected reality took some time, but eventually jumped out of a chart of *where* the balls were being hit out. The difference seemed to be this: A lefty could hit a ball out in either direction at Arlington Stadium, but it took a tremendous blast by a right-hander to put the ball out anywhere to the right of center field.

When a hitter pulls a ball it has more drive and less loft; hit to the opposite field, and the ball has less drive but more loft. The left-handers were pulling the ball when they hit into the wind, exposing it less to the wind by measures of height—important because of the strength of the wind—and time. When they hit the ball the other way, the wind did not knock down their lofted balls but rather just pushed them toward the short 330-foot left-field corner. The right-handed batters had only one direction to hit the ball out, to left field, and this made them very easy to pitch to. Keep the ball away from a righty, and you could generally keep him in the park. It probably did not hurt that the pitchers were also lulled into a false sense of security about throwing inside to a lefty, relying on the wind to protect them.

After the scoreboards were erected and cut off a sizable portion of the wind, Arlington Stadium went from basically a tie with Kansas City as the toughest home run park in the league to a fairly normal homer rating. The media, the fans, and even the players still relate the wind to the left-handed homer rate and believe that cutting off the wind has helped the lefties more than the righties. Again, exactly the opposite has happened. It is the right-handers who have gained more in their homer rates to center, right center, and right field.

PARK FACTORS AND BASEBALL MANAGEMENT

What role do the parks play in management's decisions, both on the field and in the front office? What are the benefits of a proper understanding of park influences? Most fans are quick to focus on exploiting the park effect in shaping the team's style of play. This obviously is legitimate, and can also be used to adjust the team's style to parks on the road. In the large playing field of Kansas City's Royals Stadium, the catcher could push the pitchers to challenge the opposing power hitters a bit more. The manager might rest one of his power-hitting outfielders in favor of a backup who was faster on defense to head off any extra doubles and triples on the artificial turf, particularly if that backup outfielder was a decent hitter in every regard but power.

But these kinds of adjustments are only a small part of how park factors can influence winning and a ball club's decisions. Baseball history identifies certain types of parks as being more conducive to winning than others. Stroll through the records since World War II and separate out the ballparks of the first-place teams; you'll find an overrepresentation of pitchers' parks and more neutral parks than hitters' parks. Look at the repeat champions and the effect becomes even greater: About 60% of them have home parks that favor the pitcher.

The most difficult part to sustain on a winning team is the pitching staff. Pitchers are extremely vulnerable not just to major injuries, but also to vagaries of performance resulting from a tired arm or a mechanical flaw. More and more research into pitching injuries and impingement or "tired arm" syndrome points to the pitches thrown when the pitcher is fatigued. A hitters' park increases the number of pitchers thrown and increases the chances of a pitcher's working past his endurance level. There are generally more batters per inning, which means more pitches per inning or more pitches to throw the "expected" number of innings for all pitching roles, whether it be as a starting pitcher, short reliever, or long reliever.

The extra pitches thrown in a hitters' park also tend to be especially demanding on the pitcher's arm. More men on base means more pitching from the stretch position, which puts more strain on the arm and shoulder than throwing from the windup. A hitters' park also creates more pressure situations in which a pitcher really has to bear down to get out of the inning.

The problem doesn't stop there. We have seen that younger pitchers, under age twenty-five, are generally more vulnerable to the ill effects of such overwork. In a hitters' park, the attrition rate among pitchers is so high that younger pitchers are frequently forced into major roles before they're ready, adding yet another element to their higher failure rate, creating a vicious cycle.

There are also certain mental factors to pitching in a hitters' park that can damage a pitcher and warp the judgment of management. A park that helps create more crisis situations is likely also to produce more cases in which a pitcher loses confidence or starts to tamper with his mechanics when there's really nothing wrong. On the management side, these apparent pitching crises tend to create a false image of their pitching staff's ability, heightening the green of the grass on the other side. Most teams in big offensive parks like Fenway or Wrigley have a history of trading pitchers below cost and being terribly disappointed with those acquired from other teams.

Fergie Jenkins's career is an excellent example. When the Cubs traded Jenkins after he won only 14 games in 1973 with a 3.89 ERA, they did not expect him to win another 135 games, including a brilliant 25–12 record the very next season. They traded Ron Santo to acquire Steve Stone to take Fergie's place in the rotation; after three seemingly mediocre seasons from Stone, the Cubs repeated their Jenkins mistake and let Steve go as a low-priced free agent. Over the next four seasons Stone went 63–38, 25 games over .500.

And what happened to Fergie Jenkins? He ended up in another extreme hitters' park with the Boston Red Sox in 1976–77. When he ran into a bit of trouble in 1977, he was traded at the end of the season for $20,000 and a utility infielder who never got a big-league at bat. What was Jenkins's crime? He got off to a 5–6 start in 1977 and was taken out of the rotation. His ERA was not that bad if you take into account the ballpark; he was actually 4–1 at Fenway, and in his five road losses the Red Sox scored a grand total of seven runs, 1.4 per loss. Jenkins's ERA in his two years at Boston was 3.63— not a brilliant mark on the surface, but it was the best ERA for a starter on a staff that won 83 and 97 games. Jenkins went on to win 18 in 1978, and 71 more games before his retirement. The Red Sox spent millions on free agent Mike Torrez to replace him; over the next five seasons, Torrez had a 4.51 ERA and five fewer victories than Jenkins did in the same period pitching for far inferior teams.

Although history backs up the logic of a pitchers' park assisting winning performance, I seriously question how far this connection can be taken. I do not believe, for example, that the more extreme a pitchers' park, the better it facilitates winning. It would seem there is a line, and that once it's crossed, the park begins to affect the consistency of the offense and sets off the same type of fallacious logic that afflicts pitchers and management in a hitters' park.

I suspect that happened to the Astros after 1980. The Astros had just set a franchise record with a .577 winning percentage to take their first divisional title. Because of the illusion of the Astrodome, most felt the Astros were pitching-rich but weak in hitting. Controlling the park's influence, the Astros' offense was about 33 runs better than the league average, while their pitching was only 20 runs better. The truth was that their pitching was good but the hitting was even better. The Astros seemed to miss this crucial point, and in 1981 they began to break up the offensive unit they felt was not strong enough. Partially through their unnecessary tinkering, the offense went from a +33 run performance to a −3 in 1981 to a −46 in 1982.

When the Astros began "juicing up" their ballpark in 1985, they helped reduce the errors of judgment commonly caused by extreme park factors. With their bringing in the fences, the Astrodome has moved much closer to the league average, though still a pitchers' park. The team that must now be on its toes is the Los Angeles Dodgers. Their stadium has always been a pitchers' park, and because it has remained unchanged while the rest of the league has made a lot of offensive park changes, the gap is becoming large enough that a large park illusion exists.

Perhaps the greatest limitation to a truly extreme park, and perhaps the best measure of when a park factor has been overdone, is when it begins to limit your potential solutions to your problems. When your ballpark becomes such a factor that you have to ask first whether a player can play in your home park rather than whether he can play, you're in trouble. Building and maintaining a good team requires the ability to make decisions—actually good decisions, but that becomes a moot point if your park has already eliminated the choice. Flexibility frees you from getting squeezed by supply and demand, and it provides the room, the space, for you to separate yourself from the pack through the exercise of your (you hope) wise judgment.

A general manager is better off when he can choose among all the available third basemen, any of whom is capable of making a mild adjustment in style to fit in well in the GM's home park. If the GM's choice is limited to specific talents who can play in his freak park, there are going to be times when he will have to wait out the bad times or perhaps pay through the nose for that rare right player. Fortunately, very few parks exert such a heavy-handed influence: the Astrodome when the fences are back and you are considering a one-dimensional power-hitter; Fenway Park when looking at your average lefty pitcher; and Kansas City and St. Louis when searching for out-fielders to patrol their vast pastures of artificial turf.

Ballparks, particularly the extreme ones, can even influence the financial side of the game. And contrary to what some fans think and how some owners act, money is a real resource in the building of successful teams; handling it well can make the difference between winning and losing.

Baseball rewards extreme performance in geometric progression—a reasonable practice, as the rarity of that performance increases geometrically. A .300 hitter with 30 homers is worth more relative to a .280 hitter with 20 homers than the .280, 20 HR man is to the .260 hitter with 10 homers. The same holds for the pitcher with the 2.50 ERA relative to the one with the 3.00 ERA relative to the 3.50 pitcher. The .280, 20 HR hitter and the 3.00 ERA pitcher are quality players, but the .300, 30 HR hitter and 2.50 ERA pitcher are one in a million (and that's what they get paid). Extreme ballparks lend themselves to extreme statistical performances that, due to the park, are not as rare or as valuable as they appear. Unfortunately, that doesn't sell well to players, their agents, salary arbitrators, or fans.

A player is inclined at contract time, or any other time for that matter, to see himself in the best light possible. If a pitcher has a 2.50 ERA for the Asros, the park is not going to be a factor in his mind when he makes his contract pitch, but the Astros hitter with fifteen homers will claim that he would have socked twenty for any other team. Some bad feelings can come out of such negotiations, the kind of ill will that leads to intemperate trades on ownership's part or the player demanding a trade or taking a free-agent walk.

And, of course, ballparks influence the appeal of the game and thus the attendance and financial resources of a team. Over and over, baseball history has told us that the fans prefer offensive games. Dig a little deeper, and I think there is a similar corollary that the fans also prefer a little variety in their offenses. They don't want an offensive team built on just power or just average. The fans love Wrigley Field and Fenway Park because they are offensively oriented, and assist both the long- and short-sequence offenses.

I have very strong ideas about what the ideal ballpark would be. Recognizing that owners, general managers, sabermetricians, et cetera, like to win even more than they like high attendance—and winning isn't hard on attendance either when you can pull it off—my ideal ballpark needs to have the offensive volume turned down a bit. It should be an overall neutral park or only a slightly offensive park. Proper handling of the pitchers should replace most of the winning benefits derived solely from having a pitchers' park.

I'd want this park to promote variety and balance in the offense. I would try to hold down the offense by removing the cheap home runs but give it back to the singles, doubles, and triples crowd. The park would have deep corners and a deep center field, but have power alleys that would allow honest home runs. That, of course, means that the walls, rather than following the modern semicircle, would jut straight over from the corners to the center-field area, more like those in the older parks. More depth in the corners and center field would mean more doubles and triples, and would generate more tension when an outfielder tried to cut off a ball. The hitting background would be exceptionally good—high, wide, and a flat, deep green (reducing reflection in hitting backgrounds is often underrated). This would produce a few more homers despite the larger field, and also help keep the singles hitters in the game. To throw in a little flavor, I would break up the outfield wall to produce a couple of nooks and crannies to mix in a few odd doubles and triples, as in Fenway Park's center-field area. Finally, we would have to face the central issue in the future of America's ballparks.

TO TURF OR NOT TO TURF

"That is the question: whether 'tis nobler to suffer the slings and arrows of these outrageous carpets or to take arms against a sea of injuries to body and spirit, and by opposing, end them. To die—to sleep—no more; and by a sleep to say we end the heartache, and the natural shocks that flesh is heir to."

Next to Dick Allen's statement, "If a horse can't eat it, I don't want to play on it," this soliloquy by Willie "Say Hey" Shakespeare is most often quoted as an example of the players' feelings about artificial turf. When the Kansas City Royals were getting ready to replace their turf with a newer carpet, a reporter polled the players on whether they would prefer a grass field to another artificial-turf surface. They voted about twenty-four to one in favor of grass. I think the one exception thought the question was whether to carpet the trainer's room. "No, man, grass would never grow in there."

The players' objections have a lot to do with "the natural shocks that flesh is heir to." Running on artificial turf day after day is very hard on the legs and back. Players complain of shin splints and aches and pains in their knee and ankle joints, basically the result of artificial turf's failure to duplicate the cushioning effect of natural grass. I know the Texas Rangers players with knee and back problems hate to play on the stuff.

Were players like Cesar Cedeno, Greg Luzinski, and Bake McBride hurt by growing up as outfielders running on artificial turf outfields? All three aged very poorly after brilliant beginnings. It's a concern that hasn't been sufficiently studied, but I personally would not want my son playing outfield on the stuff. The players also complain about how turf makes a hot day even hotter. It doesn't store and release moisture to modify its own temperature as the good Lord designed His grass to do. I remember a Cardinals player placing a thermometer on the artificial turf in Busch Stadium, and the mercury went right off the scale when the air temperature was only in the nineties.

I think the most vocal opponents of artificial turf are the paying customers. They'll give you all kinds of reasons for their dislike, but it seems to boil down to the simple fact that it makes them feel uncomfortable and distant from the game. That isn't the stuff they played on as youngsters, and we sure don't need any further separation between the players and fans; the salaries are quite enough, thank you. Things only get worse when the sham sod not only looks different but plays differently from that of our memories.

Oddly enough, the kindest words I hear for artificial turf are inspired by the fact that it plays differently. My friend Bill James has written in a couple of places that while he doesn't like artificial turf, he likes what it does to the game. He thinks turf gives variety to the game, spices it up with more steals, doubles, and triples, a greater emphasis on defense in the outfield and behind the plate.

I argue exactly the opposite, that turf takes variety *out* of the game. Baseball is meant to accommodate a wide variety of body types and skills. There's a great photo from the 1970s that shows Frank Howard at six seven, 300 pounds, playing first base with Fred Patek at five four, 140 pounds, as the base runner. Great arm, rag arm, baseball has a place for you. If you can hit the ball 350 feet, baseball can team you with a guy who hits it 600. If they time you with a camera flash or a calendar, you can play baseball.

Artificial turf upsets that balance by giving away too many jobs based on whether a player has the speed to play defense on turf. We don't have enough real players with the speed to play this turf game. We cut our options and end up with too many players with large gaps in their baseball skills who survive only because of the new emphasis on their quickness. What was Omar Moreno doing playing nine years as a regular in the major leagues? Let's get some of the tanks back out there in left field. I want to know that a Lou Boudreau would still be able to play shortstop. It is bad enough to have fake grass forced on us without giving us Monsanto ballplayers, too.

If we want to change the elements in the game, we should try to do it without destroying its balance and character. All the things that James likes about artificial turf could be brought out through other changes, many of them already suggested in this book. You can accomplish all kinds of things without taking the "park" out of ball-park.

What makes artificial turf so attractive to management, anyway? It is not the bargain that it originally claimed to be. It turns out not to be near as durable, and in 1985, *Sports Illustrated* reported that it has been more expensive in the end than grass. Why are we paying more for something that is inferior, dangerous, and so aesthetically disappointing?

Artificial turf was supposed to help if you shared your ballpark with a football team, but the two sports got along before and still manage to coexist quite nicely in the grass parks. And the trend is now toward independent stadiums for the two sports. Football and baseball share fewer stadiums today than ever before; fewer than half the teams now share their parks with a football tenant.

But it is the dome factor, not football, that has been artificial turf's biggest ally. Artificial turf got its start in 1965 because they had trouble growing grass in the Astrodome. Now we have four of these mush-rooms cluttering up the game and claiming artificial turf as a necessity. Hey, guys, it's twenty years later; we put a man on the moon over fifteen years ago. I have done some checking, talked with baseball groundkeepers. We are capable of growing grass under a dome and having it hold up under professional use as a baseball field.

The synthetic-turf people keep pointing out that their man-made mutations are constantly improving, becoming less dangerous, more like grass. Well, we are also making great strides in the care of professional grass fields. New drainage principles cut down on the rainouts and potential problems left behind by a fierce football game. The men we have caring for our fields are far more educated and qualified for their work than the old crews who were hired less for ability and more for who they knew. I think we can break the chains that bind us to this Frankenstein sod.

I am not a fanatic. I have never claimed that artificial turf causes cancer. I respect a lawsuit as much as the next guy. What I have is a dream. I have a dream that one day in grassy green ballparks the fans of the American League and the fans of the National League will be able to sit down together in the bleachers of brotherhood. I have a dream that one day even the Astrodome, suffering in its stale air between shadows and faded green carpet, will be transformed into an oasis of cool, sweet-smelling grass and memories.

I have a dream that Commissioner Giamatti will open a Salvage Carpet outlet with Bob Uecker doing the commercials from coast to coast. I am flooded with thoughts right out of W. P. Kinsella's story, *The Thrill of the Grass*, in which his baseball fans use the cover of the strike of 1981 to secretly transform an artificial turf field back into one of grass. Each night in that weird summer of no baseball in July, they sneak into the stadium at night to replace sections of carpet with God's green grace—I mean grass.

> I often remain high in the stadium, looking down on the men moving over the earth, dark as ants, each sodding, cutting, watering, shaping. Occasionally the moon finds a knife blade as it trims the sod or slices away a chunk of artificial turf and tosses the reflection

skyward like a bright ball. My body tingles. There should be symphony music playing. Everyone should be humming "America the Beautiful."

Toward dawn, I watch the men walking away in groups, like small patrols of soldiers, carrying instead of arms, the tools and utensils which breathe life back into the arid ballfield. . . .

What will the players think, as they straggle into the stadium and find the miracle we have created? The old-timers will raise their heads like ponies, as far away as the parking lot, when the thrill of the grass reaches their nostrils. And, as they dress, they'll recall sprawling in the lush outfields of childhood, the grass as cool as a mother's hand on a forehead.

"Goodbye, goodbye," we say at the gate, the smell of water, of sod, of sweat, small perfumes in the air. . . .

Alone in the stadium in the last chill darkness before dawn, I drop to my knees in the centre of the outfield. My palms are sodden. Water touches the skin between my spread fingers. I lower my face to the silvered grass, which, wonder of wonders, already has the ephemeral odours of baseball about it.

THE FAMOUS "BALLPARKS ARE LIKE COWS" ANALOGY

Ballparks. Oh, how they can make a baseball fan a little crazy. One night during a pitching change at Arlington Stadium, I started talking with the gentleman next to me about this chapter. In trying to express my feelings about ballparks, I found myself talking about cows. When I finished saying my piece—which came from God knows where— my neighbor gave me a queer look and said, "I dare you to put that in your book."

Well, I don't remember it exactly. I know I rambled a bit. I finished up talking about a cow I once saw wearing a red bandanna and how that could only happen in America—which isn't true but makes a point somewhere about something, I'm sure. When I was a bit more lucid, I said something like this: "I love ballparks, those curious cows in the background who can't help crowding up to the fence and sticking their noses into baseball's business. No one is safe. They bump against the players, step on the feet of the decision makers, and take an occasional kick while teaching us about winning. If we learn anything about them, let it be that we cannot paint this landscape without including them in the picture."

For my nameless friend, who I doubt took me very seriously, I offer this closing story of how a pennant was won over the confusion of a coin flip and the difference between Ebbets Field and the Polo Grounds. This little gem is told by Ralph Branca in the fascinating book *Bums: An Oral History of the Brooklyn Dodgers*.

For some reason, when the Dodgers won the toss for the playoffs in 1946, they elected to go to St. Louis to play the first game and then come back and play the next two in Brooklyn. I do not know who made the decision, but because of it we had to travel by train to St. Louis, which was a 26-hour trip, and we were exhausted, and of course, we lost.

And the reason I bring it up, now it's 1951, and we're in Philadelphia, and the Giants are in Boston, and we have a playoff with the Giants, and they toss a coin, and the Dodgers win the toss again. Only this time, no one is around because they are all in Philadelphia, and they call a guy named Jack Collins, who was ticket manager. Collins remembers that the '46 decision was wrong, that we went all the way to St. Louis and then all the way back, and so he makes the decision that we'll play the first game at Ebbets Field and the next two at the Polo Grounds. I'll bet you never heard this story, but in the first game Thomson hit a home run off me in Ebbets Field that would have been an out in the Polo Grounds, and the ball he hit in the third game would have been an out in Ebbets Field.

Bobby Thomson's shot heard round the world was hit to the short left-field seats of the Polo Grounds. Branca claims it went over the wall by about six inches at a distance of 300 feet. More impartial observers claim it went no farther than 316 feet. No matter; either way it was a very catchable ball—if it had been hit at Ebbets Field. If the Dodgers had made the logical choice and the ballparks had been reversed, Ralph Branca could have been the hero, not the goat. October 3, 1951—just another day in ballpark history.

Cows, I'm telling you . . .

HOUSE:
A STROLL IN THE PARKS

Fans and baseball writers have been talking about the effects of various ballparks on the game in the last couple of years. There's been an awful lot of talk about it, as though it were something they've just discovered. But there isn't a player in the game who doesn't know about how the park can affect what you're going to try to do out there.

There are two ways to get guys out if you don't have that unhittable fastball: You can do it with location, or you can do it by changing speeds. That's your choice, and the characteristics of the ballpark have a lot to do with which you stress on a given day.

Lew Burdette had a saying about playing conditions. He blamed the conditions on elephants; he said the first thing you had to know when you got to the park was which way the elephants were blowing. That'll take care of the ball in the air. Then you have to check to see whether the elephants have been stomping on the ground. Is the grass short? Long? Rocky? Smooth? All this enters into your equation as a pitcher. If the wind is blowing in thirty, forty miles an hour, you don't mind getting the ball up; that wind's going to keep it in the park. That's the day you emphasize changing speeds. Is it blowing out? Oops; better keep that ball down no matter what. Of course, your breaking stuff's going to be a bit sharper, since the extra air resistance will give your pitches a bigger break. If the elephants are blowing toward left, you'll stay inside to left-handers and outside to righties. Location; that's the key. Rocky ground? Maybe you'd better think about changing speeds again, because fly balls don't take bad hops. The conditions don't change what you're going to throw—a fastball pitcher isn't going to start throwing curves because of the wind. He'll just concentrate a little more on where he puts it.

The park has the same kind of effect. When I pitched in Seattle, they had just an eight-foot fence to go along with those ridiculously short power alleys, and so you never wanted to be in the center of the plate no matter how badly you had them fooled as to the speed.

Go into New York, and a lefty like me didn't have much to worry about thanks to that deep canyon in left center, so I'd be more willing to change speeds and just make sure the lefties didn't pull me. Even Fenway has those times when the wind is blowing in off Lansdowne Street, and the wall is pretty near unreachable, but if it's blowing out, it's location all the way.

For the most part, then, for pitchers the parks break down into the location parks and the change-of-speed parks. The location parks are those where you can get hurt real easily by the long ball or those where the grass is extra high. The change-of-speed parks are the ones where the ball in the air isn't going to hurt you too much, like Kansas City, say, or Dodger Stadium—the forgiving ballparks. So, sure, we're very much aware of the influence of the ballpark when we're out there playing the game. You'd be crazy not to; it would be like a golfer teeing off with a driver on a 150-yard par three.

"TO ONE HE GAVE FIVE TALENTS . . ."

For it will be as when a man going on a journey called his servants and entrusted to them his property; to one he gave five talents, to another two, to another one, to each according to his ability. Then he went away.

He who had received the five talents went at once and traded with them; and he made five talents more. So also, he who had the two talents made two talents more. But he who had received the one talent went and dug in the ground and hid his master's money.

Now after a long time the master of those servants came and settled accounts with them. And he who had received the five talents came forward, bringing five talents more, saying, "Master, you delivered to me five talents; here I have made five talents more."

His master said to him, "Well done, good and faithful servant; you have been faithful over a little, I will set you over much; enter into the joy of your master."

And he also who had the two talents came forward saying, "Master, you delivered to me two talents; here I have made two talents more."

His master said to him, "Well done, good and faithful servant; you have been faithful over a little, I will set you over much; enter into the joy of your master."

He also who had received the one talent came forward saying, "Master, I knew you to be a hard man, reaping where you did not sow, and gathering where you did not winnow; so I was afraid, and

I went and hid your talent in the ground. Here you have what is yours."

But his master answered him, "You wicked and slothful servant! You knew that I reap where I have not sowed, and gather where I have not winnowed? Then you ought to have invested my money with the bankers, and at my coming I should have received what was my own with interest.

"So take the talent from him and give it to him who has the ten talents. For to every one who has will more be given, and he will have abundance; but from him who has not, even what he has will be taken away."

Matt. 25: 14–29

The game of baseball has its own parable of talents. Every player comes to the game with certain raw skills, certain "talents." Yet that alone cannot bring them success. To reach their full fruition, something else is required of them. In the biblical parable it is to improve what they have been given; so it is in baseball. To those who act on this faithful desire, more is given. That is, their talents become more valuable. Of those who do not, "even what they have will be taken away." What talents they have will be diminished by their lack of faithful service.

Even the most talented player in the world cannot reach the promise of his potential without working with those talents. When he falters, it doesn't happen in a vacuum. The space he leaves is an opportunity given to the faithful: a chance to advance ahead of him in the minor leagues, or to take away his playing time in the majors, or even to take away his claim as the greatest player in the game. This is what is "taken" from "him who has not" and the "abundance" given to him "who has."

This is part of the beauty of baseball, a game with clear goals, a game in which men can be judged and rewarded in the end for their accomplishments rather than for the extent of their talents. It is a worthy system, and I view with alarm the erosion of baseball's lesson of the talents.

Baseball has been around a long time; this is both a blessing and a curse to the game. Part of the richness of the game is its sense of history and tradition, yet with that intellectual baggage we lose the honesty and openness that went with our early trial-and-error judgments. We become so confident in our knowledge that it actually insulates us from the truth. We begin to develop rules of thumb and stereotypes that bring prejudice and a false sense of certainty to our decisions.

Nowhere is this more prevalent than in how we evaluate ballplayers. Over the years we have created an image of the talents associated with the successful, and somewhere along the line we began to convince ourselves that this was the measure of a ballplayer. There have always been those who focus on a player's raw talent rather than what kind of ballplayer he is. Shucks, among the amateur free-agent scouts it's as natural as breathing; that's their job. But the problem comes when that focus begins to rule the judgment of the general manager, farm director, field manager, and coaches. And from there it seeps out into the media and into the stands.

We cannot afford to lose sight of the actual measures provided by the game itself. It is not talent that defines a ballplayer. In the context of the game, who can run the fastest, throw the hardest, hit the ball the farthest, etc.—all that is just an intermediate guess. The measure of a ballplayer is simply the quality of his contributions to winning ballgames—no more, no less.

As basic as this may seem, there is no doubt we have wandered far from this obvious truth. Consider our vision of Willie Mays. In 1981, Maury Allen wrote a book ranking the top one hundred players in this century. He ranked Willie Mays number one. Personally, that strikes me as a remarkably stupid choice. But there it is, and you can find a lot of people in Allen's generation who feel exactly the same way.

I contend that the only way you can justify such a decision is to misinterpret "the greatest baseball player" as meaning "the player with the greatest talents for playing baseball"—which Mays very well might have been. I saw both Mays and Aaron play in their prime. There is no question in my mind that Mays was more talented than Aaron. I also have no trouble saying Aaron was ultimately the better player.

Allen's argument for ranking Mays as number one suggests a confusion of talent and style with accomplishment: "[Mays's] timing, his instincts, his reflexes were unmatched in baseball's history . . . [He] ran bases with a flair unmatched in the twentieth century. . . . Mays was an entertainer. People paid to see him play and never felt cheated."

Understand that I have no argument with any of that, nor am I trying to put down Willie Mays. He was a great, great player, probably one of the dozen best in baseball history. If he failed to rise much above his talents, at least he didn't squander them. He did not develop a destructive ego or abuse himself with drink or drugs. He kept himself in shape and preserved a frame of mind that kept him fresh and enthusiastic, a key to his long, outstanding career. It is hard to fault a player whose sole weakness was a character destined more to enjoy the game than to become a baseball craftsman.

My argument with Maury Allen is that having great talent, appealing style, and being a fan favorite has nothing to do with measuring the greatness of a ballplayer. In this regard we must focus on Mays's accomplishments in the context of the game, not his potential and style. If you stop to look at Mays's record as a ballplayer, there is just too much to give you pause in considering him the greatest player ever.

Isn't it odd that the man Allen called "the best defensive outfielder the game has ever seen" kept finishing second to Richie Ashburn in most fly balls caught in a season? Only once did Mays ever lead the league in outfield catches; other ballhawks like Tris Speaker, Ashburn, and Max Carey did it eight times or more. And is it possible for "The Greatest Player Ever" to go through twenty-two seasons without ever once leading his league in RBIs?

In freeing ourselves from a vision of talent as equaling accomplishment, we need to guard against a growing prejudice about which players can play what position. It is obviously a delicate problem. Knowing what type of player generally succeeds at a specific position is a valuable piece of information, but we have to recognize the inherent dangers of such standardization. When we say a third baseman must have a cannon of an arm or that an outfielder must be fleet of foot, we are again putting talent above the reality of the game. We need to remember that, for example, a shortstop is not necessarily a quick little guy with a steady glove, strong throwing arm, and a weak bat. A shortstop is any guy of any physique or skills who makes enough of the defensive plays that, combined with his offensive contribution, has a net value comparable with or superior to other shortstops.

We must break the mesmerism of the stereotypes that rule what we believe is and is not possible. A lot of folks believe that Cal Ripken, Jr., is out of position at shortstop because of his size and the fact he started off as a third baseman. A third baseman is supposed to go to an easier position, not a harder one— to left or right field or to first base.

Yet historically there have been other fine shortstops who were unusually large for the position and started off as third basemen. Bill Dahlen was used more at third base and in the outfield his first four major-league seasons, but he went on to become one of the finest defensive shortstops of his period. George Davis spent two years in the outfield and five at third base before establishing himself as a fine-fielding shortstop who, by all rights, should be in the Hall of Fame. Bobby Wallace did make the Hall of Fame on his shortstop play, but he started as a third baseman and never played a game at shortstop until age twenty-five. And the greatest shortstop of all, Honus Wagner, did not convert to the position till he was twenty-seven years old.

All four of these shortstops carried at least 2.50 pounds per inch of height compared with the 2.35 or less we associate with shortstops like Pee Wee Reese, Phil Rizzuto, Luis Aparicio, Larry Bowa, Mark Belanger, Ozzie Smith, et al. Ripken stands out from the other four because he switched in 1982, while the other four pulled it off some eighty years earlier when the game was still young and we didn't think we knew so much.

Cal Ripken, Jr., is a capable defensive shortstop despite being six four and weighing around 220 pounds. He easily overcomes his lack of quickness with superior anticipation, excellent positioning, great infield instincts, good hands, and an outstanding throwing arm. Rather than trying to push him to third, why not give him his due and see him as he is? Shucks, the man owns the American League record for assists by a shortstop. In the last five seasons (1983–87) he's led the league in assists four times, in double plays three times, and his fielding percentage has been above average among the short-stops playing on natural grass. Maybe you could pull that off without being a good defensive shortstop, but could a poor shortstop do it?

Yet right from the start, a number of observers have been wildly critical of Earl Weaver's assessment that Ripken was more valuable at shortstop. These critics couldn't make a lot of noise when Cal was setting the league assist record, but they got awfully loud in 1986. That spring *The Sporting News* printed a letter from a Baltimore fan who repeated a statistic being widely quoted as proof that Ripken could not handle the shortstop position—that his fielding chances had fallen off by more than 100 from 1984 to 1985. To further underscore his belief that Ripken could not play shortstop, he accused the official scorer in Baltimore of neglecting to charge Ripken with all his legit-imate fielding errors.

First, it isn't unusual to see a significant drop-off whenever the comparison involves such an unusual fielding record which, quite frankly, is set generally by a convergence of circumstance, luck, and skill. In 1985 Ozzie Smith had over a hundred fewer chances than he did in 1980 when he set the National League assist record. And even with the drop-off, Ripken was still above the league average for shortstops in *all* defensive categories including chances fielded cleanly per game.

The letter's contention that Ripken was "protected by a notorious hometown scorer" also happened to be completely at odds with the available evidence. An examination of the 1985 box scores shows that the Baltimore scorer charged *more* errors to Ripken than he did to the visiting shortstops. They also show that the Baltimore scorer charged more errors per game to Ripken than did the official scorers on the road.

I have seen studies that indicate Ripken has slowed down as a defensive shortstop, but I have yet to meet a serious fielding analyst who would say Ripken is even remotely overmatched by the position. The Orioles should get down on their knees and thank their lucky stars that they are able to place such a strong hitter at a key defensive position.

You want to know what shortstops usually hit? In 1987 the average major-league shortstop hit .258 and barely averaged nine homers per 600 PA (.316 on-base average; .367 slugging percentage)—and that was a good year for shortstops! Through 1987, Ripken had a career average of .283 and 22 homers per 600 PA (.348 OBA; .475 SA).

Yet the Orioles' organization has never been completely at peace with Ripken at shortstop. Baseball organizations are not immune to the developed prejudices that run rampant through the media and the fans. Weaver had to fight hard to move Ripken from third to short, and this issue was still being hotly debated in the Baltimore hierarchy at least through the 1986 season.

This isn't unique. You don't have to look far for examples of other front-office decisions reflecting the same prejudice and actually injuring their team. The odd thing is that the media and the fans are so taken in by the same illusions that these decisions are rarely questioned as having been bad moves. Remember when the Boston Red Sox decided that Rico Petrocelli needed to be moved from shortstop to third base in 1971? And when the Texas Rangers made a similar decision with Toby Harrah in 1977?

Petrocelli was never as good as Ripken at shortstop, but they were not far apart. His adjusted range factors were generally pretty normal, he had steady hands and worked pretty well on the double play. In 1969 he led the league in fielding percentage and was second in double plays, and the Red Sox did manage to win a pennant with Rico at shortstop in 1967.

The problem was that Rico did not look like a shortstop or have the ideal skills of a shortstop. He was a little heavy for a shortstop at six feet, 180 pounds, but the real strike against him was the fact that he was a very slow runner. It also didn't help that he was a very good hitter for a shortstop. There seems to be a common belief that a good-hitting shortstop automatically loses points on the defensive scale.

Rico was twenty-eight when he was shifted to third base. The Red Sox traded Mike Andrews, a twenty-six-year-old second baseman who had just hit 17 homers and scored 91 runs, to the White Sox for thirty-seven-year-old Luis Aparicio. Aparicio not only looked like a shortstop and had the normal tools of a shortstop, he was probably the greatest defensive shortstop in the history of the game. Unfortunately, at age thirty-seven the word *was* was already operative. Luis's raw fielding numbers had looked good in 1969–70, but he was playing behind a staff that threw a lot of ground balls thanks to Joe Horlen and Tommy John, and with 42% of the White Sox innings coming from left-handers, there were a lot of extra chances for a shortstop.

See if you can tell when Aparicio took over as Boston's starting shortstop from these numbers:

BOSTON'S SHORTSTOPS

PUTOUTS	ASSISTS	ERRORS	FA	DP
299	501	20	.976	114
287	472	22	.972	92
259	439	20	.972	85
265	457	25	.967	86

The first two lines are 1969–70, Petrocelli's last two years as Boston's starting shortstop. The last two are 1971–72, Aparicio's first two years as Boston's shortstop. Boston dropped two wins the first season after the trade while the White Sox were the most improved team in baseball (23 more wins), as Mike Andrews hit .282 and led the team with a .403 on-base average.

Texas pulled off a near-duplicate of Boston's blunder in 1977. Like Petrocelli, Toby Harrah was twenty-eight years old and considered too large (six feet, 180 pounds) and not quick enough for shortstop. And he, too, was a great hitter for a shortstop. Toby was faster than Petrocelli and probably a better shortstop despite being more error-prone. In fact, the season before the move was Harrah's best in the field as he led all American League shortstops in chances fielded per game, although balancing factors placed his range evaluation behind that of Mark Belanger, Rick Burleson, Robin Yount, and Roy Smalley (who, incidentally, was a fine defensive shortstop before his back injury).

Still, Texas went out and signed free agent Bert Campaneris, the equivalent to an ancient Luis Aparicio. Campy had a strong defensive past but was thirty-five years old and headed for an accelerating defensive decline. Bert did improve the Rangers' defense at shortstop in 1977, but it was only a slight gain that couldn't even dent the offensive differences between Campaneris and Harrah.

In 1978, at age thirty-seven, Campaneris's glove and bat caved in to age. He hit .186 and fielded very poorly. Toby Harrah was called on to play 49 games at shortstop and had more clean chances and more double plays per game at short than Campy did. Harrah also had a sparkling .988 fielding percentage compared with Bert's .954.

It should not be a surprise that Petrocelli, Harrah, and Ripken were better-than-average defensive shortstops. The tendency to evaluate physical gifts over production means you have to do a heck of a job to get a real shot at a position your talents do not naturally point to. Another way to demonstrate this is in baseball's selection of physiques for pitching.

While hitters come in all shapes and sizes due to the differing physiques acceptable from position to position, there is no such confusion among pitchers. Being taller and heavier is a definite edge in pitching professionally; generally, you can throw a bit harder, use your body more, and rely less on your arm, which means fewer arm troubles. Throughout baseball history, the pitchers have been taller and heavier on average than the hitters.

AVERAGE HEIGHT AND WEIGHT BY PERIOD

PERIOD	BATTER'S HEIGHT	PITCHER'S HEIGHT	BATTER'S WEIGHT	PITCHER'S WEIGHT
1901–19	5' 10"	6' 00"	171	180
1920–45	5' 11"	6' 00"	175	181
1946–60	6' 00"	6' 01"	182	189
1961–73	6' 01"	6' 02"	185	192

If it is true that baseball has drifted to physical typecasting, the smaller and lighter pitchers would have to be better than the larger pitchers just to get a chance. To show this, I used the 1984 Neft and Cohen *Sports Encyclopedia: Baseball,* which separates out all the pitchers whose careers fall mainly into the 1973–84 period and gives their career won-lost totals through 1984. First, I separated out all the pitchers listed with a height under six feet. Their career win percentage was .507, versus .498 for those six feet tall or taller. I then did the same thing with those pitchers listed as 175 pounds or lighter. Their career win percentage was .515 versus .498 for those over 175 pounds.

In both cases the smaller, lighter pitchers were actually more productive. Rather than saying smaller pitchers have a physical advantage, I credit this as a direct effect of the prejudice that requires a smaller, lighter pitcher to be better than the larger prospects just to get the chance to pitch.

Of course, we lose sight of productive players over more things than just gaudy talents and position stereotypes of talent and physique. Style has also become a factor in our perceptions. There seems to be some confusion of baseball with figure skating. On more than one occasion I have suggested to a sportswriter that he read the rule book and note that no runs or wins are awarded for style or artistic interpretation.

I haven't quite had the guts to use that line on a member of a baseball organization, but I've been tempted. Style counts among baseball's decision makers, and the more traditional the style the better. If you try to substitute an odd pitch or weird delivery for a major-league fastball, you are sure to face an uphill climb.

You don't see a lot of mediocre knuckleballers or submariners. It's almost impossible for one to get drafted; most have to sign as free agents and then battle like crazy to get to the majors. The Braves did not call a press conference when they signed a twenty-year-old knuckleballer named Phil Niekro. Phil was two years out of high school before he could even get anyone to give him a chance. He was twenty-eight years old before he was in the big leagues for good. His brother Joe learned from Phil's experience and temporarily gave up on the knuckler. He was drafted as a conventional pitcher in the seventh round of the June draft in 1966. Charlie Hough was an eighth-round pick in the same draft, but he also entered baseball as a conventional fastball pitcher.

Gene Garber also had a normal style when he was selected by the Pirates in the thirteenth round, about the 260th player selected. At five ten, 172 pounds, he was not considered much of a prospect. He did not initially help his chances when one day in the International League he dropped down and sidearmed a hitter. Garber, a free spirit who already knew he was a long shot, liked the new delivery and continued with his sidewinding style the rest of his career. He made the big leagues for keeps in his tenth professional season and excelled as a pitcher for Philadelphia and Atlanta. He is the Braves' career leader in saves despite the fact he was already over thirty when he arrived in Atlanta in 1978.

Bruce Sutter was drafted about as low as you can get without signing as a free agent; he went in the twenty-first round. He had a conventional pitching style but not a lot of obvious talent. With a little coaching help, he developed his legendary split-fingered fastball. The Chicago Cubs were rather confused about how to evaluate this strange pitch, though they were open-minded enough not to fire the coach. In 1974 Sutter had a 1.35 ERA at Key West and was jumped to AA in midseason, where he had a 1.44 ERA for Midland.

Now after a season like that, where would you expect the Cubs to place him the next season? Why, back in Midland, of course. There he had a 2.15 ERA in 41 appearances when it finally dawned on somebody that they could evaluate this freak pitch by how well it prevented the scoring of runs. What a novel idea!

He was moved up to AAA, where he had a 1.50 ERA and 16 strikeouts in 15 innings. This amazingly earned him a boost all the way to the big leagues even though the Cubs already had a bullpen loaded with "stars" like Zamora, Knowles, Reuschel (Paul, not Rick), Garman, and Coleman. Their combined ERA was 4.32, and no one had reached double figures in saves. Sutter had an ERA of 2.71 and led the club in saves despite missing the first half of the season.

I don't know how effective Kent Tekulve was in high school or college. What I do know from the Phillies' media guide is that he threw submarine-style right from the start. That's probably why he was completely ignored in baseball's amateur drafts. He finally got a team to take a chance on him as a free agent when he was twenty-two years old. He made the majors for good at age twenty-eight and became the greatest reliever in Pittsburgh's history. Tekulve's career ERA entering 1988 was 2.72 with 179 career saves.

I know a little more about Dan Quisenberry's predraft record. As a college pitcher in 1975, he began throwing submarine as a response to arm fatigue during the season. He did not throw hard—still doesn't—but his 19 victories were the most by a collegian in 1975. He won 13 straight at one point and was named to the NAIA All-America team. Where did this twenty-two-year-old go in the draft? He didn't. The Royals ended up signing him as a free agent.

The Royals then ran into "Cubitis" as they bounced him around between Waterloo and Jacksonville even though he was always successful wherever they placed him. His ERAs from 1975 to 1978 went 2.42, 1.00 (honest), 1.34, and 2.39, yet not once did he get to throw an inning above AA. Finally at age twenty-six they let him pitch at Omaha, and by midseason he was in the majors for good.

This doesn't happen as often to hitters. Hitting has retained much of its mystery and thus preserved more of its freedom to experiment. Batters with a timing hitch or those who step into the bucket are not among the scouts' favorites, but they won't ignore them the way they will a knuckleballer or submariner. There is still a little reluctance to accept a youngster with a one-legged stance like Mel Ott or Sadaharu Oh, although hitting 511 home runs or being the greatest hitter in Japanese history seem like pretty good recommendations.

Baseball is also reluctant to encourage the extremely open stance. I cannot think of any player who came into baseball with this as his established stance. A few have worked it out on their own once they were already professionals: Dick McAuliffe, Brian Downing, and Jose Canseco in his rookie year have probably been the most radical in recent times. Rod Carew used a modification of this stance, which was also picked up by Cecil Cooper. Eddie Murray uses another adaptation, and Wayne Tolleson helped himself immensely in 1985 by opening up his left-handed stance.

This stance has its pros and cons and should be matched carefully according to such considerations as a player's vision, patience, platoon difference, and power potential. This kind of stance generally creates a larger platoon difference than normal, but it helps you judge the pitches coming in, particularly if your dominant eye is the one farthest from the pitcher, and the stance frequently adds to a batter's power. The unusual success enjoyed by its practitioners is just another example of the extra success *required* of any style that goes against the grain.

Beyond the growing reliance on raw talent, physical stereotypes, and conventional styles, our judgment has been further frozen by a statistical fascination that is locked into a set view of traditional categories to the exclusion of all else. We like to kid ourselves that by "looking at the numbers" we can curb our wandering from honest, responsible evaluations of ballplayers. Unfortunately, it doesn't work that way. A record or statistic is objective only in the sense that a word can be objective. Words can have clear objective definitions when studied individually, but that intrinsic objectivity vanishes when we use them to communicate some broader idea. Then it becomes subjective, a matter of context and interpretation.

The same thing is true with baseball records and statistics. If we do not provide the objectivity in their use and interpretation, if we do not work at understanding their meaning, they can be just another form for our developing stereotypes and prejudices.

Over the years the numbers game in baseball has developed its own sacred cows that tend to color our views just as much as a focus on talent and style over actual productivity. We have made batting average more than a benchmark or indicator; we have made it a god of offensive evaluation. In some cases we have declared it the sum of all offense. How else can we explain baseball's habit of ranking team offenses by the order of their batting average rather than their runs scored? And if batting average is the Father, home runs are the Son, and RBIs the Holy Ghost. This is baseball's holy trinity, its Triple Crown.

The power of this numerical prejudice was clearly demonstrated in 1979 when Don Baylor was named Most Valuable Player of the American League. Baylor won the award on the strength of his .296 average, 36 homers, and league-leading 139 RBIs. Playing on the same team was Bobby Grich, who hit .294 with 30 homers and 101 RBIs. It didn't seem to matter that Grich actually led Baylor in slugging percentage or that Baylor's lineup position gave him 44% more plate appearances with runners in scoring position. Even more startling was the voters' lack of interest in Grich's playing 153 games at a premium defensive position—second base—and playing it well. Baylor was essentially a designated hitter who was pressed into outfield service for 97 games only because Rick Miller had broken a hand and Joe Rudi broken a wrist.

DON MATTINGLY, 1985 MVP?

This point is probably best illuminated by the controversy over the 1985 Most Valuable Player Award in the American League. Actually, there really wasn't any controversy; Don Mattingly won the award easily, garnering 82% of the first-place votes. Maybe someday the lack of controversy will in itself become controversial.

It seems incontrovertible to me that George Brett had a far more valuable 1985 performance than Mattingly. Both were durable stars making significant contributions to fine teams. Brett's Royals even finished first in their division, while Mattingly's Yankees were second in the East. Both players were Gold Glovers on defense, but Brett did it at third base, a much more demanding position than first base.

And what about their hitting? Baseball offense is fairly simple, basically a combination of getting men on base and moving them around to score. Brett was second only to Wade Boggs in getting on base; his .436 on-base average was 55 points ahead of Mattingly's. The best batting measure for advancing base runners is slugging percentage, and Brett led the league in that category, with Mattingly almost 20 points behind. All the various "runs created" formulas agreed that Brett's performance had a higher run value, and the gap only got larger when it was made a ratio of run value per out expended. For those who don't trust such measures, Brett also led

Mattingly in runs scored plus RBIs per out expended, .567 to .550. And that was with the Royals scoring 152 runs fewer than the Yankees.

So how in the world did Mattingly crush Brett in the MVP voting? The reason is that the vast majority of the voters blindly followed the Triple Crown numbers. Brett outhit Mattingly by 11 points, but Don hit five more homers and had a lot more RBIs, 145 to 112. That was basically it; Mattingly had the edge in two legs of the Triple Crown. Ironically, even those edges were questionable. Brett's home park, Royals Stadium, is the toughest home run park in the league. Brett actually outhomered Mattingly by three dingers in 1985 road games. As for the RBIs, one has to remember that they were in very different lineups. Their situational batting statistics underscore the fact that Mattingly's RBI total was a very normal function of his line-up position in a potent offense.

1985	AT BATS	BA	SA
Mattingly, men on base	315	.321	.549
Brett, men on base	221	.367	.615
Mattingly, runners in scoring position	174	.316	.466
Brett, runners in scoring position	147	.340	.558

At least there were five voters (out of twenty-eight) who felt Brett's performance was better than Mattingly's. None of the voters accepted my contention that Mattingly wasn't even the best player on his *team*. Rickey Henderson was a better player than Mattingly in 1985, but less than a third of the MVP voters even considered him among the league's top three players. Henderson versus Mattingly, 1985: I consider this the classic battle between reality and the rampant stereotypes of talent, style, and numbers that plague baseball today.

Other than his speed, Henderson's raw talents were never all that obvious. When Rickey started off professionally, he was considered a so-so prospect, a decent bat with excellent speed, but a poor defensive outfielder with little power. He led in outfield errors his first two minor-league seasons and hit only 17 homers in 384 minor-league games.

Mattingly looked like a hitter right from the start. He hit .349 his first pro season, and the next year hit .358 to win the batting title and the Most Valuable Player award for the Southern League. He continued to hit over .300 in all of his minor-league seasons and averaged 104 RBIs for every 150 games. Neither player showed much power in their early years, but even in this traditional category Mattingly held the edge. In their first five seasons Don's home run rate was about 30% greater than Rickey's. Mattingly had his first twenty-homer season at age twenty-three; Henderson's came at age twenty-six.

Mattingly has exactly the kind of talent, style, and numbers that baseball traditionalists and statisticians—not to be confused with sabermetricians—go wild over. First and foremost, he's a high-average hitter. Then in 1984–85, he added the next most respected ornament by learning to hit for power. That combination gave him the lineup position to capture the final jewel, RBIs. If you can excel in those three departments, it really doesn't matter to most MVP voters whether you do anything else. You don't have to draw walks, steal bases, stay out of double plays, play a key defensive position, or even field well.

Let's start our comparisons between the two out in the field. I'm not going to argue against Mattingly's Gold Glove for defensive excellence at first base; I think it was well earned. But first base is first base. A superb defensive center fielder has much greater defensive value, and that's exactly what Henderson was in 1985 despite not winning a Gold Glove award. Frankly, he was robbed. In 1985 he led all center fielders, both leagues, in balls caught per game with a 3.11 mark, just ahead of Gary Pettis at 3.02. If you think that has something to do with Yankee Stadium's large center field, let me point out that Henderson is the *only* Yankees center fielder to ever do it. Stick *that* in your media guide.

An even more amazing testimony to Henderson's defense—also

completely overlooked—is that in 1981 he led the major leagues in outfield catches. It is the only time in the Live Ball Era (1920 to present) that a *left fielder* has led the way.

I personally know Gold Glove voters who say they cannot vote for Henderson because they cannot accept a Gold Glover with a weak throwing arm. This is a perfect example of what this chapter is all about. The strength of Henderson's throwing arm is not the issue here. We are not scouting some high school player and trying to predict where his talent will take him; we are long past that point. The master has returned, and it is time to see what the servant has done with the talents given him. We owe it to Henderson to judge him by his accomplishments rather than his talents.

The Gold Glove award should not be for classical form, raw talent, or even the completeness of talent. You don't win a batting title by looking good swinging the bat, hitting to all fields, or even by having a lot of hitting talent. We do not declare a team a winner because we like the way it plays, or because it excels in every area of the game, or even for having the best talent.

How freely did runners go from first to third on singles to Henderson? Were his assist totals unusually low for his position? Was his overall defensive contribution more valuable than any other outfielder? These are the legitimate questions for this issue. The evidence indicates that Henderson gets to the ball so quickly that the overall rate of runner advancement is normal despite his subpar throwing arm. Even ranking his arm as a minus, when you weigh it against his tremendous superiority in running down fly balls, his performance in 1985 was Gold Glove-caliber, or certainly at least worthy of more appreciation than his fielding has received.

There is a fielding factor here that should also count at home plate. You have to consider the law of supply and demand when comparing a center fielder's offense with a first baseman's. It's easier to find a player who can hit and play first base than it is to find one who can hit and play center field. Among the Yankees' 1985 competitors, eleven of the thirteen teams had more efficient run production out of their starting first baseman than their starting center fielder. That wasn't unusual; just about any season will produce similar results.

Using 1987 major-league data provided by STATS, the overall offensive production (run value per out expended) by first basemen was about 17% better than that of center fielders.

1987	BA	OBA	SA	HR/600 PA
CF	.276	.343	.430	15
1B	.283	.360	.482	24

But even if Henderson and Mattingly were both first basemen, Rickey was the better offensive player in 1985. Why didn't the voters see that? One reason is that Henderson's offensive accomplishments were more diversified than Mattingly's. Rickey hit 11 fewer homers and was 10 points behind in batting average, but he also walked twice as frequently to get on base more (a 40-point edge in OBA); he led the league with 80 steals and had a phenomenal success rate of 89%; and he used up 77 fewer outs than Mattingly did. That broad-based style may not produce eye-catching numbers, but it does add up, and it does count. It contributes to winning games, and that's the bottom line.

If you figure Mattingly's runs produced by the Paul Johnson formula—which favors Mattingly and is slightly more accurate in this kind of comparison than James's runs-created formula—Don's 1985 performance was responsible for approximately 127 runs. Rickey Henderson was responsible for 125, but when you consider that the Yankees scored a little more than 15 runs for every 77 outs in 1985, taking into account Henderson's sizable edge in outs used up makes his performance about 13 runs more valuable than Mattingly's (15 + 125 − 127 = 13).

1985 RUN PRODUCTION (JOHNSON FORMULA)

	RUNS PRODUCED	OUTS EXPENDED*	RUNS PRODUCED PER OUT
Mattingly	127	475	.267
Henderson	125	398	.314

*Outs Expended = Hitless At Bats, SH, SF, CS, and GDP.

Mattingly's big edge with the voters came from his big numbers in the more traditional categories. His biggest billboard was his 145 RBIs. The reverence for this category can be seen in the media blitz that tried to turn it into some kind of statistical landmark. You could punch the button on any sportswriter and hear, "No AL player has had more than 145 RBIs in thirty-six years!" (Ted Williams had 159 in 1949.)

Really, guys, that's true, but hardly as impressive as you made it sound. Geez, George Foster, a National Leaguer, had more RBIs than that just eight years earlier. It was only five more than Killebrew had in 1969, and four other American Leaguers have been in the 142–45 range since Williams. And none of those guys had the benefit of Rickey Henderson in front of them or a DH-lineup, and most didn't have a team that scored as many runs as Mattingly's Yankees.

The real irony is that Henderson's 146 runs scored was a far rarer and more significant accomplishment, but it got about one-tenth as much publicity. In that same thirty-six-year span no one in *either* league had come closer than 10 runs to Henderson's total. Only one other player in the whole history of the game has scored over 145 runs for a team scoring as few runs as the 1985 Yankees. I understand he was a pretty decent player, some guy named Ruth.

After Mattingly won the 1985 MVP award, one New York writer made an observation that was picked up by a number of sports columnists around the country. He made the point that back in May and June you couldn't turn around without tripping over a story hailing Henderson as the best player in baseball and a possible shoo-in for MVP honors. He noted that support faded after the brief strike in the middle of the season. He theorized that the MVP voters turned on Henderson when he "let" himself be delayed a day in returning from the West Coast after the strike.

Horse hockey. You don't need to indulge in that kind of speculation to see why Rickey's MVP chances ran from hot to cold. Henderson was a big MVP candidate when he had the flashy Triple Crown numbers. He stopped being an MVP candidate when those numbers were toned down and Mattingly's took off. It's as simple as that.

Look it up; when all those great Henderson stories were written, he was off to an amazing start in the statistical trinity. In the June 27 statistics, Henderson was leading the league with a .359 average. He had nine homers and 32 RBIs in 55 games. That projects to 27 homers and 94 RBIs in a full schedule; rather amazing for a leadoff man. At the same time, Mattingly was off to a rough start with a .291 average and only six homers.

In the end the writers went straight for the glitter and voted for the prettiest Triple Crown numbers, Mattingly's .324 average, 35 homers, and 145 RBIs. Henderson? Well, .314, 24 homers, and 72 RBIs won't win anything if you don't take the time to look below the surface and see things like the .419 on-base average, the 80 steals, or that he had 45% fewer at bats with men on base than Mattingly did. And yes, like Brett, Rickey hit higher with men on base than Mattingly did (.337 to .321).

Sadly, the 1985 MVP voting is only part of a trend that is worsening. When I look over the history of the MVP voting, I see a growing disregard for the value of defense, the value of offense relative to position, and the value of offensive contributions beyond the traditional Triple Crown numbers.

The 1987 MVP decisions in both leagues were a disgrace to what the award is supposed to represent. It doesn't bother me that Andre Dawson played for a last-place club. It bothers me that players like Tony Gwynn, Dale Murphy, Tim Raines, Jack Clark, Eric Davis, Darryl Strawberry, and several others were significantly better than Dawson despite his edge in playing in the best hitters' park in the country. And in the American League? Well, the selection of George Bell over Alan Trammell is one of the silliest selections in the history of the award. It's also perfectly consistent with the recent trend in MVP voting.

"FAITHFUL OVER A LITTLE, I WILL SET YOU OVER MUCH"

Having said all that, it may be hard to believe this, but it really doesn't make a whole lot of difference to me who actually gets a Most Valuable Player Award. What concerns me is what the quality of that judgment says about the state of the game. If prejudice and stereotype dictate the achievement awards, it is likely a reflection of their presence in the decisions that actually affect the game and the men who play it.

I intend this chapter to be a fight against letting these developing stereotypes take over the game. I am fighting for the recognition of players based on *how well* they do the job rather than *how* they do it. I don't count talent or potential; I count production. I'm not interested in whether a player looks the part or follows a traditional style; I'm interested in what he actually accomplishes. And I don't care how dominating he may be in one key area or another; I want the bottom line, the sum of all his contributions to winning.

Maybe I should start my own award—call it "The Dick McAuliffe Award." Besides being the baseball hero of my youth, his career epitomizes what the award is all about. He was a player who got the most out of what he had, one whose proudest achievement as a player was "that I can say I gave this game the best shot I had every day I ran on the field."

Because he ended up being so much better than the expectations from his talent, because he had an unorthodox style of play, and because he broadened his contributions in so many directions, there was a tendency to miss how good a ballplayer he really was. Ask a baseball fan about Dick McAuliffe, and he'll probably remember little more than that he was a middle infielder for Detroit in the 1960s who was known for his fiery play.

It isn't surprising that the common memory of McAuliffe as a player is so sketchy. The media didn't talk a lot about his accomplishments. Their two favorite topics were his odd batting stance and the fact that his talents fell short of what the Tigers seemed to need from him. When the Tigers were desperate for a shortstop, they said Dick didn't have a strong enough arm to play the position; when they needed a leadoff hitter, they said his batting average was too low.

I don't mean to give the impression that the media did not like Dick or that he was an unpopular player. Exactly the opposite was true. McAuliffe was very popular and highly respected by his teammates, the media, and Tigers fans. But the gist of their admiration, as nice as it was, had little to do with his actual accomplishments.

Generally the comments went along these lines: In 1973, Detroit sportswriter Joe Falls wrote that McAuliffe was one player he always admired because he was "a completely honest worker." McAuliffe was one of the few teammates Denny McLain did not rip in his bitter autobiography, *Nobody's Perfect,* but his actual point was this: "[One] with an immense desire to play, and one to whom God gave only minimal skills, is Dick McAuliffe. . . . Here's a guy who made himself a major-league player simply through hard work."

That's fine, but Dick McAuliffe was a lot more than just an honest hard worker, and he was more than just another run-of-the-mill major-leaguer. We seem to have a heck of a hard time admitting to ourselves that, come to the bottom line, he was a very good ballplayer.

Okay, maybe his arm was a little weak to play shortstop. He still played it well enough to put in over 650 games at the position before the Tigers were able to shift him to his more natural position of second base. And he was good enough to be the league's starting All-Star shortstop in 1965 and 1966. When he did move to second base he remained an All-Star. How many players have been All-Stars at both shortstop and second base?

It's great that McAuliffe worked hard to make himself a better offensive player; he taught himself to hit left-handed, to hit intelligently according to the situation, and he developed his unique wide-open stance to help himself as a hitter. But rather than just talking about what a great guy that made him, why don't we give a little recognition to what it did for him as a ballplayer?

Let's give some attention to how all that helped him to walk more and gave him surprising power for a player who was only five eleven, 175 pounds. He certainly wasn't a classic hitter, and he wasn't going to impress a lot of people with his career batting average of .247. But he did average 18 homers and 81 walks per 162 games, and he did it as a middle infielder in a time when offense was at an all-time low for the Live Ball Era. That's worthy of being part of our memory of him as a player.

McAuliffe's career can win you a lot of beers in a baseball trivia bar. Name the five shortstops with two seasons of more than 22 homers? Ernie Banks, Vern Stephens, Rico Petrocelli, and Cal Ripken, Jr., come quickly to mind, but it usually takes another ten guesses before someone says McAuliffe. Last American League second baseman to hit over 20 homers and draw over 100 walks in the same season? That was McAuliffe. The player who led the league in runs scored with the lowest batting average? McAuliffe, with 95 runs scored and a .249 average in 1968. The only player in the last 50 years to play 150-plus games in a season without grounding into a double play? McAuliffe again.

There are a lot of players out there worthy of "The Dick McAuliffe Award." I could have easily named the award after the player I now officially choose as its first recipient: Joseph Leonard Morgan.

THE BALLAD OF LITTLE JOE

Eddie Robinson was the Houston Astros' farm director when Joe Morgan was first scouted and signed. Morgan had been completely overlooked as a high school player, considered too small with too weak an arm. Robinson had hired a new scout, a former teammate from his White Sox days, a gentleman named Bill Wight. Being a novice to the scouting game, Wight had internalized few scouting prejudices. The first player he signed was Walt "No-Neck" Williams, five six, 180 pounds—not your typical baseball prospect, but he went on to play ten years in the majors.

The second player Wight signed was Joe Morgan. Robinson remembers that they used to kid Wight about signing such funny-looking players, "first Williams, and now a midget." Actually, Morgan was the same height as Williams at the time but was twenty-five or thirty pounds lighter. A lot of things had to come together for Morgan to get the chance to play professionally. He was fortunate that the Astros were an expansion team trying to fill out its minor-league rosters and willing to try anyone with reasonable promise. And Morgan was lucky enough to be seen by a scout who would not judge him solely by his size.

There were a number of similarities between Williams and Morgan. Both were ignored as high school players; both were unusually short but had surprising power for their size; both were fast runners; both had gone on to play college ball in hopes of sparking new interest among the scouts; and both had been born in Texas—which probably didn't hurt when you were scouted by a Texas expansion team.

This is not to say that Morgan wouldn't have eventually made it to the majors without the Astros or Bill Wight. If he had really played well in his remaining college seasons, Joe might have caught the eye of some other teams. We will never know for sure. Eddie Robinson remembers that in 1962 there was really no competition in signing him.

The Astros had to show a lot of patience with Morgan's fielding. Robinson remembers: "He tried to do everything too fast in the field to make up for his weak arm. We had to hit him a lot of ground balls to get him to slow down and make the play first and then throw the ball." I took a look at the old reports from the Washington Senators' scouts on Morgan in that first season. They were not very impressed. On a scale of one to five he was an overall three—a "passable" prospect at A-ball. In forty-six categories he didn't have a single one grade, not even for his speed. Defensively he was graded below average on the pivot and in his "hands" rating. He made 42 errors in 147 games at second base.

Of the three Senators scouts who saw Morgan that first season, one liked him considerably better than the other two. His written notes were especially revealing. Note how the very first reference is to Morgan's size, which was listed as five six, 150 pounds that season:

> Every time I look at this guy, I say to myself, I know he's too small, but he did everything to get the job done. I keep thinking of a live major-league fastball knocking the bat out of his hand, but I don't know. He hit the left-handers about as well as he did the right-handers. For a little guy, he has occasional good power. I saw him hit late-inning homers that defeated both Peninsula and Burlington. He was always coming up with the big play. He can pull the ball or go with the pitch. Excellent reflexes and instinct. . . . Usually runs to first in 4.1; however, can do it in 3.9. . . . [He] would help the Washington organization.

That is a remarkably farsighted and, for its time, very courageous report. Way to go, Joe Branzell.

One thing all the scouts missed is that Morgan walked a lot, 148 times in 148 games. Scouts are basically taught to ignore this. It drives me crazy that even on the forms used today, scouts are never asked to comment on this area of a player's offense. If they want, they can refer to it in their notes, but most never bother. Their organizations are basically telling them through the scouting form that they don't really care.

Morgan's walks were the most unique thing about his play in 1963, but three scouts watched him for a total of twenty-two games and never said anything like, "He's a smart hitter," or, "He's patient at the plate," or, "He's a selective hitter," or even just, "He walks a lot." Geez, he probably walked over twenty times in those games. That would be hard not to notice.

The next season everyone began to see that Houston had a real prospect. Joe Morgan won the MVP award in the Texas League. He hit .323 and led the league with 42 doubles to go along with eight triples and 12 homers. He drew 105 walks, stole 47 bases, and did not ground into a single double play. His defensive improvement was just as remarkable, as he led the league in fielding percentage.

One of the Senators' scouts picked out two of his deficiencies: "Runs real well although a little dumb on the bases. Doesn't know how to run the bases. Saw him make a couple mistakes that hurt the club. . . . This kid has a chance with the bat. The only time I saw him look bad is fastballs high inside from LHP."

The baserunning would continue to improve as Morgan matured and got a chance to study one set of pitchers rather than jumping from league to league. The hitting weakness came from his tendency to drop his back elbow. Morgan eventually developed his characteristic chicken flap with his back arm to remind himself to keep his back elbow up so he could handle the higher pitches better.

In 1965 Joe Morgan was the Astros' starting second baseman. He was named National League Rookie Player of the Year by *The Sporting News*. And—surprise—he led the National League in walks. The next year Morgan was having a fine season when he was struck by a line drive in batting practice and suffered a hairline fracture of his kneecap. It was not a career-threatening injury, but it disabled him for 41 days. He hit .285 in 122 games that season.

He hit .275 in 1967 with a bit more power. What makes 1967 stand out is that this was the season that Morgan became serious about his baserunning. Morgan had been a successful stealer against minor-leaguers; 75 steals in 96 attempts, a .781 success rate. In the majors he had been running less and getting caught more: 32-for-50, .640. In 1967 he stole a career-high 29 bases with a .853 success rate. Never again would that rate fall below .727 in a season.

The next season, 1968, would create a crisis in Morgan's career. In the fifth game, he tore ligaments in his knee in a collision at second base. Surgery was required, and Morgan didn't play again till late September when he got into five games, none at second base.

In 1969 there was talk of converting him to an outfielder. Since Morgan had arrived in the majors he had experienced a lot of trouble turning the double play. The scouting reports still harped on his weak arm and poor pivot. In 1967 he turned only 67 double plays in 130 games. Now the concern was that Joe would be gunshy around second after the injury. Morgan took that as a challenge to become a better second baseman.

He worked hard in spring training and was allowed to remain at his position. He turned 79 double plays in 132 games at second, his best mark per base runner per game in the majors thus far. He would continue to improve, and only once in his last fifteen seasons would his double-play rate be as bad as it was in his first three full seasons. Morgan had won a solid reprieve. He did play 14 games in the outfield in 1969, but they would be the last in his long career.

Morgan still had a lot of work to do on his defense. His knee had not fully recovered in 1969, and Joe had the worst range numbers of his career. One scout said it as plain as could be: "He is not a good defensive player. [He] must hit to stay in the majors." The knee did not help there either. Morgan hit for a career-low .236, though he drew a new high of 110 walks and proved he could still go near full throttle in a straight line as he stole 49 bases at a decent .778 clip.

In 1970 Morgan was back to near full strength. He hit .268, drew 102 walks, stole 42 bases, and set new career highs in doubles and runs scored. The scout who was so hard on Morgan's defense was still unimpressed in April: "poor hands—poor arm—fair range—makes a poor double play . . . is an overrated ballplayer." By August the same scout was reporting: "[Morgan] has improved as a fielder . . . just about ready to develop into a good major-league player. . . . Would help us greatly."

The defensive improvement was definitely there in the hard evidence. He set new career highs in range factor, fielding percentage, and double plays per base runner per game. What else is there?

By 1971, his last year in Houston, the fielding reports were basically positive: "His fielding is good enough for me. Arm a little weak, but he knows how to play. Hands a little stiff, but he [gets] in front of the ball and gathers it in. Saw him go out and get a relay, and he threw the runner out at the plate. Can make the double play." Offensively, Morgan hit only .258 but set a career high in power percentage (slugging minus batting), stole 40 bases in only 48 attempts (.833) and grounded into only four double plays in 160 games.

In 1972 baseball began to wake up to how good a player Joe Morgan really was. At the same time that Joe was just beginning to reach his prime, he escaped the Astrodome, then the toughest hitters' park in baseball. His first year with Cincinnati he set career highs in home runs, runs scored, RBIs, walks, steals, batting average, slugging average, and on-base average. On defense, the man who made 42 errors in his first pro season *led* the National League with a .990 fielding percentage and also led in fielding chances accepted. He was one of the top three players in the league, with only Johnny Bench and Billy Williams having comparable seasons.

In 1973, Joe Morgan made a significant breakthrough as a power hitter that had nothing to do with getting out of the Astrodome.

	POWER %	HR PER ROAD GAME
1965–1971, Houston	.135	.085
1972–1977, Cincinnati	.206	.156

	2B	3B	HR	POWER %
1971 Houston	27	11	13	.151
1972 Cincinnati	23	4	16	.143
1973 Cincinnati	35	2	26	.203

Nineteen-seventy-three is also when Joe Morgan did something that few could have conceived of just a few years earlier: He won the Gold Glove for defensive excellence at second base. Joe would win four more Gold Gloves, including one when he tied the record for fewest errors by a second baseman in 150 games or more (five). While the scouts could accept that Morgan had improved his defense, some still stubbornly resisted the idea that he could become an excellent defensive second baseman—still reporting on the talents rather than the production.

A Texas scout reported in August of 1973 that "[Morgan] does not complete a double play very well—below-average erratic arm . . . fair hands." That was rather an odd assessment, as Morgan led the league in double plays despite playing behind a pitching staff allowing the fourth-fewest base runners. Joe had just led the league in fielding percentage in 1972, and in 1973 his .990 fielding percentage was second in the league. He also led the position in chances fielded cleanly per game.

Besides being the best fielder at a premium defensive position, Morgan hit .290 , slugged .493, had an on-base average of .404, and stole 67 bases in 82 attempts (.817). In one of the craziest MVP votes of all time, Pete Rose won the award over a number of deserving candidates including Morgan, who finished fourth.

1973 MVP RANKING

	POSITION	BA	SA	OBA	RUNS PRODUCED	RUNS PER OUT
Rose	RF	.338	.437	.400	111	.234
Stargell	LF	.299	.646	.392	123	.331
Bonds	RF	.283	.530	.370	127	.262
Morgan	2B	.290	.493	.404	123	.277

Really, there should have been no contest between Morgan and Rose and Bonds. Stargell was so awesome with the bat that year that a case could be made for his winning the award. But if I had a choice between a mediocre defensive left fielder producing runs at a .331 rate and the best defensive second baseman in the league producing the same number of runs, though at a .277 clip, I would go with the second baseman every time.

The next year's MVP balloting was even harder to figure. Morgan missed a few more games and produced only 117 runs, but he was far more efficient, with .302 runs per out expended. Steve Garvey, a first baseman, won the MVP while producing only 96 runs at a .208 clip. Garvey was notorious for channeling all of his value into batting average and had only moderate power for a first baseman. With Morgan's broad offensive base, he could have matched Garvey's actual contributions while hitting .250.

Morgan also won another Gold Glove. One scout still filed a report in September saying, "[Morgan's] defensive play is average." That would be the last such report. As Morgan went on to win three more Gold Gloves, the reports began to come back with a terse "good defense."

In 1975 Morgan made yet another breakthrough in his offense. He tacked on *34* points to his previous high in batting average and became a .327 hitter. He also drew a career-high and league-leading 132 walks for an amazing .466 on-base average, the highest by a National Leaguer this side of World War II. He also stole 67 bases in 77 attempts, a career-high success rate of .870. Joe produced 127 runs while using up only 354 outs, a *.359* rate. Finally he was named the league's most valuable player; I believe the key for the voters was his finally hitting .300.

It did not seem possible that Joe could get any better, yet 1976 was his best year in many ways. He stole 60 bases in 69 tries, an .870 success rate. He grounded into only two double plays in 141 games. He hit .320 and led the league in on-base average with his second-best mark ever (.444). He was still the Gold Glove second baseman, and his runs per out expended actually went *up* to .375. But what made it a special year for Joe were two new career highs of 113 RBIs and 27 homers, and *he won the slugging title*. In the Live Ball Era there had never been a slugging leader close to Morgan's size. Hack Wilson was about the same height but forty pounds heavier. Mel Ott at five nine, 170 pounds, is about as close as you can find.

Going back to the idea that old scouting habits die hard, I came across another report on Joe Morgan written in 1977 after he had won his back-to-back MVP awards. Under "Player's Weaknesses" the scout put, "Somewhat limited because of small body." Fortunately, the Hall of Fame does not have a size requirement.

In 1977, at age thirty-three, Morgan had his last great season. He hit .288, stole 49 bases, drew 117 walks, won the Gold Glove, and hit 22 homers. Conceivably he had been the league's best player four years in a row; he was at least in the top three for the last five seasons. By my calculations his 1977 performance was still in the top five.

Morgan had a very bad year in 1978. He was bothered by nagging injuries that caused him to miss thirty-eight games without ever going on the disabled list. The final batting averages in his career were particularly poor as he seemed to seek out some of the toughest hitting parks in baseball. He put in another year at Houston, two in San Francisco, and one in Oakland. Morgan hit only .248 from 1978 to 1984, but thanks to his power, walks, and steals he would remain one of the best offensive second basemen in the game.

1978–84, AGES 34–40

	BA	SA	OBA	STEAL SUCCESS RATE	RUNS PRODUCED	RUNS PER OUT	AVERAGE SECOND BASEMAN
Morgan	.248	.387	.375	.813	462	.202	.145

PER 162 GAMES

	HR	BB	SB
Morgan	14	107	25

Morgan's continued success as a high-percentage base stealer is especially noteworthy as an example of his knack of getting the most out of his ability. Fewer than ten players have stolen one hundred after turning thirty-four. Only Davey Lopes had a higher succes rate that late in his career. Lou Brock, for example, had a .743 success rate after age thirty-three. In his seven final seasons, Lou's best mark was .781, and Morgan *averaged* .813.

In reviewing Morgan's career, it would be reasonable to assume that his attitude and example had a positive effect on his teammates. Bill James once pointed out that while Pete Rose liked to promote his image as an "impact" player, one who brings both great ability and a winning spirit to his team, Joe Morgan is probably more deserving of the title.

When Morgan was with the Astros, there were two notable periods of his absence, the 41 games he was out with the fractured kneecap, and the 157 games after he tore the ligaments in his knee in 1968. In those two seasons the Astros were 65–64, .504, with Morgan available, and 79–116, .405, while he was injured.

The Reds, with Pete Rose as a regular, played .538 from 1963 to 1971. In 1971, the year before Morgan joined the Reds, they were under .500, 79–83. In Morgan's first year they jumped to 95–59 and won the pennant. In Morgan's eight seasons with the Reds they finished first or second every year with an overall *.600* win percentage. They took five divisional titles, three pennants, and two World Championships. The last divisional title in 1979 came after Rose left the Reds.

In 1980 Morgan joined the Astros, and they won their first divisional title ever. In 1981 Joe went to the Giants, and their winning percentage jumped from .466 to .505. The next year they rose to .537 and finished only two wins behind the division winner. When Morgan left in 1983 the Giants fell to .488. For the seven-year span of 1979–85, the only two winning seasons for San Francisco were the two when Joe Morgan was their starting second baseman.

In 1983 Little Joe joined Pete Rose on the Phillies and helped move them from second place to pennant-winners. In 1984 Morgan wanted to play his final season in his old stomping grounds in Oakland. The A's improved three wins with the forty-year-old Morgan starting at second base.

After Morgan escaped the expansion blues of Houston, he played for seven first-place clubs involving three different franchises. All five clubs he joined won more games than they did the season before his arrival; that rivals the Reggie Jackson mystique or that of any other player you can name with that "winning" aura. Joe Morgan was a winner in every way conceivable.

Is Joe Morgan a Hall of Famer? I'm pleased to note that whenever I ask those likely to be voting on that question, they concede that Joe is an excellent bet to eventually make the Hall. Is he a first-ballot Hall of Famer? None of the prospective voters that I queried had an impression of Morgan as one who would command that special kind of respect. Every one of them balked at such an honor going to a player with a career batting average of .271 and fewer than 300 homers.

That is simply not just. Such a decision should be based on his accomplishments as a winning player, not how he was a winning player. I hope this chapter might change a few minds before it comes to a vote. You see, Morgan is more than deserving of going in by acclamation on the first ballot; his career value is among the greatest of all time, and he is arguably the greatest second baseman in history.

Why is it that this is so hard to see? That's what this chapter is about. It's about a scout who writes that a two-time MVP is handicapped by his size; people ignoring his strong fielding record to conclude he was not so good a second baseman because he had a weak arm; writers who fail to be impressed by an offensive accomplishment that is not accompanied by big Triple Crown numbers; and a failure on practically everyone's part to appreciate that if a player improves in every area possible, he can produce immense value, far more than a superficial observation will show.

It doesn't matter that Morgan was once considered a marginal prospect, actually "no prospect" when he graduated from high school. It doesn't matter that Joe was the smallest player in the National League during his career. It doesn't matter that he had a weak arm. It doesn't matter that there were stronger or faster players. It doesn't matter that so many of his contributions lacked visibility or popular style. It doesn't matter that he hit .271 in his career. You can hit .271 and absolutely crush a .330 hitter if you do everything else well.

Morgan's career is over. It is time to stop caring about what he should have done and concentrate on what he actually did.

DEFENSE

Holds ML record for consecutive errorless games at second base (91).

Tied ML record for fewest errors by a second baseman, season, 150 games or more (five).

Holds ML record for most seasons as a second baseman (22).

Holds NL records for second basemen in games (2,427), putouts
(5,541), assists (6,738), and chances accepted cleanly (12,034).
Played more games as an infielder than anyone in Live Ball
Era; second on all-time list to Eddie Collins.
Won five Gold Glove awards for defensive excellence at second base.

BASE STEALING

Stole more bases than any infielder in the Live Ball Era (689).
Among all players, only Lou Brock and Rickey Henderson
have stolen more bases in the Live Ball Era.
Only player in Live Ball Era to steal 10 or more bases in 18
individual seasons.
Career steal success rate of .810 is believed to be the highest
among players with 600 career steals. (Max Carey's mark is
.794 for his 715 attempts when caught stealings were recorded.
Carey has another 170 steals with no known success rate).
Morgan and Tim Raines are the only two players ever to have
six seasons of 40 or more steals with a success rate higher
than 80%.
Morgan is the only player to have 10 seasons of 20 or more
steals with a success rate of higher than 80%.

HITTING

Smallest man in height or weight to have 250 career homers
(Hack Wilson had only 244).
Lightest player in Live Ball Era ever to lead the league in
slugging percentage.
Holds ML record for career home runs by a second baseman (266).
Most career doubles by any post–World War II infielder.
Second only to Rogers Hornsby for most extra bases on long
hits among all second basemen.
More extra-base hits than any middle infielder after 1930.
Holds NL record for base on balls (1,799). Only Babe Ruth and
Ted Williams ever drew more walks.
Eight seasons with an on-base average over .400.

Eight times scored 100 runs or more, a record for postwar infielders *including first basemen.*

More career runs scored than any postwar infielder.

Scored more runs than any second baseman except Eddie Collins and Charlie Gehringer (more than Hornsby, Lajoie, or Frisch).

Despite batting leadoff in a non-DH league for most of his career, Morgan collected 1,134 RBIs, the most by a middle infielder after World War II.

Going into 1988, Morgan is the only player to hit more than 20 homers and steal more than 50 bases in the same season three times.

Morgan was also one of the best players at staying out of the double play. The only other player I know of in the Live Ball Era with fewer GIDPs per game is Richie Ashburn (.0379 to .0396). Every other player I have looked at—Brock, Wills, McAuliffe, and some thirty other likely candidates—have all been over .0430.

"Well done, good and faithful servant." There have been many, many more physically gifted players than Joe Morgan, but very few ever accomplished more in this game. He did it when and where it counted. His climb from "no prospect" to blue-chip Hall of Famer is one of the most amazing stories in the history of the game. His job is done. All that remains is for us to appreciate it. We could use the practice.

HOUSE:
· · · AND TO SOME HE GAVE FEWER THAN FIVE

The pitcher, more than anyone else on the field, is involved in the matchup of talent versus limitations. Pitching is, first and foremost, a head game, even if you have the awesome talent of a Nolan Ryan or a Roger Clemens. But there are a lot of guys with great talent and bad heads who aren't even average pitchers. The ones with the super talent and the great minds become the superstars. The rest of us are somewhere in between, balancing what our arms and minds will let us do in any given situation.

A hitter doesn't hit what you're throwing; he hits what he *sees*. If you can't hump it up there at ninety per, you've got to be deceptive. There are any number of ways you can do that. We did a motion study of pitchers who are considered sneaky-fast, and we found that they gained their extra "speed" by delaying the hitters' recognition of the release point, often by throwing up their front elbows as they came forward. Or you can change the delivery—come up top once, three-quarters, sidearm, all over the place. You can change speeds so it takes an extra moment to recognize the fastball. The minimum you can probably get away with in absolute speed in the majors is about 80 to 82 m.p.h. Deception will keep the batter from seeing and reading the pitch for just a couple of feet, but even just three feet over the fifty-two to fifty-four feet a pitch travels from release point to the plate is like a difference of three to five miles an hour in speed. That takes you up into the mideighties or from barely adequate to respectable. That's how it worked for me.

Motion studies can show you how to find that extra three feet. When I joined the Rangers, they had Dave Stewart. Great talent, could throw that good ninety-mile-an-hour fastball. But there was no deception to it, and sooner or later the hitters were going to adjust. He was taking that 3 to 5 m.p.h. away from his speed by just throwing it up there. But Stewart became aware of the need to develop something extra; he's added a move with his front elbow to his delivery, and that, combined with his new forkball, has turned him into the kind of pitcher his talent made everyone think he should be. Sid Fernandez with the Mets has that real late arm swing and leads with the front elbow, so he strikes out a lot more hitters than a guy with his 85 to 87 m.p.h. fastball should be able to.

In changing speeds, you want to keep a pretty clear ratio in the speeds of your various pitches. Your change-up should be about 18 to 20 m.p.h. slower than your best fastball, your curve 13 to 15 m.p.h. slower, your slider 8 to 10 m.p.h. These rates hold up no matter how hard you throw—no matter what your basic talent.

The single best example I've ever seen of a pitcher getting the absolute maximum out of his talent was Randy Jones when he had those super years with San Diego. He was consistently winning eighteen, twenty games with a fastball no better than mine—and that wasn't much. But he kept the hitters off balance, and he had great location—got all those ground balls. And I'll tell you another guy who got an awful lot out of not that much raw ability: Bill Lee. He had that goofy reputation, but once he got out there on the mound, he was a real shark.

Of course, when you don't have the tools, sometimes you need a little help. I don't think there's anything you can do to a baseball that I didn't try in my career. Dirt in the seams, pine tar, Vaseline, a little scuffing—if you've got bills to pay, you do what you have to do to stay in the game. And I did. With my little eighty-one-mile-an-hour fastball I needed something that would move like a screwball but off a fastball motion. Pack a little dirt into the seam, and the ball will break in the direction of the dirt. Find a scuff on the ball, and it will break away from that mark. Put a little pine tar on your thumb, and the ball will stick just a little on release, giving it the exact same kind of downward rotation you get on the spitter. Of course, the spitter works the opposite way; to get that effect you slick your top two fingers so the ball comes off them first, rolling off the thumb. Either way, downward rotation, and a ball that drops.

It's not real hard to get away with, either. I always had a spot on the back of my glove where I'd keep some pine tar, to help me get a grip when the weather was cold. Just rub a little from the pine tar rag just as the hitters do. And as for the Vaseline, well, you keep that somewhere you know the umps aren't going to rub around if they come out to the mound. (Ever see an umpire reach in between a pitcher's legs on the mound? Of course not.) And then you pick a little up on the *back* of your thumb. Then you can go to the resin bag, wipe your fingers on your shirt, anything, but that grease is still there on your thumb, waiting to be rubbed into your fingertips when you put your hand in your glove. Easy. And I saved it for when I really needed it. I never got watched too carefully, and I'm not sure anyone knew I was fiddling with the ball in my whole career.

I think so much of the speculation and outcry surrounding Mike

Scott comes from the fact that people feel he violated the unwritten law about cheating in baseball: It's okay to cheat if you have to cheat to make a living. (Jim Palmer said this exact same thing in discussing Jay Howell and his pine tar, though that's completely different; I doubt there's a guy in baseball who hasn't used pine tar at one time or other.) The implication is that it's okay for me to do whatever I have to to get by with my stuff, but the guys who can throw over ninety miles an hour have no business messing with the ball. It's just not acceptable in the code of the game. Watch closely: It's not the cheating itself that draws the complaints—there aren't a lot of virgins in the game, and I'm sure just about every team has one or two pitchers who are doing something funny just to get by—it's the guys who are too talented to have earned the right to cheat that draw all the bitching and moaning.

ONCE THERE WAS A BALLPLAYER

Once there was a ballplayer. His skills came right off the Christmas lists of little Muggsy McGraw, Cornelius McGillicuddy, Kid Weaver, and Charlie Stengel; as grown-ups, they'd be more realistic with their dreams. Surely no one player could have the speed and daring of Rickey Henderson, the arm of Roberto Clemente, the bat of Ty Cobb, the power of Babe Ruth, the glove of Ozzie Smith, and the character of Lou Gehrig.

Once there was a ballplayer. He came within a quiet whisper of being that perfect player. The game's two greatest general managers chose him as the first man they would pick from all the players who ever played major-league baseball. One said, "There is no question that [he] was the best all-around player who ever lived."

The leading manager of his day said, "[He] was the greatest all-around player who ever lived . . . the greatest infielder, one of the greatest hitters and base runners . . . had he played in any position other than the pitcher, he would have been equally great. . . . He was the nearest thing to a perfect player no matter where his manager chose to play him."

One Hall of Fame pitcher said, "[He] never had a weakness. [He] could hit any ball he could reach—inside or out, high or low. He was just a great hitter with the greatest pair of hands that baseball ever knew."

A Hall of Fame umpire with thirty-five years of active service said, "[He was] as great a man as he was a ballplayer. He was the best I ever saw—and I saw them all in the last sixty years."

This is not some bedtime story. Once there really was such a ball-player. What does have the quality of a dream—a nightmare—is how such a player, baseball's most perfect champion, could end up so forgotten today. Baseball prides itself on its memory, its ability to freeze the sun in the summer sky, keeping its immortals forever young. Yet in his case there has been a near-total eclipse.

He was considered the greatest defensive player of his time, yet in 1982 when *Sports Illustrated* ran a little article on the ten greatest fielders at his position, two of his contemporaries were ranked fourth and fifth, while this mighty warrior was totally missing from the list.

When people sit down and talk about the greatest hitters, or even just the greatest right-handed hitters, he is forgotten. The same happens when they talk about the fastest players, the best base-stealers, or the strongest throwing arms. In the 1980s we have been treated to numerous books attempting to rank the greatest players of all time. None of these authors, most of whom are quite familiar with baseball history, care to echo the sentiment once heard so frequently in baseball.

I recently saw a hundred-year baseball time line with notations about players like Cy Young, Christy Mathewson, Ty Cobb, Lou Gehrig, Babe Ruth, Joe DiMaggio, Ted Williams, Stan Musial, Mickey Mantle, Willie Mays, and Henry Aaron. Guess who was never mentioned?

In *The Bill James Historical Baseball Abstract,* the author noted that this player, who was called "The Olympian of the Infield," had been named to an all-star "chubby" team. With good humor, Bill pointed out that this "has got to be the most ill-informed and frankly stupid selection for which I am not personally responsible." Sadly, it is a very accurate testimony to our failure to preserve the memory of a man uniquely suited to capture all that is good in the game.

Once there was a ballplayer. His name was John Peter Wagner. He played from 1897 to 1917, and if there was something he couldn't do on the diamond, they never found what it was. *The Baseball Encyclopedia* lists him as "Honus" Wagner, which is also how he signed his name, and the name most used by the out-of-town newspapers, though in Pittsburgh and on the diamond practically everyone called him "Hans." (Both are derivatives of the Germanic equivalent of John, *Johannes*.) The newspapers also gave him the poetic title of "The Flying Dutchman," which was off by a country or two; he was born in America, the son of an immigrant from Bavaria.

The two Hall of Fame general managers quoted above were Branch Rickey and Ed Barrow. Rickey was probably the most recent baseball authority to openly name Wagner as the most valuable player in baseball history. Branch certainly saw his share of ballplayers in his sixty-one years on the major-league scene from 1905 to 1965, and to make his selection, he had only to swivel his chair and point; a standard feature in his office was a framed photo of Hans Wagner.

Ed Barrow's testimony is especially impressive. As a major-leaguer, Barrow was an American League stalwart. He managed for five years with Detroit and Boston, and then put in twenty-five years as the man who made the Yankees a dynasty. He was very familiar with the best the league had to offer in its glory years. He managed against Ty Cobb for three seasons, and he's the man who called in his left-handed ace pitcher named Ruth and said, "Son, starting tomorrow, you're an outfielder." Ed brought Lou Gehrig and Joe DiMaggio to the majors, and he had plenty of opportunity to study that .400 hitter in Boston. Yet Ed Barrow passed over all these players he knew so well to call Honus Wagner the greatest of all time. You see, Barrow was just as familiar with the legendary Wagner, whom he knew from his earliest minor-league days.

It was not an easy era for a boy like Wagner to find his way to the major leagues. The American Association, the Union Association, and the short-lived Players League had all gone under as challengers to the National League. There were not a lot of jobs; the NL was the only major league, and its twelve teams had rosters of fifteen to seventeen players each. Minor-league teams were responsible for scouting the amateur talent, and most of that "scouting" was by word of mouth.

Honus was a native of the coal country of Pennsylvania. By the age of twelve, he was working with his father down in the mines. Wagner played several years of hometown ball without ever being seen by a scout, and only got his first break by pretending to be somebody else. The story goes that Honus's brother Al, who was already playing minor-league ball, had recommended another brother named Will, who was known as a pretty good local ballplayer. When Will wasn't interested, young Hans showed up claiming to be Will.

As improbable as that sounds, research shows that Hans did have a ballplaying brother named Will, and Honus did sign his first professional contract as William Wagner. Whatever the case, Hans did not play his first professional game until he was already twenty-one years old.

In that summer of 1895, Ed Barrow was with the Wheeling Mountaineers in the loosely structured Iron and Oil League, which barely counted as a professional league. He couldn't help noticing a ballplayer named Wagner who vastly improved the Warren Wonders when he joined their club in midseason.

It didn't take a lot of scouting skill to realize that here was a real diamond in the rough. The local newspaper had already said what would soon be heard throughout the country: "Oh! for nine men like Wagner." The records for that first season are sketchy at best, but they suggest that Wagner hit somewhere between .340 and .370, had startling power, and was an absolute terror on the basepaths, averaging almost a stolen base a game. He played just about every position in the field and showed great range and a powerful arm.

That winter Barrow went looking for "Will" Wagner and signed Hans to play for his Patterson club in the much better established Atlantic League. Barrow continued to switch Wagner around from first base to center field to third base, but Hans still managed to hit .344 and scored 106 runs in just 109 games.

Rather than sell Wagner's contract to the major leagues, Barrow chose to hang on to Hans in hopes of driving up his value in 1897. It was a wise choice, as Honus appeared to blossom when Barrow settled him into one position as a third baseman. Wagner was hitting .379 when his contract was purchased in midseason by the National League's Louisville Colonels. Honus immediately went into the starting lineup and hit .344 the rest of the way, the second-best average on the team. He usually hit third or fourth in the lineup. He remained a regular until his final season, twenty-one years later, at age forty-three.

The manager quoted at the start of this chapter was Hall of Famer John McGraw who, like Barrow, was all too familiar with Wagner's long career. McGraw not only managed and played against Honus for several seasons, but he was also on the field with the rowdy Baltimore Orioles for Wagner's major-league debut. Honus batted third in the order and played center field. In his first at bat he rifled a single. Later in the 6–2 Louisville victory, Honus hit "what should have been a triple, but when he made the turn at first base, the Baltimore first baseman, Jack Doyle, gave him the hip. At second, shortstop Hughie Jennings forced him wide. At third base, none other than John McGraw blocked him off the bag, then knocked the wind out of him by tagging him hard in the stomach." Welcome to the National League in the 1890s.

Wagner's response came when he beat out a slow roller to McGraw, who threw across the diamond, only to discover his first baseman was no longer there. The Flying Dutchman had "dumped Doyle on his behind at first, left Jennings in the dirt at second and trampled all over McGraw's feet coming into third. [Manager Fred] Clarke was so tickled to see McGraw fuming and cussing that he came over to the coach's box and said, 'Nice day, ain't it, Muggsy?' "

A little more than a month later, on August 25, Wagner made his first appearance in the infield. Ironically, it was at second base rather than his normal position at third. Although Hans played only nine games at second versus 52 in the outfield, this set a dangerous precedent for his future. Wagner's willingness to fill in at every position put him in the unique situation of being a full-time utility player. Wagner missed only eight games over the next two seasons, yet he never had a regular position. He played third base a little less than half the time and split the rest of his games between the outfield positions and first and second base. Honus hit well enough, .331 overall with over a 100 RBIs in both seasons, but he was capable of doing much more if left at one position.

Wagner proved this in 1900 when the Colonels became the nucleus of the new Pittsburgh Pirates and Wagner became the club's regular right fielder. Oh, Honus still played 20 games in the infield, but he had 118 in right field, the first time he had played more than 75 games at one position in a season. Hans responded by leading the league in hitting (.381) and slugging (.572). Although the league reduced its schedule to 140 games, Wagner still had 107 runs and 100 RBIs, and his 71 extra-base hits easily led the league.

Wagner was now established as the best player in the National League, which made what happened in 1901 almost unbelievable. The Pirates were in the midst of the pennant race when their short-stop, Bones Ely, jumped to the upstart American League, then in its first season. Manager Fred Clarke wanted Wagner to take over at shortstop. For the first time in his career, Hans balked at being shifted yet again; he said he didn't mind moving back and forth from the outfield to third base, the two positions he had played the most, but that was it. The press and fans thought Clarke was crazy. Wagner was twenty-seven years old and established now as a star outfielder. It would have been roughly equivalent to asking Joe DiMaggio to switch to shortstop after an MVP season in the outfield.

Besides, who could imagine Honus Wagner as a regular shortstop? Keep in mind that in this era defense at shortstop was considered even more important than it is today. Because the ball was dead and the fields and gloves were so inferior, the batters worked to hit hard grounders rather than fly balls. Despite his speed and tremendous throwing arm, Wagner had an awkward style and was considered too big to have the coordination required at shortstop. Of the sixteen regular shortstops playing in 1901, the heaviest was twenty pounds lighter than Wagner, who packed two hundred pounds on his five-eleven frame.

But Clarke was adamant, and Honus, the consummate team player, finally yielded and took over at shortstop for the last 62 games. He had never played the position before in the major leagues; his last game at the position was believed to be way back in 1895, when he appeared in just ten box scores as a shortstop. But Wagner was an immediate success; a bit error-prone, understandably, but he showed great range, and his powerful throws were a real asset in turning double plays. Wagner hit .353 while leading the league with 126 RBIs and 48 stolen bases, and the Pirates won the pennant.

The next year, 1902, Wagner started off playing shortstop, but then the Pirates were hit by a rash of serious injuries. The starting right fielder, Lefty Davis, broke his ankle and missed 83 games. Fred Clarke, the left fielder, missed 28 games with a foot injury, and first baseman Kitty Bransfield was knocked out of the last 40 games of the season by a knee injury. The Pirates had a decent backup shortstop in Wid Conroy, so Honus ended up playing 44 games at short, 61 games in left and right field, 32 games at first, one game at second, and even pitched in one game.

The next year, at age twenty-nine, Honus Wagner finally had a regular position that would last. He started a string of thirteen seasons of 100-plus games at shortstop, a position that would account for 93% of his remaining major-league appearances. Wagner's hitting began to blossom with this newfound stability; in the next nine seasons, through age thirty-eight, he took seven batting titles and seven times was either first or second in slugging percentage.

Wagner continued to play for a number of years with remarkable stamina and durability. In 1915, at age forty-one, he played 151 of his team's 156 games. One hundred thirty-one of those games were at shortstop, where he led the league in fielding percentage and still had average range, 5.29 clean chances per game, compared with 5.33 for the average starting NL shortstop. He led all shortstops in RBIs, doubles, triples, extra-base hits, and slugging percentage, and was second in batting average and third in steals—all this at an age when every other great player has been either retired or in such decline that he could no longer be considered near the best at his position.

The next year, at age forty-two, he led all shortstops in batting average, was forty points over the whole league's average, and was the second-best RBI man among shortstops despite getting only 432 at bats.

FLYING ON THE BASEPATHS

Despite Wagner's size, he was an incredibly swift and smart base runner. Hall of Famer Sam Crawford, who knew a little about speed and baserunning from playing on the same team with Ty Cobb for thirteen seasons and was himself a talented runner with 366 steals and the all-time career record for triples, played four seasons against Wagner when Sam was with the Reds. He faced Hans again in the 1909 World Series, when the thirty-five-year-old Flying Dutchman stole six bases—more than the whole Tigers team combined. Crawford remembered Wagner's speed this way: "You'd never think it to look at him . . . barrel-chested, about 200 pounds, a big man. And yet he could run like a scared rabbit. Talk about speed. [He] stole over 700 bases in the 21 years he played in the big leagues."

Wagner's career total came in at 722 despite the late start to his career, the shorter schedules, and playing in a depressed hitting era when there was less chance to get on base. Wagner actually averaged more steals per time reaching first (on singles and walks) than Cobb did (.213 versus .207).

Five times Honus led the league in steals, and he was among the top five thieves nine times. New research shows that Wagner, not Cobb, as is commonly believed, holds the record for most times stealing his way around the bases—a steal of second, third, and home in just one time on base. And the Flying Dutchman's eighteen seasons of 20-plus steals is the major-league record.

How fast was Wagner? Several references claim he ran a ten-second hundred-yard dash in his baseball uniform and spikes. I don't know whether he ever really did this, but there is a detailed account of Wagner's being clocked from a standing start in the right-handed batter's box to first base in an astounding 3.4 seconds. If that figure is accurate, with a start like that Hans was probably capable of running *under* ten seconds in a hundred-yard sprint.

The intelligence and heads-up style of his baserunning is neatly captured in this newspaper account of a game between the Giants and the Pirates:

[With Wagner on second, Harry] Swacina next bounded a ball to the diligent Doyle, who made a low throw to Tenney. Wagner said farewell to second, hiking for third as fast as his parenthetical pins would carry him. Noting that the ball had escaped Tenney's grasp

Hans kept on toward the plate which he reached by a great slide. It is doubtful that any other player could have scored on such a play; few base runners would have taken such a chance, but Wagner is ever ready to take advantage of an opening.

[Later with two outs in the sixth, Clarke tripled and Wagner was intentionally walked.] . . . the doughty German again showed his right to be classed as the one and only. Instead of trying the time-honored double steal Wagner and Clarke sprang a new one on the Giants, standing the latter completely on their heads.

Naturally the Giants expected Hans to break for second on a pitched ball. Instead the big Teuton waited until Bresnahan [the catcher] had just returned the bulb to McGinnity, when with head down and legs spread like this ( ), he started for second. McGinnity, taken completely by surprise by the boldness and suddenness of the action, heaved the ball to second. Wagner continued his mad dash until within a few feet of Doyle [the second baseman], when he suddenly turned and hastened back toward first, never letting up in his speed. The ball was thrown to Tenney, who awaited the arrival of the Flying Dutchman. When within a yard of the Giant first-sacker Wagner wheeled and scudded back over the route to second. Tenney started to give chase, but seeing that Clarke had started for the plate turned and threw to Bresnahan. The latter got the ball all right, but the Pirate chieftain, by a cleverly manipulated bit of contortion, evaded the touch and slid over the plate in safety, while Wagner smiled from his perch on second.

That play alone was worth the price of admission.

Now think about that: They intentionally walked Wagner, and he still ended up turning it into a run-scoring play! You also may have picked up from this story that Wagner—with his "parenthetical pins"—was not built like most men from the waist down. He was extremely bowlegged, and few writers could resist working it into their stories. They commented that if you could straighten out his legs, Wagner would be over six feet tall. Between his bowed legs and long arms, they used to kid that he was the only man able to tie his shoelaces without bending over. They wrote that he walked like a crab, and in paying tribute to his defense they said you could roll a barrel between his legs—but not a baseball. The truth is that Wagner did not look like your run-of-the-mill star player:

No one ever saw anything graceful or picturesque about Wagner on the diamond. His movements have been likened to gambols of a caracoling elephant. He is ungainly and so bowlegged that when he runs his limbs seem to be moving in a circle after the fashion of a propeller. But he can run like the wind. When he starts after a grounder every outlying portion of his anatomy apparently has ideas of its own about the proper line of direction to be taken.

Altogether [Wagner] was a magnificent physical specimen, but in his component parts he looked as though he had been put together in a dark room by people who didn't speak the same language. His bland, pleasant face was adorned by a doorknocker of a nose. His powerful five-foot-eleven-inch, 200-pound frame featured a massive chest that might have come from a barrelmaker's shop and shoulders broad enough to serve dinner on. His arms were extremely long . . . with enormous hands, and fingers so long they could barely fit into the raggedy gloves of the day.

One can imagine it wasn't easy to see at first how great an athlete was housed in that outrageous frame. This rather quaint physique is largely responsible for Hans's unusual display of fielding versatility during his first five and a half seasons. Pittsburgh naturally wanted to take full advantage of his skills, but it was hard to believe how much he was capable of doing.

By most accounts the ability to play great defense at shortstop was probably always there. He was always considered a great defensive third baseman, but simply did not look like a shortstop. Researcher A. D. Suehsdorf discovered several newspaper references to Wagner's unusual range in the field in the handful of games that Wagner played as a shortstop in his first minor-league season:

. . . Wagner played a great all-around game and accepted chances outside of his territory . . .

Mansfield Shield

. . . Wagner, who plays all over his field and half of the adjoining sections, made the best stop of the day . . .

Adrian Daily Times

John Wagner covers a great deal of ground at short.

Warren Evening Democrat

As it was, Wagner's versatility in his early years provided him with a defensive reputation that's unique in the history of the game. Hans is the only major-leaguer to play over 50 games at every position except catcher and pitcher. Honus did pitch twice in the majors, and both John McGraw and sportswriter Ernie Lanigan believe they saw Wagner catch a few games (possibly in spring exhibition games, because there is no known record of Honus catching either a minor- or major-league game).

McGraw was not the only one who believed Honus could have played anywhere. Sam Crawford said, "When I first played against him he was an outfielder, and then he became a third baseman, and later the greatest shortstop of them all. He was a wonderful fielder, terrific arm, very quick, all over the place grabbing sure hits and turning them into outs."

Tommy Leach played next to Wagner on the Pirates' infield for thirteen seasons and remembered him this way: "Honus was the best third baseman in the league, he was also the best first baseman, the best second baseman, . . . and the best outfielder. . . . He didn't look like a shortstop, you know. He had those huge shoulders and those bowed legs, and he didn't seem to field balls the way we did. He just ate the ball up with his big hands, like a scoop shovel, and when he threw it to first base you'd see pebbles and dirt and everything else flying over there along with the ball. It was quite a sight! The greatest shortstop ever. The greatest *everything* ever."

THE ARM

Wagner pitched some in the minor leagues and was quite successful in his two major-league appearances on the mound. He struck out six in 8.1 innings, a strikeout rate better than twice the average for that period. They're still waiting for him to give up his first earned run.

As an infielder, Wagner studied famed defensive shortstop Bobby Wallace in order to learn how to field and throw in the same motion. From there, Wagner took the infield throw and turned it into a new art form, the likes of which had never been seen before.

[Wagner] charged the ball like a great bull, making impossible stops with glove and bare hand as he . . . threw out runners from every imaginable contorted posture and position.

His throws, from any position, were straight and hard, accurate as bullets. He threw overhand when he had time, or underhand, with a quick snap or a pendulum swing, depending on the situation and whether he was close or far from the bag.

. . . his overhand deliveries were cannon-shots, his side-arm pegs were bullets, and . . . when he had only time for a snap underhand throw, that ball, too, came to the first baseman humming a tune. In those mighty hands, a baseball was a model of behavior.

Believe me, I have tried to leave out some of the wilder secondhand stories. There are stories of Hans throwing out runners from deep in the hole while on his knees, and—shades of Ozzie Smith—of throws made behind his back. I tended to discount such stories until I came across an article by John B. Foster in the *1938 Spalding Official Base Ball Guide*. Foster was a sportswriter for fifty years beginning in 1887, which placed Wagner's career at the center of his own. In his article titled, "A Nine for All Time," Foster described Wagner's throws this way: "Wagner could throw from any position at any angle, underhand or overhand, jerk the ball or toss it forward like a boy[,] throwing it any way to get it away, and fast, too. *In a pinch he had been seen to toss it backward over his head, so determined was he to get the runner*" [emphasis mine].

THE BALL STOPS HERE

Harry Cross, a sportswriter for the *New York Herald Tribune,* was struck by the role of Wagner's fielding in his immense popularity with the fans of his day. He wrote, "In those days it didn't matter whether the Pirates won or lost. The fans flocked out anyway to see Wagner put on a one-man show at shortstop. Honus' territory was unlimited. He roamed from third to second and frequently took over the exclusive patrol of short left and center fields."

I always felt that historian Robert Smith had gone a bit overboard in his summation of Wagner's fielding prowess: "[Wagner] had the strength, agility, and muscular control of an acrobat, the eyes and perfect judgment of a juggler, the mighty strength in hands, arms, and shoulders that a circus strong man might be paid to exhibit . . . . He more than once made tremendous bounds out on the grass behind third base to spear a ball that had gone through the [third] baseman, then sizzled the ball across the diamond to first base almost as fast as sound. Fans used to goggle in disbelief at such plays and go home and talk about them for weeks afterward."

Does that sound like a bit much to you? Consider this play, recorded in the *New York American* in the summer of 1908: "With two men out Mike Donlin smashed what looked like a two-bagger down the line between Wagner and Leach [who was probably protecting the line]. Honus started after the ball like the cute fielder he is, and actually wrapped his big paw around it some thirty feet outside the diamond. Not content with this phenomenal stop he threw to first without even looking. . . . " Okay, to be fair, on this play Donlin beat the throw to first base, but Turkey Mike was also one of the fastest players in the league and led the Giants in stolen bases that season.

Try this throw recorded by Ernie Lanigan in the *New York Press*: "Good old reliable Honus Wagner has turned many a clever trick when opposed to the Giants, but nothing before anything quite so smooth as he sprang yesterday, in the third inning, when Willis issued his only pass of the day. . . . Tenney tried to sacrifice and the little [bunt] pop fly looked good when Leach [slipped and] sat down as he started for it. But Wagner raced in like lightning over half the distance to the plate and scooping it up with his bare hand an inch from the carpet fired to Swacina for the grandest double play ever seen in New York."

Everyone's favorite is the story told by Tommy Leach about his own arrival in the majors. To set the stage, both Washington and Louisville had made similar offers to purchase Leach's contract at the end of his minor-league season. Leach, a third baseman, was given a choice of which club he wanted to go to.

"I'll tell you," [Leach's manager] said, "knowing what I know, I'd say take Louisville. If you go to Washington, they have a man who's a darned good third baseman. His name is Wagner."

Well, I didn't know Wagner from beans. So, naturally, I chose Louisville. Our season at Auburn ended a month before the Big League season was over, so in late August of 1898 I reported to the Louisville club.

I hardly had time to get settled before it hit me that the guy Louisville had at third base was practically doing the impossible. I'm sitting on the bench the first day I reported, and along about the third inning an opposing batter smacks a line drive down the third-base line that looked like a sure double. Well, this big Louisville third baseman jumped over after it like he was on steel springs, slapped it down with his bare hand, scrambled after it for at least ten feet, and fired a bullet over to first base. The runner was out by two or three steps.

I'm sitting on the bench and my eyes are popping out. So I poked the guy sitting next to me, and asked him who the devil that big fellow was on third base.

"Why that's Wagner," he says. "He's the best third baseman in the league."

When I heard that, did I ever groan. I'm sure it was loud enough to be heard the whole length of the bench. "What chance does a tiny guy like me have here anyway?" I thought to myself. "Wagner isn't with Washington, he's *here*."

Actually, there was a Wagner at Washington playing a fine third base; it was Al Wagner, Honus's older brother. Leach's nineteen-year career got off the ground because Wagner could play anywhere and be outstanding. How is it, then, that Wagner could be left off the *Sports Illustrated* list of the top ten defensive shortstops?

It seems there was an unstated assumption in the list that you can't be a good defensive shortstop *and* be a good hitter, a criterion that Wagner could never pass. But there are other factors that have hidden Hans's fielding prowess as we look back in time.

Wagner made more errors at shortstop than any player in this century, but this has nothing to do with his ability and everything to do with the conditions of his time. The ball in play was usually a mottled dirty color, often scuffed, sometimes wet with saliva, and occasionally lopsided after a few innings of heavy battering. The fields were pockmarked with holes, ridges, and stones that produced some of the most creative bad hops to ever challenge the leather. The gloves were so small and poorly designed that playing with them wasn't much better than playing bare-handed. They say Hans, with his huge hands, only wore a glove because it was fashionable.

Any shortstop who played enough games early in this century was guaranteed to be the leader in errors. Wagner played his first game at shortstop in 1901 and ran up a total of 1,888 games at the position by the time he retired in 1917.

The truth of the matter is that once Wagner settled into the position, he was far from error-prone relative to his era. His fielding percentages were consistently above average compared with those of the other shortstops, and he led the league in fielding percentage three times.

Serious analysts of fielding statistics are often thrown by two other factors in Wagner's career. First, the number of fielding chances at shortstop began to decline in the early 1900s. As errors became less common than in the 1890s, probably due to improvements in the gloves and the field conditions, batters were less intent on putting the ball in play on the ground. There were more strikeouts, less offense, and more bunting, all of which translates to fewer fielding chances in the middle of the diamond.

As a shortstop, Wagner was not really a contemporary of Bill Dahlen or George Davis, who piled up a ton of chances in the 1890s. When their careers overlapped Wagner's era as a regular shortstop (1903 and beyond), Wagner was the one fielding more chances per game.

Also frequently overlooked is that Wagner got a very late start at the position and lasted a long, long time. The Flying Dutchman was remarkably durable, but he was still human. There were signs that he was slowing down with age just five or six years after he got started as a regular shotstop. You could see it in his hitting and stolen bases, and you could see it in the field.

While Wagner's defense slowly slipped from spectacular to excellent to good to average to below-average, the other fielding whizzes started to drop out somewhere around "good." By then, their offensive skills had slipped to a point where teams could no longer justify keeping just a good or average glove in the lineup. Not so for Wagner; his bat kept him in there long beyond the zenith of his defense. Remember that Wagner played over half his games at shortstop *after* his thirty-fifth birthday. Joe Tinker of "Tinker-to-Evers-to-Chance" fame played fewer than twenty games at short after his thirty-fifth birthday, about 1% of his 1,742 career games.

A comparison of career fielding statistics doesn't capture the defensive brilliance of Hans Wagner. I'm not asking for some special dispensation to honor Wagner's potential instead of his accomplishments. Even with the age handicap, any fair analysis will show that he was a great defensive shortstop for better than a dozen seasons covering some 1,600 games.

But I think we should recognize that when these old-timers swoon over Wagner's glove work, they had good cause. Hans had an amazing peak of performance that was separate from the broad expanse of his strong career record. Between the stories and the records from those peak seasons, we can say that if Honus had been established at the position at a younger age, his career record would have let him contend with Luis Aparicio and Ozzie Smith for the title of the greatest defensive shortstop of all time.

Yet no matter how circumstance and fate handicapped Wagner's defensive career, he has a legitimate claim as the best defensive shortstop of his period. The tracks his glove left in the game's records are as strong in their testimony as the eyewitness accounts.

First, let's take a look at 1901–02, the two seasons when Hans played 106 games at a position he hadn't played in five years—and all while playing 173 games at five other positions. The comparison includes the two other Pittsburgh shortstops, Bones Ely and Wid Conroy, six of the top established shortstops at this time, and Joe Tinker in his rookie season (1902) to give an idea of the record of another great shortstop just starting out.

You can see that Bones Ely was probably feeling his age (thirty-eight in 1901), which lends some credence to the theory that Clarke

SHORTSTOPS, 1901–02

	CHANCES FIELDED CLEANLY PER GAME	FA	DP/GAME
Honus Wagner	6.02	.909	.406
Wid Conroy	5.69	.923	.399
Bones Ely	5.43	.919	.343
Monte Cross	5.87	.925	.245
George Davis	5.79	.945	.469
Bill Dahlen	5.52	.923	.312
Kid Eberfeld	6.14	.914	.502
Herman Long	5.78	.946	.414
Bobby Wallace	6.19	.926	.494
Joe Tinker (1902)	5.61	.906	.379

was considering Wagner as a shortstop even before Bones jumped to the American League. Considering the circumstances, Wagner's range was remarkable, and he did pretty well on the double play when you realize that both years the Pirates' pitching staff allowed the fewest base runners in the league. Wagner's inexperience can be seen in his fielding percentage, but it is still higher than that of fellow "rookie" Joe Tinker.

What we're really interested in is how Wagner stacked up when he became a full-time shortstop. That puts the focus on the period 1903 to 1914. This covers Wagner's first full season at shortstop and takes him through age forty. There are four shortstops of special interest here. Two are Hall of Famers whose qualifications were built more around their gloves than their bats: Joe Tinker and Bobby Wallace. The other two are George McBride and Mickey Doolan, the two shortstops from this period who were ranked fourth and fifth on *SI*'s list of the ten best defensive shortstops. Each of these shortstops is compared with Wagner only for the seasons that both were starting at shortstop.

Okay, *SI*, tell us again why Doolan and McBride should be considered better fielders? Hans's *average* age in both comparisons is close to the age when Doolan and McBride *last* played as regulars, age thirty-five for both players. Honus also easily surpasses Tinker, who was seven years younger and also last played as a regular at age

SHORTSTOPS, 1903–14

NAME	COMMON SEASONS	AVERAGE AGE	CHANCES FIELDED CLEANLY PER GAME	FA	DP/GAME
Doolan	10	29.5	5.44	.939	.382
Wagner	10	35.5	5.63	.944	.408
McBride	9	28.8	5.56	.945	.384
Wagner	9	35.8	5.65	.944	.428
Tinker	12	27.5	5.54	.941	.394
Wagner	12	34.5	5.65	.942	.409
Wallace	10	33.5	5.67	.942	.339
Wagner	10	33.5	5.64	.939	.413

thirty-five. Bobby Wallace, just a few months older than Wagner, was the only one to edge him in range, but was the worst at getting the double play.

Wagner, with his powerful arm, had a special gift for starting and turning the double play. Four times he led the league in DPs despite the severe handicap of a pitching staff that allowed few base runners. From 1903 to 1914 the Pirate staff was first or second in fewest base runners allowed more than half the time.

Wagner also led the league four times in chances fielded cleanly per game, and missed by a difference of less than 1% in a fifth season. It should be noted that there is a bit of an illusion to Wallace's statistical edge in range for their ten common seasons. Wallace was only a part-time starter after his thirty-fifth birthday, playing 123 fewer games than Wagner, so an unusually large proportion of Wallace's games came from the period 1903–08, when fielding chances were more plentiful at shortstop. If we use just the 1903–08 period, where both were truly playing as full-time regulars, Wagner takes a slight edge in range, too (5.71 to 5.69).

HANS AT THE BAT

When we consider Wagner's hitting statistics, we begin to unravel the mystery of how we lost sight of his greatness. Most fans have trouble interpreting defensive statistics, but they know they can read a hitting line. That's true for sabermetricians, too, since batting records are much more complete and logical in design. On the surface, Wagner's hitting record is good, but not the kind of numbers of which people automatically say, "This guy was one of the best."

Wagner's career average is .329, only nineteenth best in this century. His 3,430 career hits ranks sixth. He is third in triples, sixth in doubles, and way out there in home runs with only 101.

Most fans realize that Wagner played in the Dead Ball Era, but they also know that Cobb's numbers are much better. Ty hit 38 points higher, had over 750 more hits, more doubles, more triples, and more homers. But Wagner and Cobb are not true contemporaries; Honus Wagner was almost thirteen years older than Cobb, a vast difference in the quickly changing baseball world of the early 1900s.

It's almost eerie how Wagner's career is situated perfectly to hide his accomplishments if not taken in perspective. Look again at his beginning compared to those of a Cobb or a Ruth, who were playing professionally at ages seventeen and nineteen. Cobb's family provided the money to allow him to go off to try to make it as a ballplayer. Ruth was raised in a major-league city, which made it easy for his play to come to the attention of professional teams. Wagner was a son of a coal miner with nine kids in the country town of Mansfield, Pennsylvania. Remember, he didn't play professionally until age twenty-one, while Cobb and Ruth already had years in the majors by then.

When Cobb made the big leagues in 1905, there were 50% more major-league jobs than when Wagner was coming up. There were even more in 1914 when Ruth started. Both Cobb and Ruth were playing in a league that didn't even exist when Wagner started. It took Honus an extra year to escape the minors even though he had played on par with Ruth and much better than Cobb had in his minor-league career.

Before the 1901 season, Wagner turned down a very lucrative offer to play in the American League. With that decision Hans also turned down the chance to inflate his batting statistics for the next couple years. First, the new league did not have the depth of pitching talent that remained in the established National League. Of the nine players who were NL regulars in 1899–1900 and AL regulars in 1901–02, only one failed to hit higher in the American League:

	NL BA	AL BA	DIFFERENCE
Boileryard Clarke	.274	.275	+1
Jimmy Collins	.290	.327	+37
Lave Cross	.319	.330	+11
Buck Freeman	.311	.325	+14
Fielder Jones	.300	.316	+16
Kid Gleason	.257	.262	+5
Nap Lajoie	.360	.400	+40
Jack McCarthy	.300	.302	+2
Chick Stahl	.323	.316	−7
Average	.304	.317	+13

Second, back in the 1901 National League they introduced the modern foul-strike rule, which took a big chunk out of the offense. The league batting average fell 11 points, and runs per game fell by 1.34 runs. The American League did not adopt the rule till two years later in 1903; its batting averages then declined 19 points, while runs per game were down by 1.65.

Playing baseball with the modern foul-strike rule *and* the old style rubber-core baseball produced the worst hitting conditions in the history of the game. Until the introduction of the cork-centered ball midway through the 1910 season, the game was different from anything we have ever known. Because it was a relatively short time, seven seasons in the American League and nine in the National, we don't bother to consider it a historically separate era in playing conditions.

But it has to be so considered in the context of Honus Wagner's career. Hans had more at bats in this period than any other player. It covered his career from ages twenty-seven to thirty-five, his peak years when he had finally settled into one defensive position. You want an idea how heavily favored the pitchers were? The National League's ERA for this period was 2.79—yes, two-point-seven-nine.

Consider some of the all-time records set in this period: fewest homers per game, 1907; fewest runs per game, 1908; lowest batting average by pinch-hitters, 1907; fewest walks per game, 1904; fewest doubles per game, 1907; most shutouts per game, 1908; most 1–0 scores per game, 1907.

You may have noticed that the problem got worse with time; most of those records were set in 1907–08. The pitchers were suffering fewer arm problems the longer they worked under these less demanding conditions. Because the National League adopted the foul-strike rule two years before the AL, the talent of its pitching base began to broaden earlier than the AL's, making things even tougher on the NL hitters. The National League had the lowest batting average of the period (.239 in 1908) and also set a record that year for the lowest slugging percentage by a league (.306). In 1907 it had the fewest doubles and homers, and most 1–0 games ever by one league.

No one was hitting .400 in this era. A .380 mark was spectacular and unheard of from 1905 until the introduction of the cork-centered ball of 1910. Ty Cobb averaged only .350 for his three batting championships in this period, about the same as Wagner's .348 for his six titles; the second-place hitter in Wagner's six league-leading seasons averaged just .330.

When the cork-centered ball was introduced, Wagner was thirty-six years old and already declining from his perch as his league's best hitter. Ty Cobb, on the other hand, was twenty-three, a veteran of six seasons and just entering his prime. Wagner totally missed the Live Ball Era and the outlawing of the spitball, which helped Cobb to age so gracefully in his statistics if not in his actual value.

Wagner's good health and unusual defensive value also had him playing a lot at ages when Cobb was playing part-time or was already retired. Cobb had only 9% of his career at-bats past age thirty-eight; Wagner had 21% of his at bats past age thirty-eight, and 662 of them came at an age when Cobb had retired. If Wagner had been born the same year as Cobb, at age thirty-eight he probably would have been a .350-plus career hitter with far better power numbers than Cobb.

To be sure, even when making careful allowances for their eras, Babe Ruth and Ted Williams were more valuable offensive players in their careers than Wagner. The same can be said about Cobb, but by a remarkably small margin. If you take only the fifteen-year span from ages twenty-four through thirty-eight, Wagner was actually a better offensive player than Cobb relative to his league. Wagner has a very legitimate claim to be one of the top five hitters in baseball, as well as the greatest right-handed hitter ever.

Wagner dominated his league in a fashion that only a few hitters have ever been able to match. Hans took eight batting titles, the most in NL history and the most of any right-handed batter. Twelve times he finished in the top five in batting average; twelve times he finished in the top five in slugging percentage, with eleven times in the top three, including an eight-year streak of being either first or second. For the fifteen-year period from ages twenty-four to thirty-eight his power percentage (slugging minus batting) averaged better than *twice* the league average.

Ten times Wagner was in the top three in doubles and eight times in triples. Hans often led by huge margins in these categories. In 1900 he led in doubles, 45 to 33, and in triples, 22 to 17. In 1904 he had 44 doubles when the next-best was 28. He had a 38–28 edge in 1907; 39–30 in 1908. In the forty-three-year history of the Dead Ball Era (1876 to 1919), Wagner was the only player to collect over 1,000 extra-base hits. No one else had even 900 with the "dead ball" (Nap Lajoie is second with 898).

The statistic in which Wagner ranked most consistently among the league leaders was one that didn't even exist when he first started playing: the RBI. When they began counting RBIs in 1907, Honus Wagner was the leader for three seasons in a row, which, incidentally, is still the record for most consecutive RBI titles. When they went back to dig out the RBI records for the earlier seasons, Wagner had two other titles, which gave him five, still the National League record today. (*The Baseball Encyclopedia* and *Sports Encyclopedia: Baseball* both list Wagner as second in RBIs in 1907, but *The Sporting News's Daguerrotypes* has him first, and so do the official records from the time.)

The Macmillan *Encyclopedia* also gives the top five in RBIs in each league for each season. Guess who spent more time in that top five than any player in history? It wasn't Ed Delahanty, Nap

Lajoie, Frank Baker, Sam Crawford, Ty Cobb, Joe Jackson, Eddie Collins, Tris Speaker, Rogers Hornsby, George Sisler, Babe Ruth, Mel Ott, Lou Gehrig, Hack Wilson, Johnny Mize, Joe DiMaggio, Ted Williams, Hank Greenberg, Stan Musial, Yogi Berra, Willie Mays, Mickey Mantle, Henry Aaron, Harmon Killebrew, Willie McCovey, Reggie Jackson, or Mike Schmidt. Most of those players are not even close.

Honus Wagner was the most consistent RBI man in baseball history, fourteen times in his league's top five. And that is not just a coincidental cutoff figure that captures all of Wagner's top seasons: Twice he was sixth, and in 1898 he missed the top five by a single RBI. You could win a lot of drinks with a trivia question like that.

It would be difficult to pick out Wagner's best season. He had four seasons when he led in batting average, on-base average, *and* slugging percentage, and just missed in a fifth season when he was nosed out for the slugging title. But his summer of 1908 would be hard to beat. He took the batting title by 20 points, led in on-base average, and totally dominated the power categories: first in doubles and triples, second in homers. His 68 extra-base hits were 20 more than those of the second-place finisher; he had 40 more total bases and led in slugging percentage, .542 to .452, in a league where only five men topped .400.

Hans missed leading the league in runs scored by one, led with 109 RBIs when only four players had over 70, and stole the most bases with 53. He played 151 of his team's 155 games, and the Flying Dutchman did all of this in the most hotly contested pennant race of all time. In 1908 the Cubs won by one game over New York and Pittsburgh, which both won 98 games. And the Pirates got more wins out of less talent than either the Cubs or Giants, as they had both the worst pitching and the worst offense of the three teams.

TEAM	RUNS SCORED PER GAME	RUNS ALLOWED PER GAME	EXPECTED W%	ACTUAL WIN%
Chicago	3.96	2.89	.652	.643
New York	4.15	2.92	.669	.636
Pittsburgh	3.77	3.06	.603	.636

Consider how the New York Giants viewed the 1908 race. When pitcher George "Hooks" Wiltse was asked to handicap the pennant race, he said there was one club he feared more than the Cubs: "The Pirates! Ah, there's the dig. Pittsburgh may be a one-man team, but that man is a 'dilly.' "

Hall of Famer Christy Mathewson said, "Pittsburgh, of course, must be reckoned with. But the Pirates are more or less a one-man aggregation. Without Hans Wagner Pittsburgh would have a hard time to get into the first division."

The pitching community naturally had an uncommon respect for a hitter they generally considered unstoppable. The Hall of Fame pitcher quoted at the start of the chapter was Chief Bender. His career perfectly overlapped with Wagner's, and Bender's Philadelphia Athletics played a series of spring exhibition games with the Pittsburgh Pirates every year. Later on, Bender was traded to the NL and played two seasons against Wagner. The Dutchman fascinated Bender because there was no way to pitch to him; "[He] never had a weakness. Honus could hit anything he could reach—inside or out, high or low."

Cy Young played several years against both Wagner and Ty Cobb and considered Cobb the more resourceful hitter because he could "push, pull, and bunt," but pointed out that you could at least pitch to Cobb; "He never could pull an outside pitch, [but] Wagner could."

Another Hall of Famer, Grover Cleveland Alexander, has a special memory of his struggles with Wagner. In July 1915, Alexander held the Pirates hitless until the eighth inning when the forty-one-year-old Wagner hit one out of the park for the only run and hit. With one swing of the bat, Wagner had prevented Alexander from throwing the only no-hitter of his career and kept him from setting an all-time record of 17 shutouts in one season.

No pitcher knew Wagner better than Christy Mathewson. They faced each other for seventeen seasons, and in his book *Pitching in a Pinch,* Christy admitted that, " 'Hans' Wagner, of Pittsburgh has always been a hard man for me." That was putting it mildly. In those seventeen seasons Wagner hit .324 off the great Mathewson, just five points below his career average. In 1908, one of the big stories of the season was the Pirates beating Mathewson while Wagner went 5-for-5 with two doubles. Understand that this was the season with the lowest batting average in NL history; no one was going 5-for-5 against anyone, and this was the best pitcher in the league having the greatest year of his career. That season Mathewson led in wins (37), ERA (1.43), strikeouts, shutouts, and allowed fewer than seven hits a game—which indicates the opposing batters were hitting under .200 against him.

In trying to capture the flavor of Wagner's hitting style, look to the more modern Pirates star, Roberto Clemente. There are a lot of interesting similarities between the two. Both had remarkable throwing arms, were considered the best defensive players at their positions, aged remarkably well, and were seen as the best bad-ball hitters of their generation. Actually, these last two factors are joined closely together.

Wagner wasn't as undisciplined as Clemente was, but there are more than a few stories of Wagner getting hits on pitches meant to be balls. Mathewson remembers that Honus got a hit off him once when Christy threw a pitch too close on an intentional pass. There is also a blurred photo from the 1909 World Series that shows Wagner swinging at a pitch that appears well outside the strike zone. Honus is up on his front foot, his back foot is completely off the ground, and, like Clemente, he looks as though he knew exactly what he was doing.

Late in his career Clemente improved his discipline at the plate, which seems to coincide with his unusually fine seasons then. Clemente's best season came at age thirty-three, and he nearly matched it at age thirty-five. Honus Wagner also had his best seasons after age thirty, his strongest was at age thirty-four. Clemente's walk average, relative to the league, rose fairly steadily in his early years, took a big jump at age twenty-nine, and stayed there for several years. Four of his top five relative walk averages came at ages thirty-one, thirty-three, thirty-four, and thirty-five.

That is almost a mirror image of Wagner's walk history. Honus's walk average, relative to the league, rose fairly steadily early in his career, took a big jump at age thirty, and stayed fairly high for a number of years. Six of his top seven relative walk averages came at ages thirty, thirty-one, thirty-two, thirty-four, thirty-five, and thirty-seven. Makes you wonder whether Clemente spent a lot of time hanging around the Honus Wagner statue outside Forbes Field, picking up a little ghostly coaching.

One big difference between Clemente and Wagner is that no one ever said Roberto was the strongest man in the game. It is hard to comprehend how much Wagner's power stood out in this era when everyone thought it was foolish to do any more than just meet the ball squarely.

Ed Barrow was a man who understood the implications of the "live ball," the value of the home run, and could recognize those who could hit them or be shaped to hit them. In addition to being the man who turned Frankenstein Ruth loose, Barrow came up with the American League's fourth thirty-homer man (Bob Meusel, 33 in 1925, despite being a right-hander in Yankee Stadium), and brought along the next man after Ruth to reach 45 homers (Lou Gehrig, 47, in 1927). Barrow's teams continued to lead in homers long after the Babe was gone. And what was Barrow's appraisal of Wagner's power? "If Wagner had batted against a lively ball, he would have hit fifty homers every year."

Long after his retirement, Wagner became a coach with Pittsburgh in 1933. At that time Forbes Field still had its original dimensions; they would not build Greenberg's Garden or Kiner's Korner for another twenty years. It was an extremely large park where the ball did not carry well. Yet more than one eyewitness remembers this particular blow. This is sportswriter Tom Meany's description: "I saw [Coach Wagner] one evening [in an exhibition game] against the Homestead Grays, a powerful Negro team, and on his first trip to the plate he lashed a triple off the top of the exit gates in right-center. This was as long a ball as any I ever saw hit in Forbes Field, a drive of at least 420 feet." Wagner was *fifty-nine years old* at the time.

We may have there the explanation why Wagner never took a home run crown despite his great strength and tons of extra-base hits. Both of the old Pittsburgh parks, Exposition Park and Forbes

Field, were extremely large, making a few triples out of doubles but taking away the homers. The home run factor of Exposition Park was .68 (32% tougher than the average NL park) during Wagner's career there. At Forbes Field it was a nearly identical .61. Data on the Louisville ballpark of his first three seasons have never been compiled.

Even without home runs, there is no denying Wagner's complete domination as the leading power hitter of the Dead Ball Era. To set himself so far apart from the rest of the baseball world would seem to have required more than just strength and raw talent. I have always assumed that Wagner had to be doing something different, something foreign to his time. After all, the man holds the record for most years leading the league in extra-base hits: seven. How many people know he shares that record with Babe Ruth and Stan Musial? Given that Musial sneaks in there by leading the league twice during the war years (1943–44), that leaves Wagner and Ruth—and we know Ruth was using a new style. Did Wagner develop a long-ball batting technique of his own?

Christy Mathewson saw that Wagner was taking a different swing from most dead-ball hitters:

> In the history of baseball there have not been more than fifteen or twenty free swingers altogether, and they are the real natural hitters of the game, the men with the eyes nice enough and accurate enough to take a long wallop at the ball. . . . [Wagner] takes a long bat, stands well back from the plate, and steps into the ball, poling it.

By "free swinger," Mathewson wasn't referring to Wagner as a bad-ball hitter—which would be the modern usage—but as one who took a full, powerful swing at the ball. On the same page of *Pitching in the Pinch,* Matty criticized some Giant teammates for trying to be "free swingers overnight and . . . trying to knock the ball out of the lot, instead of chopping at it."

I found another interesting description of Wagner's swing in a book that came out way back in 1950 called *Baseball's Greatest Hitters.*

Tom Meany had the good sense to include Wagner and had a detailed description of Wagner's stance and swing. What caught my eye was the following: "He crouched ever so slightly and even this was exaggerated by his trick of bending his knees as the pitcher wound up."

That's a fairly good description of a technique associated with certain power hitters, especially the lighter, smaller players with surprising power. Bill James points out it is a technique that frequently shows up on teams managed by Billy Martin, who used the same style successfully in his own career. I call it the "pop-up power stance" because the batter is popping up out of a slight crouch as he starts to swing at the ball.

Okay, Honus Wagner was neither little or light, but he was hitting a mushy baseball with a heavy core, and he was hitting it a lot harder than anyone else. We have no film of Wagner's swing, and as far as I know there is only one photo taken during his hitting stride. It is another of the blurred photos from the 1909 Series, but it does suggest that Honus was coming out of a slight crouch and bend at the knees. It also indicates that Wagner strode forward into the ball like a modern power hitter rather than starting from a spread-out stance and hitting flat-footed, the more common style for his era.

MOST VALUABLE PLAYER

What does it mean to declare someone the most valuable player in baseball history? I've discussed my view of Wagner's value with many serious baseball historians, some of whom are well versed in sabermetric methods. They've suggested that Barrow and Rickey, in declaring Wagner the best, were projecting his talents forward into the game at the time of their statements—into the Live Ball Era. They were, these historians argue, recognizing that some of Babe Ruth's value was the result of an historical fluke, the perfect case of his being in the right place at the right time.

The implication here is that, looking purely at Wagner in his own time, he wasn't as valuable as Ruth was in his. I don't know about that. While his power wasn't suited to his era, his speed sure was. In taking this view, the historians might be projecting their own assumption that no one could possibly be more valuable than Ruth onto Rickey and Barrow.

I agree that Ruth is the only real rival Wagner has as baseball's most valuable player ever. The Bambino's career is such a fantastic mixture of circumstance conspiring with immense talent that it would seem no other player could catch him on talent alone.

Still, I cannot say what was in the minds of Barrow or Rickey. I believe that they really meant Wagner was, even relative to his own era, more valuable than any other player relative to his time. I don't know that that is what they meant, but it isn't such an illogical conclusion.

Value doesn't have to be measured strictly at the career level. I expect that Barrow, Rickey, and McGraw were all extremely conscious of the value of playing Wagner at shortstop, which was not his career position. If we focus on the peak value of Wagner's career, say, his best ten-year span, then yes, he may well have been the most valuable player in history.

If you establish that a shortstop is one of the game's best hitters, how do you go about calculating the value of being able to place his offensive contribution at shortstop rather than in the outfield or at first base? It certainly cannot be considered irrelevant. Few people have the ability to play a premium defensive position and also hit well. This shortage means more demand, and just as in the marketplace, demand is a major determinant of value.

You could take three individual hitters who are all clearly better offensive players than Ozzie Smith and not be able to trade the lot of them for Smith. That is a fact. If I want to trade you a good-hitting outfielder for a good-hitting shortstop, we both understand that you are not expected to give me an equal hitter, just a good hitter compared with most shortstops. This is crystal clear whenever we talk about trades, contracts, or building a team. This most obvious and logical reality is no less a factor when you compare the values of a Ruth with a Wagner.

Wagner first became a full-time shortstop in 1903, so I expect his peak ten-year value is from 1903 to 1912. To get a feel for his value in this role, I combined the statistical totals of the other starting shortstops in the league during that period and divided by seven to create the average starting shortstop for the Pirates' competitors.

I then set out to do the same thing for Ruth's best period. Choosing the best ten-year span in Babe's career was very easy; if you start in 1920, you capture Ruth's move into the Polo Grounds as well as the beginning of the Live Ball Era. Ruth derived a terrific edge from catching the rest of the league in a transition stage, a period of adjustment to the new hitting strategies made possible by the livelier ball, the outlawing of the spitball, and the successful attempts to keep a quality ball in play by frequent replacement. Babe would be the first, and later only one of a handful, to exploit the home run potential of the 1920s.

Because Ruth was switched from left field to right field in midcareer and played over 1,000 games at each position, creating his composite comparative starter involved combining the other starting left and right fielders. Generally, the offensive levels don't differ greatly between the two fields other than by the tradition of the day. Sometimes right field is the home for the heavy-hitting outfielders, and other times left field seems to collect them.

The following chart shows the differences between Wagner and Ruth relative to their contemporary starters. Besides capturing the value of a super-hitting shortstop versus the slugging outfielder, it gives us a taste of the differences in the offensive opportunities of their differing eras. The runs-per-game estimate is the number of runs you would expect a team to score if it had nine such hitters in its lineup.

(These are based on the appropriate runs-created formulas for their eras as covered in *The Bill James Historical Baseball Abstract*. The decision to use these versions of James' runs-created formulas actually favors the Babe: In his 1985 *Baseball Abstract*, Bill pointed out that his formula does tend to overestimate slightly the production of players who combine high slugging percentages with a high on-base average. The most obvious extreme in all of baseball history would be Babe Ruth, who leads in lifetime slugging percentage and is second in on-base average.)

This chart takes a lot of the intimidation out of Ruth's numbers. The period 1920–29 was a great time to be a hitter, and the other outfielders had no trouble doing what they always tried to do, hit for

	GAMES	AB	HITS	BA	2B/3B/HR	BB	SB	R	RBI	RUNS/ GAME
(1903–12) Wagner	1,405	5,231	1,793	.343	352/143/ 58	566	572	969	911	9.32
Other starting shortstops	1,255	4,424	1,076	.243	148/ 55/ 14	344	182	476	448	3.50
(1920–29) Ruth	1,399	4,884	1,734	.355	314/ 82/467	1236	88	1,365	1,330	14.63
Other starting RF and LF	1,315	4,876	1,565	.321	291/ 85/ 87	455	117	793	747	6.74

average. What they lack is the home run power of Ruth and the walks that went along with that power.

It's also interesting to see that Ruth had a higher batting average than Wagner. One quick way to capture the difference in their eras is to remember that Hans took seven batting titles in those ten seasons while Ruth had only one. Notice further that while Ruth was more than twice as efficient in producing runs than the other left and right fielders, Wagner was more than two and a half times more efficient than the other starting shortstops.

Was this an abnormally weak-hitting bunch of shortstops? No, relative to the league average they were actually better than the shortstops during Ruth's period by a 2% margin, and that is without including Wagner, their top-hitting shortstop.

To better compare these run value differences, let's convert them to winning percentages. We know that during this period Wagner's league averaged 3.97 runs per team per game. A team of Wagners would score 5.82 more runs per game than that of the comparative shortstops. Divide that figure by nine—because Wagner is really only one man in his lineup—and you have Wagner's contribution to an average team. In other words, his team now has a 4.62 offense [(5.82/ 9) + 3.97 = 4.62].

How often should a team scoring 4.62 runs beat a team scoring 3.97 runs? The Pythagorean method (expected winning percentage equals runs squared divided by the sum of runs squared and runs allowed squared) says .575.

From 1920 to 1929, Ruth was in a league averaging 4.90 runs. Repeat the calculation using the appropriate data for Ruth, and you find he pushes a .500 team up to .582.

Even using a runs-created formula with a bias toward Ruth, they are left so close together (.575 versus .582) you can hardly tell them apart. But we aren't done yet. For one, we haven't given Wagner credit for his superior durability relative to his position. In his ten-year span Honus gave his team 150 extra games of his .573 value, while Babe gave his team only 84 extra games of his plus performance.

What is the value of a replacement-level ballplayer? If I gave you a team made up of fourth outfielders, fifth infielders, etc., how many games would you win? Fifty-five would be about right, or a winning percentage around .340. If you put a .340 player in an otherwise .500 lineup, its winning percentage would drop to .482. For the 66-game difference—which would cover 4.5% of Ruth's games—Ruth's team would be a .482 team compared with Wagner's .575 value. That would drop Ruth's overall winning percentage value to .577 while Wagner remains at .575. There is virtually no difference between a .575 and .577 team; both would be expected to win 93 games in a 162-game schedule.

Now remember that all these calculations are based on Wagner being just an average defensive shortstop and Ruth being an average defensive outfielder. Babe wasn't a bad outfielder, but he wasn't a Gold Glove type, either. When they shifted Ruth over to right field, it wasn't because of the strength of his arm—Bob Meusel was consistently cited by his contemporaries as having the best outfield arm in the league. Ruth ended up in right field because Yankee Stadium had too much room in left field for Ruth to cover as he got older, heavier, and slower.

Wagner, on the other hand, was recognized as an exceptional fielder almost immediately and was king at shortstop. His defensive excellence was also unusually long-lived; he led the league in range as late as age thirty-nine. The difference in the defensive value between Ruth and Wagner would have to weigh heavily, very heavily, in Hans's favor. There is no question in my mind that in peak value, Honus Wagner was the most valuable player in baseball history.

Would that defensive edge be strong enough that we can argue that Wagner also had greater total career value than Ruth? Now there you've got me. That's too difficult a question for me to answer with clear objectivity. Wagner was not nearly as valuable a player when he wasn't playing shortstop. Ruth was a very fine pitcher in his younger days.

You would have to do some delicate figuring of Ruth's pitching value, but it would also have to include a home park that greatly favored the pitcher. Wagner may deserve a projected extra season for starting his career when there were considerably fewer major-league jobs, and you would have to project some of Hans's numbers for playing in some schedules of 140 games or fewer prior to 1904. When you throw in Wagner's exceptional defense, all in all, I would not be surprised if that call, too, had to go to Hans Wagner.

There is another factor we haven't discussed that most managers would insist on including. If any player ever contributed to a winning through the "intangibles," Wagner is the man. Hans's character was uniquely suited to creating a sense of team unity, team goals, and team effort. Further, his own habits were a manager's dream, a shining example for enhancing one's performance and maintaining it at peak levels.

Babe Ruth's character was a near opposite. In *Babe,* Robert Creamer's excellent biography of Ruth, we get a view of this superstar that goes beyond his batting feats. Ruth was loved as just "a big kid," but he also caused a lot of problems with less endearing childish characteristics. He could be extremely self-centered, impulsive, petulant, and even cruel in the unthinking ways of a child.

Although Babe was far from mean-spirited, he had an explosive temper. In 1916 he threatened to slug an umpire and actually landed a blow before being pulled away. Rather than being an isolated incident, the exact same thing happened three years later with the same umpire. This time the umpire stayed out of range as players from *both* teams were needed to pull Babe away—and, of course, out of the game.

While it was hard to stay mad at the Babe—and he was never one to hold grudges—the momentary storms were not conducive to team harmony. He had more than one fight with a teammate and feuded at times with fellow stars like Lou Gehrig and Ben Chapman.

In 1922, Ruth broke Ty Cobb's record by being suspended five times in a single season. In one particularly ugly incident he threw dirt in an umpire's face. Hmm, could it be that Billy Martin was simply trying to bring back an old Yankees tradition?

Babe's childish selfishness was especially trying to his managers. While with Boston, he once faked an injury to avoid pitching at a time when his manager felt it would be in the best interests of the team that he pitch rather than play the outfield. In 1918, Ruth jumped the Red Sox to protest a five-hundred-dollar fine. He then jumped the club a second time and vowed to quit when he wasn't immediately allowed to play on his return. Seven years later he again promised to quit, this time in an attempt to have his manager fired.

Ruth was especially hard on Yankees manager Miller Huggins. Babe openly defied his diminutive manager in a belief that his superstardom put him above others both in power and wisdom. Until the club took action against him, Ruth often ignored the instructions given him and criticized Huggins to the press, calling him an incompetent. Ruth repeated this performance at the end of his career when he coveted Yankees manager Joe McCarthy's job. Babe went out of his way to criticize McCarthy to reporters, calling him a lousy manager.

As for the Babe's habits—well, let me put it this way, if a rookie chose him as his role model, he might not die, but his career quickly would. Babe was not one to take care of himself. He kept late hours, drank more than he should, and certainly his career suffered from his bouts with gluttony.

In 1923, his unusual sense of nutrition caused him to keel over with an abdominal abcess that required surgery. His playing weight is generally listed at 215, but after age twenty-five it was rarely below 225 and as high as 240. He sometimes reported to spring training in the 250 to 270 range. When Huggins slapped Babe with the legendary five-thousand-dollar fine and suspension, it was an attempt to control not just his insubordination but his wild behavior off the field, which Huggins felt was a bad influence on the rest of the team.

Incidentally, for those who are wondering, Ruth's teams had a record of .605 from his first full season till his last full season at age thirty-nine—.603 with Babe as an outfielder.

Wagner's teams had a record of .600 for his full seasons through age thirty-nine—.620 for the seasons he played shortstop. In that time Wagner played with just three Hall of Famers: Fred Clarke, Max Carey, and Jack Chesbro. Ruth played with eight: Lou Gehrig, Bill Dickey, Tris Speaker, Earle Combs, Harry Hooper, Herb Pennock, Red Ruffing, and Waite Hoyt. He was also managed by three Hall of Famers in Ed Barrow, Miller Huggins, and Joe McCarthy.

THE MAN

In reading the various recollections of Wagner by his contemporaries, you begin to wonder whether they are capable of answering any question about Honus without mentioning what a fine man he was. Ask about his baserunning, and they will tag on to their answer, "What a peach of a guy," as if it were as relevant as his seven-hundred-plus steals. When Wahoo Sam Crawford finished rattling off his appraisal of Wagner, he closed with, "A good team man, too, and the sweetest disposition in the world. The greatest ballplayer that ever lived, in my book."

Yet this personal side of Wagner is relevant if it was a part of his contributions to winning. And certainly it's of interest if we're curious about how he accomplished what he did, and just who this forgotten hero really was. With the passage of time, there has been a tendency to interpret Wagner as so easygoing and laid-back that he comes across as a bit of a buffoon. There have been several stories that paint him as an easy mark in contract negotiations and a player who just went along with his talents.

This is a gross misinterpretation. By all accounts of his peers, Honus Wagner had the presence of a confident man who knew what was important to him, and had the courage of his convictions to be exactly who he wanted to be. Baseball writer Art Daily said, "There is something Lincolnesque about him, his rugged homeliness, his simplicity, his integrity, and his true nobility of character."

The legends of Wagner's naiveté in monetary matters may simply be our own failure to understand his values. Consider the attention he gave to his bats in relation to his indifference to money matters. Honus would start every season by journeying to Louisville to pick out the wood for his bats. He would then tirelessly "bone" his bats, honing them with an old beef bone to press the fibers together. When he found an especially good bat, he didn't want others using it by mistake, and in the fall of 1905 he became a part of baseball trivia as the first player to have his autograph burned into a bat.

Hans cared deeply about many things; money wasn't one of them. When Hans was making twenty-four-hundred dollars a year in 1901, he turned down a twenty-thousand-dollar offer to play for New York in the American League. Although several NL stars were jumping their contracts, Wagner didn't feel it was ethical. Besides, he liked playing in Pittsburgh; it was close to his home, and it mattered to Wagner that the Pirates had treated him well in his young career and had helped his father escape life in the coal mines by giving him a job as a ticket-taker at the ballpark.

In a 1908 issue of *Sporting Life*, Pirates owner Barney Dreyfus revealed that Wagner had the right to name the figures in his contract for most of his career. Wagner set a salary cap on his own baseball earnings of ten thousand dollars a year; he went without a raise for the last ten years of his career. Hans felt it was more than adequate and as much as a ballplayer should make. He felt that if he went for more, there would be less for his teammates.

In 1908 and 1909 Wagner almost retired due to growing bouts of rheumatism and the success of his chicken farm. When the reporters wondered whether Wagner was simply setting the stage for a salary war, he pointed out that he didn't need the money and said, "My salary is satisfactory to me, and my great aim is to make it satisfactory to the people that pay me. If I thought I could no longer [earn my pay], I'd have my salary cut or quit the game."

Wagner never wrestled with whether to try promotions that would compromise his life-style or sense of right. The answer was always a simple, direct no. Ty Cobb came to Hans with a thousand-dollar-a-week offer to appear on a vaudeville stage with Ty in the off-season.

Hans turned him down with a simple: "I'm no actor, Ty, but thanks."

John Gruber, a Pittsburgh sportswriter, was offered ten dollars to obtain Wagner's consent to publish a "Honus Wagner" baseball card in a series put out by a cigarette company. Gruber still has the letter and uncashed check that Wagner sent him: "Dear John: I don't want my picture in cigarettes but I don't want you to lose the $10, so I am sending you a check for that sum."

There are hundreds of personal testimonies to the natural kindness and decency of Wagner. When umpire Bill "Catfish" Klem said, "Hans Wagner [was] as great a man as he was a ballplayer," he knew Wagner more than lived up to that very difficult comparison. Catfish often told a story of how Wagner courageously stepped in and saved Klem when he had been cornered by an angry mob after a controversial game.

Sportswriter Al Lang remembered how Hans was simply the kind of guy who naturally looked out for other people, and he had a special place in his heart for the youngsters just starting out: "[Wagner] always chose as his roommate some rookie who couldn't get anyone else to room with him. When he went home . . . he'd go out on the sandlots and show the kids how to play."

Does that sound like a gilded memory to you? It did to me until I read this account by Hans Lobert in Lawrence Ritter's book *The Glory of Their Times:*

> . . . living near Pittsburgh and all, my idol was Honus Wagner, and I tried to do everything just like he did. I even tried to walk like him. Wagner lived in Carnegie, which wasn't far from where we lived, and lots of times I'd see him out there playing baseball with the kids after the Pirates' game was over. A wonderful man, he was.
>
> . . . [Later, Lobert is in the Pirate clubhouse waiting for a tryout.] I guess I must have looked sort of lost, because all of a sudden Wagner, of all people, yells out to me, "Hey, kid, come on over here and use my locker!"
>
> "Oh, no, Mr. Wagner," I says, "I have to find Mr. Clarke [the manager]."
>
> "He won't be here for twenty minutes yet," Wagner said. "Meanwhile come on over and get dressed here."

So I did, and I really felt like a big shot then. Wagner asked me where I was from, and when he found out I lived near him and my name was John, or Johannus, the same as his, he started calling me Hans Number Two. Actually, we did look a little bit alike. Especially our [big] noses! From then on he always called me Hans Number Two, for all the fifty years we knew each other. I've always been proud of that.

Even grumpy old Burleigh Grimes fondly remembers Wagner from his rookie season in 1916. "Honus Wagner was a wonderful fellow . . . I remember the first game I ever pitched against Brooklyn at Ebbets Field. It was a tight spot, about the seventh inning, score tied 1–1, a man on first base. Wagner came over to the mound and said, 'Make him hit it to me, Kid.' Well, I didn't *make* him do it, but the guy did hit a hard grounder right to short. Perfect double-play ball. I was proud of myself and figured old Honus had to be impressed. Well, the ball bounced off Wagner's foot out into left-center [for an error]. Old Honus came over to me with his head down, looking kind of annoyed. He said, 'Those damn big feet have *always* been in my way.' "

And oh, yes, you can't listen to stories about Wagner without hearing about his off-the-wall humor. Sometimes it was pure fiction such as, "Once I was going for a ground ball and a rabbit ran across my path. In the confusion I picked up the rabbit and fired it to first base. I got the runner by a hare." Or the time he was a Pirates coach and commented that the opening day band was "[the] same band they had here when they opened the park thirty-five years ago . . . had about a hunnert pieces in the band then. 'Course, a lot of 'em has died off during the years."

Sometimes Hans just added the color a true story needed. Davy Jones shares this one in *The Glory of Their Times*:

We had a young pitcher . . . Jimmy St. Vrain . . . an absolutely terrible hitter—never even got a loud foul off anybody.

Well, one day we were playing the Pittsburgh Pirates and Jimmy was pitching . . . Frank Selee, our manager, said, "Jimmy, you're a left-handed pitcher, why don't you turn around and bat from the left side, too? Why not try it?"

. . . So the next time he went up he batted left-handed. Turned around and stood on the opposite side of the plate from where he was used to, you know. And darned if he didn't actually hit the ball. He tapped a slow roller down to Honus Wagner at shortstop and took off as fast as he could go . . . but instead of running to first base, he headed to *third!*

Oh, my God! What bedlam! Everybody yelling and screaming at poor Jimmy as he raced to third base, head down, spikes flying, determined to get there ahead of the throw. Later on, Honus told us that as a matter of fact he almost *did* throw the ball to third.

"I'm standing there with the ball in my hand," Honus said, "looking at this guy running from home to third, and for an instant there I swear I didn't know *where* to throw the damn ball. And when I finally did throw to first, I wasn't at all sure it was the right thing to do!"

Honus never lost his special good-natured ways: not to age, and not to the depression that ruined his sporting goods business. When he returned to the Pirates as a coach in the 1930s, the fondness of the players for the Dutchman was as full-hearted as in his playing days. Paul Waner was the Pirates' right fielder during those seasons. He told Ritter:

Honus was a wonderful fellow, so good-natured and friendly to everyone. Gee, we loved that guy. . . . He must have been sixty years old easy, but goldarned if that old boy didn't get out there at shortstop every once in a while during fielding practice and play that position. When he did that, a hush would come over the whole ball park, and every player on both teams would just stand there, like a bunch of little kids, and watch every move he made. I'll never forget it.

For all his gregariousness on the field, when the newsmen wanted to do a story on Wagner, he avoided them as best he could without being ill-mannered, and he routinely declined most invitations for affairs to honor his accomplishments. Al Lang noted that "Wagner was the most modest of stars. If anyone ever started praising him to his face, he'd leave the party rather than listen to it."

This modesty may have something to do with the unnatural fading of his memory in the game. The durability of Wagner's image was also hurt by the fact he was past his prime when the golden age of sportswriting began just after 1910. When Grantland Rice, Damon Runyon, Fred Leib, Heywood Broun, and Ring Lardner began writing, Wagner was in his late thirties, while Ty Cobb, to take one example, was in his early twenties. It also didn't help that Pittsburgh was a long way from the media hotspots of the day, New York and Chicago.

Having praised Wagner's character to the sky after a rather thorough airing of Babe Ruth's dirty laundry, it is fair to ask what blemishes may darken Hans's sterling image. There recently has been a claim that Wagner showed some racist tendencies when he quit a minor-league club in his first professional season. Wagner claimed that he left because he was homesick. Another story claims that he left because of differences with the field captain. Thirty-five years after the fact, the owner of the club said that Wagner left because he didn't like playing on a team that had a black pitcher and catcher.

That may or may not be so. Wagner was only twenty-one then; it was 1895, and I dare say that the majority of the players in that era wouldn't have even considered playing on a mixed team. In fact, the Adrian club was the only interracial team in all of organized baseball that year. The next year they became lily-white even though they had to dump pitcher George Wilson, who had a 29–4 record. But if the story is true, it is at odds with the great respect that Wagner showed for Negro League players later in his life.

When Hans was asked how he felt about the great black shortstop John Henry Lloyd being called "the Black Wagner," he replied, "I am honored to have John Lloyd called the 'Black Wagner.' It is a privilege to have been compared to him." A more gracious statement I cannot imagine.

There is one player from Wagner's era who did not care much for the Dutchman. That's Frank Chance, and I'm not sure that should count, as Chance didn't get along very well with anyone. He tended to refer to his champion Cubs as "dogs" and "sons of dogs" or something close to it. The biggest fight of the 1908 pennant race took place in the Cubs' clubhouse, with Chance getting his clock cleaned by Heinie Zimmerman, his own third baseman.

Be that as it may, in 1908 Chance claimed there was bad blood between Wagner and his manager, Fred Clarke, that Wagner had tried to get him fired, and that "Wagner has always been known as a player who worked for his individual record more than for the welfare of his team."

That's pretty strong stuff. Clarke was the only manager Wagner had for the first nineteen years of his career, including seven years after Chance made that statement. In all that time there must have been a tiff or two, but near as I can tell from all other reports they were good friends and had a lot of respect for each other.

It's ironic that in the same season that Chance charged Wagner with being a selfish player rather than a team player, you can find this story in a July issue of the *Pittsburgh Dispatch*:

> During the past week it was noticed that Wagner was missing chances and making more errors than had been chalked against him in many months. Yesterday an explanation of Wagner's foozles was forthcoming. He had been playing with a finger so disjointed and inflamed that when he showed it to manager Clarke the latter asked Hans to take a rest in order to have the injured member properly cared for. Hans declined, saying that he believed the team needed his services [they were in first place with Chicago only half a game back] and he would continue to do his best. How's that for gameness and loyalty?

If you're looking for further dirt on Wagner, you'll be reduced to stories about his sneaking old balls out of the ballbag and trading them for beers at the local bar. Regardless of Frank Chance's view, Honus Wagner was an excellent role model for a young ballplayer. Wagner believed in staying in condition year-round and credited his durability and long career to the fact that he always reported to the spring camp in playing shape. And Hans worked just as hard in polishing his baseball skills.

[Wagner] used to study the habits of batters, in the manner developed by Charles Comiskey, and seemed to know instinctively just where the man was going to hit the ball, even before he swung.

. . . Wagner's true [hitting] "secret," however, was no secret at all. It was simply tireless practicing. Often, even when he had had a good day at bat, he would stay in the park and persuade the rookie pitcher on his club to throw to him for extra practice until it became too dark to play.

The Pirates were known as a clever, quick-witted team, and manager Clarke, who was also a regular outfielder, relied on Wagner to run the infield. In a day when the players coached themselves on the basepaths and usually signaled directly to each other for many of their set plays, Honus was known as one of the most alert and intelligent players in the game. This newspaper note appeared in the *New York Globe* in 1908: "Can a man play ball and think at the same time? Can a player run bases, watch opposing players, tell when to start [the runners] and when not to? I think not. When he can, he is above ordinary and soon becomes a manager. Of course there is an exception every now and then—occasionally the game produces a man like Wagner, but not often."

Max Carey was one of the most intelligent players of this period and counted Wagner as his greatest teacher. Max's greatest natural asset was his speed, and he remembers how in his rookie year Wagner emphasized how important it was to keep his legs in shape in the off-season, and how Hans helped him learn how to get a jump on the pitchers and how to position himself on defense. Carey went on to set the major-league records for most seasons leading in stolen bases and most years leading in outfield catches, and he ended up joining Wagner in baseball's Hall of Fame.

Rather than being a laid-back bystander to his own talent, Wagner was a presence out there on the field. He enjoyed every aspect of the game, wanted to try it all and to throw in a new twist when he could. Maybe a new batting technique here, a new throwing style there, or a nifty delayed steal over here. Catch his quick thinking and his zest for playing even this small role in a game recorded in the *New York World*:

[Pirate pitcher Nick] Maddox had been very effective until [the eighth inning], when he walked Bresnahan and Donlin. Cy Seymour wouldn't wait and banged a fly on which Bresnahan went to third. Donlin stole second and in doing so bumped Wagner. The "Flying Dutchman" limped around as though he had been crippled for life. Nearly the whole Pirate crew gathered around to sympathize. . . . Finally Maddox tried again and almost broke Devlin's arm with a wild pitch.

When Maddox was waved out of the box and . . . [Irving] Young appeared to take his place, it dawned on the Giants and the fans that the wily Wagner had pulled off a trick. While he was apparently in agony [,] Young had been warming up like a house afire back of the stand. When the pitchers changed places Honus ceased to limp.

I've never quite been able to convince my friend Bill James that Hans Wagner was—by his actual play—baseball's most valuable player. In peak value and career value Bill's formulas keep coming up with the Bambino. At least his calculations are sharp enough to say that Wagner is number two in both lists.

Yet still he made this conclusion in his brief historical essay on Wagner:

Among the great players in the game there are all kinds of men— smart alecks, tough guys, driven men and heavy drinkers. As gentle- men, there are many who seem worthy of admiration, including Mu- sial, Mathewson, Gehrig, Johnson and Schmidt. None seems more worthy than Wagner. He was a gentle, kind man, a storyteller, sup- portive of rookies, patient with fans, cheerful in hard times, careful of the example that he set for youth, a hard worker, a man who had no enemies and who never forgot his friends. . . . Those qualities are part of the reason why, acknowledging that there may have been one or two whose talents were greater, there is no one who has ever played this game that I would be more anxious to have on a baseball team.

Branch Rickey: "If I had a choice, . . . the first . . . would be Honus Wagner."

Ed Barrow: "Wagner was the best all-around player who ever lived."

Sam Crawford: "The greatest ballplayer who ever lived, in my book."

Tommy Leach: "The greatest shortstop. . . . The greatest everything ever."

Bill Klem: "He was the best I ever saw—and I saw them all. . . ."

John McGraw: "He was the nearest thing to a perfect player. . . ."

There has never been another like him. It isn't fiction; he did exist and he was the player they said he was. Someday your children will ask about that "special player, you know, the best there ever was."

Tell them: "Once there was a ballplayer . . ."

ABOUT THE AUTHORS

CRAIG R. WRIGHT was born and raised in Lansing, Michigan, where he learned baseball at the knee of his grandfather, LeRoy Hiler, an early teammate of Charlie Gehringer's. Craig is a *summa cum laude* graduate of Alma College, and has over eight years experience working with major-league clubs as a sabermetrician and consultant, including four full-time seasons with the Texas Rangers. He is also Director of Major League Operations for the information service Sports Team Analysis and Tracking Systems (STATS). He serves on the Statistical Analysis Committee of the Society for American Baseball Research, and has written articles for various journals and magazines, including portions of *The Great American Baseball Stat Book,* for which he was an essay editor in 1987–88. He researches and writes the radio program "A Page From Baseball's Past," and is coauthor of the book *The Man Who Stole First Base and Other Tales From Baseball's Past.* He lives in Arlington, Texas, with his cat Shadow.

TOM HOUSE was born in Seattle, Washington, and attended the University of Southern California, from which he received a B.S. in marketing in 1971 and an M.B.A. in 1974. While at U.S.C., he appeared as an extra in several movies, including *The Graduate* and *Camelot.* He was selected by the Atlanta Braves in the third round of the 1967 draft, and went on to pitch for eight years in the majors for Atlanta, Boston, and Seattle. Tom has been the major-league pitching coach for the Texas Rangers since May 1985, the owner and pitching instructor at the San Diego School of Baseball, and the owner and performance analyst for Biotechniques. He received his doctorate in psychology from San Diego's University for Humanistic Studies in 1988, but is still best remembered for having caught Hank Aaron's 715th home run.